Higher Education for All

Higher Education for All

Racial Inequality, Cold War Liberalism,
and the California Master Plan

· ·

ANDREW STONE HIGGINS

The University of North Carolina Press Chapel Hill

Set in Charis by Westchester Publishing Services
Manufactured in the United States of America

Library of Congress Cataloging-in-Publication Data
Names: Higgins, Andrew Stone, author.
Title: Higher education for all : racial inequality, Cold War liberalism, and the
    California master plan / Andrew Stone Higgins.
Description: Chapel Hill : The University of North Carolina Press, 2023. |
    Includes bibliographical references and index.
Identifiers: LCCN 2022029654 | ISBN 9781469672908 (cloth ; alk. paper) |
    ISBN 9781469672915 (paperback ; alk. paper) | ISBN 9781469672922 (ebook)
Subjects: LCSH: Racism in higher education—California—History—
    20th century. | Education and state—California—History—20th century. |
    Education, Higher—California—History—20th century. | Educational
    planning—California—History—20th century.
Classification: LCC LC212.422.C2 H54 2023 | DDC 378.794—dc23/eng/20220708
LC record available at https://lccn.loc.gov/2022029654

Cover photo by Nacio Jan Brown of December 3, 1968, rally at San Francisco
State College, courtesy of the SFSU Photographic Timeline Project.

In loving memory
Brenda Medina-Hernandez
(1987–2017)
and
Felipe Estrela
(1984–2019)

Contents

Abbreviations in the Text

AAPA	Asian American Political Alliance
AASA	Asian American Student Alliance
AFT	American Federation of Teachers
ASIAN	Asian Students in Action Now
ASUC	Associated Students of the University of California
BAC	Black Athletes Committee
BAUC	Black Athletes of the University of California
BSC	Black Student Council
BSU	Black Student Union
BYC	Black Youth Conference
CCPA	Campus Committee on Political Activity
CSU	California State University
DQU	Deganawidah-Quetzalcoatl University
EOP	Educational Opportunity Program
FSM	Free Speech Movement
GE	General Electric
HUAC	House Un-American Activities Committee
ICSA	Intercollegiate Chinese for Social Action
ISC	Independent Socialist Club
ISL	Independent Socialist League
JHE	*Journal of Higher Education*
LASO	Latin American Students Organization
MASA	Mexican American Student Association
MASC	Mexican American Student Confederation
MAYA	Mexican American Youth Association

MECHA	El Movimiento Estudiantil Chicano de Aztlán
NAACP	National Association for the Advancement of Colored People
NCAA	National Collegiate Athletic Association
NDEA	National Defense Education Act
NSF	National Science Foundation
OPHR	Olympic Project for Human Rights
PACE	Philippine American Collegiate Endeavor
PL	Progressive Labor Party
ROTC	Reserve Officers' Training Corps
SDS	Students for a Democratic Society
SI	Student Initiative
SNCC	Student Nonviolent Coordinating Committee
STEM	science, technology, engineering, and mathematics
TWLF	Third World Liberation Front
UBA	Union of Black Athletes
UBSA	United Black Students for Action
UC	University of California
UCLA	University of California, Los Angeles
UCSB	University of California, Santa Barbara
UCSD	University of California, San Diego
UMAS	United Mexican American Students
UROC	United Republicans of California
USC	University of Southern California
WP	Workers' Party

Higher Education for All

Introduction

· ·

A decade after its inception, the 1960 California Master Plan for Higher Education was besieged from all sides. Admittedly, such had been the case for as many as five years. Where California governor Ronald Reagan had made attacks on the Master Plan system, and the comportment of its students, a central theme of his gubernatorial campaign, California's diverse population of working-class youth had long criticized the Master Plan for its entrenchment of racial and economic disparities. By the late sixties, even liberal centrists—the driving force behind the 1960 Master Plan—denounced the plan as outdated and discriminatory.[1] As student activists and progressive faculty promoted programs of affirmative action to help mitigate the de facto discrimination embedded in the Master Plan, Governor Reagan and his allies moved to cut the funding on which such programs depended. With financial constraints limiting the recruitment of disadvantaged youth to the University of California (UC) and the California state colleges, some Californians would come to propose radical alternatives that would move beyond the imperfect framework first established by the Master Plan.[2]

"The policies laid down in the Master Plan are inherently racist. . . . As long as the UC system insists on using the Master Plan to develop procedures that result in severely limited minority enrollment, the university will be a racist institution, helping to prolong racism."[3] With this succinct analysis, activist Fusha Hill explained her opposition to the admissions standards that kept the UC disproportionately white and wealthy, while funneling working-class students of color into comparatively underfunded two-year community colleges. Hill, a student at UC Davis, drew on a popular critique of the Master Plan that had developed on campuses in California in the previous years. In 1969, for instance, an opinion piece in the *California Aggie* proffered a ten-point condemnation of university complicity in systemic racism, arguing that "when the university systematically excludes national minority and working class young people from a university education, through discriminatory academic and financial qualifications, that is racism." Tellingly, when a professor of bacteriology took issue with this claim, he explained in his rebuttal that the university wasn't to blame for systemic racism—the Master Plan for Higher Education was.[4]

Although Hill's 1971 article—and the others cited above—focused on admissions at the UC, hers was subsequently republished by the *Daily Collegian*, the student newspaper at Fresno State College.[5] Hill's critique could speak to the concerns of student activists at both the UC and state colleges, as well as California's community colleges, because all three systems were regulated by the admissions standards that had been established by the 1960 California Master Plan for Higher Education.[6] In response to the Soviet launch of Sputnik, in the late 1950s, educators and politicians across California had developed a grouping of reforms that laid out a comprehensive blueprint for the functioning and governance of the nation's largest system of public higher education, while keeping costs at a minimum in the face of massive growth in the population of California youth. Those reforms—totaling sixty-seven agreements concerning the future of California's public system of higher education—are known as the California Master Plan for Higher Education.

In the years following the onset of the Great Recession, activists on California's public university and college campuses generally held a far rosier view of the 1960 Master Plan than that of sixties-era activists like Hill. As students and faculty organized against a dramatic series of tuition increases between 2009 and 2011, numerous speakers at campus rallies advanced a declension narrative contrasting a golden age inaugurated by the California Master Plan for Higher Education in 1960 with the underfunded and overcrowded public university campuses of the 2010s.[7] Such was certainly the case at UC Davis, where I participated in a range of rallies, marches, building occupations, and strikes in the wake of the 2008 financial crisis.

The campaign against "fee hikes," as they were often called, saw a statewide uprising from roughly 2009 to 2013. In a struggle that both predated and overlapped with the Occupy Movement, students, faculty, and campus workers organized against the neoliberal status quo while harking back to an earlier age of heavy state investment in education. For participants in that movement, the Master Plan served as a convenient shorthand for the better decades, long before budget cuts and creeping privatization. Left unexplained, however, was why the Master Plan coincided with the massive wave of student organizing that ebbed in the late 1960s.

In the heat of protest and ongoing economic crisis, the actual conditions of the Master Plan system, and the experiences of its students, seemed lost to public memory. For instance, in 2010, a group of activists writing under the name Saving UCSB posted an online petition that gathered hundreds of signatures and called on supporters to "Save UC's Master Plan!" The petition called on members of the California State Assembly to "protect and defend the Master Plan," arguing that "the University of California is the best financial investment our state ever made. Its work contributed crucially to the prosperity of our 'Golden Age.'"[8]

Activists were far from the only individuals positing a declension narrative in which an educational golden age in 1960s California was followed by subsequent decline. As early as 2003, California state librarian Kevin Starr described the California Master Plan as one of the three pillars of what he called the "golden age of public achievement" in mid-twentieth-century California.[9] In 2010, California State University (CSU) chancellor Charles Reed asked the readers of the *San Diego Union Tribune*, "Remember the 'golden age' of California's Master Plan for Higher Education, which promised educational opportunity for all students?"[10] That same year, an article written by the UC Office of the President praised the Master Plan as the document that "launched a golden age in public higher education support in California."[11]

In anticipation of the fifty-year anniversary of the Master Plan, Nanette Asimov of the *San Francisco Chronicle* published an article titled "The Golden Age: Higher Education Master Plan Getting Ignored."[12] Several years later, in 2015, Susan Gubernat, an English professor at CSU East Bay revived the trope of the golden age. Gubernat began her article with a whiff of nostalgia, writing, "Ah, the Golden Age when California was the Golden State, when the Master Plan for Higher Education enabled its young citizens to get a college degree for a few hundred bucks."[13] Another 2015 article, this time in the left-leaning website *truthout*, contrasted the "golden age of the California master plan" to then-president Barack Obama's empty call for tuition-free community colleges.[14]

Yet even in California's "golden age," not all was well in higher education. In an article published by the *Los Angeles Times* in 1998, educator Lee Birdsall noted that the "Master Plan of 1960 . . . created the largest, highest-quality, free system of postsecondary education in the world." However, Birdsall cautioned, "the benefits of this golden age of education were not equitably distributed" because the "chief beneficiaries" of the Master Plan system "were white and male." Birdsall continued, as California's percentage of young people of color steadily increased, "spending on public schools declined" until California came to rank "in the bottom 10 [states] in per-capita spending on students."[15] As the color-coded exclusions that Birdsall referred to attest, even during the first decade of the Master Plan era,

California's public colleges and universities remained far from the picture-perfect meritocracy that many misremember today. A return to the primary sources—to student newspapers, government studies, and speeches given and interviews granted by the student organizers of the 1960s—calls into question this image of a golden age.

Although the Master Plan offered free higher education to all high school graduates in California, for the majority, it limited enrollment to only the state's two-year community colleges. In preparing for the matriculation of the baby boom generation, the Master Plan aimed to increase access through the expansion of existing campuses and the construction of new ones. Simultaneously, however, the plan tightened admissions standards for the UC and state colleges, mandating the bottom two-thirds of students to locally funded community colleges focused on remedial education and vocational training.[16] In line with projected student body growth in the years from 1960 to 1975, the Master Planners tightened admissions standards such that in 1975 approximately fifty thousand students would be diverted from the UC and state colleges to the community colleges. As such, over the course of fifteen years, hundreds of thousands of students would be denied access to the two upper tiers of the Master Plan system.[17] In a state in which primary and secondary education had long been marred by racial segregation, the Master Plan served to replicate and further entrench such exclusions.[18]

With the 1960 Master Plan, the UC—the exclusive top tier already home to the most funding and the best faculty—became even more inaccessible. Although in theory, such admissions standards took no account of race or economic standing, in practice, the Master Plan resulted in a color- and class-coded hierarchy, sending disproportionate percentages of young people of color and working-class youth to community colleges. At the same time, the taxes paid by all Californians helped to maintain the exclusive UC as it became even more white and wealthy. Although the greater promotion of public higher education, in part, represented a turn away from elitism in higher education, the hierarchical nature of the Master Plan system served to re-create in miniature the very racial and class exclusions that structured the nation's decentralized network of private colleges and universities. In response, young working-class Californians of various backgrounds would organize a multiracial movement for the diversification and greater democratization of the Master Plan system.

The student activists of the late 1960s expanded access to the Master Plan system chiefly through their development, expansion, and defense of institutions known as Educational Opportunity Programs (EOPs). These programs proliferated at the UC, state college, and community college levels, but the services they offered varied from campus to campus, particularly in the early years before a push toward greater standardization was made in 1969. Chiefly programs for affirmative action, EOPs helped to recruit to campus promising youth who failed to meet the strenuous color-blind admissions standards enacted by the Master Plan.[19] More than that, EOPs provided funding to help working-class students meet the costs of their educations, ran summer programs to help students of color acculturate to life on majority-white campuses, and provided both tutoring and mentoring for new EOP students, as well as other varied services, depending on the campus in question. Although eventually the EOPs would lose their earlier autonomy and radical bent, their institutionalization nonetheless represented a real victory for students of color and their allies, as EOPs would bring many thousands of working-class youths to the Master Plan system long after the diverse student movement of the 1960s ground to a halt.

· · · · · ·

The first half of *Higher Educational for All* unfolds in a loose chronological order, from the late 1950s to the mid-1960s. Chapter 1 begins with the Soviet launch of Sputnik in October 1957 and traces subsequent debates regarding the state of education in California. In turn, the chapter explores both the passage and the substance of the 1960 California Master Plan for Higher Education, demonstrating that the Cold War context deeply influenced the content of the Master Plan. As top California educators aimed to develop education to meet the Soviet threat, they failed to consider how exclusions built into the K–12 years would impact higher education. De facto segregation simply was not on their radar. The Master Plan, then, emerged not as the meritocracy that was promised but as a hierarchical system very much divided along lines of race and class.

Chapter 2 uncovers the relationship of the 1964 Free Speech Movement (FSM) to the Master Plan, showing the extent to which the FSM was a direct critique and rejection of the Master Plan model of higher education. In particular, this chapter points to the central influence of Hal Draper, a fifty-year-old UC Berkeley librarian who emerged as UC president Clark Kerr's fiercest critic and a mentor to FSM activists. Building on Draper's analysis, students at the crown jewel of the Master Plan system came to reject the views and person of the central author of that vaunted liberal reform. In turn, the FSM's analysis of the Master Plan system would come to inform the wider analyses of Cold War academia put forth by the emergent New Left.

Chapter 3 turns to the opposite side of the political spectrum, by tying the rise of the New Right in California to its rejection of the Master Plan. First, Max Rafferty and then Ronald Reagan utilized criticism of student activism on public college and university campuses to further their political careers. Reagan and the New Right not only denied the legitimacy of student protest but also sought to introduce tuition, calling into question the entire framework of state-funded public higher education. The California Master Plan—notwithstanding all of its limitations—had aspired to provide free higher education to all of California's high school graduates. Reagan, Rafferty, and their ilk sought exactly the inverse: a scaling back of state funding and the further restriction of access to higher education. While piecing together a political coalition that offered staunch opposition to student activists, Reagan would nonetheless prove unable to stem the tide of on-campus organizing.

Chapter 4 is the first of three chapters that explore the anti-racist organizing that emerged to challenge the discriminatory impact of the California Master Plan's stringent admissions standards. Overlapping chronologically, these chapters cover the years from the mid-1960s into the early 1970s. Per the Master Plan, 2 percent of admissions to the UC and state colleges did not need to meet normal admissions criteria; this exception helped to enroll legacy students and student athletes, among others. Chapter 4 explores the experiences of a number of Black student athletes recruited to California campuses, who once there, found themselves disillusioned with on-campus racism and resulting social isolation and in response formed an early nucleus of organizing efforts dedicated to expanding the enrollment of students of color. They did so by making the expansion of EOPs for affirmative action a central demand of their ongoing protests.

Chapter 5 turns to California's largest minority population, Mexican Americans, to demonstrate how young Chicano and Chicana activists organized to improve on the Master Plan system. Beginning with local, then regional efforts, Mexican American activists eventually gathered together at UC Santa Barbara to organize a statewide response to the de facto racism embedded in the Master Plan. Drafting what they called a Master Plan for Chicanos in higher education—known today as El Plan de Santa Barbara—these student and faculty activists made the further development of EOPs a central goal of the Chicano movement in California.

Finally, chapter 6 explores the multiracial alliances that emerged to challenge both the Master Plan's admissions standards and the Eurocentric curriculums on campus. Black and Chicano students, in particular, formed alliances with each other and with other students of color, recruited white radical and liberal allies, and formed the vanguard of a movement that would change the face of California's public college and university campuses by institutionalizing EOPs across the state. Thanks in large part to the limitations of the Master Plan system, California became a central battleground in the Black, Chicano, American Indian, and Asian American student movements, fostering mutual support among diverse student organizations and launching a winning battle to democratize higher education.[20]

Beyond charting a multifaceted history of the California Master Plan, *Higher Education for All* brings into dialogue fields of study that too often are kept apart. Focusing on the long 1960s, this book draws together the historiography of Cold War liberalism, postwar conservatism, and that "movement of movements" known as the New Left.[21] At the same time, the book's latter half aims to make a modest contribution to a burgeoning field of study developing "a relational consciousness of race." As the editors of an important new volume note, such work "consider[s] the racialization and formation of subordinated groups in relation to one another. . . . Group-based racial constructions are formed in relation not only to whiteness but also to other devalued and marginalized groups."[22] *Higher Education for All* thus takes the college campus seriously, not only as a place of politicization and political organizing but as a key site in the formation and re-formation of racial identities. To that end, what follows reintegrates the histories of race-based student movements that, although they developed in unison, have too often been told in isolation.[23]

· · · · · ·

Today, socialists and liberal Democrats alike are promoting various plans to alleviate the student debt crisis and expand access to higher education. At the same time, Black Lives Matter activists are seeking to correct a sordid legacy of structural racism in the United States. In this present-day context, the history of the 1960 California Master Plan for Higher Education should stand as both an example and a warning. The Master Plan represented one of the most important and far-reaching state-level reforms of the postwar liberal consensus. Rationalizing the largest and most vaunted system of public higher education in the country, the Master Plan served not only as a model for other states to emulate but for other nations as well.[24] But much like the larger New Deal era of which it was an extension, the California Master Plan provided a boon to white Americans, while largely excluding African Americans and other people of color.[25]

The Master Plan expanded access to higher education, yet it did so in a way that exacerbated the racial achievement gap in education rather than narrow it. Only thanks to the efforts of a diverse group of students who, in the second half of the 1960s, organized for the establishment, expansion, and defense of EOPs for affirmative action did the Master Plan begin to move closer to meeting its original promise: quality public higher education for all Californians.

1   The Ghost of Sputnik

· ·

We, in Education, are just as interested as the generals and
ambassadors . . . in winning the Cold War.

—Roy E. Simpson, 1959
  (California state superintendent)

This is the time, and California could be the place, where public
interest can demand the expansion of the part education plays on the
national scene. The Russian Sputniks which startled the United States
and her allies with their fascinating orbiting could well have provided
the cue for the change.

—Dick Turpin, 1958
  (*Los Angeles Times* education editor)

The Soviet launch of Sputnik, a decade into the Cold War, shattered the
United States' assumption of technological supremacy and led to months
of searching debate in numerous corners of American society. For those
in higher education, the crisis was particularly acute. Reflecting the intense state of anxiety among patriotic educators, in 1958, the *Journal of
Higher Education* (JHE) printed no less than six articles discussing the impact of Sputnik on American higher education. Topics included "The University in the Free Economy," "Sputnik and the Universities," and "Sputnik
and the Educational Crisis in America." The following year, the *JHE* turned
its attention to the National Defense Education Act (NDEA). The 1959 issue included an editorial overview of the NDEA and an article, "Sputnik
and Student Aid," which opened with what was likely intended as an ominous allusion to the *Communist Manifesto*: "The ghost of Sputnik is still
haunting our educators." Finally, in 1961, the journal's cover story featured
the 1960 California Master Plan for Higher Education. Inside its pages, the
JHE provided an overview of the Master Plan written by T. C. Holy, an
adviser to UC president Clark Kerr and a former member of the Master
Plan Survey Team. Yet, there is much more to the story of Sputnik and the
Master Plan than could fit within the pages of a few volumes of any academic journal.[1]

The California Master Plan for Higher Education emerged in the context of the Cold War in the late 1950s. Those who drafted the Master Plan sought to close a perceived science and technology gap that had emerged as an object of concern with the Soviet launch of Sputnik.[2] In response to the threat posed by Soviet achievement in the space race, the Master Plan would streamline an educational hierarchy with the goal of connecting the brightest young Californians with the state's top researchers. While focused on such pressing international developments, the Master Plan's architects evinced no concern over the obstacles to academic achievement posed by the impact of race-, class-, or gender-based discrimination. In the wake of the Master Plan, the vast majority of working-class Californians— disproportionately people of color—would find themselves relegated to the state's locally funded community colleges.

Despite its promise of higher education for all, the Master Plan engendered a hierarchical and de facto discriminatory system as a result of its overemphasis of the Soviet threat and concerns to keep costs at a minimum as the baby boom led to a swelling college-aged population. During the years covered by the Master Plan, California's system of public higher education would steadily expand, with 491,017 students enrolled in 1960 and 1,540,925 by 1975. As such, the Master Plan would facilitate the incorporation of new UC, state college, and community college campuses, as well as the further development of preexisting ones.[3] Although such expansion was necessary to accommodate all those Californians who wished to continue their educations beyond high school, under the admissions standards imposed by the Master Plan, the Master Plan system would serve to entrench the racial disparities it inherited from a highly unequal system of K–12 education. With the interrelated goals of overtaking Soviet achievement, tailoring education to meet the needs of state and industry, and minimizing expenses, the Master Planners not only failed to combat racial and economic inequality in California, they exacerbated it.[4]

The Sputnik Crisis

The events of October 4, 1957, inaugurated a crisis of confidence over the state of the U.S. educational system and the nation's preparedness for an increasingly ominous Cold War. On that day, Soviet scientists launched the world's first operational satellite as part of the International Geophysical Year, an eighteen-month-long "year" of global cooperation in collecting scientific data and promoting technological advancements toward greater exploration of both the planet Earth and outer space. The unveiling of the sputnik (Russian for "satellite"), only three months into the International Geophysical Year, decimated what had been a widely held belief in the inherent superiority of American science, technology, engineering, and education vis-à-vis its Communist counterparts. Most commentators placed blame for America's embarrassing failure on two culprits: the military establishment and the nation's schools.[5] Despite the underdevelopment of Russia on the eve of the 1917 Revolution, Soviet technicians had not only managed to catch up with their American rivals but to surpass them, calling into question the efficiency of capitalist democracy in a global competition for power and prestige.

The Sputnik crisis unfolded within the context of a global war for supremacy in which the United States and USSR attempted to woo the newly decolonized and nonaligned nations of the third world.[6] As the *New York Times* noted the day after Sputnik's launch, "The Soviet Union is thought to be making a conscious effort to persuade people, especially in Asia and Africa, that Moscow has taken over world leadership in science." The *Sacramento Bee* summed up such sentiments with a cartoon: Uncle Sam stands in shock, grasping a bouquet of flowers and dropping his box of chocolates, as he sees Nikita Khrushchev holding the hand of a young woman in a dress labeled "lesser nations." With his free hand, the Soviet leader points to an orb in the sky labeled "Sputnik." The caption asks, "Who else can give you a moon?" Yet another *New York Times* article reported that thanks to Sputnik, "people could now see how the 'new socialist society' had turned the boldest dreams of mankind into reality." This boldest dream brought to life put to shame American aspirations, which included a satellite, still in the stage of early contemplation, only one-eighth the size of the already orbiting Sputnik.[7]

In the weeks that followed, President Dwight D. Eisenhower defended his own record in a national conversation focusing on the military implications of Sputnik. Democrats charged Eisenhower with "cut[ting] the defense budget to the point where national security was endangered." Eisenhower responded at an October 9 press conference, admitting that "it does definitely prove the possession by Russian scientists of a very powerful thrust in their rocketry, and this is important." Still, the president cautioned, there was no reason "to grow hysterical." As Democrats continued their critiques of the president, Eisenhower met with his thirteen-member Science Advisory Committee. Despite the president's calm reassurance, editorialists at the *San Francisco Chronicle* lambasted Eisenhower's meager assurances, noting that "Sputnik, orbiting overhead, is convincing proof that the Russians have developed engines beefy enough to power an intercontinental missile. . . . Does the United States possess such an engine?"[8] Such questions remained unanswered.

Noted journalist William L. Laurence, who had previously coined the term the *atomic age*, argued that Sputnik demonstrated the need for a greater emphasis on science in American schooling.[9] For scientists and educators, Laurence wrote, "the vital problem facing the nation and the free world as a whole, is the fact that Russia is training scientists and technological personnel at a pace four times that of our own and that, unless something is done about it as a large-scale, national effort, Russia will definitely surpass us in the near future, with consequences too tragic to contemplate." Laurence cited John R. Dunning, dean of Columbia University's School of Engineering, to shore up support for this position. Dunning urged the nation "'to divert more of the national income and effort' toward the problems of technology and technological education." The Communist system, Dunning warned, "has been able to produce scientists and engineers in certainly greater numbers and quite possibly of higher technical proficiency than our own." Lamentably, Laurence continued, "In a free society such as ours it is not possible 'to channel human efforts' without the individual's consent and wholehearted willingness." Calls for structural change to address America's scientific deficiencies, and the dichotomy posed between the effectiveness of a state economy directed by the Kremlin and the cumbersome nature of an ostensibly democratic economic system of free enterprise, would remain pillars of the American debate around Sputnik.[10]

On October 18, two weeks after Sputnik's launch, the UC regents made the seemingly unrelated announcement of the appointment of Clark Kerr as the UC's next president. This decision would prove highly influential to California's response to the Sputnik crisis. Born in Pennsylvania in 1911, Kerr had moved to California to pursue graduate studies at Stanford and earned his PhD in economics from UC Berkeley in 1939. Prior to his appointment as UC Berkeley's chancellor in 1952, Kerr worked as a labor negotiator and professor of industrial relations. It was in these years that Kerr earned the nickname the Machiavellian Quaker for his deceptively adroit skills of negotiation, a talent he would bring to his position as head of the UC. Interviews conducted with Kerr after he was named president point toward the course he would chart for the UC. Whereas in an early interview with the *San Francisco Examiner* Kerr debated the threat posed by Russian advancements, a *Los Angeles Times* article covering the Kerr appointment made no mention of

Sputnik, instead focusing on the anticipated growth of the UC. Already the nation's largest university, containing over forty thousand students across six campuses, Kerr envisioned an expansion of the UC to some one hundred thousand students dispersed throughout ten campuses by 1970.[11]

The *Los Angeles Times* presciently described Kerr as a far cry from the stereotypical "ivory tower" academic. Journalist Lucy Newhall noted of Kerr that "he has been involved more actively than most businessmen in the hurly-burly of economic life." Kerr himself argued that his was not a purely academic endeavor, commenting that "there is no industry in the State, nor any level of government, that is not in some way interested in and affected by the work of the university."[12] Kerr's understanding of the importance of the university to the state of California, combined with the threat presented by Soviet achievements and anticipation of massive growth in the student population, would crystallize some sixteen months later in the California Master Plan for Higher Education. That California's system of public higher education took the form it did was in large part due not only to Kerr's foresight and determination but also to his keen appreciation for both industry and government interests. As the historian Brian Balogh would later note, Kerr "epitomized Cold War liberalism."[13]

One month after Sputnik took flight, the Soviets again awed American observers by announcing the launch of a second satellite—and this one contained a passenger. Sputnik II was not only six times as heavy as its predecessor; it accommodated a dog named Laika, a mutt and former stray that Soviet scientists had retrieved off the streets of Moscow. What the world did not know at the time, and would not know until 2002, was that Laika had died in the first few hours of flight. The Kremlin's secrecy aside, the launch signaled yet another successful media coup for the Soviets who had timed their feat to coincide with the fortieth anniversary of the so-called October Revolution.[14] Moscow released an official announcement commemorating the launch, stating, "it seems the present generation will witness how the freed and conscious labor of the people of the new socialist society turns even the most daring of man's dreams into reality."[15] Sputnik II contributed additional urgency to the national debate already under way. In his column in the *Washington Post*, conservative journalist Stewart Alsop warned of future satellites that, instead of a dog, might contain sophisticated spy equipment or even a nuclear bomb. Sounding an ominous note, Alsop posed the question, "If one such weapon-satellite can be launched, why not dozens, to form above the world a universal Sword of Damocles, controlled from Moscow?"[16]

Throughout November 1957, the public debate over the now-plural Sputniks increasingly honed in on the state of the nation's schools and the significance of the STEM disciplines of science, technology, engineering, and mathematics. The *New York Times* noted Eisenhower's "surprise" at being "told by a group of eminent scientists that what they were worried about was not the sputnik but the state of scientific education in the schools and universities of the nation." On November 7, Eisenhower began a series of speeches focusing on science and national defense. In the first, the president admitted that the United States had not given "high enough priority to scientific education and to the place of science in our national life." Although critical of the president's efforts thus far, Democrats "pledged support . . . for 'any real, effective' science speed-up program." At the same time, a government study commissioned to report on Soviet schooling noted the dilapidated state of America's science and mathematics education when compared with the robust emphasis placed on those fields by their Communist adversaries.[17]

By early November, national debate had decidedly turned toward the role of education in winning the Cold War. The *New York Times* emphasized that the existence of "great deficiencies and weaknesses" in science and mathematics "threatens to assure Soviet scientific dominance in the future unless we correct our deficiencies. The task will not be easy, but the sputniks have done us a service in assuring that now we shall begin really to work on this problem." The article also argued for the provision of economic incentives to attract "able young people" to the right fields of study.[18] A front-page article in the *Washington Post* reported similar conclusions drawn from an interview with rocketry expert Wernher von Braun. The Nazi war criminal behind the V-2 rocket and the crown jewel of Operation Paperclip, von Braun stated that "I can only hope that [Sputnik] will give the United States science education program" a great boost.[19] By December 1957, the *New York Times* noted that all of the agitation on the question of science education had begun to take effect: the National Science Foundation (NSF) "seems certain for the first time in its seven-year history to obtain from the Administration and from Congress all the money it wants." As such, the NSF announced plans to triple its 1957 research grants.[20]

The *Los Angeles Times* Interrogates Sputnik

As the need for greater funding of education and a new emphasis on STEM was trumpeted throughout the nation, Dick Turpin of the *Los Angeles Times* brought together a group of influential California educators for a discussion of Sputnik and higher education. The daily's education editor, Turpin conducted interviews with top educators in the state for a series consisting of six articles in January 1958. Interviewees included president-elect of the UC system Clark Kerr, UCLA chancellor Raymond B. Allen, California Institute of Technology president Lee A. DuBridge, University of Southern California (USC) chancellor Rufus B. von KleinSmid, and Stanford University president Wallace Sterling. Turpin intended the series to serve as a realistic diagnosis of the state of education in California and the United States with, as he put it, specific appraisal of "its strengths and its weaknesses as it meets the ominous challenge of advancing Soviet technology."[21] Turpin's series greatly enhanced the in-state dialogue on higher education that culminated in the development of the California Master Plan for Higher Education the following year.

Marshaling the prestige and authority of leading educators and conveying the urgency of their perspectives in California's paper of record, the *Los Angeles Times*'s Dick Turpin worked to push the state's political and economic elites to embrace education reform. Turpin's series began three months to the day after the launch of Sputnik, opening with a frank concession: "The United States, with begrudging acknowledgement, has been ushered into the Space Age by unheralded Russian scientists."[22] Turpin forewarned that "a second Pearl Harbor, conceived in the classroom and the laboratory, appears in the aftermath of visible, orbiting evidences of Soviet technology, and shatters wishful illusions of an American monopoly on brainpower." Much as "the national myths of invincibility" were dashed "on a Sunday morning in 1941, the beep-beep-beep of the world's first man-made moon, with its smug Kremlin trademark" forced on the people of the United States an honest discussion of their own intellectual and educational preparedness.[23]

More than anything else, Turpin's series sought to uncover why the Soviets had succeeded where the United States had failed. In their attempt to answer this question, the interviewees came up against an uncomfortable possibility: paradoxically, to combat the Communists they so hated, Americans had to become more like them. The envy with which many American elites viewed the effectiveness of the Soviet system, coupled with their nods to the importance of democratic governance, proved a staple of post-Sputnik debate. As UCLA chancellor Raymond B. Allen argued in his interview with Turpin, "the Soviet Union in 40 years has converted an agrarian society into a powerful scientific, technological, industrial community . . . [a] historic achievement [that] was accomplished by brutally imposed sacrifices of the long-suffering Russian people—but the achievement stands."[24]

The presidents of Stanford and the UC, Wallace Sterling and Clark Kerr, joined Chancellor Allen in confronting this paradox. Kerr lamented that "the Russian challenge has placed pressure on our freedom-of-choice system [of curriculum] and the swing now must be away from it." Stanford University's Sterling agreed with Kerr, decrying that "with too much freedom of choice, our system has become a cafeteria for elective subjects."[25] Continuing the theme, UCLA chancellor Raymond Allen responded to the Soviet threat by proposing a five-year plan of his own: "The world will belong to those who know discipline. . . . We have the greatest free-enterprise system ever known but we—and I mean citizens, industry and government—must accomplish in five years what would have taken 20 years."[26] Free enterprise and democratic governance were to continue but made harder and more effective.

The interviewees located one of the key sources of democratic "softness" and inefficiency in the influence of the philosopher John Dewey. Dewey, best known for his progressive theory of education, was the only individual singled out for criticism by the educators interviewed by Turpin. For Dewey, secular and noncoercive schools should function as the principal site of the reproduction of a democratic citizenry.[27] In the eyes of conservative critics whose critiques of Dewey long predated the Sputnik crisis, progressive education was responsible for a host of ills in American public schools and in society at large. In the post-Sputnik moment, such commentators found an increasingly large audience.[28] Yet in the gap between progressive education as Dewey envisioned it and as educators practiced it and in the chasm between frontline educators and their conservative critics, Dewey's impact on American schools was both magnified and distorted.[29] Surveying the responses of his interviewees, Turpin noted their shared belief that "learning through experimentation has been carried too far" by social scientists enamored of Dewey's theories and that "pupils have been given more freedom of choice in their subjects than has been good for them."[30]

The relative merits of the STEM fields, in contrast to the social sciences and humanities, provided yet another theme for Turpin and his commentators. Later changes to education funding, which promoted STEM at the expense of the social sciences and humanities, would reflect their views. Although Turpin bemoaned the American educational system's deficiencies vis-à-vis the Soviets in the STEM fields, he maintained that the Communists were still clearly hamstrung "in areas where political ideologies" existed.[31]

Turpin condensed the arguments of his interviewees to highlight the need to "shore up and sharpen the precise subjects—mathematics, science, and languages. Sift out of the curriculum the expendable softness."[32] Once again stressing the importance of the hard sciences against a more traditional curriculum aiming to prepare students for civic participation, Turpin summed up the views of the five educators: "Science must not be overdone at the sacrifice of the liberal arts *but,* they chorus firmly, if the best American brains are to contribute to the promising fruits of the peaceful Space Age, they must be found, guided, and exhorted at an early age."[33]

Many of Turpin's interviewees stressed the need to maintain separate curricular tracks so that more advanced students would not be dragged down by their slower classmates. Their concerns would find remedy in tracking systems, standardized tests, and the three-tiered educational hierarchy later enshrined in the Master Plan, which would send the majority of California college students to community colleges for remedial and vocational training. UCLA chancellor Raymond Allen, fresh off a visit to Moscow, complained that "Russian students are far more advanced than ours in the education fundamentals. We have continually underestimated the capacity of children to learn. By gearing our schooling to the slow learners, we've wasted our brighter ones."[34] Clark Kerr, stressing the need for high schoolers to have a sufficiency in English, foreign languages, and math, forewarned that beginning in the fall of 1958, the UC would "become more stringent about entrance exams and graduation requirements," thus putting the pressure on early educators to produce results.[35] As Caltech president Lee A. DuBridge, a science adviser to both Harry S. Truman and Eisenhower, put it, "There is a definite need to lift up the educational system all the way back to the elementary grades. There is too much time wasted. . . . For a long time our attention has been directed at the handicapped students. The gifted children must now receive as much direction."[36] In order to beat the Russians, some American children would need suffer benign neglect so that the gifted few might realize their true talents.

Stanford University's Wallace Sterling took direct aim at the tensions over equality that these five educators confronted as he honed in on the theme of gifted students. As if to preempt his critics on the progressive left, the Stanford president admonished that "it is not undemocratic to find our better young minds and push them along."[37] Sterling, Turpin noted, "state[d] that talk about equality and democracy for all sounds well from the rostrum but that history and examination show that all students and all people are not equal in ability in a republic or under a dictatorship." Sterling, "like

many other men of letters, accepts the reasoning that no amount of schooling or any other training can eliminate the differences inherent in a person's genes."[38] Such intellectual elites took as a given that certain young
Americans were simply not college material and that low achievers must
make way for the cream to rise to the top.

The chancellor of USC took Sterling's view of human variability to its
uncomfortable logical end point. Rufus von KleinSmid, with his provoca-
tively trimmed mustache and aristocratic German name, has long dogged
accusations of antisemitism and Nazi sympathies.[39] Although no clear
evidence on that exact point exists, von KleinSmid was a fierce proponent of eugenics and forced sterilization programs who in 1928 cofounded the eugenicist Human Betterment Foundation. A hotbed of
eugenics, California sterilized some twenty thousand people between
1909 and 1960, accounting for one-third of the nation's sterilizations.[40]
The USC president and author of *Eugenics and the State* (1913) argued in
Turpin's article that "the truth cannot be evaded, falsified or denied and it
is a stern teacher. . . . Let's realize we cannot bluff our way about everything being equal." Now paraphrasing von KleinSmid, Turpin began, "It
is vital [von KleinSmid] says . . . to 'separate the weak and the strong'
students and find worth-while occupations for both."[41] Although von Klein-
Smid was likely the only active eugenicist in the bunch, that his views
dovetailed so nicely with those of others interviewed by Turpin should
give pause. What was envisioned by these titans of education was not an
egalitarian leveling of educational opportunities for all Californians but
a plan for how to best facilitate the achievement of the most gifted students so as to effectively realize America's Cold War aims.

On January 10, Dick Turpin concluded his series on Sputnik and higher
education by emphasizing the recommendations of these experts to focus education on meeting the threats of the Cold War. According to Turpin,
central to his interviewees' concerns was the need to place the "greatest
stress" on "the precise subjects—science, mathematics, and the languages."
Turpin paraphrased Clark Kerr, who pointed toward the example set by the
Soviets to argue against a "crash" program and in favor of a more sustained structural readjustment: "We can't have a hurry-up program, [Kerr]
adds. Russia had an evidently thorough system, giving its students 10 years of
compulsory education including five years of foreign language, five years
of physics, six years of mathematics, four years of chemistry, and three
years of biology."[42] Turpin ended his series of articles by noting contentedly

that State Superintendent of Public Instruction Roy E. Simpson had called for a meeting to move toward revising the state's public school curriculum.

Turpin followed up his series with two articles providing commentary given by Roy Simpson, and other superintendents, who called on American educators to outperform their Soviet counterparts.[43] The three superintendents reiterated themes touched on by earlier interviewees while maintaining their defense of the state's public schools. Los Angeles County Superintendent C. C. Trillingham lamented that the Los Angeles schools' teacher-to-student ratio of one to thirty-five paled in comparison to the Soviet Union's one to seventeen ratio but argued that "the American solution is not to copy the Russian brand of education, which is overemphasis on science, underemphasis on the humanities and twisting the individual to meet the militaristic needs of the state . . . but to improve our own brand of learning."[44] Trillingham saw no need to worry, however, about the ways in which corporations might influence public education, lauding the increase in "co-operation between secondary schools and industry" in Southern California.[45] Such close cooperation between schools and big business would become a key target of student protests as a new generation of Californians ascended to the state's public colleges and universities in the 1960s. Finally, Turpin reported on Simpson's enthusiastic description of a new experimental program aimed at determining the "types of instruction best suited to high-IQ students."[46] In the coming year, Simpson would emerge as a key figure in the development of the Master Plan for Higher Education, surpassed only by Clark Kerr in his individual influence on that influential reform.

The Sacramento Conference

On February 24 and 25, 1958, State Superintendent of Public Instruction Roy Simpson convened a conference in Sacramento focusing on the teaching of science and mathematics in response to the threat posed by Sputnik. Born in Santa Rosa in 1893, Simpson had attended business school and served in the army before becoming a high school principal after World War I. Having worked his way through various superintendent positions since 1927, Simpson became state superintendent, the single most important education official in California, in 1946.[47] Simpson's 1958 conference brought a number of individuals from California's schools and businesses together with bureaucrats from the nation's capital. In addition to Simpson and his co-interviewees from the Turpin articles—C. C. Trillingham and Ellis Jarvis—the conference featured talks by California Associate Superintendents of Public Instruction Jay D. Connor and J. Burton Vasche; Superintendent of Stockton City Schools Nolan D. Pulliam; associate director of the Radiation Laboratory at the University of California Glenn T. Seaborg; and the owner and chief executive officer (CEO) of the El Monte–based Hoffman Electronics Company, H. Leslie Hoffman. From Washington, DC came the executive director of the Scientific Manpower Commission, Howard A. Meyerhoff; Deputy Assistant Secretary of Labor Aryness Joy Wickens; and Kermit Mohn from the Office of the Assistant Secretary of Defense. The conference took place over the course of two days in the State Education Building in the heart of downtown Sacramento.[48]

Roy Simpson addressed attendees at the opening and closing of the conference, and as evidenced by his introductory remarks, Sputnik was a topic of central concern. The California superintendent began by addressing the collective sense of crisis generated by the Soviet advance, while simultaneously defending his turf. Simpson assured the attendees that "long before the Soviet satellite jarred the complacency of our American public and brought on an acute sense of neurosis, our public schools were giving emphasis to the increased need for more concentrated training in the physical and technological sciences. . . . We must keep in mind that our need for educated men and women to build a nation to live as Americans is independent of any competition with the Russian philosophy."[49] Still, Simpson noted, Americans would only receive the educations that they were willing to pay for. It appears that this was more than rhetoric aimed at protecting his own reputation. In the postwar era, reformers and proponents of increased national funding to schools were thwarted by a significant opposition wary of federal control and the threat of federally mandated integration. Yet the Sputnik crisis, according to historian Barbara Barksdale Clowse, "temporarily neutralized much of the opposition. . . . In this interim of crisis, champions of federal aid to education established a beachhead" with the passage of the 1958 National Defense Education Act.[50] In California, they would secure the Master Plan.

Presenters to the conference repeatedly drew attention to the role that education might serve in meeting a perceived "manpower" shortage and in bolstering the nation's economy. Much like commentators in the nation's leading newspapers, those who spoke at the conference lamented the Soviet Union's unique ability to mobilize a vast population and tailor education to meet the needs of the state while, at the same time, they praised the virtues of democracy and stressed the importance of education to meeting the needs of American industry. Aryness Joy Wickens, an economist and statistician from the Department of Labor, spoke to the federal government's concern with maintaining a public education system geared to facilitate an advanced capitalist division of labor within the context of the nation's Cold War rivalry. Wickens called for mass participation and action to address the concerns of the "space age." Warning listeners that "there can be no question of the seriousness of the situation," Wickens proclaimed that "the key to this race is people—our human resources. . . . We know too that how they use their talents will determine who wins this scientific competition, and that in a democracy performance depends upon the free decision of millions of individuals."[51] Despite distancing herself from the Soviets' social engineering, Wickens went on to outline a plan for best meeting the manpower needs of industry and the armed services—admitting that ultimately, what was needed was an education that molded students to fit the needs of capital and the state.

Hoffman Electronics' owner and CEO H. Leslie Hoffman, the only conference presenter from the private sector, offered the most candid advice for what needed to be done. Having transitioned years earlier from producing consumer appliances to making industrial and military electronics, Hoffman embraced a military Keynesianism that shaded into war profiteering. The El Monte–based CEO offered an enthusiastic assessment of the lucrative opportunities to be opened up by an extended Cold War, stating, "The electronics industry has become the second largest employer in the southern California area. The significant fact of this growth is that most of the work in which we are engaged today is on ideas, products, and services that were not known or thought about before the war. . . . Most of us feel that this is just starting and that we are on the threshold of an even greater horizon providing we can secure from our educational processes competent men to take advantage of these tremendous opportunities."[52] Not only did Hoffman champion the sort of Cold War complicity that students would reject with the coming of the New Left, but he also utilized the very sort of language young activists would heatedly denounce. After repeatedly using the term *product* to outline his ideas for education, Hoffman explained his use of the word: "When I talk about our product I'm talking about the product of our high schools and our colleges, in other words, the graduate that we see." The product, Hoffman explained, suffered from a "lack of uniformity of quality," had a poor "attitude of mind," and was in need of "stricter discipline" and a stronger work ethic.[53] The vision of education Hoffman championed thus both dehumanized students and stripped them of their individuality to the benefit of big business.

To a large extent, even the educators attending the Sacramento conference embraced the language, logic, and ideas of corporate America.[54] Nolan D. Pulliam, the Stockton superintendent of city schools, happily reported to the conference that "industry has found it profitable to devote increasing sums to research," while his counterpart in Los Angeles lauded the role that local industry played in helping to develop the curriculum for the region's seven community colleges. For greater Los Angeles's two-year colleges, Ellis Jarvis noted approvingly, content is "adjusted to meet changed need of industry" based on annual meetings with local employers.[55] Prefacing his advice with a quote he attributed to Joseph Stalin—"Education is a weapon"—Stockton Superintendent Pulliam advised that "it does seem evident that education must be considered a potentially powerful weapon in the arsenal of freedom."[56] Adopting from the example of the nation's archenemy in the Cold War, Pulliam proposed the use of Soviet educational methods to achieve the American aim of boosting the capitalist economy.

The educators gathered for the Sacramento conference believed that California could meet the challenge posed by Soviet advances by trimming the proverbial fat and better tailoring education to suit the needs of industry. As had a number of interviewees in Dick Turpin's *Los Angeles Times* series, Los Angeles County superintendent of schools C. C. Trillingham called on universities to "tighten up their entrance requirements." "Public schools have to accept all," Trillingham noted. "Universities don't." The twin goal of education, he insisted, must be "to move forward our economy and to defend our freedoms."[57] Jay D. Connor, California associate superintendent of public instruction, likewise pointed to the necessity for educators to address "the changing needs of American industry, agriculture, and business," a moving target he acknowledged would be difficult to hit. This could be accomplished, in part, Connor remarked, through "better coordination of the offerings of the high schools and the colleges of our state; with particular emphasis for these superior and gifted children . . . permitting . . . faster progress into the areas of specialization for those who can . . . demonstrate capacity."[58] Trillingham and Connor stressed the need for universities to be both more selective in their admissions and more accommodating of the business community in their curriculum.

At the same time, some attendees offered unheeded warnings regarding the abandonment of California's young women and people of color. In an era prior to the legislative climax of the civil rights movement and the early stirrings of women's liberation, both populations remained underrepresented in California higher education. While simultaneously urging more strenuous entrance requirements, C. C. Trillingham called for greater appreciation of the potential role of women, who, he noted, would make up half of an incoming cohort of some ten million workers. To beat the Soviets, the United States would need to "consider making use of the services of this big source of womanpower."[59] Where Trillingham looked to women, another educator cautioned those present to remember California's often neglected communities of color.[60]

A Nobel Prize winner and the former director of plutonium research for the Manhattan Project, Glenn Seaborg was the only speaker who addressed the important issue of California's large nonwhite population.[61] At the end of a particularly long talk, Seaborg noted that "native intelligence is not the special monopoly of the white race, and we must not overlook the potential . . . among our Mexican, Negro and Oriental ethnic groups." Several years into the wave of organizing and protest we know as the civil rights movement, Seaborg declared the need to "stress more strongly the importance of the education of the Negro and the Mexican-American not only to the individual, but to the state of California."[62] As the only commentator at the conference to address the impact of racism, Seaborg had the prescience to anticipate one of the major student critiques of the education reform which followed in the wake of the Sputnik crisis.

The National Defense Education Act

Following the February conference in Sacramento, Californians, and Americans more broadly, continued to debate Sputnik's implications for the realm of education. Some six months later, legislators reached a breakthrough at the national level. The National Defense Education Act (NDEA) was passed on September 2, 1958, the result of almost a year of post-Sputnik debate.[63] The bill aimed to improve education through the graduate school level while inaugurating a period of greater federal involvement in the nation's educational system—all geared toward the defense of the United States in the Cold War context.[64] As such, the NDEA provided a useful example for California's Cold War liberals.

The NDEA represented the largest federal commitment to higher education since the Morrill Act of 1862, establishing federal expenditures of slightly under $1 billion over the next four years. The NDEA was comprised of three major components. First, a fund totaling $295 million, focused on students in science, mathematics, and foreign languages, offered yearly loans of $1,000 for up to five years. Fully half of such loan debts would be forgiven for those students who became teachers, and all students would have an eleven-year period in which to pay off their loans. Second, the act provided for an additional $280 million in federal funds to match local purchases of science, math, and foreign language equipment in schools, whether private or public. Third, the NDEA allocated nearly $60 million for 5,500 graduate fellowships in the fields of engineering, science, and foreign area studies, or in any other field deemed to contribute to national defense.[65]

Despite the fact that this legislation represented a major breakthrough in the realm of education, when compared to greater defense spending, the NDEA funding was relatively miserly. Whereas the act secured almost $1 billion over the next four years, at the same time legislators added several billion more to a national defense budget that already surpassed $40 billion.[66] The limited funding, however, did not hinder the celebration that followed the bill's passing. Senate majority leader Lyndon Johnson labeled the act "an historic landmark." The preamble to the bill itself proclaimed that "the security of the Nation requires the fullest development of the mental resources and technical skills of its young men and women. . . . The national interest requires . . . that the Federal Government give assistance to education for programs which are important to our national defense."[67] Back in California, Roy Simpson described the NDEA as "a one billion dollar, four-year answer to post-Sputnik criticism of American schools."[68] Both the NDEA influx of federal dollars and the example of successful reform encouraged ongoing debates over the colleges and universities in the Golden State.

Toward the Master Plan

In the wake of the lucrative opportunities for funding research opened up by Sputnik and the Cold War, the Master Plan emerged as a by-product of the competition for funds between the UC and the California state colleges. In particular, state college presidents who sought to challenge the UC's long-standing monopoly on state-funded research could now use the threat of Soviet technological advancements to leverage their goals. In an effort to prevent, or at least circumscribe, the increased role aimed for by the state colleges, newly inaugurated UC president Clark Kerr set out to find a path toward the reorganization of California's higher education system that would preserve the privileges of his elite UC. To do so, Kerr had to navigate the rivalries and alliances of the state's Liaison Committee, which consisted of the UC regents and the members of the state board of education, who represented the state colleges. As UC president, and therefore a member of the Board of Regents, Kerr himself served on the committee. Since California governor Earl Warren created the group in 1946, the Liaison Committee had overseen the 1948 Strayer Report and the 1955 "Restudy of the Needs of California in Higher Education," as well as the 1957 "Study of the Need for Additional Centers of Public Higher Education in California."[69] Yet, the recommendations included in those reports went unheeded in the years prior to the launch of Sputnik.

Beyond its Cold War context, the Master Plan responded to the significant increase in school-aged Californians brought about by the postwar baby boom and rising in-migration from other states. From 1940 to 1959, California births rose 210 percent. As early as 1947, a California Department of Education memorandum warned that "an emergency exists in the provision of facilities in publicly supported institutions of higher learning" and stressed an "urgency for action." In 1947, enrollment for California's public and private institutions of higher learning stood at 171,785, yet officials estimated an increase of fifty thousand students in the next three years alone. What's more, California residents living in areas served only by two-year community colleges had begun to demand their expansion into four-year state colleges.[70] Beginning their work in mid-1947, researchers focused the Strayer Report on the division of educational labor between the UC, state colleges, and community colleges, on projected growth, and on planning for future campus sites and expanding academic programs.[71] As noted by historian of California education John Aubrey Douglass, "the Strayer Report articulated the purpose and responsibilities of each segment of the tripartite education system that would, some twelve years later, form the basis for the 1960 Master Plan."[72] Until the spark provided by Sputnik, however, such plans remained confined to the bureaucratic labyrinth.

Several years after the release of the Strayer Report, state officials commissioned a "restudy" to focus on the optimal enrollment for the state's three tiers of higher education and on the governance of the then–largely autonomous California state colleges. The 1948 Strayer Report had warned that when university campuses and state colleges grew beyond ten thousand and five thousand students, respectively, they would become "impersonal and mechanical . . . in the treatment of students."[73] Despite the Strayer

Report's earlier findings, the 1955 restudy argued that "there is no evidence that the quality of education at the large campuses of the University of California suffers in comparison with that at the smaller state colleges."[74] In addition to its dismissal of concerns about institutional size, the restudy defined public higher education along vocational lines, associating the community colleges, the state colleges, and the UC with "technical training," "occupational training," and "professional training," respectively.[75] Finally, the restudy recommended the formation of a board of trustees for the state colleges, rather than have them remain under the state board of education. This suggestion would be taken up by the Master Plan.[76] Even though the Master Plan eventually incorporated a number of the restudy's recommendations, lacking an impetus to action in 1955, both the UC regents and the state board of education declined to endorse the restudy.

Despite the immediate failures of the Strayer Report and the restudy to provide the motivation for qualitative reform, the state had already begun to respond to its growing population through the expansion of campuses at the UC, state college, and community college levels. In the years prior to the 1960 Master Plan, these three levels of public higher education operated autonomously and without coordination. In 1947, officials opened state college campuses in Los Angeles and Sacramento. A state college in Long Beach followed the next year. In 1957, the California state colleges expanded yet again, opening campuses in Fullerton, Hayward, Northridge, and Stanislaus. Among others, Clark Kerr pointed to the creation of a new campus in rural Stanislaus County as representative of the haphazard expansion of the state college system prior to the Master Plan. The UC president noted sardonically that the legislature was "being pressed to create colleges at every crossroads. And one did get by—Turlock. The turkey capital of the world got its own" state college. As future CSU president Donald Gerth would note, the "Stanislaus State campus at Turlock was a direct result of the fact that the then Speaker of the Assembly . . . was from there."[77] For California communities off the beaten path, the development of a new state college could mean a financial windfall.

The expansion of the UC also continued, albeit at a slower pace. In 1951, Berkeley's farm school at Davis, operating since 1905, expanded into a full campus. Riverside, since 1907 the UC's Citrus Experiment Station, followed suit in 1954. Completing the triad was the former Scripps Institute of Oceanography, part of the UC since 1912, which became UC San Diego in 1959. UC Irvine, created ex nihilo, joined the rapidly expanding UC in 1960. (UC Santa Cruz would join, after the passage of the Master Plan, in 1962.) Not to be outdone by the state colleges or the university, community colleges expanded at an extraordinary rate. Following the California department of education's 1947 call to action, twenty new community colleges were founded, bringing the total number of two-year institutions to sixty by the onset of the Master Plan. As Clark Kerr later noted, "We recommended that there be a community college within commuting distance of every person in the state, except in the most remote areas."[78]

In December 1958, Clark Kerr attended his first Liaison Committee meeting. There, Kerr continued to promote the establishment of a plan for the reorganization of California higher education that would maintain the privileges of the UC while offering limited concessions to increasingly determined state college administrators. The first state college, the California State Normal School, was founded in San Francisco as a teachers' college in 1862. Later campuses joined the state college system under the purview of the state board of education. In 1935, the legislature reclassified teachers' colleges as "state colleges" to reflect the expansion of the curriculum beyond teacher training. From 1948 to 1959, enrollment at the state colleges doubled, and administrators began clamoring for greater funding and the accreditation of certain disciplines theretofore limited to the UC. At his first Liaison Committee meeting, Kerr made a conciliatory gesture, embracing the efforts of San Jose State to gain accreditation for its engineering program and stating his support for increased funding toward research conducted at the state colleges. Kerr's overture helped clear the way for a path to progress during a 1959 California legislative session clogged by "some 23 bills, 2 constitutional amendments and 3 resolutions" calling for a restructuring of the state's system of higher education. In particular, Kerr's recommendation of a joint meeting of the UC regents and the state board of education resulted in the approval of two such meetings that would take place in March and April 1959.[79]

At the behest of Clark Kerr, Bakersfield assemblywoman Dorothy Donahoe introduced Assembly Concurrent Resolution 88, paving the way for the eventual passage of Master Plan legislation. The UC president had previously sent UC lobbyist James Corley to visit the Bakersfield Democrat and gain her approval for Kerr's vision of the Master Plan. Donahoe consented and brought to the state assembly the draft of a resolution Corley had given her. The resolution called on the Liaison Committee "to prepare a master plan for the development, expansion, and integration of facilities, curriculum, and standards of higher education, in junior colleges, state colleges, the University of California, and other institutions of higher education of the State, to meet the needs of the State during the next 10 years and there-after." Despite ongoing clashes between Kerr and Roy Simpson over the pre-rogatives of the UC and state colleges, movement toward the Master Plan gained the backing of the newly inaugurated governor, Democrat Edmund "Pat" Brown. The state legislature approved Donahoe's resolution the week following the UC regents–state board of education meeting of April 15.[80]

The next months witnessed efforts by Kerr and Simpson to find a middle ground that would satisfy their competing ambitions and bolster their respective systems while moving forward on the Master Plan. In May 1959, the two came to an agreement on the creation of a Master Plan survey team. According to that agreement, the survey team would research questions concerning potential student enrollment up to 1975; the educational divi-sion of labor to be established between the three tiers; a tentative timeline and priority list for the development of new UC and state college campuses; a costs estimate for public higher education in the decade to come; an ap-praisal of the potential of the state to pay for further developments in its public higher education system; and plans for "the organization, control and administration" of the Master Plan system. To ensure equity, the team it-self was to be comprised of two representatives of each of the state's three tiers—the UC, state colleges, and community colleges. During a Liaison Committee meeting on June 3, 1959, Kerr and Simpson contacted the presi-dent of Occidental College, Arthur G. Coons, who agreed serve as chair.[81] A representative of the state's private colleges and universities, Coons was thought to provide an impartial perspective, equally sympathetic to the aims of both UC and state college boosters.

Whereas the Master Plan survey team itself was made up of only 7 mem-bers, some 125 individuals contributed toward the development of the plan.[82] This larger group included individuals from the UC, the state colleges, the community colleges, independent colleges, the state department of educa-tion, California high schools, the California Association of School Admin-istrators, the California Association of Adult Education Administrators, and a number of state politicians. Of those 125 participants, two were women: Mabel E. Kinney of the state board of education and Assemblywoman Donahoe, one of the nine politicians invited to "sit with" the Liaison Com-mittee for discussion.[83] Not a single member was tasked with exploring the circumstances and needs of women or the state's minority populations—two diverse groups vastly underserved by California's system of higher education.

In the seven months that the Master Plan survey team had to complete and present its research to the state legislature, tensions soared regarding the appropriate roles of the UC and state colleges. In particular, Glenn Dumke of the state colleges and Dean McHenry of the UC sparred as proxies for their institutions and superiors, Roy Simpson and Clark Kerr, respectively. Dumke, then president of San Francisco State College, pushed an amendment to secure for state colleges the doctorate, heretofore the prerogative of the UC. Kerr's former graduate school roommate, Dean McHenry, was quick to combat Dumke's attempt to, in McHenry's words, "make passes at the Crown Jewels" of the UC system and promised "the firmest resistance." In addition to the doctorate, Dumke sought for the state colleges what Coons called "adequate state support of faculty research."[84] Finally, some within the state colleges pushed to free themselves from what they viewed as the strictures of the California department of education through the creation of a board of trustees that would function in a manner analogous to that of the UC Board of Regents.

Thanks to the determined partisanship of Clark Kerr, the state colleges could not easily secure the changes they so clearly desired. However, a compromise engineered by Kerr, and accepted by Dumke and other representatives of the state colleges, allowed the Master Plan survey team to avoid an impasse. Kerr proposed that the state colleges offer a joint doctorate in tandem with the UC.[85] The representatives of the state colleges accepted the UC president's suggestion, with the condition that they be granted a greater role in state-funded research. Last, the Master Plan, in the words of Glenn Dumke, "recommended that the state colleges establish their own board, modeled somewhat on the Board of Regents of the university . . . and that systemwide governance be set up under a chancellor who would be the executive officer of the board."[86] With these three compromises, the Master Plan survey team reached an agreement on the report, the "Master Plan for Higher Education in California: 1960–1975," that Simpson and Kerr would present to the California state legislature on February 1, 1960.

In March, liberal Democrat George Miller, a state senator from Contra Costa, introduced the bill that would enshrine an attenuated version of the proposed Master Plan. By striking down the proposal that key elements of the Master Plan be written into California's state constitution, Miller sought to reserve for legislators the right to more easily modify the Master Plan system. Assemblywoman Donahoe, a staunch proponent of the Master Plan, began work on minor revisions to Miller's bill before abruptly falling ill and dying of complications related to pneumonia on April 5, 1960. Donahoe's unexpected passing at age forty-nine led Senator Miller to rename his legislation the Donahoe Higher Education Act. The assembly and senate ratified the bill, and nine days after Donahoe's untimely death, Governor Brown signed the Donahoe Act while standing alongside Clark Kerr, Roy Simpson, Arthur Coons, and George Miller.[87] Only three months prior, the liberal Democrat Brown had couched his support for the Master Plan in the context of the Cold War, informing the California legislature that "if—as we all pray—the epic contest in which the world is involved is not settled on the battlefield, it will be settled in the classrooms and laboratories. . . . It is here that we can best serve the cause of freedom."[88]

The California Master Plan for Higher Education

Reflecting on the Master Plan in 1971, future CSU Sacramento president (1984–2003) Donald Gerth wrote that "like most public documents, it represented some substantial compromises. It has been interpreted by some in California as a ratification of the status quo and by others as a peace treaty." In Gerth's view, the latter assessment is more correct. The chair of the Master Plan survey team, Arthur Coons, agreed, noting in 1968 that "how the University, the State Colleges, and the junior colleges were to be organized and governed, what responsibilities each was to possess, and how they were all to be kept in orderly relationships to each other was the central and most important item for the Master Plan Survey to settle."[89] From this perspective, the Master Plan represented a successful balancing of the privileges granted the UC and the possibilities open to the state colleges. California's community colleges, with no real political movers and shakers fighting in their corner, largely took what they were given—the promise of additional income from the state to supplement paltry local funding and the possibility that their more gifted students would be able to transfer up to one or the other of the state's four-year systems.

Rather than a single entity, what we have come to know as the California Master Plan for Higher Education was composed of three key parts. The Master Plan included first, the recommendations of the Master Plan survey team which had been approved by the state board of education and the UC Board of Regents; second, the Donahoe Act, passed on April 14, 1960, which secured in law several of the main provisions of the Master Plan; and third, a state constitutional amendment that established the California state college board of trustees. In total, the three components of the Master Plan established sixty-seven agreements concerning the future of California's system of higher education, a comprehensive pact for education reform.[90]

In addition to establishing a board of trustees for the state colleges, effectively removing them from the purview of the state board of education, the Master Plan incorporated three major functions. First, the Master Plan created a fifteen-member board, known as the Coordinating Council for Higher Education, to act as an advisory panel to oversee the functioning of California's three-tiered system of higher education. This aspect of the Donahoe Act provided the greatest level of coordination ever brought to bear on the state's previously unwieldy public colleges and university. Second, the Master Plan clearly defined the functions of each of the three levels of public higher education in California in an attempt to avoid the types of turf wars that had plagued the UC and state colleges in previous decades. By delineating the purposes of the three tiers, the state aimed to save money wasted on the duplication of efforts.[91] Finally, the Master Plan set entrance requirements for the UC and state colleges while promising that all three levels would remain tuition-free for California residents.[92] The state would not hinder the various campuses from charging student fees to cover certain costs, and it would still charge tuition for out-of-state students.[93]

The Master Plan covered a wide range of aspects related to the UC and the community colleges, yet the California state colleges experienced the greatest transformation under the plan. With the passage of the Master Plan, the state colleges gained a board of trustees, a joint doctorate program with the UC, and greater funding for research, which was especially important within the context of the Cold War. The plan secured the formal removal of the state colleges from the auspices of the state board of education, yet the state colleges' new board of trustees failed to gain the same level of autonomy from the state which characterized the UC Board of Regents. In the realm of funding allocations, in particular, state college campuses remained tethered to the whims of politicians in Sacramento. The politicization of the board of trustees that would occur during the overlapping Reagan governorship and Dumke chancellorship intensified this trend. The joint degree failed to develop over the course of the 1960s, leaving some faculty in the state colleges feeling decidedly empty-handed. Although two of the Master Plan's promises to the state colleges remained largely pyrrhic victories, the plan still represented a promising change from past practice.[94]

The Master Plan had long-lasting implications in the realm of admissions and planning for future enrollment, enacting changes that would ultimately work to the detriment of California's diverse population of working-class youth. To better prepare for the surge of college-age students that would continue to engulf California in the coming years, the UC and state colleges trimmed their acceptance rates. Previously, the UC had accepted the top 15 percent of graduating high school seniors from California, and the state colleges had taken on upward of the top 45 percent.[95] After the Master Plan, the UC would begin to curb admissions to the top 12.5 percent of students, while the state colleges set a firm limit of 33 percent.[96] The remaining 67 percent—up from 55 percent prior to the Master Plan—were consigned to community colleges in an effort to pinch pennies for the state budget. Importantly, the Master Plan limited exemptions to its admissions standards to 2 percent of those admitted, down from 10 percent previously.[97]

The Master Plan saved money in the face of the baby boom by sending ever greater numbers of young Californians to two-year community colleges for vocational training and remedial educations.[98] As noted in a 1960 article by Burton R. Clark, a UC Berkeley professor of education, the community colleges largely served a "cooling-out" function designed to "mollify those denied [achievement] in order to sustain motivation in the face of disappointment and to deflect resentment."[99] Even though the community colleges were trumpeted by their supporters as transfer points to the UC or state colleges, the majority of community college students—nearly 80 percent—would never transfer up.[100] As projected by the Master Plan survey, estimated costs per student averaged out to $7,043 at the UC and $4,026 at the state colleges, compared to $2,833 at the community colleges. Unlike the UC and state colleges, community colleges were principally financed locally.[101] In addition to the new admissions standards, the Master Plan recommended that applicants to California's system of public higher education be mandated to take a standardized admissions test.[102] Finally, the Master Plan set enrollment ranges to be attained on the various campuses in the coming seven to ten years.[103]

Troubles to Come

The conflicts that emerged between the UC and the state colleges during the development of the Master Plan should not detract from the fact that key figures on both sides, Clark Kerr and Roy Simpson in particular, saw the world and the place of education within it in remarkably similar ways. That the Master Plan reformed public higher education as it did was the result of this confluence. Both educators geared their vision of reform toward meeting the challenge of Soviet advancement, and both believed that a three-tiered system tracking students into an ostensibly appropriate level represented the best method for beating the Communist threat. At no point did either man commit to paper any consideration of the extent to which de facto racial segregation and discrimination would influence the outcome of their supposedly meritocratic system. The passage of the California Master Plan for Higher Education, half a decade before the twin legislative peaks of civil rights era, was the product of some 123 men and 2 women who placed an instrumentalist vision of educational attainment above any consideration of the effects their system would have on California's large and diverse minority population. Although the results of such obliviousness would return to plague the Master Plan system, in the post-Sputnik hysteria of the late 1950s, these educators simply had other things on their minds.

More than anyone else, the Master Plan was a result of the efforts of Roy Simpson and Clark Kerr. However, historical treatments have focused almost exclusively on Kerr, often omitting entirely the role of Simpson. Arthur Coons, the chair of the Master Plan survey team, witnessed and lamented this misrepresenation early on. In his 1968 memoirs, Coons wrote that "I am glad the Master Plan is known by its real name and does not bear the name of any individual, because I truly believe that the credit for the successful completion of the Master Plan belongs to more than one person. However, *Time* magazine gave the credit to President Clark Kerr (a cover story, October 17, 1960) with no mention of Dr. Roy Simpson." In his 1970 history of the UC, historian Verne Stadtman likewise noted that Kerr and Simpson together should rightly be "regarded as the architects of the Master Plan." Finally, in Kerr's 2001 memoirs, the former UC president granted that "Roy was an essential building block of the Master Plan. Without him, it would never have been achieved."[104] It was Simpson, after all, who played the foil to the UC's Kerr, fighting for the place of the state colleges while at the same time planting his feet on the substantial common ground that existed between him and Kerr.

In the years between the launch of Sputnik and the implementation of the Master Plan, Clark Kerr and Roy Simpson traveled the state delivering speeches which offer a window into their understanding of the role of public education in Cold War California. Simpson, like Kerr, viewed his goal as facilitating a system of education that would train workers, at varying levels, to defeat the Soviet threat and help grow the U.S. economy, all while keeping the cost of education to a minimum. The bluntness with which Simpson laid out his goals points to the commonality of views that existed within the California educational community at that time. Speaking in San

Diego, a city that largely owed its existence to the largesse of the military-industrial complex, Simpson assured his audience of the California Labor Federation that school reform carried out in the wake of Sputnik was "evidence that we, in Education, are just as interested as the generals and ambassadors, and you in the Labor movement, in winning the Cold War." The enthusiasm with which Simpson set out to gear the state's system of public education toward the goal of American preeminence in the Cold War reflected his belief—which he shared with Kerr—in the necessity of social engineering in meeting the complex demands of an advanced capitalist system. Referencing the report "Manpower: Challenge of the 60s" by U.S. labor secretary James Mitchell, Simpson called for California youth to receive "the training to make them effective workers in an increasingly technical society." Foreshadowing the concept of a knowledge economy in which information would come to play a bigger role than the physical labor that had dominated the industrial era, Simpson remarked on the "snowballing accumulation of knowledge" that characterized the age and noted that "a society ever more dependent on both white and blue collar skills will require more comprehensive education."[105] Simpson would bring this same Cold War pedagogy to bear on the development of the Master Plan for Higher Education.

One month before the passage of the Master Plan, Superintendent Simpson spoke at a Sacramento conference for California elementary school principals and superintendents. Here, Simpson extended the ideology and strategies that he brought to the Master Plan into the realm of early education. In his speech, Simpson noted the impact of Sputnik, even for California's youngest students: "For us in public education," he warned, "our jobs can never be the same again. Sputnik has opened the space age. We must prepare our students to live, work, play and serve in that space age." In the same speech, Simpson endorsed standardized testing for elementary school students, claiming that "uniform, comparative tests" could demonstrate the attainment levels of individual students, thus preparing Californians at a young age for the standardized assessment tests the Master Plan recommended for acceptance at the UC and state colleges.[106] Despite his near-constant conflict with Kerr regarding the proper role of the state colleges vis-à-vis the UC, Kerr and Simpson shared much in common.

Although Kerr was far more active on California and national lecture circuits than Simpson, the remarks he delivered in the years between the launch of Sputnik and the implementation of the Master Plan bore a strong resemblance to those of the state superintendent. Like Simpson, Kerr envisioned a new knowledge economy. Kerr placed especially strong emphasis on technocratic expertise, as did Simpson, but he also remarked on the possibility of much more leisure time thanks to envisioned advances in technology. Such expanded time for relaxation and self-development were only possible, in Kerr's eyes, with increased government spending. Several months after Sputnik's launch, Kerr noted disapprovingly that the United States spent only "15 percent of our gross national product on new investment. In Russia they are spending 30 percent. And part of the competition of the future will be not only in the area of science and military equipment, but also in how much of the national income of Russia and of the United States will be spent on investment for the future." Although Kerr was far off the mark in his prediction that the coming decades would bring more leisure and greater economic equality, he was correct to note the extent to which the United States would invest in science and the military and, as a by-product of that, education.[107]

In the speeches that Kerr gave in this period, he elaborated on a vision of public education as social engineering for a hierarchical Cold War America. In various speeches, the UC president drew from Adam Smith's 1775 *Wealth of Nations*. Kerr argued that Sputnik proved the validity of Smith's pronouncement that, as Kerr put it, "the real wealth of nations" resides in the education and cultivation of a nation's human resources. One year after Sputnik's launch, stressing the need to meet the challenge of the space age, Kerr argued that the United States had "an acute need for an aristocracy of talent." In order to prepare such a group, Kerr demanded that educators "identify gifted students early in their educational training" and work "to make the entire period of formal education more productive, from kindergarten through high school."[108] Such sentiments were readily shared by Simpson and other post-Sputnik education reformers.

Yet Kerr's rhetoric praising educational efficiency, ostensibly in the service of democracy, at times crossed a line into the blatantly undemocratic. In an April 1964 speech before the American Philosophical Society, Kerr laid out a rather disturbing vision for the future. With the increasing centrality of technical knowledge in the economy, Kerr envisioned what he described as "a society much like a modern university—highly competitive, essentially undemocratic, effective." Likewise, an earlier speech Kerr had delivered to students, first at Pomona College and then again at San Jose State, offered a revealing look into the type of society Kerr foresaw—rationally planned and benevolently guided by a technocracy of philosopher kings. "There may in fact be instances," Kerr admonished, "when it is better for a country to have a temporary military dictator who is honest and progressive . . . than a democracy which is run by corrupt and bungling politicians." He continued, now hitting closer to home, "Though we cherish self-government, we should be realistic about both time and place. Degrees of 'guidance' from above may be inevitable in some situations today, and should be both expected and accepted."[109] Just what degree of guidance, Kerr left unclear.

The 1960 California Master Plan for Higher Education, a reform that stressed technocratic planning and training students for preestablished roles in the Cold War, was not simply "accepted" by Kerr's underlings at the UC, nor by students attending the California state colleges. Despite Kerr's confident pronouncements, indeed in part because of them, many of those who inhabited the newly streamlined Master Plan system revolted against the vision of its founders. That Kerr spent so much time in this period traveling the country and making grand statements about the decades to come provided a wealth of incriminating evidence when in the hands of the student rebels who would soon climb into the trenches at UC Berkeley. Kerr, Simpson, and the rest of the Master Planners shared a clear vision for the future of 1960s California; yet, the students of the New Left envisioned otherwise.

2 Striking the Knowledge Factory

. . . .

> "Education for All" became one with "Survival," and closing missile
> gaps became the aim of education. . . . The California Master Plan for
> Higher Education (engineered into existence by Kerr) dominates the
> entire educational apparatus of the state.
>
> —Brad Cleaveland, 1964
>   (student activist, UC Berkeley)

> The history of the adoption of the Master Plan . . . show[s] that faculty
> members and students are consistently excluded from those groups of
> legislators, bureaucrats, and businessmen which make the most far
> reaching decisions concerning the development and reform of the
> University. Those of us whose lives are directly involved are denied
> any effective voice in these decisions which structure and pervert
> our immediate, daily environment.
>
> —Mario Savio, 1966
>   (Free Speech Movement leader)

"There is only one proper response to Berkeley from undergraduates: that
you *organize and split this campus wide open!*" In his manifesto titled
"A Letter to Undergraduates," UC Berkeley graduate Brad Cleaveland threw
down this challenge only four days before an administrative crackdown on
student political organizing that would lead to the Free Speech Movement
(FSM). Cleaveland continued, declaring that "MY INTENTION IS TO
CONVINCE YOU THAT YOU DO NOTHING LESS THAN BEGIN AN OPEN,
FIERCE, AND THOROUGHGOING REBELLION ON THIS CAMPUS."
Denouncing the Cold War university as "not an educational center, but a
highly efficient industry" producing "bombs" and "other war machines,"
Cleaveland launched into an attack on UC president Clark Kerr and the
Board of Regents. He concluded with an eight-point list of demands culmi-
nating in the "resignation of Clark Kerr" and the "reconstitution of the
Board of Regents."[1]

Along with his manifesto, Cleaveland produced and disseminated a pamphlet, "Education, Revolutions, and Citadels," in which he clarified his

critiques of contemporary education and trumpeted the need for reform. Cleaveland lamented the fact that "the California Master Plan for Higher Education (engineered into existence by Kerr) dominates the entire educational apparatus of the state." In Cleaveland's view, the UC, as the "multiversity" sitting at the apex of Kerr's Master Plan, had "used the noble banner of education for all while cynically overthrowing education in the name of training for the contingencies of the Cold War." A Korean War veteran, Cleaveland bemoaned a world in which "closing missile gaps became the aim of education," and he called on Berkeley students to imagine otherwise.[2]

Cleaveland's passionate attempt to engage with the UC Berkeley student body seems generally to have been ignored at the time, much as it has largely been overlooked by historians. Yet within the next week, the Berkeley campus would witness the beginnings of the FSM with the formation of the United Front, a broad coalition of student groups concerned with the limitations that administrators placed on student political organizing and advocacy on campus. After four years in the navy, Cleaveland spent seven at Berkeley studying political science. By the fall of 1964, he had earned both bachelor's and master's degrees and had turned to activism full time. Cleaveland was well read and a fierce critic of modern education, yet his diatribes somehow missed their mark with the young undergraduates on campus. As sociology graduate student Max Heirich recalled, Cleaveland's manifesto "did not create much stir in student circles." Tom Weller, a campus activist who edited Cleaveland's letter, noted that "Cleaveland was full of ideas about educational reform and could convey a great sense of enthusiasm to a group of people face to face. . . . But he couldn't write worth a darn."[3] A jumble of capital letters, exclamation points, and underlining, Cleaveland's letter failed to resonate with students in the way that other more succinct critiques soon would.

Where Cleaveland would be remembered by FSM activist David Lance Goines as a failure, "the campus rabble-rouser manqué," campus librarian Hal Draper would become known as the éminence grise of the FSM.[4] Like Cleaveland, Draper was not a student. Unlike Cleaveland, Draper's analysis of Clark Kerr and the state of modern education had a major impact on the student body. Nearly three weeks after Cleaveland published his manifesto, Draper delivered an off-campus talk that provided movement participants with an intellectual framework for understanding the clash between student protesters and the university administration. In large part, Draper did so by popularizing two concepts that would become central to students' conceptualization of the FSM.

In a talk hosted by the Independent Socialist Club, Draper introduced his audience to the "multiversity" and the "knowledge factory." Both terms derived from Clark Kerr's publications and became mainstays of the oratory and analysis of the FSM. Together, these two terms served as a shorthand for all that was wrong with mass higher education in the eyes of movement participants. Yet, the concepts were analytically distinct. Where the multiversity referred primarily to an institution—a modern and massive research university—the knowledge factory referred to its function. In serving as a producer of knowledge for the Cold War state and industry, the multiversity operated as a knowledge factory. Tracing the use of these twin concepts, this chapter demonstrates how leading FSM activists understood the movement in which they took part and how they explained their critiques of modern education. Focusing on the influence of Draper on FSM participants—above all, on student leaders Mario Savio and Jack Weinberg—illuminates how student activists turned Clark Kerr's analysis of modern education on its head, enunciating a staunch rejection of the thinking behind the California Master Plan for Higher Education.[5]

Students active in the FSM firmly rejected Kerr's vision for postwar higher education as embodied in the Master Plan and elucidated in Kerr's 1963 *The Uses of the University*. FSM activists denounced Kerr's cherished California Master Plan for Higher Education in substance, if not often in name. With the important exceptions of Mario Savio and Brad Cleaveland, FSM participants seem to have rarely mentioned the Master Plan by name. Instead, student protesters organized by reference to Kerr, the multiversity, and the knowledge factory. In doing so, they rejected the California Master Plan in content as they simultaneously repulsed the administrative efforts of UC president Kerr as he sought to contain the emerging movement on campus.

From Harvard to the Multiversity

In his 2001 memoirs, Clark Kerr enumerated the honors bestowed on UC Berkeley in the wake of the successful completion of the Master Plan. Among other accolades, Harvard University asked the UC president to present their annual Godkin Lectures in 1963. As Nicholas Lemann notes of the honor, "that [Kerr] had been invited to deliver the Godkin Lectures, a venerable endowed series that was usually given by a leading social or political thinker, was a remarkable tribute in itself. . . . It was a sign of Kerr's prestige at the time that in addition to being the administrator of the biggest educational system in the world and the recent winner of a signal political victory, he was also considered an intellectual giant." Celebrated both at home in California and by the veritable East Coast elite at Harvard, Kerr presented a three-part lecture series that would become *The Uses of the University*, published on October 24, 1963, by Harvard University Press.[6]

A close reading of *The Uses of the University* demonstrates that for Kerr, the history of higher education culminated in his own creation, the Master Plan multiversity, which he believed represented a synthesis of the best models of eras past. Only fifty-one years old and the recipient of much recent praise, Kerr delivered an unabashedly bold vision of the future of higher education in his 1963 Godkin Lectures at Harvard. Lemann, in analyzing Kerr's lecture series, explains that "Kerr delivered a dazzling *tour d'horizon* encompassing the entire history of higher education—Athens, Oxford, Bologna, Berlin, Johns Hopkins, Chicago—and coming to rest at its culmination, its apotheosis, the California Master Plan." The product of the Godkin Lectures, Kerr's *The Uses of the University* was, in the words of one contemporary reviewer, "the work of a deeply satisfied man."[7]

In late April 1963, Clark Kerr presented the three lectures that would introduce the multiversity, Kerr's conceptualization of the modern university. Kerr's April 23 lecture became the basis for his book's first chapter, "The Idea of a Multiversity." At the start of that first lecture, Kerr explained that although the "the modern American university" derived from the "ideal types" of the past, "it is not Oxford, nor is it Berlin; it is a new type of institution in the world. As a new type of institution, it is not really private and it is not really public; it is neither entirely of the world nor entirely apart from it." By defining even his own public UC as "not really public," Kerr acknowledged early on the role of the multiversity in servicing private industry and, reciprocally, the influence of private industry on the university. As Kerr noted, with "operating expenditures from all sources of nearly half a billion dollars," the UC maintained "some form of contact with nearly every industry . . . in its region."[8] Clearly, Kerr's multiversity was not the old public university of American nostalgia.

Exuberant in his recent successes, Kerr traced the genealogy of the multiversity all the way back to ancient Greece, weaving his history through the most exalted heights of Western civilization. Among the Greeks, Kerr placed the multiversity on the side of the Sophists and the Pythagoreans, as opposed to Plato's academy, which Kerr criticized for being "devoted to truth largely for its own sake." In contrast, he proclaimed, the Sophists "taught rhetoric and other useful skills—they were more interested in attainable success in life than they were in the unattainable truth." In addition, the Pythagoreans' emphasis on "mathematics and astronomy" became for Kerr an ancient affirmation of his elevation of the STEM fields.[9]

Beyond ancient Greece, Kerr surveyed the universities of medieval Europe and post-Reformation Germany, demonstrating how the best qualities of each era found a new home in the multiversity. Aligning the multiversity with Oxford and Cambridge, Kerr praised the emergence of the medieval university as "a center for the professions, for study of the classics, for theological and philosophical disputes" but lamented their decline into "centers of reaction" set against the emerging Renaissance and Reformation. Against such decline, Protestant northern Germany became home to the Berlin university model, which Kerr cited as an antecedent to the multiversity. In Kerr's retelling, the establishment of the University of Berlin by Wilhelm von Humboldt in 1809 contributed to a much needed "emphasis on philosophy and science, on research, on graduate instruction, on the freedom of professors and students." From there, the Berlin model captured the rest of Germany, carrying with it "two great new forces: science and nationalism."[10]

Kerr charted a westward journey of freedom and truth, from post-Reformation Germany to the United States, where the Berlin model would prove a decisive influence on the future of American higher education. Bypassing the significance of Harvard, the University of Pennsylvania, and the University of Virginia, which he argued were premised on the outdated models of Oxford and Cambridge, Kerr noted the impact of Humboldt's Berlin model on Johns Hopkins University, founded in 1876. The "Hopkins idea," which Kerr credited with influencing American state universities, "brought with it the graduate school with exceptionally high academic standards . . . the renovation of professional education . . . and also the great proliferation of courses." To the Hopkins idea Kerr paired the land grant movement, two models of higher education that "turned out to be more compatible than might at first appear. The one was Prussian, the other American; one elitist, the other democratic." For Kerr, the land grant model reached its apex in the Progressive Era, as the "Wisconsin idea" introduced a model of university service to "the whole state."[11]

It is through this dizzying array of past precedents that Kerr cobbled together his view of the triumph of history: the multiversity. As Kerr saw it, from ancient Greece to medieval Europe, from Reformation Germany to

Progressive Era Wisconsin, all previous models of higher education contributed to the multiversity hybrid: "Out of all these fragments, experiments, and conflicts a kind of unlikely consensus has been reached. Undergraduate life seeks to follow the British, who have done the best with it, and an historical line that goes back to Plato. . . . Graduate life and research follow the Germans, who did best with them, and an historical line that goes back to Pythagoras. . . . The 'lesser' professions (lesser than law and medicine) and the service activities follow the American pattern, since the Americans have been best at them, and an historical line that goes back to the Sophists." For Kerr, then, the multiversity approaches the most perfect synthesis of the history of higher education. The chief architect of the Master Plan posited that "a university anywhere can aim no higher than to be as British as possible for the sake of the undergraduates, as German as possible for the sake of the graduates and the research personnel, as American as possible for the sake of the public at large." It is this hybrid that Kerr aspired to as "the central mediator," the "Captain of the Bureaucracy" of the UC.[12] Kerr's teleology thus rested on the Master Plan's UC, a modern multiversity that Kerr himself did much to create.

Far less ambitious in its scope, Kerr's April 24 lecture served as the basis for his book's second chapter, "The Realities of the Federal Grant University." In the history of American higher education, Kerr maintained, "two great impacts, beyond all other forces, have molded the modern American university system." Those forces were the land grant movement, inaugurated by Abraham Lincoln's passage of the Morrill Act of 1862, and the great wave of "federal support of scientific research during World War II." Kerr focused on the latter. Pointing, in particular, to the efforts of the University of Chicago, MIT, and UC Berkeley, Kerr argued that with World War II, "the major universities were enlisted in national defense and technological development as never before." This influence, Kerr noted, outlived the war itself as "in addition to the stimulus of Germany, there was Russia—for Russian scientific achievements both before and after Sputnik were an immense spur to the new departure."[13] From the National Defense Research Committee established in 1940, to the postwar GI Bill, to the National Defense Education Act of 1958, the federal government involved itself in higher education as never before, magnifying the impact of what Kerr previously identified, in the context of German higher education, as the two great forces of science and nationalism.

Where Kerr's first lecture analyzed the past and his second the present, on April 25, Kerr turned to look toward the future. A hodgepodge of predictions and prophecies, warnings and assertions, Kerr's lecture titled "The Future of the City of Intellect" provided much fodder to the unruly students who would make their dissatisfaction with Kerr's vision known in the coming year. Kerr argued that the American university was in the midst of its "second great transformation," which he predicted would span 1945-70, the latter being the final year covered by the campus enrollment ranges set by the California Master Plan for Higher Education. In these years, Kerr noted, "the university is being called upon to educate previously unimagined numbers of students; to respond to the expanding claims of national service; to merge its activities with industry as never before." Yet even beyond "merging" with industry, Kerr argued that the university had become an industry in its own right, "the knowledge industry."[14]

With the onset of the Cold War, Kerr proclaimed, the modern university had "become a prime instrument of national purpose." Noting the impact of the space race, and fears "of Russian or Chinese supremacy, of the bomb and annihilation," Kerr made a bold pronouncement: "knowledge has certainly never in history been so central to the conduct of an entire society. What the railroads did for the second half of the last century and the automobile for the first half of this century may be done for the second half of this century by the knowledge industry: that is, to serve as the focal point for national growth." Describing the university as sitting "at the center" of the knowledge industry, Kerr also projected that the new "truly American university" would come to serve as "a model for universities in other parts of the globe."[15] Bringing his earlier genealogy of the multiversity together with his emphasis on the significance of the knowledge industry, Kerr thus affirmed the work he had done toward creating the California Master Plan and steering the UC in a new direction.

Yet, alongside Kerr's embrace of the recent history of higher education came a warning. In his closing remarks on April 25, Kerr rather accurately predicted some of the troubles that would plague his future career as president of the UC. Returning to an early theme, Kerr explained that "the university and segments of industry are becoming more alike. As the university becomes tied into the world of work, the professor . . . takes on the characteristics of an entrepreneur." Kerr enumerated a number of changes to the traditional role of the professor—from lower teaching loads and a new emphasis on faculty research, to larger classes and the use of "substitute" teachers for the regular faculty—and he warned that such restructuring of the university would contribute to "an incipient revolt of the undergraduate students against the faculty; the revolt that used to be against the faculty *in loco parentis* is now against the faculty *in absentia*."[16] Such frustration with change, Kerr noted, might easily lead to increased student protest.

Worries over the potential of "a minor counterrevolt" aside, Kerr defended his own vision as being the best one suited to meet the needs of the late-twentieth century United States. Noting that "the great university is of necessity elitist—the elite of merit," Kerr posed the question of how best to justify such hierarchy in public education: "How may the contribution of the elite be made clear to the egalitarians, and how may an aristocracy of intellect justify itself to a democracy of all men?" For Kerr, the answer was simple. Despite its inegalitarian hierarchy, according to Kerr, the "great university" found its true purpose in protecting the perceived interests of the American people in the Cold War. For as Kerr noted, in concluding the last of his Godkin Lectures, "intellect has also become an instrument of national purpose, a component part of the 'military-industrial complex.' . . . In the war of the ideological worlds, a great deal depends on the use of this instrument."[17] The uses of the university, Kerr maintained, were crucial to the very survival of the United States as a free, prosperous, and ostensibly meritocratic republic. Journalists covering Kerr's lectures and reviewers of *The Uses of the University* were generally enthusiastic in their embrace of Kerr's conceptualization of the university as a bulwark in the Cold War. Yet, the reception Kerr's ideas would receive from certain students was anything but. What Kerr had foreseen as "minor" student protests would soon grow into something much larger as students challenged the UC for both its elitism and its complicity in the Cold War economy.

Toward a United Front

In the years stretching from the Sputnik scare and the debate over the California Master Plan for Higher Education to the publication of Kerr's *The Uses of the University*, Berkeley was home to a small but growing student left. First formed in 1957, the student organization known as Slate grew to somewhere between one hundred and two hundred students, becoming the largest of all political groups on campus. An "issue-oriented coalition," Slate captured control of UC Berkeley student government in the spring of 1959. As described by UC Berkeley sociology graduate student Max Heirich, "Although it was intensely critical of established arrangements, Slate did not engage in partisan ideological rantings." Slate brought "large numbers of vaguely liberal students into dialogue with committed radical students" and served "to make radical political positions and acts more nearly *respectable*."

The organization quickly gained the support of a large sector of the graduate students. Slate's dominance in student electoral politics was challenged, however, when Berkeley administrators barred graduate students from participating in student government elections in May 1959.[18]

In October 1959, additional administrative changes known as the Kerr directives further aggravated campus activists. Kerr had only recently replaced Robert Gordon Sproul, who served as UC president from 1930 to 1958. Among other things, Kerr's new rules "enjoined student government from taking positions on off-campus political, religious, economic, international, or other issues of the time without permission of the chancellor."[19] Although the directives were, in part, a reaffirmation of long-standing policy, given the recent disenfranchisement of the graduate students, many students interpreted the Kerr directives as yet another attack on Slate and the growing spirit of student activism. The UC-wide Kerr directives drew strong condemnations from students across the state.

In the coming years, tensions between students and the Kerr administration deteriorated further. In 1960, nearly the entire staff of the *Daily Californian*, Berkeley's on-campus newspaper, resigned in protest when the administration "clamped down on the newspaper's endorsement of Slate candidates and its attention to 'off-campus' issues." Two years later, in 1962, a critique of the Kerr directives written by a group of Slate activists drew on Kerr's 1960 publication *Industrialism and Industrial Man* and anticipated some of the key analyses of the FSM. In "Theodicy of 1984: The Philosophy of Clark Kerr," Bruce Payne, David Walls, and Jerry Berman criticized Kerr's view of education as what they called "the production of individuals with particular skills required by the existing industrial order more than preparation for citizenship."[20]

In late April 1960, the House Un-American Activities Committee (HUAC) announced new hearings scheduled for May in San Francisco's city hall. Berkeley students who had become active in Bay Area civil rights organizing understood the HUAC hearings to be part of a coordinated effort aimed at painting the civil rights movement as subversive and thereby cooling organizing efforts. As graduate student Max Heirich explained, "HUAC was unpopular because it was associated with 'McCarthyist' efforts to force political conformity on universities across the country . . . and because many of its members were well known for their segregationist sympathies and had attempted to demonstrate a link between the Communist Party and civil rights agitation in the South."[21] Student displeasure with HUAC increased immeasurably with the news that HUAC had subpoenaed Douglas Wachter, a Berkeley undergraduate and Slate member. In response, Wachter's supporters organized as Students for Civil Liberties, circulating a petition denouncing HUAC and setting plans to picket the hearings.[22]

On the second day of picketing HUAC, police officers armed with firehoses attacked some two hundred students who were unable to enter the cramped hearing chamber, washing them down the thirty-six marble steps at the entrance to city hall. As Jo Freeman later recalled, "When the wet, bedraggled students began to sing 'We Shall Not Be Moved' at the foot of the stairs, the police attacked them with billy clubs." Police arrested sixty-four students, thirty-one of whom attended UC Berkeley. The brutality of the arresting officers further politicized those attending the hearings, helping to develop what Heirich described as "a core of students who considered themselves to have 'become committed' to direct action for civil rights." Soon after, HUAC produced and disseminated a film, *Operation Abolition*, which attempted to portray the protesters as Communists. Subsequent conflicts between the administration and Slate, who wanted to host a critical screening of the film, led to the loss of Slate's "on-campus" status. The administration barred the organization from organizing on campus and from using the university name for official purposes.[23]

Student activism around civil rights and civil liberties during the 1963–64 school year proved crucial to the emergence of the FSM.[24] In 1963, national and local attention increasingly turned to the civil rights struggle. In May, police used fire hoses and dogs to attack nonviolent demonstrators in Birmingham, Alabama; in June, a white supremacist assassinated Medgar Evers, the National Association for the Advancement of Colored People's field secretary for Mississippi; and in August, the March on Washington brought some 250,000 participants to rally in the nation's capital. Closer to home, Berkeley activists were inspired by talks given by a number of visiting Black activists, including James Baldwin, James Farmer, and Malcolm X.[25] In the middle of the fall semester, a young student named Mario Savio began attending meetings of the Bay Area Friends of SNCC.[26] In March 1964, Savio participated in a sit-in at the Sheraton Plaza. His subsequent arrest led to a fateful decision to participate in the SNCC-sponsored Mississippi Freedom Summer.[27] The summer project, which suffered violent attacks by white supremacists including the brutal murders of young organizers James Chaney, Michael Schwerner, and Andrew Goodman, did much to inspire a new wave of off-campus organizing by Berkeley students in the fall of 1964.

On September 2, 1964, Berkeley student activists announced their intention to picket William Knowland's *Oakland Tribune* for engaging in discriminatory hiring practices. Knowland, the "standard-bearer for [the] emergent suburban Right," had begun to work at his father's conservative newspaper after a failed run for governor in 1958.[28] On September 4, the protests began in full. In response, according to students, someone from the *Oakland Tribune* "phoned [UC Berkeley chancellor Edward Strong] to ask him whether he was aware that the *Tribune* picketing was being organized on university property."[29] One week before the start of the fall semester, with Chancellor Strong in Hawaii and President Kerr on a business trip to Japan, Vice-Chancellor Alex Sherriffs was left in charge to handle a potentially disruptive situation.

The administration responded to student participation in the civil rights movement by closing off the Bancroft Strip, a small area of space allotted to students for the purposes of political organizing.[30] For several years, the sidewalk on Bancroft Way, by the intersection with Telegraph Avenue on the southern edge of the campus, had served as the de facto organizing space for campus groups engaged in tabling, fundraising, and other political activities. The space served as terra nullius, with the administration claiming it belonged to the city and the city acting as though it belonged to the campus. This administrative loophole had allowed those student organizations banned from campus by the 1959 Kerr directives access to the greater student body. The Bancroft sidewalk was, in fact, campus property, and at least some administrators had always known this was the case. Dean of Students Katherine Towle, for one, viewed the strip as "sort of a safety valve" and thought that "there was no harm in what [students] were doing."[31] But on September 14, by order of Chancellor Strong and Vice-Chancellor Sherriffs, and against her own better judgment, Dean Towle announced the closure of the Bancroft sidewalk to student political organizing. The decision resulted in what President Kerr would call "a three-month series of disruptions."[32] For the students, it was a declaration of war.

In response to the ban on political action, approximately twenty student groups came together as the United Front. This broad-based organization was formed by a diverse array of groups, including Slate, Campus CORE (Congress of Racial Equality), University Friends of SNCC, the Independent Socialist Club (ISC), Students for a Democratic Society (SDS), University Young Democrats, University Young Republicans, Cal Students for Goldwater, and Campus Women for Peace, among others. The ad hoc organization quickly established contact with the campus newspaper, scheduled a meeting with Dean Towle, and planned protests for Monday, September 21. When Towle denied the students' formal request for newly regulated use of the Bancroft Strip, the United Front moved forward with their plans. The Monday protest was followed by another on Wednesday and a third on the subsequent Monday. Students picketed and set up tables in front of Sproul Hall, the campus administration building, in an explicit rejection of orders to cease tabling and other forms of political advocacy on campus. The administration soon responded with the threat of disciplinary action targeting prominent student organizers.[33]

Behind the Ban

On the night of Tuesday, September 29, the movement received an unexpected boost when several leading participants, including Mario Savio and Jack Weinberg, attended a talk by Hal Draper. The gathering was organized by the newly formed ISC, a small but influential presence in the large and ideologically diverse United Front, at an off-campus location known as Stiles Hall.[34] The speaker, Hal Draper, was a cofounder of the ISC and a UC Berkeley campus librarian then unknown to the vast majority of Berkeley students. Draper's talk, "Behind the Ban: Clark Kerr's View of the University as a Knowledge Factory," soon became the basis for a widely distributed pamphlet titled "The Mind of Clark Kerr." As presented in his talk and pamphlet, Draper's analysis changed the way student activists spoke about the conditions at UC Berkeley and introduced the key concepts that organizers would use to elucidate and inspire student struggles on campus, throughout California, and beyond.

Draper remains a minor presence in most histories of the FSM. At the time of his talk, Draper had just turned fifty years old. He had been deeply involved on the American left for over thirty years and possessed a remarkably sophisticated, if heterodox, analysis of mid-twentieth century American society. Draper was born in 1914, the son of Ukrainian Jews who immigrated from the Russian Empire to Brooklyn.[35] As a young man, Hal met his life partner, Anne, in the student movement of the 1930s. Finding a political home on the Trotskyist left, Draper was active in the Student League for Industrial Democracy and the Young People's Socialist League as early as 1932. After nearly a decade of youth organizing, in 1940, Draper split with Trotsky to cofound the Workers' Party (WP), which would later become the

Independent Socialist League (ISL). Dedicated to a democratic interpretation of Marxism, the WP, in the words of one scholar, "developed an analysis of the Soviet Union as neither a 'workers' state' nor state capitalist but a new form of exploiting class society, bureaucratic collectivism."[36] The WP-ISL critique of the agency and potential autonomy of state bureaucracy would later inform Draper's analysis of Clark Kerr as a Cold War liberal.

Draper presented Berkeley students with a third path between a racist and imperialist Cold War America and a decidedly authoritarian Soviet alternative. Equally set against both the United States and the USSR, Draper popularized his own interpretation of "socialism from below" and would later interrogate the Marxist tradition with his four-volume *Karl Marx's Theory of Revolution*, three-volume *Marx-Engels Cyclopedia*, and a wide range of lesser works. With this oeuvre, Draper established himself, in the estimation of Alan Wald, as "one of the foremost Marxist scholars in the world."[37] In the years before he came to Berkeley, Draper honed his analysis and organizing skills as a leader of the WP-ISL.[38] After relocating to Berkeley and securing work as a campus librarian in 1958, Draper was honored by student organizers as an exception to the rule: the FSM catchphrase "'Don't trust anyone over thirty,' originally had a second clause, 'except Hal Draper.'"[39] As one such student organizer put it, Hal "didn't demand agreement or conformity, he was always open to serious new thought."[40]

The mentorship and intellectual guidance Draper provided to students, and in particular the relationship he developed with Mario Savio, greatly influenced the course of the FSM.[41] Savio would later write the introduction for Draper's 1965 analysis of the FSM, *Berkeley: The New Student Revolt*. Savio noted of Draper that "'don't trust anyone over thirty' became a motto of the Free Speech Movement when Jack Weinberg was quoted to that effect. Hal Draper is one of the few 'over thirty' who were familiar with the events of the struggle from the very beginning, and who understood well enough to take the students seriously. He has always been ready with encouragement but has consistently refrained from giving inappropriate and unsolicited 'vintage 1930' advice. This is far from common with our 'fathers.'" Draper, Savio concluded, "has been a friend."[42] Decades later, in an oral history interview, Savio credited Draper with helping him come to the realization that he, like Hal, was a socialist.[43] Particularly tender evidence of the relationship Draper and Savio developed is found in correspondence the two maintained when Savio relocated to Oxford, England, after the conclusion of the FSM. Writing to inform Draper of the birth of his first child, Mario opened up to Hal regarding the hardships of raising a child so far away from home, all while attempting to enter a new program of study. Savio also requested, and Draper subsequently provided, analysis to keep him up to date with new developments at Berkeley, particularly regarding the Vietnam Day Committee. Finally, Savio asked for news of Anne, Hal's wife, and an update on her involvement with the United Farm Workers' struggle back in California.[44]

On the night of Tuesday, September 29, 1964, Draper's "Behind the Ban" presented his listeners with an analysis of the works of Clark Kerr that would prove crucial to the development of the FSM. Draper's impact owed to his critical readings of Kerr's 1963 *The Uses of the University*, based on his Godkin Lectures at Harvard, and his 1960 *Industrialism and Industrial Man: The Problems of Labor and Management in Economic Growth*.[45] As one student activist would later note, Draper's synopsis was the closest most students would come to reading Kerr's work for themselves. David Lance Goines, a classics major who in the early nineties published his memoirs of the FSM, commented on Draper's analysis of Kerr: "Regardless of how he was quoted or to what end, there was no doubt that Kerr was profoundly arrogant and out of touch."[46]

In addition to elucidating Kerr's texts, Draper introduced those present to the twin concepts of the multiversity and the knowledge factory. The term *multiversity* came directly from Kerr's *The Uses of the University*, whereas *knowledge factory* was a neologism of Draper's own. Although Kerr had introduced the term *multiversity* in the Godkin Lectures, he later clarified, after the word had "become, on the lips of some, a term of opprobrium," that "the word was not really new with me," having been utilized previously by at least four other professors or administrators at colleges across the nation.[47] Likewise, in distancing himself from Draper's popularization of the phrase *knowledge factory*, Kerr notes in his memoirs that he hadn't coined the phrase *knowledge industry* but rather borrowed it from the economist Fritz Machlup.[48]

In introducing the concept of the "knowledge factory," Draper combined Kerr's use of the phrase *knowledge industry* with an increasingly popular denigration of the large modern university. In 1962, one Berkeley graduate student noted that "students refer to a school that is so large that any human contact between professors and students is strictly accidental, so that the struggle for knowledge takes on the character of an assembly line from lecture to lecture, from exam to exam, as a 'factory.'"[49] Draper, analyzing the place of the university in the Cold War economy, presented what he called "the assumption which permeates" Kerr's thinking, that "the use of the university, or the role of the multiversity, is to have a relationship to the present power structure, in this businessman's society of ours, which is similar to that of any other enterprise. There are railroads and steel mills and supermarkets and sausage factories—and there are also Knowledge Factories, whose function is to service all the others and the State."[50] Leading FSM activists would come to explain their own movement against Clark Kerr's university while relying heavily on Draper's analysis of the multiversity and the knowledge factory.[51]

Draper's talk explored the central contradiction embedded in Kerr's works. As Draper noted, Kerr encouraged professors to conduct research beneficial to private industry and the Cold War state, while at the same time castigating students for their involvement in off-campus affairs. Highlighting this contrast, Draper sought to elucidate the reasons "behind the ban" on student political activism. Kerr had written that thanks to the Cold War, "the university is being called upon . . . to merge its activity with industry as never before."[52] In response, Draper commented on a seeming paradox:

> There seems to be a wide gap between Kerr's published theory about
> the "merger" of the university and "society," and his moves toward
> restricting student involvement in political and social action off
> campus. On the one hand he tells us we must accept the integration
> of the university with the state and industry in this Cold War
> (in fact, with what has been called the Military-Industrial Complex)
> and must erase the boundary lines; on the other hand, he tries to
> muzzle and rein in student activity on campus which tends to step
> beyond the boundary line—which, as his administration puts it,
> "mounts" political and social action off campus—while at the same
> time other "constituencies" in the university community are lauded
> for doing just that.

For Draper, the obvious solution to this paradox lay in the fact that Kerr's university existed to serve "the present power structure." As demonstrated by his own work toward the Master Plan, Kerr viewed higher education as a weapon in the Cold War and firmly believed that education could best serve this role by working to strengthen both the US economy and the state. Draper posited that for Kerr, "society" was identical to the "leadership groups in society." Therefore, civil rights protests targeting the Bank of America or the *Oakland Tribune* were not attacks on "the Giannini financial empire of the Bank of America . . . or [*Tribune* owner William]

Knowland. . . . They are 'attacks on society.'"[53] For those students who had imagined the university as a place to challenge the status quo and work toward a more equitable and peaceful world, Draper's elucidation of the mind of Clark Kerr was nothing short of disturbing.

Having introduced the key concepts that would guide the FSM and explored the seeming contradiction in Kerr's thought, Draper shifted toward an analysis of Kerr's vision for the future. Draper argued that "behind Kerr's vision of the university-factory is a broad-gauged worldview, a view of a Brave New World (his term) or Orwellian *1984* toward which all this is headed."[54] Here, Draper's many years as a theorist of bureaucratic collectivism came to most influence his analysis of Kerr. As read by Draper, the future of Kerr's imagination is one of *"full-blown bureaucratic (or managerial) elitism."* Quoting liberally from Kerr's *Industrialism and Industrial Man*, Draper noted Kerr's assertion that "turning Marx on his head, [bureaucrats and managers] are the vanguard of the future."[55] In the book's last chapter, Kerr had assured his readers that in the future, "the age of ideology fades . . . the benevolent political bureaucracy and the benevolent economic oligarchy are matched with the tolerant mass. . . . Not only all dictatorships but also all democracies are 'guided.' . . . Society has achieved consensus. . . . There will not be any revolt, anyway, except for little bureaucratic revolts that can be handled piecemeal."[56] Rejecting Kerr's vision as "an orgiastic dream of the Bureaucrat's Paradise," Draper cautioned that "students must not accept Kerr's vision of the university-factory, run by a Captain of the Bureaucracy as a parts-supply shop to the profit system and the Cold War complex."[57] By exposing and critiquing Kerr's vision of the future, Draper did much to help contribute to the more-than-minor revolts that would soon erupt.

In examining the future envisioned by Clark Kerr, Draper posed to students the question of their own role in the world to come while highlighting some of Kerr's musings on the unique place of intellectuals. In *Industrialism and Industrial Man*, Kerr opined that "the intellectuals, (including the university students) are a particularly volatile element . . . capable of extreme reactions to objective situations . . . more extreme than any group in society. They are by nature irresponsible. . . . Consequently it is important who best attracts or captures the intellectuals and who uses them most effectively, for they may be a tool as well as a source of danger."[58] In so blithely insulting the very individuals over whom he served, Kerr opened the door to an uprising against his own administration. Simply by presenting the students with their university president's own words, Draper helped to inspire the dedication and organizing that would be necessary to stand down both the administration and waves of police. In closing his talk and pamphlet, Draper posed to students a moral choice that resonated with the existentialist current then popular among certain college students, "Kerr believes that the student's relationship to the Administration bureaucracy can be only that of a tool or a danger. . . . Which will it be? Everyone must choose, and it is a matter of life or death: life as an independent human being, or death as a man."[59]

In the following two days, the moral question presented by Hal Draper was answered resoundingly by two of the students who had attended his Tuesday night talk. On Wednesday, Mario Savio addressed those assembled for a sit-in at Sproul Hall with his own spin on Draper's critique of Clark Kerr and the multiversity. Referring to Chancellor Strong's announcement of the suspension of eight FSM activists, including Savio himself, Savio stated his intention "to connect *that* [the suspension] with statements that have been made by President Kerr in his book on the multiversity." Drawing directly on the previous night's talk, Savio intoned that "President Kerr has referred to the University as a factory; a knowledge factory—that's his words—engaged in the knowledge industry. And just like any factory, in any industry—again his words—you have a certain product. They go in one side, as kind of rough-cut adolescents, and they come out the other side pretty smooth. . . . Well, this machine, this factory here, this multiversity, its parts are human beings. And, sometimes when *they* go out of commission, they don't simply break down, but they really gum up the whole works! (*Scattered laughter*) That's what we're all doing here."[60] In addition, Savio took aim at Kerr's endorsement of the university status quo, arguing that "it's really an institution that serves the interests and represents the establishment of the United States. And we have Clark Kerr's word on it in his book on the multiversity. As I said before, the purpose of the university is simple: it's to create a product. The product is to fit into certain factories. You go out and take part in the Establishment and that's why there is a university!"[61] The following day, Savio and Jack Weinberg would capture the attention of the world with their starring role in a campus confrontation.

On Thursday, October 1, local police confronted student activists who had set up tables in front of Sproul Hall. During a temporary moment of calm, Jack Weinberg delivered an impromptu speech in which, as he later recounted, "I talked about the university factory. I was essentially trying to fit some of what was happening into [Hal Draper's] theoretical framework."[62] As Weinberg himself noted, his speech was heavily influenced by the talk he had attended only two days before. Weinberg proclaimed to those assembled that "I want to tell you about this knowledge factory. . . . It seems that certain of the products are not coming out to standard specifications. And I feel the university is trying to purge these products so that they can again produce for the industry exactly what they specify. . . . This is a mass production; no deviations from the norms are tolerated."[63] Whereas Draper had analyzed Kerr's view of knowledge as the university's "invisible product," Weinberg—like Savio the day before—took the analogy a step further, with students themselves serving as the product that the university would deliver up to industry.

When police returned to the scene with reinforcements and shoved Weinberg in the back of a squad car, student activists—schooled in the techniques of the civil rights movement—simply sat and surrounded it, beginning what would be a prolonged sit-down strike.[64] The ranks of participants grew from two or three hundred into the thousands as classes came to an end, and Mario Savio stooped to remove his shoes and carefully climbed atop the immobilized police car to address the crowd. Savio announced the three demands of the protesters: the reversal of the eight student suspensions, an end to what he called "arbitrary restrictions" of on-campus speech, and the promise of no disciplinary actions targeting those engaged in the ongoing protest. After a back-and-forth with a worried representative from the student government, Savio introduced the first in what would be a long line of speakers addressing those assembled from the roof of the police cruiser, an inconspicuous fifty-year-old campus librarian. As graduate student Max Heirich described the scene, the crowd cheered as "Hal Draper climbed up on the car and gave a brief resume of his review of Kerr's book. The definition of the situation had been set."[65] For thirty-two hours, students sat around the police cruiser with Weinberg locked inside, debating and delivering speeches from the impromptu open mic set up on top of the car. The long protest came to an end with "the Pact of October 2." Signed by Clark Kerr and nine students, this cease-fire set the stage to move forward with negotiations.[66] As Hal Draper noted, in a successful attempt to cheer up a somewhat despondent Jack Weinberg, "you have essentially won a recognition as a collective bargaining agent, and that's a real victory."[67]

Two important developments followed the end of the police car sit-in. In what has been described as a "euphoric meeting" of the ISC following the success of the protest, Hal Draper set on a course to produce a pamphlet based on the talk he had given on September 29 and the synopsis he had provided from atop the police car. Within the next forty-eight hours, Draper produced, and the ISC published, the pamphlet *The Mind of Clark Kerr*. Twelve pages of text, split into two columns per page, the ISC printed 1,500 copies of the pamphlet which at twenty-five cents apiece promptly sold out the first morning they went on sale. Calling Draper's work "the most successful agitational pamphlet I've ever worked with," ISC and FSM leader Joel Geier described its impact from the vantage point of forty years, noting of the FSM that "all the speakers at rallies refer to 'the university as factory' and 'the knowledge factory'—everybody takes from it. [Draper] becomes the ideologist of [the FSM] insofar as it has one and that is because of his pamphlet."[68] Mario Savio, for his part, later noted that "*The Mind of Clark Kerr*, contributed mightily to the movement's understanding of the extent and depth of injustice by which the 'multiversity' runs."[69] As ISC members busily printed and distributed Draper's pamphlet, a meeting of the United Front led to the creation of the newly christened FSM on October 3. The two days that followed the triumph of the police car sit-in thus saw both the emergence of the FSM proper and the publication of what graduate student Mike Parker noted "was often called the Bible of the Free Speech Movement," Hal Draper's *The Mind of Clark Kerr*.[70]

Bodies upon the Gears

The weeks following the formation of the FSM on October 3 witnessed intense debates. The militant speeches and direct action of the United Front days gave way to negotiations between the FSM and campus administrators. Where the FSM organized executive and steering committees, Chancellor Strong formed a ten-member Campus Committee on Political Activity (CCPA) to speak on behalf of the administration. As explained by Max Heirich, the FSM executive committee took votes on policy decisions while the steering committee met "daily to plan negotiating strategy" as well as negotiate with the administration.[71] Student organizers quickly realized that the chancellor's CCPA existed to achieve little more than thwart the student advance and defuse potentially disruptive eruptions. As explained by the steering committee's Bettina Aptheker, the administration attempted "to use the committee to stall . . . in the hope that in the ensuing weeks FSM would somehow disappear. . . . It became clear that the only way to secure the rights of the students was to exercise them."[72] Accordingly, the relative calm that had reigned on campus throughout much of October and early November came to an end with a renewal of tabling, a calculated violation of the administration's ban on political activity.

After a nearly monthlong moratorium on direct action, new clashes with administrators and the threat of disciplinary measures swiftly reinvigorated the lagging FSM. On November 9, students set up tables in front of Sproul Hall, in direct violation of administrative rules. In response, a team of assistant deans took down the names of seventy-five individuals who had helmed the tables. That such administrative maneuvering only sparked more resistance became clear the next day, when the Graduate Student Coordinating Committee organized 196 graduate students to take over the tables placed in front of Sproul Hall. When the chancellor's office announced disciplinary action against those whose names had been recorded, these graduate student supporters of the FSM met to discuss the creation of a teaching assistant union. By the end of the week, hundreds of students had signed various petitions to the administration affirming that they, too, were guilty of manning the tables and thus violating university policy.[73]

Having faced down campus administrators, police officers, and even a brief appearance by unruly frat boys, the FSM trained its sights on one of the most powerful and influential forces in California, the UC Board of Regents. As chance had it, the monthly regents' meeting set for November 20, 1964, was scheduled to occur on the Berkeley campus. Frustrated with administrative repression targeting students and inspired by the possibility of swaying the regents' hand, as many as five thousand students rallied at noon on the Sproul Hall steps before marching across the campus to University Hall where the regents were meeting.[74] In an attempt to mollify the regents, protesters fully embraced the politics of respectability. Many donned suits, and an American flag was positioned beside the microphone on the Sproul steps. As graduate student Max Heirich recalled the event, "speeches were short and simple . . . and talked about the importance of defending the U.S. Constitution."[75] Yet, the besuited students failed to sway the regents, who voted to support Kerr and Chancellor Strong against the FSM and to maintain the eight suspensions ordered by campus administrators. The regents' refusal to let either the student government or FSM representatives speak at their meeting left students "angry and disappointed."[76] The experience set the stage for increasing agitation around the regents that would expose the conflicts of interest between their role as administrators of public education and their positions within the economic and political power elite that ruled California.[77]

Unsure of itself, the FSM faltered in the wake of the regents meeting. On Monday, November 23, a rally on the Sproul steps degenerated into an argument over the advisability of a building occupation. Against the protestations of some of the FSM leadership, perhaps three hundred students moved into Sproul Hall to commence what would become known as the abortive sit-in.[78] Debate continued even as students settled in. Some, including movement leaders Jack Weinberg and Bettina Aptheker, pushed for an end to the occupation, against the wishes of Mario Savio and others. Eventually, the steering committee voted six to five to end the sit-in when Sproul Hall closed at 5:00 P.M. As Max Heirich recalled, "It was a badly demoralized and split group. . . . A number of persons on the Executive Committee, as well as friendly observers of the movement, opined privately that the FSM was dead."[79] In the following days, students returned to their apartments and family homes for the Thanksgiving break, unsure of what would remain of the FSM when they returned to campus.

Over Thanksgiving weekend, four FSM leaders received letters from the UC Berkeley administration informing them of disciplinary actions that opened up the possibility for their expulsion. Hal Draper has argued that coming at what has been described as the nadir of the FSM, "there were few other moves by the administration which could have so thoroughly united all the diverse elements of the FSM."[80] The suspensions of Mario Savio, Brian Turner, Jackie Goldberg, and Art Goldberg stemmed from the police car sit-in that had occurred nearly two months earlier, in the opening days of the movement.[81] With the exception of Savio, those targeted were known as FSM "moderates." As David Lance Goines noted, "One pleasant consequence of these disciplinary letters was to provide a bridge for reconciliation" between the feuding Savio and Jackie Goldberg, and between the moderate and radical factions, more generally.[82] As classes resumed after the Thanksgiving weekend, the FSM issued a call to Chancellor Strong to drop the charges, a suggestion Strong quickly rejected. In response, students began organizing for what would be their biggest demonstration to date.

At noon on December 2, as many as six thousand FSM supporters rallied in front of Sproul Hall.[83] It was at this massive rally that Mario Savio delivered what would become one of the most famous speeches of the decade, an impromptu seven-minute talk that has since wound its way into posters, documentaries, comic books, songs, and more. Savio biographer Robert Cohen notes that this, Savio's most famous speech, has "been linked to the influence" of a diverse array of thinkers including Henry David Thoreau, Walt Whitman, Mahatma Gandhi, Leo Tolstoy, Charlie Chaplin, Martin Luther King Jr., C. Wright Mills, Herbert Marcuse, and Albert Camus. But, as Cohen notes, it seems more realistic to attribute to his words an influence closer to home. Reaching back to the end of September, Mario Savio resurrected the concepts he had first heard at Hal Draper's talk "Behind the Ban," giving a force to Draper's rhetoric that would continue to inspire those struggling for justice, even decades later. For, as Cohen notes, Savio's speech represented "a scathing indictment of the political compromises and educational failings of the university."[84]

Building on Draper's castigation of Kerr and the knowledge factory, Savio introduced those listening to his timeless critique of the university:

> We have an autocracy which runs this university. It's managed! We were told the following: If President Kerr actually tried to get something more liberal out of the regents in his telephone conversation, why didn't he make some public statement to that effect? And the answer we received, from a well-meaning liberal, was the following: He said, "Would you ever imagine the manager of a firm making a statement publicly in opposition to his board of directors?" That's the answer! Well, I ask you to consider: If this is a firm, and if the board of regents are the board of directors; and if President Kerr in fact is the manager; then I'll tell you something. The faculty are a bunch of employees, and we're the raw material! But we're a bunch of raw materials that don't mean to be, have any process upon us. Don't mean to be made into any product. Don't mean, don't mean to end up being bought by some clients of the University, be they the government, be they industry, be they organized labor, be they anyone! We're human beings!
>
> There's a time when the operation of the machine becomes so odious, makes you so sick at heart, that you can't take part! You can't even passively take part! And you've got to put your bodies upon the gears and upon the wheels, upon the levers, upon all the apparatus, and you've got to make it stop! And you've got to indicate to the people who run it, to the people who own it, that unless you're free, the machine will be prevented from working at all![85]

Savio concluded his moving speech by calling for the occupation of Sproul Hall and introducing the crowd to folksinger Joan Baez.[86] Baez sang as perhaps 1,500 student protesters marched up the steps of Sproul Hall into the building.

Later that day, Savio delivered yet another impromptu speech inside the building. Offering a critique of the mid-twentieth century United States, Savio focused his ire on the place of the university in contemporary society and the role of "impersonal bureaucracy."[87] In doing so, Savio once again resurrected the well-known themes of the theoretical framework introduced by Hal Draper. Savio began his talk with a critique of bureaucracy. Calling "depersonalized, unresponsive bureaucracy" perhaps "the greatest problem of our nation," Savio attacked the "bureaucratic mentality," arguing that "impersonal bureaucracy is the efficient enemy in a 'brave new world.'"[88] Savio also put forward a critique of Clark Kerr's vision of the university, demonstrating his familiarity with Kerr's *The Uses of the University*. "Campus students," Savio proclaimed, "are not about to accept it as fact that the university has ceased evolving and is in its final state of perfection, that students and faculty are respectively raw materials and employees, or that the university is to be autocratically run by unresponsive bureaucrats."[89] Kerr, who was in many ways the target of the sit-in itself, came to find himself the explicit target of Savio's speech as well.

Continuing on, Savio attacked Clark Kerr through his resurrection of a binary first posed by Hal Draper and, like Draper, put forward a moral call for students to answer. "One conception of the university," Savio argued, "suggested by a classical Christian formulation, is that it be in the world but not of the world. The conception of Clark Kerr by contrast is that the university is part and parcel of this particular stage in the history of American society; it stands to serve the need of American industry; it is a factory that turns out a certain product needed by industry or government."[90] Here, Savio completes the move initiated by Draper. For Clark Kerr, the multiversity represented the means of production in the knowledge industry, and Draper transformed Kerr's industry into the knowledge factory. Finally, for Savio, the university is simply a factory, with graduates, not knowledge, serving as the final product. Returning to a more existentialist critique and bringing back an idea that he himself had introduced in a speech more than two months before, Savio lamented that "the university is well structured, well tooled, to turn out people with all the sharp edges worn off."[91] Finally, like Draper's pamphlet, Savio's speech concluded with a challenge: "The 'futures' and 'careers' for which American students now prepare are for the most part intellectual and moral wastelands. This chrome-plated consumers' paradise would have us grow up to be well-behaved children. But an important minority of men and women coming to the front today have shown that they will die rather than be standardized, replaceable and irrelevant."[92] Building on his mentor Draper, Savio impressed and inspired those around him with the strength of his words and the rigor of his analyses. The speeches, discussions, songs, and films came to a close as day turned into night, and those remaining in the building began to drift slowly into sleep.

Abruptly, at 2:30 A.M., the lights were turned on as organizers on megaphones gave the warning to prepare for arrest. Over the course of twelve hours, police cleared those protesters who refused orders to disperse from Sproul Hall, resulting in 773 arrests. Whereas the first arrests proceeded slowly and were relatively gentle, as the night wore on the police became increasingly violent. Citing the testimony of those arrested, Hal Draper described how "male students were generally dragged and bumped down the stairs, arms twisted, strong-armed, or kicked. Female students were dragged into the elevator and bundled down with less overt violence until they reached the basement. . . . A number of policemen hid their badges to prevent identification. . . . A few students, particularly recognized FSM leaders, were deliberately roughed up."[93] Bettina Aptheker vividly recalled that "a booted officer kicked me hard in the stomach. . . . I was met by more officers. Two, one on each side of me, held my arms . . . while a third pummeled me in the stomach and breasts with his fists." One officer, recognizing Aptheker, launched into an antisemitic tirade, denouncing the FSM leader as "a goddamn Russian Jew!"[94] With the eruption of such police violence, yet another administrative misstep had ensured a reinvigorated wave of support for the FSM.

The week following the arrests at Sproul Hall witnessed the most widespread participation yet in the FSM, as graduate student teaching assistants went on strike and undergraduates boycotted classes.[95] Even faculty members participated, convening an impromptu meeting and eventually throwing their weight behind the striking students. Pickets commenced on the morning of December 3, while police were still busy arresting the remaining students in Sproul Hall. After a slow start at 6:00 A.M., truck drivers belonging to a Teamsters local refused to cross the picket lines, as did the carpenters working on a new campus building. With the majority of the steering committee under arrest, a new line of leadership largely consisting of graduate students took command.[96] Max Heirich, then among the mass congregated in Sproul Plaza, recalled, "I estimated perhaps five or ten thousand people might be crowded together on the plaza by noon. . . . People were pressed shoulder to shoulder, chest to back."[97] Graduate student Steve Weissman addressed those massed with a list of demands. The most far-reaching demands to date, they included the withdrawal of all charges, administrative and legal, against student protesters, an end to the restrictions on free speech on campus, an end to police brutality and police interference in campus affairs, and the resignations of Chancellor Strong and President Kerr.[98]

Berkeley faculty, heretofore largely confined to the margins of the movement, organized an emergency meeting on December 3, the morning of the Sproul Hall arrests. With some nine hundred faculty members in attendance, one professor remarked that the meeting had twice as many participants as a typical meeting of Academic Senate.[99] Henry May, chair of the history department, put forward a three-part resolution in favor of the FSM to great applause. Franz Schurmann, a noted sinologist, appealed to those assembled for action, arguing, "I have not been an active participant, but events of the last few days have changed my mind. The faculty are largely to blame: in a sense we *have* become a factory, dependent upon a bureaucracy for leadership." Schurmann's words, of course, called to mind Draper's earlier critique, and those assembled met his speech with "enthusiastic, prolonged applause."[100] Political scientist Herbert McClosky followed up with two additional demands, bringing the total to five. Voting began and the faculty overwhelming approved both the May and McClosky resolutions. Thus, the faculty voiced their support for "new liberalized rules for campus action" and an end to administrative actions against both on- and off-campus student protest.[101] In addition, Roger Stanier of the department of bacteriology read out a petition to Governor Edmund Brown denouncing the police presence on campus and calling for the "prompt release" of arrested students. Some 361 faculty members signed the letter to Brown. Hal Draper described the faculty mutiny, noting that "this was the first time the faculty had spoken *up* strongly, and it occurred precisely at the point where the students were engaged in their strongest action."[102] With such a large section of the faculty coming out in support of striking students, the meeting marked the beginning of the end of the FSM.

The student strike that began on Thursday, December 3 continued through the weekend and into Monday. On Saturday and Sunday, a telephone survey conducted by the FSM found that 55 percent of randomly contacted students supported the FSM and the strike. Hal Draper, who argued that "one TA [teaching assistant] striker . . . equaled in effectiveness many undergraduates," noted that "a majority of the [teaching assistants] went on strike; in the humanities and social sciences, 90 percent. The FSM's over-all report was that 900 out of 1200 struck."[103] Even the right-wing student magazine *Man and State* admitted to the success of the FSM action: "Attendance at classes severely dropped. . . . Student opinion solidified behind FSM." Draper, who in a reversal of roles found his inspiration in Mario Savio's words, wrote that "the gears, wheels and levers of the Multiversity had been effectively checked."[104] The FSM strike of December 3–7,

1964, effectively outmaneuvered President Kerr, his administration, and the UC Board of Regents. The students had won over not only the student body but a majority of the faculty. At this point, the only question left would be how the revising of university rules would proceed.

In a last-ditch attempt to retake control and shore up support among the faculty, UC president Clark Kerr visited the Berkeley campus to address a convocation of all students, faculty, and staff. On Monday morning, between thirteen and twenty thousand attendees crammed into and around the campus's outdoor Greek Theatre for the 11:00 A.M. meeting. [105] Applause erupted and approximately half of those assembled gave a standing ovation when Mario Savio was spotted toward the front of the theater. Savio had requested permission to address the assembly, a request that Professor Robert Scalapino, who had organized the event along with Kerr, turned down. In addition, Scalapino denied representatives from the Associated Students of the University of California (ASUC) student government a chance to speak. Kerr delivered what he believed to be a conciliatory speech, embracing the proposals of department chairs for amnesty. Yet to many of those assembled, what seemed like deliberate vagueness on the part of Kerr opened up the possibility for the continued persecution of activists.[106] What students would remember most about the Greek Theatre episode, however, came at the end of Kerr's remarks when Mario Savio attempted to take the stage. As one front-page article read, "The leader of the Free Speech Movement was dragged from a microphone today on a stage in front of 13,000 students and faculty."[107] Even decades later, Clark Kerr remembered the feeling of bitter disappointment as his plans for the convocation "went all for naught. The crowd had seen Mario Savio dragged from the scene and that was all it remembered."[108] After a brief detention, Savio was released and addressed the crowd to inform them of plans to rally in front of Sproul Hall. Perhaps as many as ten thousand FSM supporters attended the triumphant gathering.[109]

From December 7, 1964, through the end of the semester, the FSM continued to amass victories. In particular, two different electoral successes marked the triumphant completion of the fight for political organizing on campus. First, and perhaps most importantly, for the first time the entire Berkeley faculty registered its formal support of the FSM. On December 8, the day after Kerr's Greek Theatre tragedy, nearly a thousand members of the faculty turned up for a meeting of the Academic Senate. In the midst of intense debate, Professor Joseph Garbarino, chairman of the pro-FSM Committee on Academic Freedom, presented a five-point resolution. Most importantly, the committee proposed the withdrawal of all disciplinary actions stemming from the FSM, the end of regulations on speech and advocacy on campus, and that future disciplinary measures be determined not by the campus administration but by a newly formed committee of the Academic Senate.[110] The vote was a landslide. Of those faculty assembled, only 115 voted against the resolution while 824 voted in favor.

The faculty had registered their voice, and they stood with the FSM. So, it seems, did the student body. Throughout the movement, the ASUC student government had consistently taken the side of the administration. Yet the ASUC elections, held on December 8, registered widespread student support for the FSM. Pro-FSM candidates, organized under the Slate banner, swept the elections. What's more, turnout was twice the usual size, with 5,276 votes cast.[111] As Max Heirich recalled, "December 8 had been quite a day. Supporters of the FSM had been given control of the student government; the faculty had passed a resolution basically supporting the position the FSM had been advocating all fall; and the faculty had taken charge of the campus governing machinery."[112] After a long and exhausting fall semester, the FSM came to a close.

While maintaining a show a strength in the face of increasingly unruly subjects, the UC regents recognized that the times had changed. At their December 18 meeting in Los Angeles, the regents began with a call for law and order and a reminder that "the ultimate authority for student discipline within the university is constitutionally vested in the Regents, and is a matter not subject to negotiation." This was a clear swipe at the proposals overwhelmingly affirmed by the Berkeley faculty on December 8. The regents also announced a study and, somewhat confusingly, warned that "existing rules will be enforced." Yet at the same time, the regents issued a statement to university faculty conceding the inevitable. In the midst of pablum and equivocations, the board announced that "the Regents affirm devotion to the First and Fourteenth Amendments to the Constitution."[113] Despite all their threats to the contrary, they had relented on the one matter that had been central to the struggle from the beginning. What's more, on January 2, 1965, at an emergency meeting of the Board of Regents, the regents dismissed Chancellor Strong, under the cover of "a leave of absence to recover his health."[114] Martin Meyerson, who Max Heirich described as "one of the more sympathetic proponents of student concerns within the administration," was named acting chancellor.[115] Strong would never return to his post.[116]

Despite ongoing legal troubles and the occasional flaring up of old issues, the FSM had won. It was an unequivocal victory for the students and a sound defeat for the administration. For Bettina Aptheker, the daughter of Communist Party USA members who throughout her life had lived with the ominous threat of McCarthyism and political persecution, the victory was especially sweet. Reminiscing on what she saw as the final nail in the coffin of an earlier, repressive era, Aptheker's memoirs describe the scene at the climax of the December 8 Academic Senate vote in support of the FSM: "Many of us were crying, and so were many of them, these stolid, mature, often elderly, white men. At this moment many of us, faculty and students alike, understood that the days of the loyalty oaths and speakers' bans and anti-Communist witch hunts were finally over."[117] And despite the need to rest and rejoice, despite the hardships imposed by a six-week-long trial for the nearly eight hundred students arrested at the occupation of Sproul Hall, despite ongoing tensions with the campus administration and the regents, those activists formed in the fires of the FSM continued to organize, they analyzed and taught others what they had learned over the course of the fall semester, and they set their sights on a much bigger target than on-campus political advocacy: the war in Vietnam.[118]

A series of post-FSM talks, pamphlets, articles, and books helped to popularize Hal Draper's critique of Clark Kerr far beyond the Master Plan system itself. Only days after their victory on campus, FSM leaders Mario Savio, Bettina Aptheker, Suzanne Goldberg, and Steve Weissman were flown to New York City for an interview on the *Les Crane Show*, a popular late-night program on ABC.[119] In the coming weeks, FSM leaders, "singly and together" Aptheker recalled, "spoke at Columbia, Queens College, Harvard, and the Universities of Chicago, Minnesota, and Wisconsin."[120] At his old haunt of Queens College, Savio denounced Kerr as a captain of bureaucracy, while giving Draper credit for a term that was actually Kerr's own.[121] At Harvard, Savio described Kerr as an "able practitioner of managerial tyranny" who sought to make UC Berkeley a "knowledge factory." "Kerr's university," Savio lamented, "is a university plugged into the military and the industrial—but not to truth."[122]

In the movement's wake, Draper worked to convey the roots and significance of the FSM to the burgeoning New Left. Draper's *Berkeley: The New Student Revolt* was published by Grove Press on September 15, 1965, in an initial run of twenty-five thousand copies.[123] Alongside his own extended analysis of the FSM, Draper's 246-page book included important speeches from FSM organizers and a thoughtful introduction by Mario Savio.[124] Following the book's publication, Draper took up correspondence with the Chicago-based national secretary of SDS, Paul Booth, informing him that

Grove Press was willing to provide free copies of *Berkeley* to key members of SDS. Draper and Grove Press also offered steep discounts of up to 45 percent off any additional copies purchased by SDS national offices.[125] Booth took up the offer, providing a list of 275 key local contacts who would receive free copies of Draper's book. In a letter to the 275 SDS members, Booth described Draper's work as "quite an important book for our organizing purposes. . . . Draper's analysis of the causes of the rebellion, and of the sources of student alienation, is an analysis with clear implications for student action throughout the country."[126] Finally, Draper's influence spread even beyond the American New Left, as the London-based *Solidarity* magazine included an enthusiastic six-page review of Draper's "The Mind of Clark Kerr" in a volume dedicated to what they called "the battle of the Berkeley campus."[127]

Jack Weinberg also helped to further spread Draper's analysis of the FSM. Weinberg produced a concise analysis of the movement for the benefit of the Student Union for Peace Action, the most important organization in Canada's New Left. The Canadian group's "impact on other [Canadian] youth organizations was legendary," and the Student Union for Peace Action itself was largely influenced by the writings of the American New Left in addition to decolonization theory and European Marxism.[128] "The Wildcat Strike and the Knowledge Factory," a succinct analysis provided by Weinberg in January 1965, was well timed for a Canadian organization that saw its chief impact from 1965 to 1967. Weinberg began by describing the "free speech issue" as a "vehicle enabling students to express their dissatisfaction with so much of university life" but quickly refocused his ire on the larger society. "The University of California," he argued, "is a microcosm in which all of the problems of our society are reflected." "Throughout society," Weinberg wrote, "the individual has lost more and more control over his environment. . . . He has become more and more a cog in a machine, part of a *master plan* in whose formulation he is not consulted, and over which he can exert no influence for change. . . . The bureaucratization of the campus is just a reflection of the bureaucratization of American life."[129] With his pamphlet, Weinberg brought to the most influential student organization in Canada a radical critique of mid-twentieth century society that was heavily influenced by Draper's analysis of Clark Kerr and the Cold War multiversity.

In what were likely the most widely circulated analyses of the FSM by a movement participant, Mario Savio conducted a post-FSM interview with *Life* and published an article in *Harper's* magazine. Savio's *Life* interview had all the hallmarks of his earlier speeches in support of the FSM, including denunciations of Clark Kerr and of the multiversity, an institution carefully calibrated, Savio maintained, to support the smooth functioning of the military-industrial complex. Yet it was Savio's piece for *Harper's*, "The Uncertain Future of the Multiversity," published in October 1966, that broke new ground. In it, Savio trained his sights on the 1960 California Master Plan for Higher Education itself. Savio wrote that "I personally believe [that the continuation of] the Master Plan would only hinder improvement of undergraduate colleges—and that it should be radically redesigned or simply abandoned." Further, he lamented that "the worst features of the system of large lectures and perfunctory grades will be emphasized . . . and under the Master Plan the average size of undergraduate classes will increase." The Master Plan, Savio argued, had been "force[d]" on Californians by Clark Kerr, the regents, the legislature, "and others who inhabit the stratosphere of educational high finance." Savio connected the Master Plan to the same sort of technocratic arrogance that led to the FSM, arguing that "the history of the adoption of the Master Plan . . . show[s] that faculty members and students are consistently excluded from those groups of legislators, bureaucrats, and businessmen which make the most far reaching decisions concerning the development and reform of the University. Those of us whose lives are directly involved are denied any effective voice in these decisions which structure and pervert our immediate, daily environment."[130]

Savio embedded a warning in his denunciation of the Master Plan: "If this Plan is not stopped soon . . . the great enthusiasm for reform generated by the Free Speech Movement will be lost." Still, he noted optimistically, "some opposition is developing among the more independent state college faculties."[131] Savio was quite correct to note the discontent brewing in California's state colleges. Within the next two years, faculty and students would contribute to a series of struggles on campuses including Fresno, San Fernando Valley, San Jose, and San Francisco State, among others. At the same time, campus rebellions would meet stiff resistance on the part of California's New Right. In November 1966, Ronald Reagan won the California governorship in large part by riling his conservative base through constant criticisms of student protests. From the governor's mansion, Reagan would challenge what had been a bipartisan consensus regarding state-funded higher education, calling into question the Master Plan itself.

3   The New Right Takes Aim

· ·

Too many [students] show up for the commencement exercises fresh
out of jail, breathing fiery and four-letter contempt for anything
smacking of decency or morality and looking as though they had
neither bathed nor combed their hair since they were freshmen.

—Max Rafferty, 1965
  (California state superintendent of public instruction)

The governor, in other words, has demanded the repeal of the Master
Plan of Higher Education. . . . If he prevails, Ronald Reagan will have
won a Pyrrhic victory that California will long regret.

—Editorial Board, 1967
  (*Los Angeles Times*)

At the height of an apparent revolution powered forward by a broad coalition
of Black Panthers, anti-war protesters, and Chicano nationalists, California's
conservatives increasingly fixated on an unlikely figure: a septuagenarian
philosophy professor. Having fled fascist persecution in Nazi Germany, Herbert Marcuse had eventually found what appeared a safe haven in sunny San
Diego. Upon his arrival in the United States, Marcuse had spent the war
years working for the U.S. Office of War Information, the Office of Strategic
Services, and finally, the U.S. Department of State.[1] As the world returned to
a postwar normalcy, Marcuse found employment at Brandeis University before relocating to an emerging University of California, San Diego (UCSD)
campus that was trying to establish its academic credentials. Only a few
years later, however, this critical theorist and senior citizen would find himself the target of an anti-communist campaign promoted by right-wing local
media, encouraged by California's new conservative governor, and likely or-
chestrated by none other than J. Edgar Hoover, the long-standing director of
the Federal Bureau of Investigation (FBI).[2]

In May 1968, the *San Diego Union* newspaper began a series of editorials
critical of Marcuse, calling the seventy-year-old philosopher a "dangerous man" whose salary was paid by California taxpayers.[3] The FBI had
begun an official program of surveillance on Marcuse two years earlier to

investigate his ties to the student movement and anti-war activism. By the end of September 1966, the FBI's San Diego office had produced a full report on Marcuse for national director J. Edgar Hoover. In 1968, the bureau placed Marcuse "under heightened surveillance."[4] Given such timing, it seems likely that the articles critical of Marcuse in the archconservative *San Diego Union* originated with the FBI's Mass Media Program. That program, according to investigative journalist Seth Rosenfeld, consisted in the cultivation of "special relationships with more than three hundred cooperative members of the news media, leaking them information from confidential FBI files to produce stories advancing bureau interests and in some cases even drafting the articles and editorials these journalists published under their own names."[5] Whatever their origin, the stories critical of Herbert Marcuse developed into a full-blown crisis over UC faculty autonomy and political intrusions by Governor Ronald Reagan and the Board of Regents.

In the wake of the series of *San Diego Union* editorials, Marcuse received both death threats and an extended bout of harassment by Governor Reagan and the UC regents. On July 1, 1968, Marcuse received a letter warning him: "leave the United States, 72 hours, Marcuse, and then we kill you." The handwritten note was signed, simply, "Ku Klux Klan." Although no clear evidence connects organized Klansmen to this threat, far-right militias plagued San Diego in the late sixties.[6] Just two days later, Marcuse discovered that his phone service had been disconnected. Before the end of his seventy-two-hour deadline, Marcuse and his wife left the country for their customary summer in Europe. Rather than condemn the threats on Marcuse's life, San Diego conservatives stepped up their campaign against the elderly philosopher. Republican state senator Jack Schrade demanded that UCSD terminate Marcuse's contract, a demand subsequently endorsed by the *San Diego Union* and echoed by Governor Reagan. Marcuse, for his part, announced his plans to return to San Diego for the fall semester. Throughout the 1968–69 school year, Marcuse would face continuing harassment from California conservatives but received unflinching support from his colleagues and campus administrators.[7]

Marcuse's case represents a typical episode in the culture war that conservatives waged in the post-McCarthy era. Collaborating across a host of institutions, the far-right wing of the Republican Party harassed leftist faculty throughout the Master Plan system. In his first term as governor, Ronald Reagan—along with state superintendent of public instruction Max Rafferty—would use his institutional power and influence in an attempt to cancel courses and void teaching contracts held by a host of better- and lesser-known academics. Those targeted included Marcuse's graduate student Angela Davis, San Francisco State sociologist Nathan Hare and graduate student George Murray, Fresno State professors Robert Mezey and Marvin X, and new hire Harry Edwards and guest lecturer Eldridge Cleaver at UC Berkeley, to name but the most prominent cases.

In a successful attempt to further their control in the wake of the Marcuse controversy, Reagan, Rafferty, and their allies on the Board of Regents stripped the UC chancellors of their long-standing authority of tenure appointments and promotions. The vote, taken in April 1969, systematized what had heretofore been a haphazard series of political intrusions.[8] The actions taken by Governor Reagan and the regents dovetailed nicely with the aims of the FBI, which had long been concerned with combating ostensibly communist influences on college campuses. In the late sixties, the bureau's Faculty Involvement in New Left Activities Program targeted left-leaning professors across the nation. In Reagan, the FBI found a willing ally at the highest echelon of California state politics.[9]

As Governor Reagan consolidated his control of the UC Board of Regents and state college trustees, campus administrators noted the emergence of a clear pattern of political intrusions into matters of faculty hiring and retention across the Master Plan system. As UCSD chancellor William McGill lamented in his memoirs, "the original plan of the multicampus system envisioned by Clark Kerr had been founded on decentralized decision-making, but . . . Governor Reagan and his followers on the board became increasingly reluctant to yield to local campus officials." George Zenovich, a Democratic assemblyman from Fresno, accused Reagan of leading "a total takeover" that "goes against all basic concepts of higher education in this state." Rather than try to build and improve on the imperfect framework established by the California Master Plan, Reagan would work to tear it down. For Reagan and his allies, UCSD chancellor McGill correctly noted, the Marcuse affair was a single front in a larger war. As McGill wrote, "Governor Reagan and State Superintendent of Public Instruction Max Rafferty were expressing a simple diagnosis and a simple remedy: we are in a revolution; we must crush it with force."[10]

· · · · · ·

In California, opposition to the provision of free higher education was central to the emergence of the New Right. Those California conservatives who rose to prominence in the 1960s did so through deliberate attacks on the system established by the California Master Plan for Higher Education. Such opposition comprised a major part of their fierce dedication to anti-communism in the post-McCarthy era.[11] Epitomized by California governor Ronald Reagan, New Right conservatives harbored deep misgivings about the role of state and federal governments as providers of social services, including public education. Although previous scholars have astutely analyzed debates over race and the welfare state as central to the New Right's emergence, close study of the California Master Plan for Higher Education suggests that battles over the provision of public higher education were just as important to the rise of the New Right.[12]

In contrast to former president Dwight Eisenhower and the "modern Republicans" who had made a relative peace with the New Deal order, New Right conservatives maintained an ideological commitment to scaling back the scope of government intervention in society.[13] As one commentator at the time noted, "In a sense, the Democratic Party was the party of big business in California; Reagan's constituency was weighted with marginal entrepreneurs, on whom the cost of government weighed most heavily."[14] Reagan's efforts toward the privatization of public goods—in the case of higher education through the failed introduction of tuition and subsequent successful increases in student fees—coincided with their assault on students and faculty who sought to expand access to the highest tiers of the Master Plan system. On the campaign trail, Reagan and his fellows challenged the legitimacy of publicly funded higher education, helping to pave the way for California's taxpayer revolt, which would reach its apex in 1978.[15] Once in office, the governor and his administration attacked the Master Plan financially, while simultaneously expanding their authority through administrative proxies on individual campuses. Through their combined efforts, by the 1970s, New Right conservatives would throw into question the survival of the liberal framework established by the 1960 Master Plan for Higher Education.

Rafferty for Superintendent

Although Ronald Reagan remains the best-known exemplar of New Right conservatism, his rise to power in California and the success of his attacks on higher education owed much to a coterie of archconservative ideologues. Although now much forgotten, the "superconservative" Max Rafferty served as one of Reagan's most committed allies in his long-running battles with campus activists.[16] Prior to his political career, Rafferty worked his way through a number of isolated counties and educational posts, from teacher, to vice principal, principal to superintendent.[17] In the early sixties, Rafferty held forth against John Dewey's theory of progressive education while working in various conservative Southern California school districts. As former California state librarian Kevin Starr has noted of this "fiercely anti-progressive" critic of the New Deal, "Rafferty hammered away at his anti-Dewey message, linking progressive education to a larger drift towards collectivism."[18]

From 1962 to 1970, the Republican Rafferty served as state superintendent of public instruction. Like the governor, the "ultraconservative" Rafferty sat on the boards of both the UC regents and the state college trustees by virtue of the office he held.[19] In the wake of the 1964 Free Speech Movement (FSM), Rafferty gained wider acclaim on the right by lambasting the early stirrings of California student activism. Rafferty consistently represented a far-right voice on the California political spectrum until successive electoral losses in 1968 and 1970 led to his decision to relocate to Alabama.[20]

Rafferty's successful initial foray into politics represented the thorough politicization of the historically and officially nonpartisan office of the California state superintendent of public instruction. The occasion for Rafferty's campaign was the retirement of Roy E. Simpson, the longest serving state superintendent in California history. Governor Earl Warren had appointed Simpson to his first term in November 1945. In the late fifties, Simpson emerged as a coauthor of the California Master Plan for Higher Education, his influence on the Master Plan overshadowed only by that of UC president Clark Kerr. At the age of sixty-nine, Simpson decided to end his four-term seventeen-year reign as California's state superintendent of public instruction.[21] A moderate Republican, Simpson initially pledged to remain neutral, offering no endorsement in the race to replace him.

Nine candidates faced off in the nonpartisan primary race for California state superintendent of public instruction in June 1962. Of those nine, Ralph Richardson and Max Rafferty advanced to the November runoff for the highest educational post in the state. Richardson, a Democrat, worked as an associate professor of English at UCLA. For more than five years, Richardson had served as the president of the Los Angeles city school board, governing the state's largest school district.[22] Richardson emerged from the primary as the clear leader of the pack, having received 737,578 votes. Rafferty, in turn, barely eked out a second-place finish, receiving 660,537 votes—less than 1 percent more than the third-place finisher.[23]

Behind in the polls, Rafferty turned toward the mobilization of his GOP base. Rafferty was well positioned to gain the support of his fellow archconservatives, particularly in the conservative suburbs of San Diego, Los Angeles, and Orange Counties. Courting this hard-right voting bloc in the primary, Rafferty denounced "our [nation's] Columbia University philosophers, our educational psychologists, and our state department consultants" for what he claimed was the abysmal state of American education. With a nod to Sputnik, Rafferty blamed progressive educators for an era in which "our world position degenerat[ed] so abysmally that a race of lash-driven atheistic peasants can challenge us successfully in our own chosen field of science." Although here Rafferty spoke to a broadly held concern, such rhetorical excesses did little to endear him to the then-dominant moderate wing of the Republican Party.[24]

Born in 1917 and raised in Iowa, Rafferty moved with his parents to California as a young teen. After graduating from Beverly Hills High School, he attended UCLA, majoring in history and graduating with a C+ average.[25] It was there that Rafferty first engaged in an aggressive politics that bordered on the extreme. In the midst of the left-leaning student movement of the 1930s, Rafferty found a home on the far right, joining the UCLA Americans, a conservative student group formed in opposition to liberal and leftist student organizing on campus.[26] In 1937, a fellow student publicly accused Rafferty of "trying to spread Fascist propaganda over campus . . . under the name of Americanism and democracy."[27] As yet another fellow student would note, Rafferty's group was "largely fraternity men" and possessed "a kind of vigilante spirit," known to patrol the campus at night, "carrying torches and flags."[28]

Rafferty came to serve as a leader within the UCLA Americans, an experience he would later recall fondly. Speaking to the press in the late sixties, Rafferty compared his own years with the UCLA Americans to the contemporary student movement, claiming that "the only difference is that in those days the school administrator and the Chancellors were on our side, not with the Communists."[29] Some of the group's history, however, Rafferty preferred to keep quiet. In 1970, Hollywood producer Stanley Rubin, a former editor of the *Daily Bruin*, remembered the UCLA Americans' frustration with that campus newspaper. Recalling an angry young Rafferty, Rubin noted that the future superintendent once "came crashing into the office in his ROTC uniform and boots, looking every bit the stormtrooper. He had two big football players with him" and began "physically attacking me."[30] From such beginnings Rafferty became a darling of California's radical right.

In the months prior to the runoff election for state superintendent, Rafferty courted the Republican vote. The conservative educator rose to prominence in the early sixties while working as the first superintendent of schools for La Cañada, a wealthy Los Angeles suburb.[31] In the summer of 1961, Rafferty gained wide acclaim for his speech "The Passing of the Patriot."[32] The June speech attacked those Rafferty called "the phoney sophisticates who clutter up our colleges" and blamed Dewey's theory of progressive education for producing "unwashed, leather-jacketed slobs, whose favorite sport is ravaging little girls and stomping polio victims to death." Denying that "indoctrination" was "an ugly word," Rafferty declared that "if it is ugly to teach children . . . to hate communism and its creatures like hell, then I say let's be ugly and let's revel in it!" Despite, or perhaps because of, the hyperbole, Rafferty's speech was a hit and was subsequently published in the October 1961 edition of *Reader's Digest*. The wake of his speech witnessed the opening of a "draft Rafferty" movement in Orange County, and the combative educator was summoned to a meeting in Los Angeles with no less than "nine heads or executives of major oil companies and leading state banking and real estate figures."[33] With ample funding at hand, the aspiring candidate hit the Republican circuits delivering talks across California and beyond.

As early as 1961, Rafferty had captured the support of the conservative wing of the Republican Party, a faction that would later embrace Arizona senator Barry Goldwater for the presidency and Ronald Reagan for governor of California. Like those conservative figures, Rafferty struggled to cope with widespread charges of extremism. In November 1961, Rafferty spoke to some two thousand attendees at an anti-communist "Crusade for Americanism" rally in archconservative Glendale.[34] The *Los Angeles Times* would later describe the LA suburb as, in the 1960s, "a magnet for white supremacists" and home to both "the commander of the American Nazi Party's Western Division" and "the Grand Cyclops of the state Ku Klux Klan."[35] In April 1962, Rafferty again found himself in far-right territory, speaking alongside similarly minded Republicans Joe Shell and John Rousselot. Where Shell was then running to be the Republican candidate for the governor of California, to the right of Richard Nixon, Rousselot was one of only two self-avowed Birchers in Congress. Although Rafferty long denied membership in and collusion with the John Birch Society, the far-right organization's conspiratorial and rabidly anti-communist views aligned closely with those of Rafferty.[36] Because of such associations, throughout the campaign Rafferty and his subordinates repeatedly found themselves fending off charges of extremism.[37]

By December 1961, Rafferty's astringent conservatism had alienated an important potential Republican ally, the retiring state superintendent of public instruction Roy Simpson. In his opening remarks to the annual conference of the California Association of School Administrators, Simpson denounced "irresponsible criticism" and warned that the "Communist cause is being served by those who create unwarranted suspicion among loyal Americans." Honing in on the target of his critique, Simpson noted that Max Rafferty's famous speech, "The Passing of the Patriot," had cast doubts "upon the patriotism of young Americans as well as upon the effectiveness of public schools in developing patriotic attitudes in our young people." Unlike Rafferty, Roy Simpson was a military veteran and had proven his anticommunist credentials in his efforts to shape California schools to meet the Soviet challenge. While Max Rafferty was "busy tearing down our educational system," Simpson charged, "we were concerned with building it up. . . . We have upgraded the whole field of public education."[38] A venerated Republican educator, Simpson had no time for Rafferty's Bircher-like aspersions. Herbert McClosky, a professor at UC Berkeley, echoed Simpson's remarks to those assembled, warning that "extreme rightists, cloaking themselves in the mantles of super-patriotism, threaten academic freedom and weaken the democratic case against communism."[39]

Despite speaking out forcefully against his fellow Republican, Roy Simpson initially refused to endorse Rafferty's opponent, Ralph Richardson. While Richardson racked up endorsements from the California Association of School Administrators and nine out of ten members of the state board of education, Rafferty fought off claims that he was the preferred candidate of the John Birch Society.[40] Finally, with only two weeks left before the election, Simpson publicly endorsed Richardson. In an interview sixteen years later, Simpson would recall that "I didn't support anybody until about the last two weeks, when Rafferty started to lambast the public schools by making us look like a bunch of ninnies."[41] Reaching across the aisle, the Republican Simpson embraced the liberal Richardson, calling him "the better man for the job." Yet, Simpson's endorsement of Richardson read more as a rejection of Rafferty. Simpson claimed to be "disturbed because of the many inaccuracies and unfounded statements" made by Rafferty and noted that "the man has displayed a great ignorance of the responsibilities of the office." In addition to pointing to several examples of Rafferty's ignorance of the duties and basic functions of the post he sought, Simpson critiqued Rafferty for making "derogatory statements" about the California's Department of Education and maintained that its staff members were both "competent and dedicated." As *Los Angeles Times* writer Daryl Lembke noted of the endorsement, "Simpson, a Republican, said he has kept politics out of his office . . . and feels Richardson, a Democrat, would do the same. Rafferty is a Republican."[42]

Despite Richardson's impressive string of endorsements, on November 6, Rafferty pulled off a narrow upset victory, winning 52 percent of the vote in an election generally unfriendly to Republicans.[43] Having thoroughly alienated much of the educational establishment in California, Rafferty turned to the uneasy transition from candidate to officeholder.[44] Roy Simpson noted to a reporter, upon hearing news of Rafferty's victory, that the office of superintendent "is one with considerable influence but little power. . . . Rafferty can recommend policies endlessly but they can't be put into effect without the approval of the state board." As such, the incoming state superintendent began an uphill battle to find common ground with the ten-member state board of education he had so thoroughly alienated in months of campaigning.[45] Rafferty quickly released a seven-point plan, which stressed phonics in reading and an emphasis on children's literary "classics" and downplayed what were then known as "life adjustment" courses. Rafferty promised a new emphasis on "the great heroes, stories and facts of American history . . . from the first grade on."[46] Wary of Rafferty's arrival, Thomas Braden, president of the state board of education, promised cooperation in "toughening up the school curricula. 'But if he comes up with all this stuff about indoctrinating school children in patriotism and the dangers of communism, he's going to incur opposition from us.'"[47]

In early 1963, Rafferty settled into what would be a two-term stint defined by harsh rhetoric and internal conflicts with the board of education. Eventually, in 1970, Rafferty would lose his reelection bid to Wilson Riles, a Democrat and the first African American ever elected to statewide office in California. As Riles would later note of the Rafferty years, when "Max became superintendent, you had a virtual shootout between" Rafferty and Governor Edmund "Pat" Brown. "That did no good for education. Education was in the paper a lot, but it was a contest, an adversary relationship between Max and the board [of education]." Not until Ronald Reagan began his gubernatorial term in 1967 would the board begin to turn in a conservative direction more amenable to Rafferty's leadership.[48] Yet even before Reagan ascended to office, Rafferty did his best to combat the rising tide of activism on California campuses, opposing both student protest and teacher unionization.[49]

When the FSM erupted at UC Berkeley, Rafferty rode the crest of a wave of conservative censure. Prior to the December 1964 UC regents meeting which would debate the topic of the FSM at Berkeley, Rafferty warned that "to permit" such protest was equivalent to "abdicating the right to control crime on campus." The state superintendent sought to close the door to future student activism through such equation of political protest to criminal activity.[50] By 1965, Rafferty had dialed up his rhetoric, denouncing nonviolent FSM activists as "rioters" participating in "a veritable orgy of childish malevolence which . . . would have raised eyebrows in an institution for the emotionally disturbed." Rafferty placed the blame for such campus activism on parents who "yank their kids out of school and put them on picket lines" and professors who "in the name of academic freedom . . . promote in [their] classes one particular ideology."[51] In his weekly syndicated column for the *Los Angeles Times*, Rafferty attacked student activists as those who "defy the taxpayers who are subsidizing their educations, wreck police cars and bite the legs of campus cops."[52]

As the FSM gave way to anti-war organizing, Rafferty once again stood in the vanguard of political reaction. Calling such political protest "downright treason," the conservative educator commenced to engage in more of his characteristic hyperbole. In his column, which ran under the headline "Disciplining Academic Freedom," Rafferty warned of a taxpayer and parental revolt, writing that "the crisis is compounded when Dad and Mom read every day about Prof. Benedict showing Junior how to lie down in front of troop trains, while Prof. Arnold gives him lessons in how to tear up his draft card."[53] By engaging in such sensationalism, Rafferty sought to make his vision of taxpayer revolt a self-fulfilling prophecy. Finally, upon running for reelection in 1966, Rafferty reminded his potential supporters that "I didn't vote to permit riot and anarchy on the Berkeley campus."[54] Rafferty was certainly not the only California politician to wager that running against student activism was a winning proposition.

The Rise of Ronald Reagan

As many have observed, Ronald Reagan arrived in Sacramento having promised to "clean up the mess at Berkeley." Like Max Rafferty, Reagan defied what were then common observations regarding California's moderate to liberal politics. Finding a base in the staunch conservatism of Southern

California, Reagan would serve two terms as governor, picking up the mantle of conservative stalwart in the aftermath of a disheartening rebuke for the far right in the 1964 presidential election. Where Barry Goldwater had failed abysmally, Ronald Reagan would eventually succeed as president between 1980 and 1988, turning back the clock on the New Deal and ushering in a new conservative age of American politics. In the early days of his gubernatorial campaign, however, many, if not most, political observers viewed Reagan as something of a joke.

Reagan's campaign for governor emerged in the context of a years-long effort to push the Republican Party of California to the right. At least since Governor Hiram Johnson in the 1910s, California had been known as a progressive state with a history of moderate Republican leadership.[55] Shortly after the 1962 elections, the conservative wing of the California Republican Party gained greater strength with the founding of United Republicans of California (UROC). The organization wasted no time in gearing up for the 1964 president election, as UROC laid the basis for support of Barry Goldwater's anticipated presidential bid. In order to do so, UROC moved to outmaneuver the enemy closest at hand: moderate Republicans.[56] UROC sought to elevate the fiercely anti-communist and anti–New Deal politics of the conservative Arizonan above the more moderate views of former Republican president Dwight Eisenhower and his ilk. By early 1964, such efforts bore fruit in California, where, as Matthew Dallek writes, New Right conservatives "achieved a stunning political coup, ousting Republican moderates from their positions . . . [and] electing conservative stalwarts to leadership posts in the California Young Republicans (YRs), the California Republican Assembly (CRA), and the Republican party state Central Committee."[57] Some twelve thousand members strong, UROC utilized their newly found power and assembled an army of volunteers to deliver the 1964 California Republican presidential primary to Barry Goldwater. The Arizona senator defeated the moderate New Yorker Nelson Rockefeller 51.6 percent to 48.4 percent in California. Goldwater's stronghold in the southern counties of Los Angeles, Orange, and San Diego secured his victory.[58]

Even as Lyndon Johnson trounced Goldwater in the November 1964 general election, Ronald Reagan emerged as the great white hope of California conservatives. One week prior to Goldwater's landslide defeat, Reagan delivered a speech called "A Time for Choosing." The October 27, 1964, talk marked Reagan's emergence as a nationally recognized rising star of conservatism, yet the speech was one he had been delivering and honing for many years.[59] Ronald Reagan was born on February 6, 1911, in

Tampico, Illinois, population 849. The story of the future president's early years is relatively well known. Reagan came of age in a succession of small Illinois towns and cities, playing football, working as a lifeguard, and acting in a high school play. In the fall of 1928, Reagan enrolled at Eureka College, a tiny Christian school of fewer than two hundred students.[60]

Reagan's formative years at this small conservative college contributed to his lifelong prejudice against large public research universities. Journalist William Trombley noted in 1974 that, as governor, Reagan "increased state scholarship spending from $6 million to $43 million a year, a boon to the private schools because they get half the students and 75% of the money." In addition, "Reagan assisted the private schools by forcing the University of California to charge [higher fees] . . . making it easier for private institutions to compete for students."[61] Historian Gerard De Groot notes that, as governor, Reagan made clear "his preference for private education on the small liberal arts college model," often denouncing student protest in speeches delivered at such campuses.[62] Reagan himself confirmed his dislike for the multiversity model in an October 1969 speech at a fundraiser for the small private Eisenhower College located in New York State. There, Reagan appropriated the FSM's critique of the Master Plan, noting that students "refuse to become numbers in a computer in some kind of diploma factory. . . . These young people want a re-ordering of the priorities—let 'publish or perish' and research come along behind teaching in the order of importance."[63] Despite Reagan's fondness for his tiny alma mater, as an undergraduate "by his own account, studies rarely intruded on [his] breathless schedule" which included sports, student government, and other extracurriculars. Reagan biographer Garry Wills notes cuttingly that the future president "only did the minimum studying necessary on the easiest courses available."[64] Having "barely eked out passing grades," Reagan graduated in 1932 with a 1.37 GPA and a bachelor's degree in economics.[65]

Reagan relocated to California in 1937, after several years working as a radio sports announcer. This early career, in combination with subsequent decades in film and television, well prepared Reagan for his later life of politics and public speaking. The future president scored his first acting gig in 1937 and appeared in seventeen films over the next two years. According to his longtime biographer Lou Cannon, in his earliest films, Reagan played characters who were "earnest, brave, and not too bright," and landed "lead roles in several B-pictures and bit parts in a few A-films."[66] Yet as the United States slowly lurched toward participation in World War II, Reagan took early steps toward the development of what would be a long and mutually advantageous relationship with the FBI. In late 1941, Reagan received word that he needed to report for military service. The military denied Reagan's employer's initial request for deferment. Yet Warner Brothers did not relent, and through the use of a former FBI agent, William Guthrie, working as a studio liaison to the military, Reagan secured draft deferments and an eventual role producing propaganda films for the military. Yet Warner Brother's obtainment of Reagan's deferment seems to have been less than aboveboard, as "the FBI opened a file on Guthrie titled 'Fraud Against the Government—Bribery.'"[67]

Through a more-than-thirty-year legal battle with the FBI, journalist Seth Rosenfeld uncovered a sordid history of collaboration and mutual back-scratching between Ronald Reagan and FBI director J. Edgar Hoover.[68] The bureau reached out to Reagan for information in 1943 and 1945 but did not seek to cultivate the actor as an informant until 1946.[69] In March 1947, with no knowledge of the actor's ties to the FBI, the Screen Actors Guild elected Reagan as president of their 8,500 member organization. Within a month, Reagan began to abuse his new position of power, betraying fellow actors by naming them to the FBI as potential communist sympathizers. Meeting with FBI agents in his home in April 1947, Reagan passed along the names of ten actors and actresses, disproving his later claims of never having "pointed a finger at any individual." Rather than protect his union brothers and sisters—as was his pledge—Reagan endangered their careers and reputations in the early days of the postwar anti-communist witch hunts. Subsequent investigations by the House Un-American Activities Committee destroyed the careers and lives of at least six of those ten individuals Reagan denounced.[70] Such early anti-communist collaboration with the FBI presaged the reactionary politics that would flourish under Reagan and Rafferty in 1960s California. With his own acting career on the downslope as he entered his mid-forties, Reagan continued to cultivate his relationship with the FBI and took on a new job in public relations at General Electric (GE).

It was serving as the television host of *General Electric Theatre* and visiting GE factories around the country that Reagan first developed the speech "A Time for Choosing," which would catapult him to conservative political fame in 1964.[71] According to journalist William Kleinknecht, in 1954, for an annual salary of $125,000, "Reagan virtually sold his identity to General Electric, becoming the public face of one of America's biggest corporations." For the next eight years, much of Reagan's career consisted of visiting GE factories and delivering motivational and anti-union speeches to workers.[72]

"The Speech," in its earliest format, showcased all the facets of Reagan's reactionary ideology—anti-tax, anti-union, anti–New Deal, and anti-communist.[73] Yet Reagan's appeal stemmed, in part, from the fact that his vision was not solely negative. While denouncing welfare state collectivism, Reagan praised the free market, entrepreneurial spirit, and the rights of the individual. Reagan's charisma and optimism would prove a winning contrast to the ominous pessimism of Barry Goldwater. Like Goldwater, Reagan posited a conservative vision of a holy war between the forces of capitalist liberty and communist totalitarianism, but he did so in a way that would reassure and inspire voters, rather than alienating or frightening them away.[74]

Following Reagan's "A Time for Choosing" speech and Goldwater's seemingly momentous defeat in 1964, a group of conservative California millionaires regrouped around the actor turned corporate salesman. In particular, three men emerged at the head of a campaign to draft Reagan: Holmes Tuttle, the owner of a chain of Ford dealerships, and oilmen A. C. Rubel and Henry Salvatori.[75] Tuttle and Salvatori had already worked to plug Reagan into the failed Goldwater campaign, inviting him to speak at a $1,000 per-plate Goldwater fundraiser and paving the way for his October 27 speech. Flush with cash, a Hollywood smile, and better name recognition than money could buy, Reagan's backers sought to turn a washed-up actor into a winning political proposition. As a final touch, Reagan borrowed a campaign slogan from a former car salesman and disgraced Texas minister by the name of William Steuart McBirnie. By then a pastor and radio evangelist based in conservative upper-middle-class Glendale, McBirnie coined the phrase "the creative society" to describe a philosophy that could "show all Americans that there existed in California 'the human resources to solve any problem—without the growth of bureaucracy.'"[76] Armed with this optimistic entrepreneurial vision—which he counterposed to bureaucratic efforts like Roosevelt's New Deal, Kennedy's New Frontier, and Johnson's Great Society—Reagan set out to capture the Governor's Mansion.

Yet in order to win the governorship in 1966, Reagan would first need to secure the nomination of the Republican Party. In the wake of Goldwater's defeat, five Republican hopefuls vied for the office of governor in California: moderates Tom Kuchel and George Christopher, and conservatives Joe Shell, Max Rafferty, and Ronald Reagan. Soon enough, the race narrowed, as Kuchel decided to remain in the Senate and Rafferty opted to run for re-election as state superintendent. A far-right extremist lacking Reagan's charisma, Shell quickly fell behind as the primary developed into a race between Christopher and Reagan. A former two-term mayor of San Francisco, Christopher represented the sort of moderate Republicans who, in the hyperbolic words of Reagan, were "pledged to the same socialist philosophy as our opposition."[77] Although early polls showed Christopher outperforming Reagan against Governor Brown, Reagan slowly chipped away at the ex-mayor's front-runner status.[78] One question-and-answer session in Santa Barbara encapsulated moderate Republicanism's ultimate problem. Where Christopher responded to a question about budget deficits by drawing on his experience and knowledge of political procedure, Reagan retorted that he would simply "eliminate 10 percent of all state employees," drawing loud cheers from the crowd.[79] Despite early stumbles and charges of extremism, Reagan eventually pulled ahead of Christopher, in large part thanks to an underhanded smear campaign conducted by Governor Brown's reelection team. Brown, quite mistakenly, thought that Reagan would make for an easy road to victory in the November 1966 election.[80]

Even before defeating Christopher to secure the nomination, Reagan began to plan for an eventual run against Governor Brown. Reagan sought at once to disarm charges of extremism and to turn his outsider status into a positive. With regard to the latter, as Reagan's campaign manager Bill Roberts admitted, "we decided not to show brilliant knowledge, which he did not have"; instead, "we tried to operate on the level that he is not a professional politician, that he is a citizen politician. . . . It turned into a real asset. At the end, Brown was defending himself against being a professional politician."[81] It didn't hurt that this nonpolitician also had such a widely recognized face. Reagan campaigner Gordon Luce later acknowledged, "We took advantage of his celebrity status and rather than apologize for it, we utilized it."[82] Few in Governor Brown's camp recognized the severity of the threat posed by such an opponent. Manning Post, a fundraiser for Democrat Jesse Unruh, warned Brown to no avail: "He's the guy with the white hat. He's the Shirley Temple of the male set. This sonofabitch is going to beat the shit out of you. . . . You take an actor who had the image of a good guy; man, you can't overcome it. You just can't make him a bad guy."[83] When combined with his name recognition, Reagan's claim to political innocence won wide support in an era of a gathering anti-government backlash.

Although Reagan remained unable to turn his ties to right-wing extremists into a positive, he did manage to mitigate their negative impact. The John Birch Society posed the most troublesome question about connections between Reagan and the far right.[84] By the mid-1960s, between one-fourth and one-third of all Birchers—an estimated ten thousand members—resided in California, most of them in the Los Angeles suburbs and Orange County.[85] By 1966, Reagan had years-long connections with the far right that his campaign now sought to downplay. As early as 1961, Reagan delivered a keynote address at a fundraiser for John Birch Society member and California congressman John Rousselot. The Bircher Rousselot, in Reagan's own words, was a "warm personal friend." Beyond Birchers, Reagan had lent his celebrity status to a number of white supremacist southerners, including committed segregationists Orville Faubus, Ross Barnett, and Charlton Lyons. Historian Matthew Dallek has found that as late as the early sixties, Reagan "was more than willing to associate himself with racists and conspiracy theorists."[86] Yet by 1965, California conservatives were well aware that they simultaneously needed to rally their base—which included Birchers—while, in the words of one Orange County Republican, avoiding the "abrasive approach of these fire eaters."[87] As Reagan sought out the California governorship, he began to moderate his tone, arguing that he would accept the support of Birchers and other extremists but "by persuading them to accept my philosophy, not by my accepting theirs." Learning from Richard Nixon's mistakes in the 1962 gubernatorial race, Reagan refrained from denouncing the John Birch Society members who made up a crucial segment of his most enthusiastic supporters.[88]

Finally, on the campaign trail, Reagan focused his ire on the three key issues of race, the Vietnam War, and public higher education. Despite their distinction on a theoretical level, the three issues converged on California's streets and campuses in the months leading up to the 1966 election. Protests peopled by California youth challenged the traditional hierarchies that conservative Californians, whether Republican or Democrat, had come to cherish. Political theorist Corey Robin has argued that "Conservatism is the theoretical voice of . . . animus against the agency of the subordinated classes." Those Californians who railed against protests in both city and college sought, to paraphrase one prominent contemporary conservative, to stand athwart history yelling "stop!"[89] Reagan's supporters shared not only a concern with law and order but an acute hostility to social movements, which in their minds threatened their most intimate and cherished possessions: their homes, their nation, and their children.[90]

Protests toward greater civil rights and against the Vietnam War challenged white California's uncontested rights to private property and what many viewed as their nation's patriotic mission in Southeast Asia. In California, the civil rights movement centered on efforts to end discrimination in hiring—often in small businesses like local restaurants—and to secure open housing legislation. The Republican Party in California, alongside less reputable conservative organization such as the John Birch Society and White Citizens Councils, provided staunch opposition to such antidiscriminatory efforts. As the head of the California Republican Assembly would argue at the time, "The essence of freedom is the right to discriminate. . . . In Socialist countries they alas take away this right."[91] By the early 1960s, civil rights activists—including many from UC Berkeley, San Francisco State, and other public campuses—engaged in mass demonstrations targeting a host of hotels, restaurants, and other businesses.

Civil rights organizers' and liberal politicians' attempts to secure fair housing legislation, most importantly the 1963 Rumford Fair Housing Act, engendered intense hostility from conservative white Californians. With the passage of Proposition 14 in 1964, a supermajority of California voters overturned the Rumford Act, which targeted property owners who refused to rent or sell to people of color. Despite the strength of such a white backlash, the California Supreme Court in turn repealed Proposition 14 in 1966, thus reestablishing fair housing in California. A staunch opponent of the Rumford Act, Reagan benefited greatly from white resentment against not only open housing but also welfare programs, the 1965 Watts Rebellion, and burgeoning campus-based protests against the war in Vietnam.[92]

By the late 1970s, Reagan would assert that the issue of campus protests was thrust on him by enraged voters, yet the evidence available does little to bear out his claim. Reagan focused special ire on the protests emanating from California's college campuses, and Berkeley in particular, in an attempt to shore up his Republican base and poach conservative white Democrats. Over a decade after this initial gubernatorial run, Reagan maintained that "the opposition tried to make out that I was persecuting the university for political purposes. I wasn't. I had never mentioned Berkeley as an incident, or as an issue, until those question and answer sessions" on the campaign trail.[93] However, Reagan's campaign manager at the time, Stuart Spencer, argued just the opposite, claiming of student protest that the wily Reagan had "escalated it into an issue" in order to drum up support.[94] Noting that frustration with campus unrest at Berkeley "never showed up in our polling data," Spencer recalled discussing the issue with his candidate. "Reagan had strong feelings on that [the Berkeley protests] and he talked about it. He'd pound that issue. . . . By God, he pounded and pounded. This was without a big TV ad campaign. This is just one guy running around the state of California kicking the hell out of the hippies in Berkeley."[95] Journalist

Seth Rosenfeld seems to confirm Spencer and disprove Reagan. According to Rosenfeld, the FBI had "encouraged Reagan to push the Berkeley issue hard." In order to entice him to do so, FBI plants working on the Berkeley campus passed Reagan insider information during the campaign.[96] The FBI, not the people of California, pushed the issue of Berkeley campus protests on Ronald Reagan, who then made it a central topic of his campaign.[97]

Reagan focused attention on California campuses—particularly the UC—throughout his campaign. In a move sure to infuriate campus activists seeking to expand access to the UC and state colleges, Reagan appropriated a critique of Master Plan admissions standards, while training his supporters' anger on student activism. At a campaign stop on December 4, 1965, Reagan lamented that with "a great university built by the people of California," too many California parents now "see many of their children denied admittance because of a lack of space while that same great university has been brought to its knees and humiliated by a neurotic, dissident minority."[98] Thus, the shortcomings of the liberal Master Plan had become a winning talking point, however hypocritically, for the aspiring conservative governor.

In March 1966, Reagan again attempted to rile up his base by repeating and embellishing what turned out to be inaccurate thirdhand reports about a Vietnam Day Committee–sponsored dance at UC Berkeley.[99] Speaking in front of the largest crowd of his campaign tour thus far, Reagan described a darkened dancehall filled with three thousand people and featuring an abundance of underage high school students, three rock bands playing simultaneously, movie screens portraying nudity, clouds of marijuana smoke, and in allusion to sexual activity, "other happenings that cannot be mentioned here." Reagan argued that the purported acts stemmed from an abdication of responsibilities on campus that "began a year ago" with "so-called free speech advocates." "What in heaven's name," Reagan asked, "does 'academic freedom' have to do with rioting, with anarchy, with attempts to destroy the primary purpose of the university, which is to educate our young people?"[100] In the coming months, Reagan continued to speak publicly about the lurid details of the dance at Berkeley, now joined to the promise that if elected, he would appoint former Central Intelligence Agency chief John McCone to investigate why the school had "become a rallying point for Communism and a center of sexual misconduct."[101] A later report by the Alameda County district attorney found earlier news coverage "highly inaccurate" and Reagan's claims to be much exaggerated.[102] Nonetheless, Reagan's distortions and mistruths served their purpose.

Reagan defeated the incumbent Democratic governor Pat Brown in November 1966 through some combination of voter dissatisfaction with liberalism and, more specifically, the issues of student protest, civil rights legislation, and anti-war activism. A good dose of charisma and celebrity name recognition surely padded the former actor's comfortable margin of victory. The final count tallied to 3,742,913 for Reagan and 2,749,174 for Brown, a difference of nearly one million votes. Although Reagan defeated Brown in fifty-five of California's fifty-eight counties, he fared worse off than his fellow Republican Nixon would in 1968 in both Black communities and college towns.[103] The evidence would suggest that the central factor in Reagan's victory was not so much campus protest specifically but law and order mixed with racial backlash. After all, Reagan won the gubernatorial race by the same margin of votes that conservative Democrat Samuel Yorty had received in the primary against Brown.[104] A three-term mayor of Los Angeles, Yorty had run to the right of the incumbent Democrat, promoting what Matthew Dallek calls "a conservative, law-and-order approach to race, crime, and social upheaval."[105] It would not be surprising, then, if the majority of Yorty's supporters—disproportionately located in Southern California—defected to Reagan in the general election. Two important works, by the California political historians Dallek and Lisa McGirr, both embrace this assumption.[106] Unsurprisingly, Reagan found his key bastion of support in Yorty's own backyard, winning "huge pluralities" in Los Angeles, San Diego, and Orange Counties.[107]

Governor Reagan

Immediately upon coming to office as governor, Ronald Reagan found himself at the center of a higher education controversy of his own creation. During budget discussions held in the opening days of his tenure, Reagan announced plans for a new budgetary policy toward the UC and the California state colleges. First, the new governor proposed to trim a full 10 percent off the previously approved UC and state college budgets for the 1967–68 year.[108] Second, Reagan announced a plan to charge tuition for the first time ever in California public higher education. Reagan proposed a $400 annual tuition for the UC and $200 a year for the state colleges.[109] Beyond simply pinching pennies, Reagan himself admitted at the time that his plan had a political dimension. Introducing tuition, Reagan noted, would help to "get rid of undesirables" on campus. "Those there to agitate and not to study might think twice before they pay tuition." The governor continued, "They might think twice [about] how much they want to pay to carry a picket sign."[110] Reagan's higher education proposals formed part of a larger budgetary strategy of simply chopping 10 percent off all state department and agency budgets. Democrats and Republicans alike derided the plan, noting that it "would have penalized departments that operated frugally and rewarded those with padded payrolls."[111] Yet, it was Reagan's attack on the world-renowned UC and his plan to introduce tuition that raised the most ire.

As concerned observers immediately warned, Reagan's plan effectively undercut the 1960 California Master Plan for Higher Education. Those who had drafted the Master Plan in the late fifties did so in the knowledge that student enrollment and budgetary needs would increase throughout the 1960s and into the '70s. The central purpose of the Master Plan had been to account for those changes and to keep costs down. The plan did so through the introduction a strict division of labor to eliminate the duplication of effort across the three-tiered system and, significantly, by tightening admissions standards to channel more students into community colleges, rather than the UC and state colleges. As the *Los Angeles Times* editorialized, Reagan's proposal "could gravely imperil the quality of higher education which Californians have come to expect" and "does violence to the intent of the Master Plan for Higher Education."[112] The former chairman of the Master Plan survey team and current president of the state Coordinating Council for Higher Education, Arthur Coons, warned that "there are two principles of the master plan that I fear the current administration has overlooked. One is that there be the widest possible opportunity for higher education in California. The other is that this education should be of high quality."[113] With Reagan's budget cuts and tuition plan, Coons warned, maintaining the Master Plan's most basic principles would prove impossible.

Students, faculty, and administrators alike vocally rejected Reagan's attacks on the framework established by the California Master Plan. By abandoning the Master Plan's emphasis on tuition-free higher education, they warned, Reagan would force many students at the UC and state colleges to relocate to the community colleges or to enroll only part time in order to increase their working hours.[114] UC regent Dorothy Chandler and chairman of the UC Berkeley Academic Senate Arthur Kip both noted flaws in Reagan's plans. Chandler pointed to Reagan's goal of eliminating the upcoming introduction of summer courses, noting that such summer sessions would "save millions of dollars of taxpayers' money in the long run." Kip, a professor of physics, argued for the importance of the UC to maintaining a strong state economy, explaining that "for every dollar put in, the state gets a number of dollars back. . . . I can't feel this is anything but short sighted."[115] The UC president and architect of the Master Plan, Clark Kerr, denounced the move in coverage provided by the *New York Times*. In an article that highlighted Reagan's threat "to end a century-old tradition of free education," Kerr exclaimed that "generations of Californians have benefitted from tuition-free higher education, and the benefits they have received individually have become one of the great public resources of the State of California."[116]

With a broad and vocal swath of Californians arrayed against tuition, several influential figures called for a halt on tuition plans to provide more time to study the issues involved. Democrat Jesse Unruh urged a two-year delay to accommodate a financial study by the Joint Legislative Committee on Higher Education. After all, Unruh noted, "The state isn't going to fall to pieces in two years."[117] Later that week, Albert Ruffo, the chairman of the state college board of trustees, asked for at least a one-year delay on tuition and budget cuts, warning that "indiscriminate slashes . . . might set California higher education back many years."[118] In an indication of the broad support for public higher education in the state, California labor leaders came out against Reagan's reactionary cocktail of tuition and budget cuts. Peter Remmel, the executive secretary and treasurer of the Orange County Central Labor Council, and John Kulstad, president of the Communication Workers of America Local 9510, both denounced Reagan's plans during a rally at Fullerton State College.[119] By threatening the foundation of the Master Plan for Higher Education, it seemed that Governor Reagan had touched the third rail of California politics.

The UC Board of Regents first sought compromise with the adversarial governor. Meeting in Santa Barbara in early February 1967, the regents proposed to trim their requested budget but refused to consider introducing tuition until the fall of 1968. Elaborating on the potential impact of the compromise, *Los Angeles Times* education writer William Trombley warned that the regents' new budget would "bring about a major change in the state's Master Plan for Higher Education by limiting enrollment of qualified students." In particular, the regents' budget would result in a decrease of at least 3,500 students in the coming year. At the same time, Trombley noted, the state colleges faced cuts of up to twenty thousand students. Budget cuts would also prevent the employment of the vast majority of six hundred new professors the UC had planned to hire in the coming year. Because of such limitations, the Board of Regents itself had been greatly divided over the idea of a compromise. Regent Norton Simon, a millionaire businessman based in Los Angeles, warned that "the University is the greatest industry in the state . . . and it is being needlessly held back." His fellow regent William M. Roth, a State Department official, argued that "it is not up to the regents to attempt to say what the state can afford to pay for higher education. It is up to the regents to say what it takes to run a quality university." Despite the attempt at compromise, Reagan refused to endorse the regents' proposal.[120]

With Reagan refusing to budge and the UC regents divided over how best to proceed, the editorial board of the *Los Angeles Times* offered its assessment of what they termed the "Crisis in Higher Education." "Governor Reagan," the paper warned, had already "won the first major skirmish in his determined and dangerous assault upon California's great system of higher education." While the UC had "never before" turned away a qualified student, Reagan's proposals demanded exactly that. "The Governor, in other words, has demanded the repeal of the Master Plan of [*sic*] Higher Education—the pledge by the people of California that a tuition-free college education will be available to every qualified resident. . . . The enormous contributions—tangible and intangible—that higher education has made to this state's economic and social progress fully justify the continuing investment. Gov. Reagan seems incapable of comprehending this, even though it is obvious that the excellence of education and the number of those educated cannot be maintained if heavy, arbitrary cuts in spending are imposed." Noting the ongoing status of the battle for public higher education, the editorial board warned that "if he prevails, Ronald Reagan will have won a Pyrrhic victory that California will long regret."[121] The following day, the *Los Angeles Times'* Richard Bergholz released a column further castigating Reagan for his attack on higher education. If Reagan succeeds, Bergholz wrote, "the full onus for the damage to California's educational system falls directly and personally on Reagan. No one else. If the system's quality is impaired, as critics say it surely will be . . . the damage may be felt literally for generations."[122]

Under attack from a host of critics for almost two months, Governor Reagan finally moved to compromise. To be sure, he did so from a position of strength. Although he tempered his initial proposals, Reagan still insisted upon UC and state college budgets far below those requested by the regents and board of trustees.[123] Further, in acknowledgment of the authority of the Board of Regents, Reagan abandoned his initial goal of imposing tuition in the coming school year. Despite the seeming concessions, the *Los Angeles*

Times remained steadfast in its opposition to Reagan's plans. In yet another fiery editorial, the daily warned that thousands of students would still be turned away thanks to budget cuts. Further, the editorial clarified that "The Times strongly believes that this breach of the state's Master Plan for Higher Education would be a disaster for California" and for the "system of higher education that is the state's greatest resource."[124] University officials likewise urged caution moving forward, warning that by awaiting "the regents' decision on a permanent tuition policy before deciding on a final 1967–1968 appropriation for UC, the governor is holding a 'club' over the university's head."[125]

Beyond simply threatening the education budget, Reagan earned the disdain of many when he stated his belief that taxpayers should not be "subsidizing intellectual curiosity." Speaking at a press conference in Sacramento, Reagan warned that "there are certain intellectual luxuries that perhaps we could do without." Pressed to expand, Reagan made the dubious claim that students at UC Davis were "receiving academic credit for staging political demonstrations" and "hanging the governor in effigy."[126] As yet another example of "intellectual luxuries," Reagan pointed to an unspecified Midwestern university that supposedly offered a master's degree in repairing band instruments, and thus, the governor "implied that similar courses of dubious intellectual quality are offered at UC." Scorning Reagan for "the emptiness of his argument," the *Los Angeles Times* warned that the governor's proposal would "violat[e] the promise of the Master Plan." The *Times* continued, noting, "When the rest of the country is looking to California for leadership in [higher education], how paradoxical it would be for California to retrogress!"[127]

In the early weeks of the tuition and budget cut controversy, Ronald Reagan engineered the dismissal of UC president and Master Plan architect Clark Kerr. The much-anticipated firing of the top administrator of the UC came during Governor Reagan's first meeting with the UC Board of Regents on January 20, 1967. There, the regents dismissed Kerr by a vote of fourteen to eight.[128] At least since his gubernatorial campaign, Reagan had coupled his criticisms of Berkeley student activism with hostility toward the UC president. In early January, Kerr had encouraged resistance to Reagan's proposed tuition and budget cuts, promising to defend "the best system of education the world has ever known."[129] In the week prior to Kerr's firing, Reagan responded, criticizing the administrator for having "unnecessarily disturbed and even frightened" parents and students by publicly discussing the idea of an enrollment freeze in order to deal with the proposed budget cuts.[130] Reagan repeated the charge on the opening day of the UC regents meeting.[131] It was particularly jarring, then, that the governor would later express his "surprise" at the board's ouster of Kerr.[132] Subsequently, Reagan denied any political motive behind the firing, maintaining that "none was involved," and claimed that "this Governor has no intention of ever trying to overrule the Regents and engaging in arm twisting."[133] Decades would pass before the full story behind Kerr's dismissal emerged.

The relationship that Ronald Reagan had developed with FBI director J. Edgar Hoover in the 1940s proved useful to him as governor, when the pair conspired to fire Clark Kerr as UC president in 1967.[134] To that end, Hoover had sent agents to Reagan's home to brief the new governor just weeks before Kerr's ouster.[135] During the meeting, which took place in the governor's bedroom, Reagan requested FBI intelligence reports pertaining to Kerr, liberal members of the Board of Regents, and upcoming student protests. Hoover worked to aid the conservative governor while simultaneously covering his tracks, fearing potential embarrassment should the FBI be publicly linked to Reagan's crusade against Kerr.[136] Reagan would claim innocence vis-à-vis the Kerr firing for the rest of his life. As Seth Rosenfeld notes, Reagan "maintained that he had not maneuvered behind the scenes to remove Kerr. And he made no mention of his secret bedroom meeting with the FBI agents." Reagan's collusion with the FBI would continue throughout his years as governor and beyond, well past J. Edgar Hoover's death in May 1972.[137]

In the coming months, Governor Reagan resumed his push for tuition with the far-fetched argument that charging tuition would make it easier for working-class students of color to enroll in the UC and state colleges. To that end Reagan misleadingly parroted critiques of the racial exclusions inherent to the Master Plan that had been made by campus and community activists. Decades later, Reagan biographer Lou Cannon made note of contemporary complaints of Black community leaders that the UC admissions standards "severely restricted the percentage of minority students," who in 1966 made up only 2 percent of the student body.[138] In support of tuition, one Reagan administration mailing quoted the pioneering neoliberal economist Milton Friedman, who asked, "Why should the families in Watts pay taxes to subsidize the families in Beverly Hills who send their children to U.C.L.A.?"[139] In late July 1967, the governor stated that the branches of the UC "have become almost closed campuses, available mainly to those who come from upper middle class white families. . . . It is obvious that we are doing a poor job of providing higher education for our lower income groups."[140] Reagan proposed solving the problem with the creation of a scholarship program to be funded through tuition. Reagan's tuition proposal included a balance of loans—to be repaid with interest—and grants to working-class students.[141] As the *Los Angeles Times* astutely observed, months after first introducing tuition as an attempt to economize, Reagan now emphasized that his "basic desire was to help students from poor families get into higher education."[142] Not surprisingly, the governor's critics remained unconvinced.

Even before Reagan's tuition rebranding, a number of California labor leaders had forewarned of the impact tuition would have on working-class students. In a display of progressive solidarity, Cesar Chavez and some two hundred members of the United Farm Workers participated in an anti-tuition march followed by a rally at the state capitol. Chavez walked amongst the crowd raising a handmade picket sign that read "*Huelga* [Strike] On Tuition." Later that day, speaking to a massive crowd of ten thousand demonstrators, Chavez stated that his working-class and predominantly Mexican American cohort joined the march because "we're opposed to tuition. We're the first to be hit by it."[143] Around the same time, California labor unions began a campaign against Reagan's proposal for tuition and budget cuts. Sigmund Arywitz, secretary of the Los Angeles County AFL-CIO Labor Federation, wrote to Reagan, warning the governor that the locals and the workers he represented "are strongly opposed to any program of charging tuition." In a letter to the UC regents, California's AFL-CIO executive secretary, Thomas L. Pitts, lamented that "economic discrimination in higher educational opportunities has long existed, but until now the philosophy of both our state and nation has been to minimize it rather than maximize it." As such, in lieu of charging tuition, Pitts called for tax increases on big agriculture and other corporations who benefited from the research conducted by the university. If successful, Pitts warned, Reagan's move to charge tuition would "hit the educational hopes of youths from families in the lower income brackets."[144]

As *Los Angeles Times* education writer William Trombley reported, those most attuned to questions of access and diversity in California higher education voiced their skepticism at Reagan's proposal for scholarships to offset tuition. Kenneth Washington, director of the Educational Opportunity Program (EOP) at UCLA, warned that Reagan's schema of tuition, grants, and loans, would create "a world of trouble. . . . What we have now is much better than that."[145] Washington's UC Berkeley EOP counterpart, Bill Somerville, likewise criticized Reagan's plan. "Loans are not attractive to low-income people," Somerville argued. "They are already in debt and they have no intention of going further in debt." While affirming that the UC and state colleges needed to do more to enroll working-class students of color, Somerville pondered, "What indication is there that [minority enrollment] would go up with greater costs?" Finally, Kenneth Martyn, an administrator at Los Angeles State College—and the author of the upcoming report *California Higher Education and the Disadvantaged*—warned that "the money [Reagan] is talking about so far would not be enough to increase significantly the number of low-income minority students."[146]

A subsequent *Los Angeles Times* article by Jack McCurdy reported on concerns with Reagan's plan as voiced by public high school officials in minority and working-class districts. As McCurdy summarized, "They believe that the tuition-loan system will present a serious 'roadblock' which would reverse the present trend of encouraging more youngsters of poor families to attend the university and colleges." Ernest Ono, the head counselor at Fremont High School, noted that "going into debt to get an education would not appeal to a large majority of students. . . . I know we need to send more students to college from our area but the aid should be in the form of scholarship grants" not loans to pay off new tuition charges. Aaron C. Wade, the principal at Compton High School, contrasted Reagan's plan with ongoing efforts to expand access to higher education, plainly advising that "I definitely think this (loan program) would be a bad thing." Speaking of campus efforts toward developing EOPs, Wade argued that Reagan's tuition would "contradict and defeat" EOP, which he described as "the type of program we need to draw the disadvantaged and undecided students to college."[147]

Conceding defeat in his yearlong quest to introduce tuition, Governor Reagan shifted to talk of "raising fees for particular services."[148] Faced with a recalcitrant bloc of anti-tuition regents, Reagan ultimately accepted that a new student fee would serve the same goal as introducing tuition.[149] Beyond the subtle privatization of public higher education represented by the introduction of new student fees, Reagan continued his attacks on those students and faculty advocating for the expansion and better funding of the campus-based EOPs which provided recruitment, tutoring, and financial aid for young working-class Californians. Yet, not only the EOPs fell within Reagan's crosshairs. A whole host of campus-based activist initiatives would become the focus of conservative counterrevolution. Student struggles toward ethnic studies programs and against the Vietnam War would soon make headlines to rival those generated by the new governor's efforts to introduce tuition. On UC, state college, and community college campuses, students organized to counteract the racialized exclusions and Cold War complicity of the California Master Plan for Higher Education while simultaneously attempting to hold back the tidal wave of conservatism represented by Governor Reagan.

Despite Reagan's failure to introduce tuition as such, the governor's conservative coalition, which spread across the UC Board of Regents and state college board of trustees, soon moved on to other battles. In particular, California conservatives reopened old wounds stemming from the Cold War–era faculty loyalty tests in an effort to contest, sometimes effectively, the employment status of UC and state college professors deemed subversives.[150] Additionally, the board of trustees, created in 1960 by the Master Plan, moved to stifle burgeoning efforts toward faculty unionization at the state colleges. Finally, the board asserted greater control over student funds at the increasingly tumultuous state college campuses. Although conservatives succeeded in terminating the employment of a number of leftist faculty at the UC and state colleges, such actions also backfired, inspiring denunciations and greater progressive mobilization across California campuses.

By the late 1960s, Governor Reagan had succeeded in establishing conservative blocs within both the UC regents and the state college trustees.[151] Former San Francisco State president John Summerskill lamented of the board of trustees that its members "almost always belong to the governor's own political party. . . . It was much more politics than higher education."[152] In early 1969, UC Berkeley's chancellor Roger Heyns likewise denounced the increasing politicization of the Board of Regents.[153] Having successfully marshaled sufficient power to eliminate Clark Kerr as UC president, Reagan and his regent and trustee allies turned to a host of leftist instructors and faculty members across California. To note only some of the most controversial cases, these California conservatives targeted Robert Mezey and Marvin X at Fresno State College, George Murray and Nathan Hare at San Francisco State, Eldridge Cleaver and Harry Edwards at UC Berkeley, and Herbert Marcuse and Angela Davis at UC San Diego.[154] Reagan justified such breaches of academic freedom by projecting his own actions onto those he sought to remove, arguing that "many who wrap themselves in the mantle of defenders of academic freedom are, in reality, those who would destroy it. . . . There is no academic freedom in the philosophies of the George Murrays."[155] At the same time, Reagan promoted a crackdown on student protest, tightening "laws against unlawful assembly" and suspending financial aid to those convicted of participating in "campus disturbances."[156]

At the state college level, conservatives among the board of trustees clashed with faculty members seeking to improve their working conditions. Where the UC benefited from its position at the top of California's higher education hierarchy, the advent of the Master Plan relegated the state colleges to a perpetual secondary status. As Herbert Wilner, a San Francisco State professor of English, wrote of the Master Plan system in 1971, "The state colleges . . . would provide for more students but be second best in quality and resources."[157] Even as UC faculty were given both the time and material support for advanced research, the Master Plan left faculty at the state college level comparatively underfunded with much greater teaching loads. It is not surprising, then, that many state college faculty complained that the Master Plan had trapped their campuses in a legislated mediocrity. Faculty members who bristled under the Master Plan and the rule of the conservative state college–wide chancellor, Glenn Dumke, organized as locals of the American Federation of Teachers. Locals formed at the state college campuses in Chico, Hayward, Humboldt, Pomona, San Francisco, San Jose, and Sonoma. Unionization, and subsequent faculty strikes at San Francisco State and San Jose State, further exacerbated tensions between the board of trustees and state college faculty.[158]

In the 1968–69 school year, the board of trustees raised state college students' ire through the debate and eventual passage of a resolution placing student funds under the control of the board itself. Previously, such funds had been controlled by the elected student governments on each campus. A November 1968 article in San Francisco State's *Daily Gater* noted that with the proposed change, "student power for California State College students may be drastically undercut" and that "any program 'not consistent with Board of Trustees and college policy' could be legislated out of existence."[159] At San Francisco State, such programs included the Black Student Union, the countercultural newspaper *Open Process*, the nation's first experimental college, and a community tutorial program, among others.[160] Prior to their 1968–69 strike at San Francisco State, the coalition known as the Third World Liberation Front correctly warned that "the Trustees are preparing to . . . seize [student government] funds."[161] Student activists at San Fernando Valley State likewise fought back against the proposal. As noted in their campus newspaper, the revision would mean that student "governments will no longer be able to fund projects themselves." Instead, all student programs would need to pass an informal but effective political litmus test administered by the board of trustees.[162]

Despite protests, the board of trustees revised Title V of the state college system's administrative code in April 1969, confirming the trend toward greater political surveillance and control of previously autonomous campus functions. Funds once controlled by the students themselves now fell under the purview of Governor Reagan and the state college board of trustees.[163] This move at the state colleges coincided with investigations by the UC Board of Regents into the content of student newspapers. In response, the editors of six UC newspapers published a joint editorial warning against efforts "to intimidate the traditional freedom of the university's campus newspapers."[164] Beyond the regents' investigation of student newspapers, Reagan himself exercised control through his close surveillance of developments on campuses at both the UC and the state colleges. The governor's interference ran the gamut from such banal matters as the staging of ostensibly offensive theater productions to the promotion and encouragement of conservative administrators like San Francisco State's S. I. Hayakawa and Fresno State's Karl Falk.[165]

First as Tragedy, Then as Farce

Historian Gerard De Groot argues that there exists a paradox at the heart of the Reagan governorship. Having observed that "during his first term, unrest escalated sharply," De Groot notes that Reagan "was more effective at radicalizing students than at taming them." Surely, the protests of the FSM that had so inflamed conservative sentiment appear timid in comparison to the campus rebellions of 1969 and 1970. When running for reelection, a reporter posed this conundrum to Reagan at a press conference. Pressed as to why student protest had so obviously escalated over his four-year term, Reagan claimed that "he never suggested that he knew how to solve the problem" of campus disruption. In De Groot's reading, student unrest was "an issue now which Reagan could not lose. If he won a skirmish with students, Californians cheered, but if he failed to control unrest, his failure merely underscored the threat of militancy and the need for greater vigilance."[166] Yet, such an analysis would suggest that Reagan, and his fellow hardliners, would gain in popularity over the tumultuous years of the late 1960s. Instead, the opposite occurred.

Both Ronald Reagan and Max Rafferty, the vanguard of law-and-order-on-campus sentiment, became less popular while maintaining their fierce opposition to late-sixties campus radicalism. Reagan's rhetoric may well have deepened his base's animosity toward the provision of public higher education, yet it apparently did nothing to help that base expand. Reagan won the 1966 gubernatorial election with a total of 3,742,913 votes, or 57.55 percent of votes cast. Four years later, the incumbent Reagan received three hundred thousand fewer votes, for a total of 3,439,664, or 52.84 percent of votes cast. Reagan lost almost a third of a million votes between 1966 and 1970 despite the fact that California's population had grown by 1.11 million in those same years.[167]

For state superintendent of public instruction Max Rafferty, the situation turned still worse. Despite taking an even harder stance than Reagan against campus disruptions, Rafferty lost his run for the Senate in 1968 and lost his reelection campaign for state superintendent in 1970, effectively ending his political career. Although certainly other issues were at play in Reagan's unimpressive reelection, Rafferty had built his career on being *the* archconservative educator. Yet, he lost his Senate race to liberal Democrat Alan Cranston and his state superintendent race to Wilson Riles, the first African American elected to statewide office in California history. Anti-protest rhetoric might have secured for Reagan and Rafferty a conservative base in the mid-1960s, but it did nothing to increase that base over the course of intensified campus uprisings from 1968 through 1970.

Reagan, like Rafferty before him, garnered support through broad attacks on an ostensibly overpermissive liberal educational establishment. In office, Reagan, Rafferty, and their allies chipped away at the foundation of the California Master Plan for Higher Education through a range of budget cuts and administrative power grabs backed by the threat of yet more financial strangulation. As a result, the *Los Angeles Times* noted that at the UC "the student-faculty ratio has risen steadily" and "state funding for research has been reduced," while at the state colleges "student-faculty ratios have climbed steadily, expenditures per student have declined and faculty teaching loads have increased."[168] On campus, Reagan allied with conservative administrators to target progressive faculty and untenured instructors and to inflict harsh disciplinary punishment on student organizers. But as the following chapters confirm, even Governor Reagan could not stem the tide of fierce student activism that erupted during his first term in office, 1967–71. In these years, diverse coalitions of student activists flourished across the UC, state colleges, and community colleges as organizers sought to rectify the de facto racial exclusions of the California Master Plan for Higher Education.

4　Black Skin, White Campus

Archie had an enlarged photograph in his dormitory room. It was taken at a football game, and Archie had his arm around this white boy's neck. Underneath the picture he had an inscription: My name is Archie Chatman. I don't answer to "boy."

—Les Johns, 1971
　(undergraduate, San Fernando Valley State)

When I arrived on San Jose State's campus there was a long-established joke circulating: When campus police find a Negro on campus after dark, they throw a football at him. If he fumbles it, they throw him a basketball. If he fumbles that, they throw him in their squad car.

—Harry Edwards, 1980
　(sociology professor, UC Berkeley)

On October 16, 1968, two Black students from San Jose State College captured the eyes of the world. In the smoggy morning sunshine of Mexico City, sprinters Tommie Smith and John Carlos stood on the Olympic podium with their heads bowed and fists raised high. Having captured the gold and bronze medals, respectively, for the two hundred–meter dash, Smith and Carlos drew the ire and respect of the world. Their silent but powerful protest represented the culmination of a movement that had first gained traction under the tutelage of San Jose State alumnus and professor of sociology Harry Edwards.

Harry Edwards, himself a former star athlete, had taken the first step in the marriage of sports and activism that he would popularize as the revolt of the Black athlete.[1] In September 1967, Edwards and Ken Noel, another Black student athlete, had organized a boycott of the season-opening San Jose State football game to protest anti-Black racism on campus. Edwards, Noel, and their organization, United Black Students for Action, targeted discrimination and segregation in campus housing and fraternities, as well as the debilitating impact of the admissions standards first established by the 1960 California Master Plan for Higher Education. In the coming months, their protest expanded beyond campus, laying the foundation for the Olympic Project for Human Rights, one component of the larger revolt of the Black athlete. At the same time, and much like their counterparts at the UC and other state colleges, the small number of Black students at San Jose State organized to increase the matriculation and retention of African American students on their overwhelmingly white California campus.

The revolt of the Black athlete, originating at San Jose State College, represents one outgrowth of the diverse student movement grounded in the structural reality of the Master Plan hierarchy in California public higher education. The new admissions standards enacted by the 1960 California Master Plan restricted entry into the UC and California state colleges to the top 12.5 and 33 percent of students, respectively. These new standards also came with an important caveat. Only 2 percent of all those admitted to the UC and state colleges did not need to meet the stringent admissions standards first introduced by the plan. Prior to the Master Plan, special exceptions accounted for up to 10 percent of admissions. UC president Clark Kerr later reflected on the inclusion of the 2 percent exception embedded into the Master Plan, noting that "I did think—as critics said—about places for 'tackles on the football team.' But I was interested too in students who could make special contributions to campus life, as in music, theatre, and leadership (for example, high school class presidents); and students who had shown ability to overcome disadvantages and deserved 'equal opportunity' consideration." In that expansive list, Kerr omitted the important components of legacy students and, as one researcher put it, the "progeny of influential state figures who would not have gained admission into the University through their scholastic achievement alone."[2]

The de facto racial exclusion resulting from the new admissions standards enacted by the Master Plan helps explains the emergence of widespread protest by Black student athletes in California in the 1960s. Across sixties' California, a portion of the 2 percent of students enrolled through the Master Plan's special admissions helped minority students, among others, to gain entrance to the state's best schools.[3] Yet in the first half of the 1960s, admissions exceptions were not typically directed at minorities as such but rather at minorities as athletes. Because of this, Black male student athletes brought to the UC and California state colleges formed an early nucleus of Black activism in a mass of white faces.[4] Often the majority of Black students on campus, these athletes formed organizations and enacted protests that would open the doors to increasing numbers of minority students through the development of what became known as Educational

Opportunity Programs (EOPs). These programs helped Black activists and their allies to redirect the small numbers of exceptions to the Master Plan admissions standards from Black athletes to promising young students of color.[5]

Black Man on Campus

The passage of the California Master Plan coincided with historic shifts in the color line in amateur and professional sports. Prior to the Supreme Court's 1954 ruling in *Brown v. Board of Education,* Black athletes' opportunities to gain higher education in southern and border states remained limited to historically Black institutions of higher learning.[6] Yet, public colleges and universities in California had long welcomed Black athletes especially to the top-notch teams at UCLA. In the 1930s, Black Los Angeles native James LuValle ran track for UCLA. In 1936, LuValle traveled with Jesse Owens and other African American athletes to participate in the Olympic Games held in Nazi Germany, where he won three bronze medals.[7] In addition to baseball, Jackie Robinson played football for the UCLA Bruins alongside Kenny Washington and Woody Strode. In 1946, Washington and Strode integrated the National Football League, one year before Robinson did the same for Major League Baseball.[8] In 1947, UCLA basketball's Don Barksdale became the first African American to earn All-American status in the National Collegiate Athletic Association (NCAA). He subsequently broke the color barrier for both the US Olympic basketball team and the National Basketball Association's All-Star Team.[9]

The decades-long legacy of integrated athletics at UCLA would motivate a young Kareem Abdul-Jabbar to commit to the school despite offers from competitive basketball programs across the country.[10] Abdul-Jabbar, then known as Lew Alcindor, matriculated to UCLA in the fall of 1965. Although UCLA rules then forbade college freshman to play on varsity teams, Abdul-Jabbar scored a remarkable fifty-six points in the first varsity game of his sophomore year. The young center so dominated the league that the NCAA outlawed the slam dunk at the end of his first season, inaugurating what many referred to as the Lew Alcindor rule. Nonetheless, Abdul-Jabbar led his UCLA squad to three national championships while maintaining a demanding course of study in history and English. Despite his fame on the court, Abdul-Jabbar faced unrelenting racism on the UCLA campus. For Abdul-Jabbar and other Black athletes at the majority-white school, this included the open racism of fellow students and that of area landlords, many of whom refused to rent to African Americans.[11] Beyond the ostensibly integrated UCLA campus, the historian Donald Spivey notes, trailblazing Black student athletes "all suffered racial abuses and discrimination at the hands of opponents, teammates, fans, coaches, the student body, and the wider establishment of sports writers and bowl committees."[12] In the 1960s, Black student athletes across California's Master Plan system began to organize against such maltreatment.[13]

By 1960, San Jose State College had earned a national reputation for recruiting top Black sprinters.[14] Nicknamed Speed City, San Jose State enrolled some of the fastest people on earth, where they trained under legendary coach Bud Winter. Winter began coaching track and field at San Jose in 1941 and published the book *So You Want to Be a Sprinter* in 1956. By the time he retired in 1970, Winter had trained 27 Olympians, 37 world record holders, and 102 NCAA All-Americans.[15] Yet, not all was well in Speed City. Black student athletes at San Jose State complained of "second-class treatment" while suffering from a wide array of discriminatory practices.[16] By the summer of 1968, San Jose State sprinters Tommie Smith, John Carlos, and Lee Evans would become world famous, not as much for their medal-worthy performances as for the protests that followed them.

The racism and isolation experienced by Black student athletes in the Master Plan system spread far beyond San Jose State and UCLA. Protest by Black athletes became so common on campuses in the 1960s that one San Fernando Valley State professor included "fire the football coach" and "investigation of athletic department practices" in a condescending article containing his list of "inevitable 'issues'" to be raised by student protesters. As early as 1963, before transferring to San Jose State, Ken Noel encountered staunch racism at San Jose City College, where he organized his fellow Black athletes to fight back. As Noel later recalled, "In 1963, a black athlete at City was looked on as a performing animal. I thought it was degrading . . . so I organized the basketball team to go on strike." When his role as an organizer of athletic labor generated intense conflict with his coach, Noel decided it was time to transfer.[17]

In early 1968, Black student athletes at UC Berkeley joined in the tradition of the Free Speech Movement and the Vietnam Day Committee to demand change on that vaunted California campus. African American students from Berkeley's varsity sports teams organized themselves as the Black Athletes of the University of California (BAUC) in late January, threatening an athletic boycott. BAUC charged the "athletic department with practicing racial discrimination toward Negro athletes in several areas" and demanded the firing of the head basketball coach, two assistant football coaches, and the department's business manager. A spokesman for BAUC provided reporters with a resolution outlining "favoritism toward whites in financial aid"; "derogatory comments and ridicule" of Black athletes by athletic staff; a tendency of coaches to dismiss Black players' injuries; the practice of "stacking" Blacks in certain positions so as to limit their numbers on the team; the absence of Black coaches; the failure to provide promised assistance in securing housing for Black athletes who faced residential segregation; and "inferior academic advice and counseling."[18]

The hostility of white players on the basketball team, who vocally supported their coach and denounced BAUC, furthered exacerbate the situation. According to *Los Angeles Times* reporter Dwight Chapin, the attitude of white players was that Black athletes who were "in effect getting an education because they can pass, shoot or hit a ball better than others, shouldn't snap back at the men who have bestowed the scholarships upon them."[19] Across the 1960s, the number of Black athletes at UC Berkeley had grown from five to nearly forty. Such change had convinced many whites, players and coaches alike, that "we'd been making real progress in race relations," as Athletic Director Pete Newell explained. Newell would announce his resignation some six weeks later. When asked if the BAUC protest had influenced his decision, he denied any connection.[20] One month later, Berkeley's varsity basketball coach announced his own resignation, conceding that "the Negro situation was a factor."[21] In the wake of the resignation, Berkeley chancellor Roger Heyns elevated the freshman coach Jim Padgett to the varsity squad and announced the hiring of Earl Robinson as his assistant. Robinson himself was a former Black student athlete who had played on Berkeley's baseball and basketball teams in the 1950s.[22]

Despite BAUC's victory for the basketball team, racial tensions continued to plague the football team at Berkeley and at UCLA as well. In May 1968, Black student athletes boycotted spring football training at UC Berkeley. The *Los Angeles Times* reported on football coach Ray Willsey's insistence that "the demands related solely to the playing of Negro athletes and their positions, not to any coaches."[23] Willsey's remarks referenced "the common practice of 'stacking' on white college campuses." As sports scholar Michael Lomax explains, "Black players were channeled into one position or another to limit their numbers on the team." Often coaches stacked Black players into stereotypically Black positions, while leaving star positions like football quarterback, or point guard in basketball, open to white players.[24]

Seemingly in response to Black players' worries, Berkeley announced the hiring of John Erby as an assistant football coach. Erby, a Black Vietnam veteran, had played football for Berkeley in the early 1960s.[25] Further south, tensions flared on the UCLA football team as Black players charged that their athletic department and coaching staff preferred to work with white players, failed to help Black athletes secure apartments in a discriminatory housing market, refused to take Black players' injuries seriously, and doled out perks to white players that Black athletes were denied.[26]

At UC Santa Barbara (UCSB), the development of a student movement inaugurated by the Black Athletes Committee (BAC) culminated in the creation of a department of Black studies. There, Black student athletes charged the UCSB athletic department with racist "attitudes, policies, and intolerable conditions." On October 1, 1968, BAC met with the campus chancellor and demanded the hiring of Black coaches and administrators. The following week, more than four hundred UCSB students attended a rally jointly held by BAC and the campus's Black Student Union. With the administration stalling, Black students on campus turned to direct action. Two weeks after BAC's meeting with the chancellor, twelve Black students entered, occupied, and barricaded the campus computer center in North Hall. Over the course of the day, approximately one thousand people visited North Hall to show their support, including members of the campus branch of the United Mexican American Students (UMAS). Although the administration refused the occupiers' demand to fire the campus athletic director, Chancellor Vernon Cheadle committed to establishing Black studies at UCSB.[27]

Across the Master Plan system, Black student athletes organized against racism in athletics and on campus. At Fresno State College, the campus branch of the Black Student Union originated as the Union of Black Athletes (UBA) in 1967. According to the campus newspaper, the UBA formed when Black football players overheard their coach remark that he "hated all niggers." Osby Davis, the first president of the UBA, had come to Fresno State to play baseball. When he arrived on campus, in 1966, out of only sixty-seven Black students on campus, "most were out-of-town athletes" recruited through the Master Plan's 2 percent exception rule.[28] And at San Francisco State, Black athletes formed an important part of the Black Student Union–led coalition whose five-month-long strike culminated in the creation of the nation's first College of Ethnic Studies.[29] But it was at San Fernando Valley State and San Jose State that the struggles of Black student athletes developed the most intensely.

The Valley State Nineteen

At San Fernando Valley State College, concerns about racism in the athletic department led to a four-hour-long occupation of the administration building in early November 1968. In turn, Black student activists who participated in the occupation soon found themselves the victims of mass felony convictions.[30] Despite the state repression these activists incurred, their protest directly led to the expanded recruitment and enrollment of Black and Chicano students at Valley State and to the expansion of Valley State's Black and Chicano studies programs. In the late 1960s, Black student activists and their Chicano allies would develop the largest EOP in the state college system at what had previously been known as the whitest of all state colleges.

San Fernando Valley State College began operations as an independent part of the California state college system in September 1958.[31] Between 1955 and 1958, the Northridge campus had operated as a satellite of Los Angeles State College.[32] Early planners had originally envisioned a new state college campus in Pacoima, a predominantly Black and Mexican American working-class community in the San Fernando Valley. Instead, in 1954, the state acquired a substantial property in Northridge, a conservative, middle-class, and overwhelming white suburb of Los Angeles.[33] With an allocation of over $20 million in state funds, the San Fernando Valley State campus would expand its physical plant in a five-year construction project running through 1964.[34] The campus's inaugural year, 1958–59, began with an enrollment of 3,300 students and a faculty of just over one hundred instructors.[35] By the 1960–61 school year, those numbers increased to 5,800 and 210, respectively.[36] Both would continue to grow.

Throughout the early and mid-1960s, the student body remained—like Northridge itself—almost entirely white, relatively wealthy, and fairly conservative. Most students hailed from Northridge or, as the *Los Angeles Times* noted, from nearby "upper-middle class areas along the San Diego Freeway, including beach towns." The parents of Valley State students reported incomes higher than those of their counterparts at the other state colleges, with 9 percent earning $20,000 a year or more—compare that to less than 3 percent at Los Angeles State College. Speaking to a reporter in late 1968, sophomore David Robman endorsed the prevailing view of Valley State as "less liberal than all the other state colleges . . . and less aware politically."[37] African American and Mexican American students were a rare sight at Valley State, and the campus community was largely isolated from the population and problems of nearby Pacoima, not to mention the other diverse, working-class neighborhoods of the Los Angeles metropolitan area. According to one account, during the 1966–67 school year, there were only thirty Black students out of a population of eighteen thousand.[38] In 1967–68, that number decreased to twenty-three out of almost twenty thousand.[39] That same year, Mexican Americans accounted for a similarly low number of students—roughly twenty.[40] The first EOP students would not arrive at Valley State until the fall of 1968.

When Archie Chatman transferred to San Fernando Valley State in early 1967, he joined a fluctuating population of twenty-some African Americans, making their way in a sea of white students. Born in 1947, Chatman was raised in South Central Los Angeles. In 1966, he enrolled at Los Angeles Community College, studying history and literature, while playing football and running track. When Valley State offered him a football scholarship, Chatman transferred and set on a course to major in history.[41] Along with Les Johns and Art Jones, Chatman was one of only three Black players on the Valley State varsity team. As Jones complained, the attitude of the white football coaches, who routinely pitted their Black players against one another in practice, seemed to be "let's see the niggers kill each other."[42] Black activists would also accuse the athletic department of a broad pattern of anti-Black discrimination, including the use of racial slurs.[43] The concerns of these Black student athletes, and those to come, would later provide the spark for the most confrontational Valley State protest of the entire decade.

It was in the 1967–68 school year that the small community of Black students at San Fernando Valley State took steps to begin to organize politically. Bill Burwell, a sociology major, and Jerome Walker, a psychology major, formed a Black Student Union (BSU) in November 1967. Both Burwell and Walker hailed and commuted from nearby Pacoima, where they were active as organizers in the Black community. Their first recruits were the student athlete Archie Chatman and a young woman named Genie Washington. Within a couple of weeks, the fledgling Valley State BSU had grown to twenty-five, meaning "nearly all the black students on campus had been enlisted."[44] Previously, political action on the relatively conservative and overwhelmingly white campus had been dominated by the antiwar organizing of the Students for a Democratic Society (SDS), particularly their protests against on-campus recruiting by the Central Intelligence Agency and Dow Chemical. But as the Valley State Black Student Union grew in size and stature, the student body increasingly came face-to-face with confrontational Black protest.

Black Student Union organizing at San Fernando Valley State grew out of the alienation experienced by Black students on campus. Even the *Los Angeles Times* noted the school's long-standing reputation as "one of the most lily white of the state colleges."[45] As undergraduate Teresa Tolliver reflected, "I came to this school in good faith and I did not know what racism really was until I came. . . . What I felt upon entering San Fernando Valley State was isolation. . . . Being there as a black student set me apart."[46] Or as another Black student put it, whites "think that we don't belong in this area and that we will contaminate their valley. . . . They stare at us as they are driving down the street. And it's almost impossible to find accommodations." Like their fellow African American students at San Jose State, Black students at Valley State found it extremely difficult to secure off-campus housing due to discrimination by white landlords.[47] Such a feeling was far from subjective—a survey conducted in the summer of 1968 showed that only twenty out of some six hundred apartment managers surveyed were willing to rent to Black students.[48] Feeling unwelcome on campus and in surrounding Northridge, the burgeoning Black Student Union at San Fernando Valley State set on a course to keep Black students involved in the African American community in nearby Pacoima.

Early organizing by the Valley State BSU reflected the cultural nationalism of the Los Angeles–based activist Maulana Karenga, who in 1965 founded the organization known simply as "US". At least one Valley State BSU member was a former member of US, and Karenga himself visited and spoke on campus.[49] Rather than focusing on changing conditions on campus, the BSU first turned its energies to involvement in the Pacoima community, organizing classes for Black youth that focused on self-defense, culture, and political education. In addition to providing instruction in karate and Swahili, Black Valley Staters taught and discussed the writings of a range of anti-racist, anti-capitalist, and anti-colonial thinkers, including W. E. B. DuBois, Frantz Fanon, Malcolm X, and Kwame Nkrumah.[50] Over time, the BSU added campus activism to its program of community involvement.

On-campus organizing by the Valley State BSU sought to increase Black enrollment despite the Master Plan's strict admissions standards. In that context, campus administrators announced plans to begin an EOP program in the spring of 1968. The inaugural EOP class was slated to include just fifteen students on a campus of twenty thousand. Frustrated with such a paltry gesture, BSU activists organized for a larger incoming cohort. BSU cochair Archie Chatman met with campus administrators and faculty to argue for an expanded EOP and the introduction of for-credit Black studies classes. One BSU member recalled of Chatman at the time that "he was always going to meetings with the faculty. . . . It was around this time that he became the dominate figure in the BSU, and it was mostly because of the pressure he put on the faculty that the EOP was expanded."[51] Chatman's efforts paid off when the administration announced that instead of fifteen EOP students, Valley State was open to welcoming three hundred, split evenly between African Americans and Mexican Americans.[52] The administration placed the responsibility for recruiting those students in the hands of the BSU and UMAS.[53] In addition, the school proposed a total of four Black studies courses for the fall of 1968, focusing on Black sociology, psychology, history, and literature.[54] Valley State would also offer four Mexican American studies courses during the 1968–69 school year.[55]

The expansion of the Valley State EOP provided the opportunity for Black and Mexican American student organizers to push back against the de facto discriminatory admissions standards enacted by the Master Plan for Higher Education. During the 1967–68 school year, approximately forty African American and Chicano students attended the college.[56] In the spring of 1968, the BSU and UMAS set about to organize for an influx of new students. The BSU established a committee consisting of seven permanent members to evaluate applications from Black high school seniors. At the same time, UMAS organized a parallel system for Mexican Americans under the leadership of chapter president Mike Verdugo.[57] With only two months left in the school year, BSU members established contact with predominantly Black schools in the area, talked with teachers and counselors, and in combination with UMAS, interviewed over one thousand potential EOP recruits. By June 1968, both the BSU and UMAS had selected their EOP students for the fall.[58]

Despite constant worries about funding and the reception Black and Chicano students might receive from the campus and the greater community, the BSU and UMAS did their best to prepare for the influx of EOP recruits. The Community Involvement Project, a liberal and predominantly white organization, aided in the EOP efforts.[59] Approximately ninety EOP students spent the summer at Valley State, attending an eight-week "head start" program to acclimate them to life in such a white and wealthy environment.[60] The director of the program, Dudley Blake, a Valley State professor of education, explained that the program sought "to enhance intellectual skills needed for successful college work" and aimed at "bridging the environmental gap between ghetto life and college life."[61] During those eight weeks, students lived on campus and attended classes in social science, philosophy, English, and biology—all focused around the theme of "Man in Contemporary Society." In addition, nine student counselors worked with the incoming students, discussing coursework and everyday problems as they arose. In this way, the program helped these ninety EOP students to gradually acclimate to campus life. Although, as Blake noted, perhaps the bigger challenge would be in educating "the predominantly white, upper middle-class community of Northridge to the realities of minority group life with a view towards modifying racist attitudes."[62]

In September 1968, 220 EOP students arrived at San Fernando Valley State for the new school year.[63] By then, the Valley State EOP was the largest such program in the state college system. The first problem the incoming students faced was financial. Over the summer, Governor Ronald Reagan had vetoed a bill that would have provided the EOP with state funding. Although the federal government was willing to match state funds dollar to dollar, Reagan's tight purse threatened the emergent program. As Valley State's vice president of academic affairs, Delmar T. Oviatt, lamented, "Now we can admit them, but we have no funds to help them. . . . For the state to play politics with it is just horrible."[64] Despite the threat of funding running dry in the coming year, BSU and UMAS organizers set about to introduce the new EOP students to campus life. They also continued their push to develop degree-granting programs in Black and Chicano studies. Even with faculty support, and solidarity from the Community Involvement Project and SDS, a conflict originating in the athletics program would soon lead to an all-out crisis on campus.

Much like their counterparts across the Master Plan system, Black student athletes at San Fernando Valley State struggled with campus racism on and off the field, eventually leading them to acts of resistance. In the fall of 1968, as the first EOP students settled into campus life, all three of the Black players on Valley State's varsity football team quit to dedicate themselves to the BSU full time. The departure of Archie Chatman, Les Johns, and Art Jones followed earlier frustrations among Black athletes on campus as well as ongoing conflicts with an all-white coaching staff and athletic program director.[65] After the resignation of Valley State's Black varsity football players, Black players remained on the school's junior varsity team.[66] And on October 17, 1968, long-simmering tensions came to a boil when the junior varsity football coach physically struck one of his Black players during a game. According to witnesses, during a tense moment in the second half, coach Donald Markham grabbed and kicked George Boswell, one of the three Black players on the junior varsity team, while attempting to remove him from the playing field. More than twenty members of the BSU, in the stands watching the Thursday night game, witnessed Markham's attack.[67] In addition to coaching, Markham, who was white, worked as a police officer in Los Angeles.[68]

For BSU activists and sympathizers, Markham's violent outburst publicly confirmed long-standing complaints about racism in athletics at Valley State. Such complaints, broadly put, included "large differences [that] exist between treatment of non-white athletes" and their white counterparts.[69] The following day, BSU members held a meeting where they decided that the athletic director Glenn Arnett needed to fire Markham from his post as a football coach.[70] Noting both Markham's violent attack and a larger pattern of racist behavior, the BSU scheduled a meeting with Arnett, to be facilitated by Stanley Charnofsky, the white faculty director of the campus EOP.[71] BSU members who arrived for the meeting on the morning of Monday, November 4 were surprised to discover that it was to be a closed meeting, rather than one open to the organization's entire membership. As such, BSU chair Archie Chatman, along with EOP newcomers Eddie Dancer and Robert "Uwezo" Lewis, entered the athletic department offices to speak with Arnett. The athletic director quickly declared that he could not—and would not—fire Markham, explaining that only the school's acting president, Paul Blomgren, could do so. As such, all those assembled, and the more than one hundred BSU members outside, walked the seven-hundred yards from the athletic department to the administration building. Along the way, the planned meeting transformed into a four-hour occupation of the building.[72]

Once inside the building, BSU members put forward a short list of demands reflecting both immediate and long-term problems faced on campus. First, they demanded the ouster of both the junior varsity football coach and the athletic director as the result of Markham's racist outburst and Arnett's stated unwillingness to deal with anti-Black racism within campus athletics. Second, the BSU demanded that the campus administration make efforts to rectify a coming budget crunch that threatened the continuation of the campus EOP program. Finally, like their counterparts then active at San Francisco State College, the occupiers demanded that the administration fight back against the board of trustee's proposal to take control of student funds heretofore handled by elected student governments across the state college system.[73] Jim Dailey, a graduate student in political science, warned of the potential erosion of campus autonomy represented by the board of trustees' proposed change. Speaking with the on-campus newspaper, the *Daily Sundial*, on the day of the BSU occupation, Dailey lamented that "when the trustees meet this month and pass that law, it will come without the consent of the student governments, and those governments will no longer be able to fund projects themselves."[74] With their demands made, the occupiers exited the buildings less than four hours after having entered.

Although many campus protests in the late sixties evolved into overnight building occupations, the relatively brief BSU occupation at Valley State resulted in mass arrests, a wide range of trumped-up charges, and the first mass felony prosecution of student activists in U.S. history.[75] Approximately thirty BSU members occupied the building's fifth floor, home to the president's office and those of other top administrators, while 150 mainly white SDS members and sympathizers settled into an occupation of the first and second floors.[76] In the wake of the occupation, the BSU members would face a range of felony charges including kidnapping and false imprisonment, while white SDS members escaped with only misdemeanors. This racial imbalance led many to charge the local district attorney—a conservative former protégé of J. Edgar Hoover—with both racism and political aspirations. As the BSU's Robert "Uwezo" Lewis argued, "It was clear to us from the beginnings that District Attorney Evelle Younger and Judge Mark Brandler were in on a conspiracy with Ronald Reagan to make political gain at our expense."[77] Such a view seems to be confirmed by a comment made by the deputy attorney who later stated that "I would expect that militants all over the country were watching the results of this trial. . . . It could have a crippling effect on campus militancy in this state, if not throughout the country."[78] Although the local power structure came down hard on BSU organizers, such political repression did not stifle campus protest in California or even at San Fernando Valley State.

Judge Mark Brandler eventually declared nineteen BSU activists guilty of a wide range of counts including conspiracy, kidnapping, and false imprisonment.[79] The second and third charges stemmed from the fact that administrators and staff had been present during the occupation. What Judge Brandler condemned as kidnapping, the BSU explained as an attempt at face-to-face dialogue. Even Valley State's president, himself present for the occupation, testified that "he did not consider himself to be either kidnapped or falsely imprisoned."[80] Sixteen of those charged received varying lesser sentences that included some combination of a $150–$250 fine, two to five years' probation, and up to one year in the county jail. But BSU leaders Archie Chatman, Eddie Dancer, and Robert "Uwezo" Lewis each received an open sentence of one to twenty-five years in state prison. It was, at the time, "the most severe individual penalty ever given a campus activist."[81] Although their charges would stand, only three months after they had been sentenced, every one of the nineteen was out on bail, including Chatman, Dancer, and Lewis. Los Angeles superior judge George M. Dell granted the trio a five-year probation period and barred them from reenrolling at Valley State.[82] None of the Valley State nineteen would go on to serve any additional time for the occupation.[83]

Even as the Valley State BSU dealt with trials and imprisonment, school administrators moved to meet eight of the twelve demands presented during the November 4 occupation. Among other victories, these included a BA-granting Black studies department, a BSU–run tutorial program for EOP students, and the admission of five hundred Black EOP students every year until Valley State's student body came in line with racial demographics nationwide. Not only that, but the successes of the BSU helped UMAS to win parallel gains.[84] Within a year of the November 4, 1968, occupation, San Fernando Valley State would expand its ethnic studies offerings from four Black and four Chicano studies courses to eighteen of each. Those isolated courses would be unified in degree-granting and independent Black and Chicano studies departments.[85] Finally, the administration announced plans for the admission of 350 Black and 350 Chicano EOP students in the fall of 1969.[86]

At the end of the 1970s, Bill Burwell and former student athlete Archie Chatman sat down for interviews with a writer from the *Los Angeles Times* to reflect on the BSU victories at Valley State from the vantage point of a decade. In the resulting article, journalist Bob Baker noted that the young Black activists had successfully forced "a virtually lily-white campus . . . to become one of the first in the nation to create departments for the study of black and Chicano cultures and to drastically increase minority admissions." By 1979, Valley State, by then known as Cal State Northridge, boasted what Baker noted was "the largest [Black studies program] in the California state university system in terms of full-time equivalent students. It has seven tenured faculty members, 10 part-time instructors, offers 50 to 60 courses a semester and grants degrees to a handful of majors each year." What's more, from the paltry twenty or so African Americans on campus during the 1967–68 school year, a decade later as many as 1,800 Black students were enrolled.[87] Despite the temporary repression visited upon BSU organizers, Burwell, Chatman, and the rest successfully challenged the climate of complacency and conservatism at Valley State, helping to make it a home for thousands of Black and Chicano students in the coming decades by forcing administrators to move beyond the admissions standards established by the Master Plan.

From San Jose to Mexico City

Much like their counterparts at Valley State, the small number of Black student athletes at San Jose State College aimed to increase the recruitment, matriculation, and retention of African American students on their majority-white California campus. Founded in 1857, San Jose State is the oldest institution of public higher education in California.[88] By the early 1960s, it was one of the largest schools in the state.[89] From six thousand students in 1951, the campus grew to twelve thousand in 1961. It would increase to twenty thousand by 1963 and to twenty-four thousand by the start of the 1967–68 school year.[90] Despite its large size, San Jose State was home to a very small and fluctuating population of Black students, the vast majority of them male student athletes.

Throughout the early 1960s, the Black student population at San Jose State was kept to a minimum by the strict admissions standards enacted by the California Master Plan for Higher Education. According to both professor Harry Edwards and undergraduate Tommie Smith, most Black students on campus were athletes brought in under the Master Plan's 2 percent exception rule.[91] Edwards first came to San Jose State on an athletic scholarship in the fall of 1960. Born and raised in East St. Louis, Illinois, Edwards lived with family in California while attending Fresno City College.[92] When Edwards transferred to San Jose State in 1960, the school already had a reputation for enrolling top Black sprinters.[93] But as soon as he arrived on campus, Edwards realized that although they were more than happy to recruit young Black men as athletes, the historically white campus was less than comfortable with the relatively new phenomenon of Black men as students.

The small number of Black students at San Jose State in the 1960s experienced broad-based discrimination in the realm of academics. Although Edwards would go on to earn his PhD from Cornell and serve on the faculty for many years at UC Berkeley, he found on arrival at San Jose State that the school practiced an informal policy of steering Black athletes into the physical education major. That department, Edwards insinuated, doled out grades in an effort to keep athletic scholarships functional. As Edwards would later explain, San Jose State expected its Black student athletes to focus on athletics while ignoring their studies. A similar situation prevailed at UCLA, where Kareem Abdul-Jabbar noted that "I quickly got the impression from some of my teachers and fellow students that not a lot was expected out of me in the world of academics. . . . There seemed to be a clear assumption that I wouldn't be up to the work."[94] Reflecting on the early sixties from the decade's end, Edwards noted that "no Black athlete at the time I entered could recall any recent Black athlete who had graduated" from San Jose State. Edwards continued, "There were fewer than sixty full-time Black students on campus. Most of these were either currently active athletes or athletes who had used up their athletic eligibility but who were still trying to graduate."[95] If the Black student athletes accepted under the 2 percent exception rule were to learn and to graduate, they would have to do so through their own determination, set against the best efforts of their respective coaches to keep them focused on their sport.

Off the field, Black student athletes faced a wide range of discrimination at the hands of their fellow students. Black students found their options for both housing and social life extremely limited. As Edwards ruefully explained, "Though San Jose State had acquired a 'party school' reputation, it was no place for Blacks looking to party. . . . Fraternity row was off limits for Black students twenty-four hours a day." The de facto discrimination practiced on college campuses meant that Black students paid student fees that subsidized white extracurriculars which excluded African Americans.[96] What's more, because the vast majority of Black students on campus were male athletes, there was a real paucity of African American women on campus in an age before the 1972 Title IX expansion of women's sports. Edwards remembers only three Black women among full-time students, all of whom were recent transfers. The lack of Black women led to tensions on campus, given the strict, yet often unspoken, prohibition against interracial dating. According to Edwards, the warning was clear enough: "Don't be caught even talking to a white girl, much less dating one."[97] A Black student's best bet for companionship, platonic or otherwise, was to visit the nearby cities of Richmond, Oakland, and San Francisco. Edwards summed up his experience as follows: "By the end of my first semester at San Jose State, all illusions of California as a super-liberal, interracial promised land had evaporated."[98]

Black students were invariably disappointed by the racism they encountered at San Jose State, but discrimination was a particularly bitter pill to swallow when it came at the hands of those they depended on, like white teammates, coaches, and area landlords. Upon arriving on campus, Edwards wasn't initially able to move into the dorms because the school administration couldn't find a white student willing to have a Black roommate. At the same time, African Americans attempting to live off campus were turned away by white landlords.[99] In his 1969 sociological study, *The Revolt of the Black Athlete*, Edwards noted that "like other blacks, black athletes find housing, recreational facilities, clubs, and off-season jobs closed to them."[100] Beyond such discrimination, Edwards singled out fraternities as a key locus of racial discrimination. Compounding such racist exclusion, "many of the black athlete's white teammates may and usually do belong to these racist clubs." Edwards relayed his personal experience that "white 'teammates' can practice with you five days a week for hours on end yet at night refer to you as 'coon,' 'nigger,' and 'jiggaboo' and then jump all over you on Saturday afternoon talking about team spirit."[101] In all aspects of campus life, and even off campus, racial intolerance and discrimination was the norm at San Jose State in the 1960s.

As San Jose State College grew along the guidelines established by the Master Plan, the number of African American students rose slightly, although their low percentage in and exclusion from an overwhelmingly white student body remained constant. San Jose State would not begin experimenting with an EOP focused on recruiting and retaining Black students, beyond just small numbers of athletes, until student organizers forced white administrators and their fellow students to confront the issue of racism on campus.[102] When Harry Edwards started at San Jose State in 1960, he placed the Black student population at "fewer than sixty" in a school of approximately ten thousand.[103] Recruited to campus in 1963, Tommie Smith estimated there were "definitely no more than 30" in the surging student body of twenty thousand.[104] Although it remains unclear whether the Black student population decreased from sixty to thirty in the years stretching from 1960 to 1963, such a decrease would mirror the Black exodus that occurred at San Francisco State in the wake of the enactment of the 1960 Master Plan's new admissions standards. Either way, San Jose State was an incredibly white campus, featuring only a smattering of Black athletes. As Smith noted, "If you were a black person on campus at the time, the odds were overwhelming that you were an athlete."[105] These isolated Black student athletes continued to compete and attend to their studies but at the same time were increasingly aware of race-based struggles taking place across the nation, especially, but not exclusively, the civil rights movement then ongoing in the South.

In June 1964, Harry Edwards graduated from San Jose State and, having won the prestigious Woodrow Wilson Fellowship, moved across the country to Cornell University to study "race relations and social stratification." The fellowship aimed to increase the nation's supply of college professors through the recruitment of gifted undergraduates.[106] Edwards would visit California in the summer of 1965 to conduct research, and he returned to California for good after completing his master's degree in the spring of 1966.[107] In the meantime, Black student athletes like Tommie Smith continued to grapple with pervasive anti-Blackness at San Jose State. As Smith recalls, "Facing that [racism] every day created camaraderie among the black athletes. . . . We all developed a bond with each other."[108] In the spring of 1965, such camaraderie helped provide the basis for a protest march in support of the southern civil rights movement. As Black San Jose State students and their supporters marched more than forty miles from campus to San Francisco, Smith recalls, whites in automobiles harassed them, "called out from their cars, jeered us, called us niggers. . . . A few threw objects at us, bottles and other things."[109] That experience, coupled with ongoing tensions on campus, led to fervent discussions among San Jose State's Black student athletes; "the most prevalent topic," according to Smith, "was the black athlete's plight on the college campus—how black athletes could, and must, survive and prosper academically in an environment that discourages, even resents, their doing anything besides performing for the university's benefit."[110] Such discussions would soon bear fruit in the form of sustained campus protest.

As Black student athletes at San Jose State continued to grapple with campus racism, they took a page from African Americans elsewhere and began to organize. However, unlike other Black activists, student or otherwise, these student athletes would pioneer the use of their athletic prowess as a fulcrum with which to move school administrators to action. While still working toward his doctorate from Cornell, Harry Edwards returned to San Jose to teach during the 1966–67 school year. Edwards remembers being "increasingly disturbed over the circumstances of blacks on campus." He was then "one of only four Black instructors on a faculty of over a thousand" and "Black students were outnumbered by foreign students twenty to one." Most of those Black students, he notes, "continued to be current or former scholarship athletes."[111] Disillusioned with his return to San Jose State,

Edwards began an ongoing dialogue with Ken Noel, a Black master's student in sociology who, like Edwards, was a former San Jose State College athlete.[112] As Edwards remembers, "It suddenly dawned on us that the same social and racial injustices and discrimination that had dogged our footsteps as Freshman at San Jose were still rampant on campus—racism in the fraternities and sororities, racism in housing, racism and out-and-out mistreatment in athletics, and a general lack of understanding of the problems of Afro-Americans by the college administration."[113]

Frustrated by the lack of substantive change in the years stretching from 1960 to 1967, Edwards and Noel took their concerns about campus racism to the administration. They were ignored. In response, Edwards and Noel organized a "Rally on Racism at San Jose State." The protest coincided with the first day of classes on Monday, September 18, 1967.[114] Over seven hundred people attended the rally which witnessed the birth of San Jose State's first Black student organization, United Black Students for Action (UBSA).[115] What's more, Edwards and Noel served notice that should their concerns be ignored, UBSA was ready to engage in more drawn-out and confrontational methods. In particular, Edwards and Noel organized a boycott of San Jose State football's upcoming season opener by the team's Black players. In announcing the boycott, Edwards outlined a list of nine demands addressing the ongoing crisis of racism at San Jose State. Those demands included calls for the "public deliberation of *all* problems" of minority groups on campus and for the desegregation of housing, fraternities, sororities, and other on-campus organizations.[116]

Most crucially, the UBSA protest took aim at the de facto discriminatory admissions standards introduced by the 1960 Master Plan for Higher Education. Edwards, Noel, and UBSA criticized structural racism and the 2 percent admissions exemption rule used to facilitate the enrollment of Black athletes. UBSA called for the San Jose State administration "to expand the 2% rule to bring underprivileged minority group members to [campus] as students at least in proportion to their representation in the general population of California." Further, they demanded the establishment of "a 'tutorial' type program aimed at the recruitment of minority group members, and, secondly, that [the administration] show *proof* by the deadline admission date for the spring '68 semester that it has worked effectively."[117] The rally itself drew praise and support from both faculty and the student government, including the passage of a resolution against racial discrimination by the Academic Council, and a promise from the acting student body president to investigate instances of on-campus racism.[118] At the same time, the proposed football boycott forced a wide range of persons, from administrators and alumni, to white athletes and sports fans, to confront the allegations of racism at San Jose State.

The boycott organized by Edwards and Noel succeeded in forcing the San Jose State community to confront the issue and impact of racism. As Edwards later reflected, "We had done our homework. . . . We knew that the sports program was a focal interest for faculty, students, athletes, administrators, fraternities, sororities, and the community at large, and so our strategy would draw all these varied forces into a pressure situation."[119] With much on the line, San Jose State College president Robert D. Clark ordered the cancellation of the season opener against the University of Texas, El Paso. Rumors had been circulating that Black football players on both teams were planning to sit out the game.[120] In addition, President Clark feared the possible involvement of off-campus members of the Black Panther Party, an organization with which Edwards maintained good relations and of which he had briefly been a member.[121]

Having canceled the season-opening football game, President Clark also made several other moves in opposition to racism on campus. The president promised to make real efforts toward mitigating discrimination in housing and campus social life, including the notoriously segregationist fraternities. Clark also proposed, and would soon deliver, the creation of two new administrative posts. A new campus ombudsman would, in Clark's words, "conduct a continuous and aggressive campaign against racial discrimination" at San Jose State. Taking special note of criticisms of the 2 percent admissions exception rule, President Clark also promised the appointment of a new administrator who would serve as "a director to recruit and instruct minority students." Dr. Clark's admission of a real campus problem and his immediate efforts to resolve them defused what was until then a rapidly developing crisis. Yet, where Harry Edwards took the president's actions as proof that the UBSA had chosen the right course of action, California conservatives took the game's cancellation as an ominous portent of things to come.

As would occur on campus after campus across California, student organizers at San Jose State battled with Governor Ronald Reagan and other conservatives to secure the support of campus administrators. Governor Reagan came out strongly against the cancellation of San Jose State football's season opener, arguing that what was needed was "the necessary force and law enforcement" instead of what he viewed as "appeasement." State superintendent of public instruction Max Rafferty did the governor one better, calling the game boycott "blackmail" and claiming that were the decision up to him, "if I had to call in the U.S. Marine Corps, that game would have been played."[122] For Reagan and Rafferty, the game's cancellation was just the first in a long line of battles waged with current San Jose State and future UC Berkeley professor Harry Edwards.

Edwards himself recognized that the game's cancellation marked the opening of an important new era of Black student protest, one grounded in the strategic position of athletes. By threatening the flow of sports-generated revenues, Black student athletes were in a unique position to force their colleges and universities, and the nation at large, to face the deleterious impact of racism on all African Americans, including star athletes. Edwards noted in *The Revolt of the Black Athlete*, published two years after the threatened boycott, that "all totaled, the cancellation of the football game had cost the San Jose community and college somewhere in the neighborhood of $100,000 in direct game receipts and anticipated business income."[123] Years later, Edwards would reflect on the larger implications of the game cancellation in his 1980 memoir: "At San Jose State, the mold had been forged. By exploiting the sports arena, we had compelled long-overdue change. . . . We had learned how to generate political leverage through action based upon sound analysis. We had discovered the utterly untapped power potential inherent in Black involvement in America's collegiate sports institution."[124] Soon, Edwards and a number of Black student athletes at San Jose State would take that lesson to even bigger arenas.

The revolt of the Black athlete was grounded in the experience of isolated Black students on a campus whose Master Plan admissions standards shut out most African Americans while allowing a tiny minority of star athletes to gain admission. With startling rapidity, San Jose State's Black athletes, in concert with Professor Harry Edwards, would take their protest to the highest stage of sport: the Olympics. Even before the September 23 football game cancellation, Black student athletes at San Jose State had informally discussed the possibility of boycotting the upcoming 1968 Olympic Games in Mexico City. In 1963, the comedian and civil rights activist Dick Gregory had floated the idea of a Black boycott of the 1964 Olympic Games. In the following years, Edwards and Ken Noel discussed the possibility of a boycott with the Black student athletes at San Jose State.[125] And in early September 1967, sprinter Tommie Smith set off a press frenzy when he casually mentioned the idea of a boycott during an exchange with a Japanese reporter in Tokyo, where he was participating in the World University Games.[126] If boycotting a football game could win much needed reforms on campus, San Jose State student athletes wondered if such an experiment could be replicated on a much bigger stage to advance civil rights across the United States.

With the success of the UBSA protest behind them, current and former student athletes from San Jose State set on a path to bring their campus-based movement to the global stage. In the immediate aftermath of the canceled season opener, Harry Edwards, Ken Noel, and other partisans of the struggle at San Jose State began to focus their efforts on the proposed boycott of the 1968 Olympics. As Edwards recalled, "After consulting with other Black activists and a number of well-known Black athletes [off campus], we dubbed the venture The Olympic Project for Human Rights (OPHR), based upon our belief that the role of Blacks in American sports was intimately interdependent with our overall struggle for human rights in American society."[127] Although Edwards would not, in the end, be present in Mexico City for the 1968 Olympics, he played a major role in the first meeting to organize the OPHR. In fact, that October 7 meeting was held in Edwards's home.[128] Tommie Smith would later recall that "Harry led the meeting; Lee [Evans] and I were there. . . . Harry had talked to me throughout the years about social issues, but the stage was much bigger now."[129] Lee Evans, a year below Smith, was yet another Black San Jose State track star. Also present were graduate student Ken Noel; George Ware of the Student Nonviolent Coordinating Committee; Bob Hoover, a Black activist and counselor at San Mateo Community College; and Jimmy Garrett, the chairman of San Francisco State's BSU.[130]

After protesting San Jose State's season opener in late September and organizing as the OPHR in early October, San Jose State's Black activist athletes took their movement off campus. The 1967 Los Angeles Black Youth Conference (BYC) took place on November 22 and 23.[131] San Jose State student athletes involved in the OPHR traveled to Los Angeles to present their proposed boycott to BYC participants. The conference had drawn a wide range of participants, including movement leaders like Martin Luther King Jr. and Black Panther Party cofounder Huey Newton.[132] Also present at the BYC were a number of top-ranked Black student athletes whom Edwards and the San Jose State contingent had invited to a workshop on the proposed Olympic boycott. Noted attendees included the high jumper Otis Burrell from the University of Nevada at Reno as well as Kareem Abdul-Jabbar, Mike Warren, and Lucius Allen, of UCLA's basketball team, the defending NCAA champions.[133] Abdul-Jabbar was, at twenty years of age, already a nationally recognized sports star. He was also one of the dismally few Black students attending UCLA. Abdul-Jabbar wholeheartedly endorsed the boycott, noting that "I've served UCLA, amateur sports, and this country well—millions of dollars, scores of jobs, and hours of pleasure have been generated by my team's playing ball."[134] Edwards noted that Abdul-Jabbar's "moving and dynamic statements on behalf of the boycott . . . drew a five-minute ovation from the more than 200 persons" present for the boycott workshop.[135] As the most famous college athlete of the era, Abdul-Jabbar's endorsement of the boycott served to legitimize it in the eyes of many.[136] At the end of the workshop, those present voted almost unanimously in favor of boycotting the Summer Olympic Games, which were scheduled for October 1968.[137]

Participants in the OPHR sought to address a range of racial concerns, both concrete and amorphous. Harry Edwards, the boycott's driving force from the start, outlined four major aims of this Black athlete's revolt: "(1) to stage an international protest of the persistent and systemic violation of Black people's human rights in the United States; (2) to expose America's historical exploitation of Black athletes as political propaganda tools in both the national and international arenas; (3) to establish a standard of political responsibility among Black athletes vis-a-vis the needs and interests of the Black community; and (4) to make the Black community aware of the substantial hidden dynamics and consequences of their sports involvement."[138] More specifically, these Black athletes sought to voice their concerns regarding the position of Avery Brundage, president of the International Olympic Committee, and the participation of the apartheid state of South Africa. South Africa's invitation to the Olympic Games was eventually revoked, thanks in large part to the threat made by a number of postcolonial African states and Eastern Bloc nations to withdraw should South Africa be included.[139]

Reigning International Olympic Committee president Avery Brundage was widely known as a racist and antisemite.[140] In the early 1930s, Brundage had publicly praised Hitler and successfully thwarted a proposed boycott of the 1936 Olympic Games held in Nazi Germany.[141] According to historian David Clay Large, Brundage then "began to see in this opposition a diabolical Jewish plot to subvert the entire Olympic enterprise." The Nazis, in 1936, "had a friend in Avery Brundage."[142] By the 1960s, Brundage was part-owner and served as president of the Santa Barbara Country Club, which barred African Americans as members. Additionally, Harry Edwards noted, as the head of the International Olympic Committee, Brundage had "been in the forefront of efforts to sustain South Africa's participation in the Olympic Games" despite that nation's brutal practice of apartheid.[143] Although South Africa's participation in the games was blocked, the OPHR was unsuccessful in removing Brundage from his post.

As the games approached, the initial project of a boycott transformed into the idea of using the Olympic Games as a stage on which to make a political demonstration in front of the whole world.[144] Kareem Abdul-Jabbar and his Black UCLA teammates Mike Warren and Lucius Allen proved exceptions to this change and followed through with the original commitment to an Olympic boycott.[145] In the end, three Black student athletes from San Jose State—Tommie Smith, John Carlos, and Lee Evans—competed in the Olympics. The trio turned their medal award ceremonies into platforms to protest against anti-Black racism in their home country and to call for human rights on a global scale. When Smith and Carlos raised their fists on the podium, effecting one of the most iconic images of the 1960s, they drew the immediate ire of Avery Brundage and most of the Olympic and sporting establishment. Under threat by Brundage, the U.S. Olympic Committee expelled Smith and Carlos from the Olympic Village.[146] The two sprinters evacuated their Olympic housing for a hotel in Mexico City, before being stripped of their visas and returning to the United States.[147] Two days after Smith and Carlos's podium stand for the two-hundred-meter dash, San Jose State sprinter Lee Evans won the gold medal in the four hundred meter. Evans also won a second gold medal in the 4×400-meter relay. Despite warnings of "'severe' penalties" for "any further protests," Evans and his fellow gold medalists donned berets in the style of the Black Panther Party and briefly raised their fists in solidarity with the OPHR and their teammates Smith and Carlos.[148]

Although their protest reached far beyond its on-campus origins, the OPHR originated in the concerns of the small group of Black student athletes at San Jose State in the 1960s. Harry Edwards, Ken Noel, Tommie Smith, John Carlos, and Lee Evans, all represented the tiny 2 percent of students who could gain admittance to the state college system without meeting the stringent admissions standards of the California Master Plan for Higher Education. Only months before the 1968 Olympics, on-campus organizing at San Jose State and other California schools successfully pressured the state college board of trustees and the UC regents to accept an increase in the admissions exception rate from 2 percent to 4 percent.[149] The revolt of the Black athlete inaugurated real changes at San Jose State College and inspired similar efforts elsewhere, in California and beyond. These Black athlete activists helped to spur the development of a robust EOP that would bring at first hundreds and eventually thousands of African Americans and other minority students to the San Jose State campus. For Harry Edwards, the protests he envisioned, organized, and inspired helped pave the way for a long and fruitful career in academia.

The revolt of the Black athlete had a wide-ranging impact on San Jose State College. As *Los Angeles Times* education editor William Trombley noted in August 1969, "Following racial trouble in 1967, the college committed itself to EOP in a big way." For the 1968–69 school year, San Jose State admitted 425 students through its new EOP, 225 African Americans and 200 Mexican Americans. Despite the hardships that many had faced in comparatively underfunded and de facto segregated high schools, these EOP students performed "very comparable to the freshman class as a whole." As such, San Jose State administrators increased the EOP to 600 students for 1969–70, including 250 Blacks and 350 Chicanos. This total would represent nearly 20 percent of the incoming freshman class.[150] No longer would the small number of Black students on campus be comprised almost entirely of athletes. By 1969, the conditions prevalent since Harry Edwards's arrival at San Jose State in 1960 were no more.

Black protest at San Jose State succeeded not only in increasing minority enrollment and retention, but it also helped spur the institutionalization of ethnic studies on campus. Prior to the development of Black studies and other ethnic studies courses, the curriculum at San Jose State remained thoroughly Eurocentric. As Harry Edwards himself noted, in all his years at San Jose State, "I'd never been assigned so much as an essay by or about a Black American. In four college-level courses in American history and enough sociology classes to fulfill the course requirements for an undergraduate major . . . I had never been exposed to any survey of Black social or political thought."[151] When San Jose State opened its Black studies department in the fall of 1969, the *Los Angeles Times* rightly noted that "much of the credit . . . goes to Harry Edwards."[152] Even before the opening of the Black studies department proper, San Jose State had begun to move in the direction of ethnic studies. In the 1968–69 school year, the college offered eight courses in Black studies and five in Chicano studies. In the following year, the school was set to add an additional twelve new courses in Black studies and fifteen in Chicano studies.[153]

Finally, in January 1970, UC Berkeley announced the appointment of Harry Edwards as an assistant professor of sociology.[154] With characteristic modesty and insight, Edwards noted that "the job had grown out of student and progressive faculty demands for increased minority administrative, faculty, and student representation and involvement in the university. More generally, it turned out, I owed my job offer to what was called the Third World Strike, a student-faculty strike that virtually brought university business to a halt over the issue of institutional racism." Itself modeled on the example of the Third World Liberation Front strike at San Francisco State, the UC Berkeley third world strike won, as one of its victories, the hiring of Harry Edwards.[155] At UC Berkeley, Edwards would join his old coconspirator Ken Noel, who was by then working toward his doctorate in the sociology department.[156] Perhaps unsurprisingly, California conservatives met Edwards's hiring with hostility. Noting that he opposed the appointment "unequivocally," Governor Reagan promised Edwards would be "a prime topic of discussion at the next Regents' meeting." Max Rafferty, for his part, warned that "bringing Edwards to Berkeley is like pouring gasoline on a forest fire . . . and I couldn't care less about Edwards' academic credentials."[157] Edwards would remain a popular professor and prodigious scholar until his retirement in 2000.

At San Jose State and San Fernando Valley State, Black student athletes led the way in developing confrontational protest movements to challenge both institutional and interpersonal racism. At UCLA, UC Berkeley, and UCSB, and at Fresno State, San Francisco State, and San Jose City College, Black student athletes formed important parts of larger coalitions dedicated to creating change. The early organizing efforts of Black student athletes in the Master Plan system contributed to the establishment of programs of ethnic studies and the development of EOPs. Yet Black student athletes, and Blacks students more generally, were joined by a diverse array of allies in the struggle to democratize the Master Plan system. The following chapters turn first to the development of the Chicano student movement in California and then to the broader phenomenon of interracial solidarity at the UC, state college, and community college levels. Typically led by Black and Chicano students, coalitions formed across the Master Plan system bringing African Americans and Mexican Americans together with radical whites, Asian Americans, Natives, and Latinos to increase the matriculation of working-class students of color through the expansion of the admissions exceptions embedded in the Master Plan for Higher Education.

5 A Master Plan for Chicanos

· ·

The three-day Chicano conference of students, faculty, staff and
community was an historic *encuentro*. There was *hermandad*, there was
intercambio de ideas, there was even *chingaderas*, most important there
was work on the issues affecting higher education and Chicanos in
California. . . . The conference, not an end in itself, was a strong and
crucial step forward toward putting together what we all agree is
necessary at this point: a Chicano master plan for higher education.

—Jesus Genera, 1969
    (Educational Opportunity Program counselor, UC Davis)

A point to be remembered in evaluating the Master Plan is that it
was written before a significant number of Chicanos were enrolled
in public higher education. . . . The dramatic increase in enrollment
of Chicanos and other minorities (most of whom are economically
disadvantaged) has created difficulties and misunderstandings since
the Master Plan provides no policy for their accommodation by
higher education.

—Ronald Lopez and Darryl Enos, 1972
    (California State Legislature Joint Committee on the Master Plan)

For three days in April 1969, more than one hundred Chicanos and Chicanas gathered together at UC Santa Barbara. The month prior, a small group
of Chicano activists across California—students as well as young faculty and
administrators—had released a call for a "Chicano Student/Faculty workshop on Higher Education" that, in their words, would seek to "develop a
'Master-Plan' for Chicanos in higher education." The organizers envisioned
a series of workshops in which one hundred invited participants would labor
toward the creation of "a document that can be used as a guide to recruit
Chicano students, faculty and administrators to campus; [and] to deal with
support programs, curriculum," and more, while addressing the "needs of
the Chicano community, as it relates to higher education."[1] As such, this
"'Master-Plan' for Chicanos" would seek to negate the structural inequalities institutionalized by the California Master Plan of 1960.

The conference would prove an enduring success, producing a rough draft of what would become *El Plan de Santa Barbara* and birthing both the Chicano Coordinating Council on Higher Education and El Movimiento Estudiantil Chicano de Aztlán (MECHA). Where *El Plan de Santa Barbara* would provide a blueprint for continuing activism, the recruitment of Chicana/o undergraduates, and the development of Chicano studies on campuses in California and beyond, the coordinating council united Chicano and Chicana faculty and administrators, and MECHA sought to merge existing Chicana/o student groups into a single nationwide organization. Moving forward and guided by *El Plan*, the council and MECHA would organize for greater Mexican American representation on college and university campuses. As such, the conference at UCSB proved a remarkably productive one, the result of more than one hundred scholar activists and student activists who spent three days tackling nine distinct workshops fueled by a hearty supply of "pan dulce y cafe."[2]

Through the 1969 Santa Barbara conference and the resulting *Plan de Santa Barbara*, Chicano and Chicana activists registered their discontent with the impact of the 1960 California Master Plan for Higher Education. Conference participants committed themselves to increasing the matriculation of Mexican Americans to California's institutions of higher education, to promoting and supporting Chicana/o faculty and staff, and to redirecting college and university resources to those who remained off-campus, dwelling in California's *barrios y colonias*, toiling in its factories and fields. The 1960 Master Plan for Higher Education had pledged universal access to California's public colleges and universities, and the participants in the state's Chicano student movement organized to ensure that Chicanos and Chicanas would be equal beneficiaries of that promise.

Much as any history of the Master Plan for Higher Education would be incomplete without an assessment of its impact on California's Mexican American population, so too the history of the Chicano movement is incomplete without an understanding of the centrality of the Master Plan to Chicana/o student organizing in California.[3] Although much has been written on the *Plan de Santa Barbara*, scholars have yet to place the conference that resulted in its drafting in its proper context, that of the 1960 Master Plan for Higher Education and its impact on Mexican Americans. Largely consigned to underfunded segregated schools throughout their early lives, Chicano youth were further hindered in their attempts to obtain college educations by the Master Plan's new admissions standards and its concurrent restriction of special admissions from 10 to 2 percent. The de facto racial exclusions embedded in the 1960 California Master Plan for Higher Education thus drove Chicano and Chicana youth to organize for equal access, culminating in a substantial increase in Mexican American enrollment at the UC, state college, and community college levels.

The long-standing practice of segregation in education and the resulting low rates of enrollment at the college level exacerbated by the admissions standards enacted by the 1960 Master Plan inspired Mexican American youth in California to organize as part of the emergent Chicano movement. Through the 1969 conference at UCSB, and the Chicano student movement more generally, organizers worked toward a future in which California's colleges and universities would be representative of the percentage of Mexican Americans statewide. By 1969, Mexican Americans made up 13 percent of California's total population. Chicanos formed an even higher percentage of the population in certain areas. For instance, Chicana/os made up 17 percent of K–12 students in Los Angeles city schools, and in Fresno County, Mexican Americans were 20 percent of the total population.[4] Yet despite being California's largest minority population, throughout the 1960s, Mexican Americans were highly underrepresented in the ranks of students in the Master Plan system.

Official efforts tracking the racial identity of public college and university students in California did not begin until the early 1970s, yet examining a range of contemporary sources gives a sense of the underrepresentation of Chicana/os in higher education. Unsurprisingly, Mexican Americans were least represented at the UC, the top tier of the Master Plan system. At UC Berkeley, Chicanos made up approximately 0.25 percent of the student body in the 1966–67 school year.[5] Estimates for 1967 place Chicanos at slightly above 0.2 percent of the UCLA student body.[6] In 1968, Chicanos made up about 0.8 percent of students at UCSB.[7] At most state colleges, Chicanos' numbers were not much better. Mexican Americans made up 0.2 percent of San Jose State in 1966; 0.1 percent of San Fernando Valley State during the 1967–68 school year; 2 percent of Fresno State in the same year; 0.5 percent of Los Angeles State in 1969; and despite making up 14 percent of San Francisco's population, Latinos of all national backgrounds comprised only 1 percent of San Francisco State students in 1969.[8] As late as 1971, Mexican Americans even remained underrepresented in California's community college system. Only one two-year community college, located in a heavily Mexican American neighborhood, bucked the trend. As early as 1967, Chicanos had come to make up 40 percent of the student body at East Los Angeles College.[9] Like their Black counterparts, when Chicanos managed to enter the Master Plan system, they tended to do so at the bottom rung.

Juan Crow California

The practices that resulted in Chicano exclusion from higher education had deep roots in California history. Much like African Americans, Mexican Americans and Mexican nationals residing in the United States had long suffered from segregation in education. Where in the Jim Crow South such segregation was written into state laws, in California segregation of both African Americans and Mexican Americans was achieved through a combination of methods, both de jure and de facto. Local and state practices across the American Southwest guaranteed the separation of children of Mexican descent from their white peers. Although segregation would come under fire in the 1940s and 1950s, Mexican youth in the late 1960s, like their Black counterparts, still struggled to achieve equality of opportunity in education.[10]

Mexicans, of course, predated the United States in the vast territory that would become California and the rest of the American Southwest. California's population stood at approximately 110,000 at the end of the US-Mexico War. With the Treaty of Guadalupe Hidalgo in 1848, Mexican nationals were given a choice: remain and become U.S. citizens or abandon their homes to relocate south of the new border and retain their Mexican citizenship. The vast majority chose to remain in what was from then on the United States. As such, California's Mexican American population became what one historian describes as "a 'colored,' Spanish-speaking, Catholic minority in a white, English-speaking, Protestant society."[11]

School segregation developed as Mexican immigration to California and the American Southwest shot up in the opening decades of the twentieth century. From 1900 to 1930, over 1.5 million Mexicans immigrated to the United States.[12] It was in those years that most communities with substantial numbers of Mexican residents began to practice segregation. Although the five southwestern states lacked laws mandating the segregation of ethnic Mexicans, white school administrators consistently segregated pupils of Mexican descent from their white counterparts. Between 1910 and 1950, as historian Gilbert Gonzalez explains, "many members of the dominant society commonly looked upon [Mexicans and Mexican Americans] as aliens or cultural outcasts whose principal function was to sell . . . their labor, in the lowest-paid occupations. Consequently, the American community perceived educational opportunities for Mexicans as a burden and of little value."[13] As such, parallel and unequal systems of education developed and solidified across California and the Southwest in the first half of the twentieth century.

Schooling for pupils of Mexican descent developed according to the dictates of the regional economy and to the perceived capacities of a racialized population. Across the Southwest, Mexican students were forced into underfunded schools often housed in dilapidated buildings. The white teachers assigned to such Mexican schools were usually either new to the profession or had been sent there as punishment for their poor performance at white schools. Finally, such teachers and administrators developed an informal practice of directing students of Mexican descent into vocational or remedial classes.[14] Conditions for the children of migrant farmworkers were particularly dreadful. As Carey McWilliams noted in his seminal 1935 work, *Factories in the Field: The Story of Migratory Farm Labor in California*, "Migratory children were herded together in garages, school corridors, and abandoned barns, with as many as 125 children for one instructor. . . . Children were made to attend school from 7:30 A.M. to 12 o'clock so that they might then be excused to work in the fields. The policy back of this type of discrimination was announced as an attempt to 'adjust the child to the crop.'"[15] Such policies reverberated from remedial schooling to higher education. For instance, Merton Hill, a superintendent in Southern California, called in 1924 for a "scientific study of the Mexican . . . the temperament of the race." Hill continued, "Their capacities to perform different types of service should be set forth [so] that their employers may utilize them to the best interests." Hill would soon thereafter be named the head of admissions for the UC.[16]

In the 1940s, parents in "at least a dozen southern California communities" challenged the racial segregation of Mexican pupils that had solidified over the previous two decades.[17] Even earlier, the 1931 decision in *Roberto Alvarez v. the Board of Trustees of the Lemon Grove School District* struck a preliminary blow against the segregation of Mexican students.[18] In March 1945, a group of parents living in Orange County filed a class action lawsuit against four local school districts. Representing the efforts of a broader group, Gonzalo and Felicitas Mendez of Westminster gave their name to the case that would successfully challenge school segregation. Two years later, on April 14, 1947, the U.S. Court of Appeals in San Francisco upheld a decision in favor of the plaintiffs in the case of *Mendez et al. v. Westminster School District of Orange County*. The following school year, the all-white Franklin School targeted by the Mendez family was integrated. In retrospect, the

Mendez decision represented an early strike against the doctrine of separate but equal established by the 1896 U.S. Supreme Court decision in *Plessy v. Ferguson*. However, the *Mendez* ruling left open the possibility that school districts could continue to segregate Mexican students on the basis of their proficiency in English but not their race or ethnicity.[19] The victory for school desegregation notwithstanding, as Gilbert Gonzalez argues, "schooling for Mexican children continued to come under the significant influence of pseudoscientific intelligence testing" coupled with the practice of tracking students of Mexican descent into slow learner and vocational classes.[20]

Despite legal victories against de jure racism, de facto segregation would remain the norm for California's Mexican population, and as such, racism embedded in early education would follow Chicano youth as they attempted to pursue higher education within the Master Plan system.[21] The majority of Californians of Mexican descent remained in predominantly Mexican neighborhoods due to racially discriminatory housing covenants. Mexicans had the dubious distinction of being the most segregated racial group in California, and most Mexican youth would continue to attend predominantly Mexican schools.[22] In such schools, white administrators and teachers continued the practices of assigning pupils to subordinate educational tracks and of punishing students for speaking Spanish. Finally, all of California's students confronted a Eurocentric curriculum that erased the century-long presence of Mexican Americans in U.S. history.

The Oakland-based Chicano movement newspaper *La Hormiga* would succinctly describe the situation in late 1968: the typical segregated "barrio school spends less money on its students, has the least competent teachers, the most overcrowded classrooms, and above all the most irrelevant curriculum."[23] As the political climate of the early Cold War gave way to the social upheavals of the long 1960s, a new generation of Mexican Americans would come to challenge these practices and more through a vibrant wave of youth activism.

The Chicano Student Movement

As evidenced by the *Mendez* case of 1947, previous generations of Mexican Americans had not simply acquiesced to second-class citizenship. Since at least the turn of the century, Mexicans in the United States had formed *mutalistas* (mutual aid societies), joined unions, and organized politically.[24] By the 1930s, Mexican Americans and Mexican migrants alike participated in diverse labor and political organizing across the Southwest. Such efforts helped lead to the founding of El Congreso de Pueblos de Habla Español in 1939 and the Asociación Nacional México-Americana in 1949.[25] In the 1940s and 1950s, influential organizations typical of what historians have termed the Mexican American generation included the League of United Latin American Citizens, the American GI Forum, and the Mexican American Political Association. Their efforts were informed by the experiences of discrimination in the Great Depression, patriotic sacrifice in World War II, and the reactionary political climate of an emerging Cold War. As such, these comparatively conservative organizations worked within an assimilationist framework as they sought equal rights for Mexican Americans.[26] The early 1960s, however, marked a qualitative shift in Mexican American activism, from liberal calls for inclusion to subversive dissent.[27]

While resurrecting the radical Mexican American politics of the 1930s and 1940s, the Chicano student activists of the 1960s drew inspiration from a range of ongoing struggles, including the civil rights movement. But perhaps no struggle had a greater impact on the emergence of Chicano student activism in California than that of the United Farm Workers. From 1965 to 1970, countless young Chicanos and Chicanas would be inspired and politicized by the United Farm Workers' grape strike and boycott. This was true of students on urban campuses and, as discussed below, of those attending college in agricultural areas like the students at Fresno State. To take but one example, in October 1968, police arrested eleven members of the Mexican American Student Confederation at UC Berkeley, when they occupied the office of UC president Charles Hitch, demanding that the UC halt its purchases of scab grapes for campus cafeterias.[28] As farmworkers organized across rural California, Chicana/o students organized in tandem throughout the Master Plan system.

The first student organization founded by and for students of Mexican descent in the United States was Student Initiative (SI) at San Jose State College. Founded by San Jose State undergraduate Armando Valdez in 1964, SI filled an important niche in the robust activist community developing on that massive South Bay campus. Valdez was a member of the Students for a Democratic Society, an active supporter of the Student Nonviolent Coordinating Committee, and like Cesar Chavez, a former organizer with the Community Service Organization. SI connected students at San Jose State to the ongoing farmworker struggle in California. On campus, SI placed pressure on administrators to increase the recruitment and retention of Mexican American youth. Students at nearby San Jose City College joined SI as well.[29]

After three years, SI would rename itself the Mexican American Student Confederation (MASC) as it expanded out of its initial base in San Jose.

Mexican American student organizations proliferated across California a couple of years after the organization of SI. In January 1967, Mexican American activists organized the Mexican American Student Association (MASA) at East Los Angeles College. Students at Fresno State would first organize under the same name, MASA, but agreed to a merger with MASC after a November 4, 1967, meeting in Berkeley. Beyond San Jose and Fresno State, student organizers founded MASC chapters in 1967 on Northern California campuses including San Francisco State, Hayward State, Sacramento State, and UC Berkeley. Around the same time, the United Mexican American Students (UMAS) organized chapters across Southern California, including at UCLA, UCSB, Los Angeles State, Long Beach State, San Fernando Valley State, and private colleges Loyola University and the University of Southern California. At UC San Diego, San Diego State, and San Diego City College, student activists formed chapters of an organization they named the Mexican American Youth Association (MAYA).[30]

One of the most important spurs to Chicana/o student activism emerged not on college campuses but in high schools, albeit with the support of activists from local colleges. In a series of demonstrations beginning in March 1968, nearly ten thousand Mexican American high school students would walk out of their classrooms to protest the poor conditions in their largely segregated schools. The so-called blowouts began on March 3 at Lincoln High School in East Los Angeles.[31] At Lincoln High, more than a thousand students participated in the massive walkout. From there, protests spread to fifteen schools across the Los Angeles school district and even inspired similar demonstrations as far away as Texas and Colorado.[32] As noted by one Los Angeles–based movement newspaper, the blowouts "incontestably prove a new political consciousness among our Raza youth."[33] Among other demands, protesters called for meaningful action to combat high dropout rates, efforts to ameliorate overcrowding and substandard facilities, and a more relevant curriculum that would illuminate the history of Mexicans in the United States.[34]

Members of UMAS took a leadership role in organizing their high school counterparts and participated enthusiastically in the walkouts.[35] By 1968, UMAS was an established presence at several Southern California colleges and universities, including UCLA and Los Angeles State College. Each campus branch, in turn, was paired to a local high school, where it would support budding student activists.[36] According to Carlos Muñoz—then a UMAS organizer at Los Angeles State College—UMAS served as "the leading force" behind the famed high school protests. As the Los Angeles–based movement newspaper *Chicano Student News* put it, UMAS, itself "a product of those high schools, helped, aided, assisted, and advised their younger brothers and sisters in their protests for better education." UMAS's prominent role in organizing the walkouts even led the organization to begin establishing new chapters at area high schools.[37]

In the early years of on-campus organizing, Mexican American student groups operated autonomously or as part of larger citywide efforts, yet new developments increasingly spurred ever larger networks of Chicana/o activism. In December 1967, UMAS held a two-day meeting attended by approximately three hundred Chicana/o student activists. At the University of Southern California, MASC activists from the Bay Area connected with UMAS organizers from greater Los Angeles and two special guests representing the Black Student Union. According to movement historian Arturo Rosales, "this was one of the first occasions Chicano students from both Southern and Northern California met within a movement context." Such cross-pollination laid bare important questions about movement ideology and strategy, as MASC embraced a loose socialism and third world solidarity with other people of color, while UMAS appeared to be in transition from the assimilationist politics characteristic of the earlier Mexican American generation toward a form of Chicano nationalism. Despite such differences, attendants to the December 1967 conference found common ground in their rejection of the racist educational status quo.[38]

Finally, forty-year-old activist Rodolfo "Corky" Gonzales hosted the first Chicano Youth Liberation Conference in March 1969 in Denver. Over a thousand young activists attended the Denver conference, the majority students, with most of them hailing from California.[39] The key by-product of the Denver conference, a concise three-page manifesto known as the *Plan Espiritual de Aztlán*, was a cultural nationalist call to arms. Aztlán is a Nahuatl word for the mythico-historical homeland of the Aztec peoples of central Mexico, believed by movement participants and others to be located in the contemporary American Southwest. For Chicana/o activists, the *Plan Espiritual* validated Chicanos as the region's rightful inhabitants and called on a "free and sovereign" people to struggle "against the foreigner 'gabacho' who exploits our riches and destroys our culture." The nationalism inherent in this Chicano "plan of liberation" would prove a highly influential strand within the burgeoning Chicano movement.[40] What's more, the *Plan Espiritual de Aztlán* set an influential precedent within the Chicano movement with its call to make education relevant to Chicanos and its demand for Chicano community control of "our schools, our teachers, our administrators, our counselors, and our programs."[41] All the while, as committed Chicana/o organizers met in Denver and at other movement summits, much larger numbers of activists continued to demonstrate and to build their organizations at the local level.

The Santa Barbara Conference

Even as young Mexican Americans across California took up the moniker of Chicano and set to organizing against racism, their enrollment rates at the UC and state colleges remained stubbornly low. Because of this, a small group of Mexican Americans who had found precarious homes at those institutions as graduate students, new instructors, and low-level administrators began a movement toward drafting what they called "a 'Master-Plan' for Chicanos in higher education."[42] Well aware of the role that the 1960 California Master Plan had played in maintaining the exclusivity and disproportionate whiteness of the UC and state colleges, these activists sought to democratize the Master Plan system and to make higher education a welcoming home for the state's large population of Mexican Americans.

The idea of developing a Master Plan for Chicanos began with Rene Nuñez, an activist and recruiter of underrepresented minorities to the UC and state colleges. As an adult undergraduate at UCLA, Nuñez worked as the director of the Educational Clearinghouse.[43] Based in south central Los Angeles, this program recruited "high potential" Black and Chicano high school students to the upper tiers of the Master Plan system. Working in such a role and as a Chicano student at UCLA himself, Nuñez was forced to confront the Master Plan admissions standards that kept most young Mexican Americans out of the top tiers of the Master Plan. As such, Nuñez and a group of likeminded acquaintances organized a formal planning committee to work toward a three-day workshop that would be held April 11 to 13 in Santa Barbara. In the weeks leading up to the Denver Chicano Youth Liberation Conference of March 1969, the planning committee drafted and mailed letters to selected Chicano activists—mainly educators and administrators—across California.[44]

The conference planning committee emerged in the heady aftermath of the high school walkouts of spring 1968 in which Nuñez himself had participated.[45] The planning committee consisted of twelve Chicano organizers active across the state, from San Diego to Sacramento. In addition to Nuñez, planning committee members included Armando Valdez, Paul Sanchez, Jesus Genera, Eliezer Risco, Tony Munoz, Jesús Chavarría, Fernando de Necochea, Carlos Jackson, Juan Gómez-Quiñones, Bert Rivas, and Frank Sandoval. The all-male committee in part reflects the gender imbalance in academia in the 1960s—those Mexican Americans who had managed to secure employment in the Master Plan system were disproportionately men. Yet, the conference steering committee and the Chicano Coordinating Council on Higher Education—founded at the conference—would include important Chicana scholars and activists.[46]

In their attempt to bring together Chicano and Chicana activists from across the state, the planning committee sought out a rough middle ground in Santa Barbara. Located in between the activist hotbeds of greater Los Angeles and the Bay Area, the small central coast city could serve as a sort of neutral territory. Rene Nuñez approached the Santa Barbara campus branch of UMAS about hosting the conference.[47] UCSB had joined the UC system in 1958 and grew from two thousand to twelve thousand students over a ten-year period. Yet, Mexican Americans only made up approximately 0.8 percent of UCSB students ten years into that campus growth spurt. Having suffered in isolation as racial minorities on the predominantly white campus, Mexican American students in Santa Barbara organized as UMAS in January 1968.[48] Although the campus branch of UMAS would not play a central role in organizing the conference, the group secured the physical space in which the conference took place—the Francisco Torres residence halls—and its members served as "workshop facilitators" assigned to take notes during all workshop sessions.[49]

In the six months leading up to the conference, the planning committee met multiple times to select invitees and to plan the nine workshops that would facilitate the drafting of a Chicano Master Plan. In the words of the committee, "every participant [was] selected because of his commitment to La Raza and because of his expertise in the field, thus each person participating is expected to participate in the development of the final statement or master plan that will issue from this workshop and contribute to the implementation of any action or political programs that are created to carry out the 'Master-Plan.'" Conference organizers aimed to limit the number of participants to ten to twelve individuals per workshop so as to keep them "small enough so that each can develop its contribution to the master plan." The committee sought out one hundred participants for the conference, split between fifty-eight student representatives of MASC, UMAS, and MAYA chapters based on twenty-nine California campuses and forty-two slots "filled by faculty, administration and involved community— *puros chicanos*."[50]

By March 12, 1969, the planning committee had drawn up a list of thirty-four individuals to invite to the Chicano conference that would take place at UCSB the following month. The organizers requested that invitees reply within the week, indicating their first and second choice of workshop. Rather than jumping from one discussion to the next, the committee expected invitees to "participant in [their] assigned workshop through the weekend." The planning committee geared workshops toward two broad targets: "Technical Operations" and "Political Operations." The technical workshops focused on recruitment, student support programs, funding, curriculum, and "university-community programs," while the political workshops targeted "organizing campuses," "statewide communication and coordination," political action, and legislation.[51] These nine workshops would form the basis for the eventual publication of *El Plan de Santa Barbara*, a Master Plan for Chicanos focused on increasing Mexican American enrollment in California colleges and universities and on building Chicano studies programs.

Despite the detailed plans drawn up by the committee, in the end, far more than the one hundred invitees participated in the conference. Workshop participant Carlos Muñoz later noted that although the committee limited invitations to only two students per campus organization, "when [other] students found out about it," they decided that "they were going anyway."[52] According to the postconference "Operations Report," the costs of the conference included "meals for 140 people." This suggests some forty extra participants attended—likely those student activists who crashed the conference, joining the student movement representatives, faculty, administrators, and community members who had been formally invited. The enthusiastic and spontaneous arrival of the uninvited students led to an imbalance in attendance—approximately forty-two faculty, staff, and community members to one hundred or so student activists. Thanks to this unexpected ratio, far more attention would be paid to the question of organizing Mexican American students than the conference planners had anticipated, with important consequences for the future of the Chicano student movement.[53]

In the end, the conference at UCSB accomplished three major tasks. As noted in an early report produced by conference participants, first and "most importantly," the individual conference workshops "produced reports which will ultimately make up a *Chicano* master plan." Following the conference, those workshop reports were to be edited and compiled into a single document, "an organic Master Plan . . . which will then be printed and distributed." Second, steering committee members and other workshop leaders formed what would become the Chicano Coordinating Council on Higher Education. Consisting of faculty and administrators, this organization would, according to conference organizers, represent "the statewide organization of our movement" in the coming years. Following the conference, coordinating council members would further revise the workshop reports, ultimately producing the document known as *El Plan de Santa Barbara*. Armando Valdez, who in 1964 had founded the nation's first Mexican American student organization at San Jose State, committed his Oakland-based La Causa Publications to publishing *El Plan*.[54]

Thanks perhaps to the unexpectedly high number of student participants, the conference produced an important new student organization—MECHA. In 1969, Mexican Americans were still highly underrepresented on college campuses as faculty and staff.[55] Yet, the first years of Educational Opportunity Program (EOP) efforts had slightly increased the number of Chicana/o undergraduates on California campuses. Those undergraduates were divided among a range of different organizations including MASC across Northern California, UMAS around greater Los Angeles, MAYA in San Diego, and MASA at East Los Angeles College. Because of this, the students who gathered at UCSB committed themselves to uniting within a single new organization. The decision to do so seems relatively spontaneous—it was not one of the original goals set by the planning committee—and appears to reflect the influence of the larger-than-expected participation of student activists at the conference. As Carlos Muñoz later remarked, "The conference in Santa Barbara was not organized to deal with the student movement" proper; instead, its principal aim was to organize toward the greater matriculation of Mexican Americans at the UC and state colleges.[56]

Student organizers at the Santa Barbara conference agreed to combine forces as MECHA. As they explained in *El Plan de Santa Barbara*, conference participants believed that "all student organizations should adopt one identical name throughout the state and eventually the nation" as a first "step toward greater national unity which enhances the power in mobilizing local campus organizations."[57] Despite their general agreement that activists should unite within a common organization, it was at first unclear what name they should take. One conference participant, from MASC at UC Berkeley, pushed for the use of Spanish for the organization's new name. Carlos Muñoz, then a graduate student teaching at Los Angeles State

College, proposed CAUSA, in homage to La Causa of the United Farm Workers.[58] Other suggestions included COSA (Chicano Organization for Student Action) or RAZA. A number of comical and even vulgar acronyms scrawled on the back of a conference handout reflect both the exhaustion and good humor that characterized the late-night rap sessions that followed the daytime workshops.[59] In the end, MECHA hit all the right notes: it was in Spanish, it included the words *student movement*, and it referenced Aztlán, the Chicano homeland, which had so recently been popularized at the March 1969 Chicano Youth Liberation Conference in Denver.

The Santa Barbara conference served to give the Chicano student movement in California an even stronger sense of direction and greater unity as student activists worked to address the shortcoming of the Master Plan system. In the months following the conference, student attendees continued their work on campus and in the community. In particular, Chicano student activists worked to help build programs of ethnic studies on multiple campuses. As Carlos Muñoz later noted, "Students were really the people who were researching, who were looking for faculty, who were doing a lot of the legwork, meeting with academic senate people, meeting with the administration," and working on community outreach. "That's where the energy went after Santa Barbara."[60]

At the same time, the faculty, staff, and community organizers who made up the Chicano Coordinating Council on Higher Education continued meeting and working to prepare their Chicano Master Plan, *El Plan de Santa Barbara*, for publication. In the immediate aftermath of the conference, the conference steering committee and other select conference participants began editing to produce the final drafts of workshop reports.[61] Meeting in Santa Barbara, Los Angeles, and Oakland, they formed an editorial board tasked with "full responsibility for finishing a manuscript for publication." The board consisted of Rene Nuñez, Fernando de Necochea, Paul Sanchez, Juan Gómez-Quiñones, and Armando Valdez. The board charged Gómez-Quiñones and Valdez with completing the final editing.[62] Despite hopes to publish what organizers called their Master Plan by late May, meetings toward publication continued into the following months.[63]

In early April 1969, a small group of educators had declared their intention to make public higher education accessible and welcoming to Mexican American youth by coming together to draft and disseminate a Master Plan for Chicanos. Six months later, it was ready: in October 1969, the Chicano Coordinating Council on Higher Education published *El Plan de Santa Barbara*. The final product was more than 150 pages and included an opening manifesto, a bibliography and various models for Chicano studies programs, suggested courses, and a "barrio" community center. With the bulk of the publication organized into sections that derived from reports generated by conference workshops, *El Plan de Santa Barbara* was above all a group effort, the end product of some 140 conference participants. Yet in the estimation of conference participant Rodolfo Acuña, the central influences on *El Plan* "were definitely" Juan Gómez-Quiñones and Jesús Chavarría, young historians who had managed to find toeholds in the Master Plan system at San Diego State and UCSB, respectively. With regard to *El Plan*'s opening manifesto, Acuña argues that "the influence of Juan Gómez-Quiñones is all over the document."[64] By way of contrast, Carlos Muñoz claims that *El Plan*'s "analytic framework was based to a large degree" on the work of Chavarría.[65]

As the joint product of a wide group of thinkers and activists, *El Plan de Santa Barbara* synthesized the dominant perspectives of the Chicano movement on California's university and college campuses at the close of the 1960s.[66] *El Plan*'s opening manifesto begins by proclaiming a Chicano *renacimiento*, a rebirth. The authors posit that the Chicano people are now "expressing a new consciousness" of themselves, a people unique to history, armed with their own goals, "and a new resolve" to achieve equality and break with the oppressions of the past. In many ways, the manifesto is reflective of the strand of cultural nationalist thinking then making itself felt within the Chicano movement. Yet, the opening manifesto also tempers such cultural nationalism with a nod to the Marxism embraced by many activists, Chicanos no less than others, stating that "throughout history the quest for cultural expression and freedom has taken the form of a struggle." The authors recognize that such struggle has long characterized the Mexican experience in the United States. For the vast majority, life in the United States has meant serving as "suppliers of cheap labor," with Mexican neighborhoods remaining "exploited, impoverished, and marginal."[67] In order to break free from such a history of oppression, *El Plan* proposed that Chicanos organize to take advantage of a Master Plan system that had heretofore largely excluded them.

Beyond efforts to gain inclusion in the Master Plan system, the authors of *El Plan* understood their own work and organizing efforts as contributing to an even larger turning point in a long history of struggle. The term *Chicano* itself denoted an important shift. Where previously Chicano was a "pejorative and class-bound term," *El Plan* notes that contemporary usage of the term in the late 1960s "reveals a growing solidarity" and "signals a rebirth of pride and confidence." The combination of a cultural nationalist embrace of "Chicanismo" and the class consciousness reflected in a growing understanding of Mexican Americans as an exploited internal colony led to strident calls for "self-determination" for the Chicano community.[68] Ironically, such nationalism and self-determination would find remedy in institutions of higher education that were overwhelming controlled by white Americans.

For the authors of *El Plan*, higher education had an important role to play in the Chicano struggle. *El Plan* called for "a strategic use of education," noting "we believe that higher education must contribute to the formation of a complete man who truly values life and freedom."[69] The authors envisioned Chicano studies as a broad program of reform going beyond simple changes to the curriculum, arguing that it represents "the total conceptualization of the Chicano community's aspirations" as they relate to higher education.[70] As such, the authors called on "the university and college systems of the State of California" to make improvements including greater "1) admission and recruitment of Chicano students, faculty, administrators and staff, 2) a curriculum program and an academic major relevant to the Chicano cultural and historical experience, 3) support and tutorial programs, 4) research programs, 5) publications programs, 6) community cultural and social action centers." In addition to releasing *El Plan* for public consumption, conference organizers planned to mail copies to UC president Charles Hitch, state college chancellor Glenn Dumke, the UC Board of Regents, Governor Ronald Reagan, and more.[71] In total, *El Plan* represented a comprehensive series of demands on the power structure in California.[72]

El Plan de Santa Barbara represented a direct critique of the racial composition of higher education in California and, as such, of the 1960 Master Plan for Higher Education. The authors thus called on California's colleges and universities to "truly live up to their credo, to their commitment to diversification, democratization, and enrichment of our cultural heritage and human community." In this way, the authors of *El Plan* married a critique reminiscent of the Free Speech Movement's analysis of the modern multiversity as an alienating knowledge factory to the racialized exclusions embedded in a color-blind Master Plan for Higher Education. Firmly grounded within the long political traditions of the Mexican diaspora, the authors closed *El Plan*'s opening manifesto with a quotation they attributed to the revolutionary-era Mexican writer and philosopher Jose Vasconcelos: "At this moment we do not come to work for the university, but to demand that the university work for our people."[73]

Like Free Speech Movement activists before them, the authors of *El Plan de Santa Barbara* turned to the written record of Master Plan architect Clark Kerr in order criticize the system he had done so much to establish. To do so, *El Plan* quoted directly from Kerr's 1963 book, *The Uses of the University*. Drawing on Kerr's influential text, the authors of *El Plan* argued that "the inescapable fact is that Chicanos must come to grips with the reality of the university in modern society. . . . So far reaching is its power that the university today is widely acknowledged as being the single most important factor in social and economic growth."[74] Yet at the same time, *El Plan* took direct aim at Kerr's cherished Master Plan system. For instance, in *El Plan*'s section on student support programs for Chicanos, the authors noted that the California legislature's Joint Committee on Higher Education "has shown that students who are eligible for higher education do not enter a college or university because of insufficient financial support." The Chicano activists who gathered in Santa Barbara sought to move beyond the Master Plan's normative vision of a white middle-class student and called on the state to make higher education available to California's diverse working class by covering student fees and providing living stipends.[75]

According to *El Plan de Santa Barbara*, the full democratization of higher education depended on much greater Chicana/o enrollment. Where the Master Plan had tightened admission requirements for the UC and state colleges nearly a decade earlier, the Chicano Master Plan envisioned expanded access. In particular, the authors called for schools located in areas with a high population of Chicanos to enroll the same percentage of Chicano students as existed in the school-age population. For campuses located in areas with few, if any, Mexican Americans, they called for the enrollment of Chicano students at rates equivalent to their school-age population across California. What's more, *El Plan* appealed to administrators to become proactive in recruiting Chicano students. The authors denounced the "'standard' admissions criteria" as "culturally biased" and thus as "not reliable indicators of college success for Chicanos." Finally, beyond simply admitting more Chicano and Chicana students, *El Plan* demanded the hiring of Mexican American faculty, staff, and employees at all levels.[76]

Although most Chicanos had long viewed colleges and universities as elite and alienating institutions, *El Plan de Santa Barbara* demanded that they be made both accessible and beneficial to the Chicano community, and not solely to white, middle-class California. As such, although they promoted the greater matriculation of Chicana/os in higher education, the authors of *El Plan de Santa Barbara* still maintained fierce critiques of the educational status quo. The point was not simply to join the ranks of college graduates but, further, to change how higher education functioned. The authors recognized that "colleges/universities must be a major instrument in the liberation of the Chicano community." In part, student activists could utilize the university to that end by using "the resources open to the school for the benefit of the Barrio at every opportunity." Through such strategic action, El Plan's authors sought to realize an important goal: "our people must understand not only the strategic importance of the university, however; they must above all perceive the university as being our university." Through the establishment of Chicano studies and "the strategic application of university and college resources to the community," these Chicana/o activists hoped that the Chicano community might "come to benefit from the resources of the institutions of higher learning."[77]

Rather than a set of isolated suggestions for improvement, El Plan de Santa Barbara envisioned a series of reforms that would operate in concert to make higher education work for the Chicana/o community. Many scholars have rightly understood El Plan as an important document in the emergence of ethnic studies, yet its authors also imagined Chicano studies as one part of a larger whole. For instance, El Plan argued that "the elaboration of Chicano curriculum should be directly linked to the appointment of new Chicanos to the faculty." Further, they called on the university to grant credit "for community service when the service is correlated to course work." As such, Chicano studies would help promote the advancement of Chicana/o scholars and improvement in the lives of community residents. The authors also recognized the central role of student organizers and Chicano staff to the full functioning of Chicano studies programs, arguing that "the mutual accountability of student organizations and staff in these programs is clear: it is their responsibility to protect the program from influences which will co-opt the focus of the program." Thus, El Plan envisioned that students and student organizations, faculty, staff, and barrio residents would come together in a mutually reinforcing and self-supporting system to uplift the entire Chicano community.[78]

While calling for greater in-group solidarity among la raza, the activists behind El Plan de Santa Barbara recognized both the importance and potential pitfalls of engaging in interracial coalition building on and off campus. In the months that preceded the April 1969 Santa Barbara conference, Chicana/o student activists at San Francisco State had participated in the nation's longest student strike, from November 1968 to March 1969. As part of the Third World Liberation Front, members of MASC struck alongside the Black Student Union, the Latin American Student Organization, the Philippine American Collegiate Endeavor, and the Intercollegiate Chinese for Social Action. MASC activists at UC Berkeley also participated in a third world strike on that campus, from January to March 1969. Despite such recent examples, the authors of *El Plan* cautioned that "a careful analysis must precede the decision to enter into a coalition." What's more, they drew up a list of "questions [that] must be asked and answered before one can safely say that he will benefit and contribute to a strong coalition effort" on campus.[79] Armed with such an awareness, Chicana/o student activists participated in a host of formal and informal coalitions alongside Black, Asian, Native American, and white leftist counterparts across the UC, state college, and community college systems.[80] For instance, at Fresno State College, Mexican American and African American students would organize alongside one another to combat the structural racism inherent in the Master Plan system.

Envisioned as a "Chicano master plan for higher education," the 1969 *Plan de Santa Barbara* enumerated the shortcomings of the 1960 California Master Plan for Higher Education, while proposing concrete suggestions to overcome its racial exclusions.[81] *El Plan* called on colleges and universities to hire Mexican Americans as faculty, administrators, and staff; it proposed directing school resources to Mexican American barrios; and it called for the establishment of programs of Chicano studies. More than anything else, *El Plan* took aim at the Master Plan's admissions standards by demanding the matriculation of large numbers of Mexican American youth, despite the substandard educations many Chicana/os had received at segregated schools. Beyond simply calling on those in power to do the right thing, *El Plan* provided just that, a plan for effective organizing by students, faculty, administrators, and community members, to make the promise of the California Master Plan a reality—free quality higher education for all Californians, *incluyendo a Chicanos y Chicanas.*

The Struggle at Fresno State

Vibrant campaigns for change emerged as Chicana/o students and their counterparts organized on campuses across California, particularly in large urban centers like Los Angeles, San Diego, and the Bay Area. Yet even in smaller out-of-the-way cities and towns, Mexican American student activists joined in the fight. In Fresno, a medium-sized city in the San Joaquin Valley, organizing by student activists paralleled that of their counterparts on other campuses. Chicano and Chicana activists at Fresno State College organized alongside other student activists, demanding curricular changes so that their educations would better speak to the Mexican American experience and pushing for the recruitment of Chicana/o youth who did not meet the stringent admissions requirements first enacted by the 1960 Master Plan.

Interrogating the Chicano student movement at Fresno State helps to demonstrate the ways in which the concerns and strategies enumerated in *El Plan de Santa Barbara* played out in real time, while drawing attention to a city whose history has been overshadowed by that of its larger coastal counterparts. What's more, the movement at Fresno State showcases a unique struggle as student supporters of the United Farm Workers—many of whom were the children of farm laborers—sought to make a place for themselves in an agricultural school that had long catered to the needs of California's big farm owners.

On their predominantly white campus, Mexican American organizers allied with Black activists in seeking change at Fresno State. Much like at San Jose State and San Fernando Valley State, Black student activism at Fresno State began with the struggles of Black student athletes. Unlike at those schools, however, at Fresno State Chicana/o activists largely overshadowed their Black counterparts. Their influence was at least in part a reflection of their greater percentage within the student body and of the approximately 20 percent of Fresno County's population that was of Mexican descent.[82] Despite their predominance both on and off campus, Chicana/o activists chose to band together with their less numerous Black counterparts in an attempt to create a more diverse, more welcoming, and less Eurocentric college experience at Fresno State. To this end, Chicana/o and Black activists recruited working-class minority students to the school through a campus EOP, created programs of Chicano and Black studies, and even took joint control of a portion of the student newspaper so as to better communicate their desires and disappointments to the majority-white student body and campus administrators.

In conforming to the enrollment goals established by the 1960 California Master Plan for Higher Education, Fresno State experienced the sixties as a tumultuous transformation from a fairly conservative rural agricultural school into a college that was at once larger, more liberal, and more well rounded academically. The state of California had established Fresno State as a teachers' college, the Fresno State Normal School, in 1911. In 1950, the California legislature secured the purchase of 880 acres to relocate the growing college, over 80 percent of which would be dedicated to the study of agriculture.[83] The new campus was operational by 1953, and the former campus site became the home of Fresno City College.[84] Finally, in 1960, the California Master Plan incorporated Fresno State into the now centrally coordinated state college system. Like its fellow state colleges, Fresno State College would experience rapid student body population growth and the erosion of its previous local autonomy under the newly established board of trustees.

Even as Fresno State College expanded rapidly, Chicano and Chicana students had to fight for their rightful place on campus. Over the 1960s, the campus faculty lept from two hundred to eight hundred professors, and the student body from four thousand to thirteen thousand students. As the institution grew, Chicana/o and Black activists worked to increase the ranks of minority students at Fresno State. In the 1967–68 school year, only 190 Mexican Americans attended Fresno State College, a tiny island in an overwhelmingly white sea of nine thousand students. African Americans fared even worse, with only sixty-seven on campus that year. Yet, thanks to the development of a robust EOP, those numbers would increase. By the spring semester of 1970, Fresno State boasted a growing population of 763 Mexican American students, 6 percent of the total student body. Fresno State College's 351 African American students, in turn, by then made up 3 percent.[85] Thus, although still relatively small, Chicana/o and Black enrollment at Fresno State represented the fruits of a well-fought collaborative struggle against the discriminatory impact of the California Master Plan.

As was the case on most California campuses, at Fresno State organized Black student activism predated similar efforts by Chicana/os. Undergraduate Osby Davis came to the campus in the fall of 1966 with plans to play baseball and study engineering. Like his Black counterparts elsewhere, Davis had trouble finding off-campus housing near the school "because I was black," noting that "my white and oriental friends went to places after we had [been turned away] and they were offered apartments." Yet it was an on-campus incident, a racist remark made by a coach about Fresno's Black football players, that led to the founding of Fresno State's Union of Black Athletes (UBA) in late 1967.[86] Davis served as the UBA's first president. When Davis had begun at Fresno State, of the sixty-seven Black students on campus, "most were out-of-town athletes" recruited through the California Master Plan's 2 percent admissions exception rule.[87] Yet, the focus on organizing Blacks as athletes quickly turned toward an organization for all Black students, with the UBA becoming a BSU, the Fresno State Black Student Union. And like their counterparts elsewhere, the Fresno State BSU soon entered into coalition with Mexican American activists in an attempt to establish programs of ethnic studies and to bring greater numbers of minority students to campus.

Mexican American students at Fresno State College first organized politically as MASA in 1967.[88] In November of that year, Fresno State MASA agreed to join the growing regional organization MASC after attending a meeting held in Berkeley. Alex Saragoza, the MASA chapter president, explained the decision to join MASC as a necessary step in organizing Mexican Americans more effectively against ongoing and systemic racism, noting that "taking into consideration the discrimination leveled against Mexican-Americans in the last 100 years, it was inevitable FSC [Fresno State College] join MASC."[89] Despite their relative geographical isolation in the middle of the state, Fresno State's Chicana/o activists would now be plugged into a burgeoning MASC network, which included chapters across the Master Plan system, from UC Berkeley to the state colleges at Hayward, Sacramento, San Francisco, and San Jose.

In the summer of 1967, a small number of Fresno State faculty began organizing to counteract the discriminatory impact of the Master Plan admissions standards. Although faculty members laid the groundwork for the program that would become known as Project 17, their effort would eventually be taken over by Black and Chicana/o student activists. The program began with an informal discussion between three faculty members, one of them Black, about the problem of racism both on and off campus in Fresno. Discussions soon expanded to include two additional faculty and five administrators. In the words of one student journalist, the program was envisioned as a way to help "alleviate minority problems." More specifically, the faculty sought to take advantage of the Master Plan's 2 percent admissions exception rule to bring more minority students to campus. The inaugural class of Project 17 admitted ten Mexican American and ten African American students to Fresno State for the 1967–68 school year. Seventeen chose to enroll, giving birth to the program's name.[90] At that point, Chicano students made up just under 2 percent of the student body, with Black students representing less than 1 percent.[91]

Over the course of the 1967–68 school year, Mexican American and African American students pressured the administration to expand their efforts at recruiting minority students, and Project 17 was reborn as the Fresno State EOP. For September 1968, the campus administration agreed to admit a combined total of seventy-six Blacks and Chicana/os through the program. The EOP had recruited these students from high schools and community colleges in the greater Fresno area. Despite flagging financial support from the state, activists hoped to further expand the program. Fresno State EOP director Katherine Panas noted growing support for the EOP mission on campus, explaining to the student newspaper that "many teachers and students" have realized "that many more students could benefit from the program and this realization had made present EOP enrollment look like tokenism."[92] In addition to their efforts to expand the EOP, Chicano activists on campus continued to organize toward other goals.

In the spring of 1968, Chicano student activists at Fresno State formulated a list of demands that aimed to alleviate their isolation on that majority-white campus. The students called on campus administrators to hire a bilingual administrator and three Mexican American professors, with more Chicana/o faculty to follow in the years to come. In addition, they demanded the creation and maintenance of a special collection of books on Mexican and Mexican American history and culture in the college library. As student activist Guillermo Martinez cautioned the campus president, "We are tired of listening to flowery rhetoric." More than promises and platitudes, those backing the list of sixteen demands wanted concrete change. As Mexican American enrollment increased on campus, student activists were committed to making Fresno State a more welcoming place.[93] As if in immediate response to the students' demands, the *Daily Collegian* released an article the following day detailing the administration's efforts to combat "de facto segregation" on campus. In particular, the student newspaper outlined the goals of an administrative committee working toward "the hiring of minority faculty, more minority literature in the Library and curriculum additions of minority studies."[94]

Despite the administration's rhetorical commitment to combating racism, new tensions flared in November 1968, as Chicana/o students called on Fresno State to boycott grapes in support of the United Farm Workers. Thanks to the campus's location in the San Joaquin Valley, Fresno State had long served as a center for the study of agriculture, the industry around which the valley itself revolved.[95] At a school sometimes jokingly referred to as Grape State Tech, the United Farm Workers boycott thoroughly angered a segment of white Aggies, some of whom came from farm-owning families. Queried by the *Daily Collegian* as to the merits of the boycott, one viticulture major responded by stating that "my father is a Delano grape grower. . . . It's not our fault the farm workers are at the bottom of the ladder." Ultimately, the student senate voted fifteen to eleven to oppose the boycott. Chicana/o activists responded with an impromptu protest with about sixty participants. As they marched across the quad, white agricultural students threw scab grapes at the protesters.[96]

Despite such conflict, campus president Frederick Ness moved to demonstrate his commitment to easing the racial burden on Fresno State's isolated Chicano and Chicana students. In February 1969, President Ness approved the development of a Chicano studies program, which would be known at Fresno State as La Raza studies. Ness took the opportunity to simultaneously approve a program of Black studies. Both new programs would be incorporated into the School of Arts and Sciences.[97] Later that month, Ness announced his appointment of Eliezer Risco as the chair of La Raza studies and the hiring of Roberto Rubalcava as the school's first Mexican American administrator.[98] An immigrant from Cuba, Risco had been an organizer of the 1968 high school walkouts in East Los Angeles and was active as a member of the planning committee for the then-upcoming April 1969 conference in Santa Barbara.[99]

Building on their early gains, Chicana/o and Black activists pushed for further institutional support at Fresno State. In September 1968, Chicano activist George Garcia had requested Mexican and African American representation in the student senate.[100] The following month, a group of Chicana/o and Black students put forward a proposal for the procurement of a room in the College Union building. The room would serve multiple purposes, including as "a central office for Chicano and black history and culture classes" and a tutorial aid center.[101] Although Garcia's bid for minority senate representation failed, the College Union board approved the activists' request for a room in the building.[102] Later that year, a coalition of Chicanos and African Americans protested Governor Reagan's proposal to cut $2.5 million in funding from the state EOP budget.[103] In response, President Ness promised to work alongside the protesters and interested faculty "to provide greater educational opportunities for minority students."[104] The following week, Fresno's MASC and BSU chapters held a joint rally, attended by approximately eight hundred students, to promote even greater administrative and financial support for the campus EOP and ethnic studies.[105]

In the spring semester of 1969, activist Guillermo Martinez successfully petitioned to secure weekly control of Fresno State's student newspaper for Chicana/o and Black students. In recognition of the social isolation faced by minority students on the white-majority campus, the Fresno State College board of publications agreed to cede control of the *Daily Collegian* once a week.[106] Alternating weeks, *La Voz* and *Uhuru* editions of the paper allowed Chicana/o and Black students, respectively, to communicate with the student body at Fresno State.[107] In the first issue of what they called a Chicano-Black coalition paper, Chicano editor John Ramirez promised that "Chicano and Black students" would seek "to use this paper to unite and not to incite . . . for together is the only real way we can seek and build a better world." With that in mind, Ramirez took the time to thank their "Black brothers and sisters" in the struggle.[108] Even as they built up their alliance with the BSU at Fresno State, MASC activists helped students at Fresno City College to organize a chapter on their own campus.[109]

Moving forward, Chicana/o and Black students continued their alliance, utilizing their weekly editions of the *Daily Collegian* to fight back against an attempted counterrevolution on campus. The turmoil began in October 1969 when President Ness terminated the appointment of Marvin X, a well-liked new hire in the burgeoning Black studies program. When word of the firing became public, some two hundred students, mainly Chicana/os and Blacks, marched on the Administration Building in support of the young professor.[110] In the coming weeks, a large coalition of students and faculty emerged to protest the dismissal; these included the student senate, the bulk of Chicana/o and Black students on campus, and the majority-white campus branch of the Students for a Democratic Society.[111] Sandwiched between liberal faculty and student protesters, on the one hand, and a conservative governor and board of trustees, on the other, the liberal president Ness resigned his post, citing "inexcusable pressures."[112] Subsequently, Chancellor Dumke appointed Karl Falk as acting president. A staunch conservative, Falk had taught for years in the Department of Economics before retiring to serve as president of a local Fresno bank.[113]

Faced with the hostility of the conservative Falk administration, Chicana/o and Black activists struggled to win the removal of the ineffective and unpopular director of the campus EOP. The students charged the director, Walker Munson, with being inaccessible to students and failing to maintain a fully functional EOP.[114] President Falk refused to meet with students, dismissing their charges and warning them that the future of the EOP itself was in danger. Furthermore, Falk advised the study body that state college chancellor Glenn Dumke's office had "verbally directed" the state colleges not to accept any new EOP students for the fall of 1970 until further notice.[115] For the Chicana/o and Black students at Fresno State, threatening the EOP in toto was simply unacceptable.

Borrowing a page from Cesar Chavez, thirteen Chicana/o activists began a weeklong hunger strike in defense of the EOP and ethnic studies on

March 1, 1970. The protesters laid out a series of demands including the admission of five hundred Chicano EOP students in the fall of 1970 and a plan to bring the percentage of Chicanos on campus up to par with the surrounding area. In Fresno, this would mean 20 percent of the student body. In addition, the hunger strikers demanded the retention and hiring of a number of Chicano administrators and the creation of eight new faculty positions in La Raza studies.[116] The hunger strikers swelled to a group of twenty who spent the week in a makeshift camp set up on the ground in front of the Administration Building.[117] On Friday, as the strikers prepared to clean up camp and end their strike, they were visited by a group of white students from the agricultural department. The two groups, campus Chicanos and campus aggies, had long sparred verbally over farmworkers' rights. The taunts that strikers had endured all week turned to fists as white students attacked the Chicanos, who were weakened after five days without food.[118] This physical violence was but the first of many blows to Chicano organizing efforts at Fresno State in the months to come.

In the spring of 1970, a range of new developments imperiled the victories previously won by Chicana/o activists and their Black allies. Toward the end of the semester, a revanchist campus administration targeted students and faculty in a campaign that a contemporary journalist for *The Nation* described as "the strangulation of Fresno State." After the National Guard massacred four student protesters at Kent State University in Ohio, a wave of protest hit California campuses. Student protesters physically attacked Reserve Officers' Training Corps (ROTC) buildings at UC Berkeley and UC Davis and at six state college campuses, including Fresno.[119] On May 12, more than five hundred Fresno State students, including members of MECHA, participated in an on-campus march against the war.[120] Later that week, and only days after police shot and killed two students at Jackson State in Mississippi, the new computer center at Fresno State College mysteriously went up in flames.

Given the rash of ROTC bombings that followed in the aftermath of the killings at Kent State, it seems likely that anti-war activists destroyed the computer center. Like other such early campus computers, Fresno State's computer center served to track students' grades, facilitating administrative efforts to keep local draft boards abreast of students' eligibility for military service at the height of the Vietnam War. Yet, campus administrators fingered a different culprit in the Black Student Union. Although administrators never explained why the BSU might target the computer center specifically, they alleged that members of the group were angry over the administration's recent announcement that eight out of twelve ethnic studies instructors would not be rehired for the coming year.[121] In the aftermath of the bombing, President Falk declared a state of emergency, brought large numbers of police to campus, presided over the arrest of forty-six students, and cut off all funding to the student newspaper, the *Daily Collegian*.[122] That done, Falk's tenure as acting president came to an end. His replacement, Norman Baxter, would begin the following school year on a conciliatory note but continued the anti-EOP and ethnic studies policies initiated by his predecessor.

At the start of the 1970–71 school year, the new Baxter administration announced the cancellation of La Raza studies for the fall semester. Administrators claimed the move stemmed from pragmatic rather than political roots—they had simply failed to hire anyone to teach the classes.[123] Yet when pressed on the issue, Baxter admitted that "philosophical differences" between the administration and La Raza studies contributed to the decision.[124] What's more, Baxter refused to consider a list of ten candidates for La Raza instructors submitted by Chicana/o students and community members.[125] In response, over one hundred Mexican American and African American students held a long protest during the fall registration for classes. When campus security forces confronted the demonstrators, the protest turned violent, and the administration suspended a mixed group of six Chicano and Black activists for their participation.[126]

The announcement of suspensions targeting key figures in the EOP and ethnic studies inflamed campus sentiment. An editorial in the *Daily Collegian* voiced the widespread opinion that the administration had singled out certain individuals in an effort to "purge key student leaders in the movement for a relevant Ethnic Studies program."[127] Those suspended included the Chicano EOP leader Richard Nieto and financial aid counselor Chris Hernandez, as well as Black EOP leaders Carol Bishop and Julius Brooks.[128] Thanks to the widespread outrage that followed the suspensions, including formal complaints by the student government and the threat of a lawsuit, President Baxter reinstated five out of the six.[129] According to campus activists, Baxter had hoped to neutralize important figures "in the Educational Opportunities Program and Ethnic Studies Program."[130] Thanks to student organizers, all but one of the suspensions were quickly overturned, yet EOP and ethnic studies activists continued to face administrative harassment.[131]

The following months witnessed what onlookers nationwide deemed a purge of liberal faculty at Fresno State, and although ethnic studies and the

EOP would continue on the campus, they remained on the defensive.[132] The spring semester of 1971 saw the return of La Raza studies after a semester-long absence in the fall.[133] Still, campus and community activists remained wary. A Chicano student community organization called La Mesa Directiva warned that La Raza studies survived at Fresno State as only "a loose composite of borrowed faculty from other departments," rather than the autonomous department activists had once envisioned.[134] An editorial in the *Uhuru* edition of the *Daily Collegian* contrasted the then-current mood on campus with that of the late 1960s, when "Fresno State College [had] promised to do everything possible to reduce the suffering for Black Americans" and "Black, Brown and White people worked together to reduce the suffering at Fresno State."[135] When Governor Reagan proposed yet another austerity budget for the state colleges in 1971, Fresno State's EOP was further imperiled. Chicano student Lalo Acevedo spoke out against the budget plans in the student newspaper, arguing that "Reagan's financial cutback of the E.O.P. is an example of institutionalized racism" and a blow to "equal opportunity in education."[136]

Despite the many obstacles they had faced, Chicana/o and Black activists at Fresno State would continue their long tradition of marching together in solidarity.[137] In June 1972, Chicana/os and all EOP activists won an important victory when Lupe De La Cruz was elected student president. The son of migrant farmworkers and an EOP student himself, De La Cruz would serve as Fresno State's first Chicano student president in its sixty-one-year history. In an interview with the *Daily Collegian*, De La Cruz promised skeptical readers that he would "be president for all of the students," not just "the minorities." Queried about plans for his life after graduation, the rising senior spoke to an important lifelong goal: "to help more poor people take advantage of government programs like EOP." He continued, noting that "I hope I won't get trapped on the success ladder. . . . Many Chicanos get their education and leave and don't put anything back into the Community. I'm proud to be a Chicano."[138]

Through the efforts of student activists like Lupe De La Cruz—Chicana/os and Blacks alike—the EOP would continue at Fresno State for many decades to come, helping to mitigate the de facto segregation embedded in the California Master Plan. Yet, such a history is not limited to Fresno State alone. As we have already seen, struggles toward the greater democratization and diversification of higher education emerged at San Jose State and San Fernando Valley State as well. The following chapter turns to the even wider emergence of interracial solidarity at the UC, state college, and community college levels. Typically led by Black and Chicana/o students, the coalitions that activists built across the Master Plan system brought African Americans and Mexican Americans together with whites, Asian Americans, Natives, and Latina/os in an effort to increase the matriculation of working-class students of color through the utilization and further expansion of the admissions exceptions embedded in the 1960 California Master Plan for Higher Education.

6 Their Struggle Is Our Struggle

. . . .

> The planners, in 1959, seemed blissfully unaware of the effects of
> racial discrimination and segregation on education. They did not even
> mention race as one of the main obstacles to the achievement of an
> adequate education.
> —Magali Sarfatti Larson, 1970
>   (San Francisco State professor of sociology)

> The demand for an entire School of Ethnic Studies, accessible to the
> entire nonwhite community, flies in the face of the Master Plan and
> the whole trend toward elitism in California education.
> —William Barlow and Peter Shapiro, 1969
>   (San Francisco State student journalists)

In January 1969, the student newspaper *Open Process* published its interview with the leaders of the Third World Liberation Front (TWLF) strike at
San Francisco State College. The strikers had recently entered into the third
month of what would become the longest student strike in the history of
the United States. *Open Process*, an underground newspaper published by
students at San Francisco State, represented the large and largely white New
Left milieu from which the TWLF drew consistent support. And although
San Francisco State in 1968–69 remained predominantly white, the leaders of the strike represented a diverse array of self-declared third world
revolutionaries.

Open Process interviewed TWLF central committee members Roger Alvarado and Tony Miranda of the Latin American Students Organization
(LASO), Benny Stewart of the Black Student Union (BSU), Jesus Contreras
of the Mexican American Student Confederation (MASC), Ed Ilamin of
the Philippine American Collegiate Endeavor (PACE), and Mason Wong
of the Intercollegiate Chinese for Social Action (ICSA). In discussing the
strike's relationship to the institutional structure of higher education
in California, LASO's Roger Alvarado noted that "the whole function of
the state educational system is to produce human resources for the industries and businesses that the [state college] Board of Trustees represent."

Furthermore, noted the BSU's Benny Stewart, "governor [Reagan] says higher education is a privilege, not a right. We say that all human beings have a right to live, therefore they must have a right to work, and it has become a reality that if one is going to work one must have an education." MASC's Jesus Contreras agreed. Pointing to the conditions faced by California's Mexican American population, Contreras lamented that "there are now more Mexican Americans in prison than in higher education in California."[1]

For the leaders of the TWLF, the principal goals of the strike were the expansion of access to higher education for young people of color and the institutionalization of autonomous departments of ethnic studies. Although people of color then made up nearly 60 percent of San Francisco high school students, Roger Alvarado argued that "this population is not reflected in Third World attendance at [San Francisco State] because Third World students are systematically excluded from colleges throughout California."[2] As Alvarado and his fellow TWLF organizers well knew, such institutional racism had been exacerbated by the 1960 Master Plan for Higher Education.[3] As such, Alvarado made note of the TWLF's goal of increasing third world special admissions to San Francisco State. Speaking to the strikers' other main demand, PACE's Ed Ilamin argued that educational institutions like the state colleges "perpetuate the racist and manipulative values that presently prevail. . . . This goes right to the heart of the School for Ethnic Studies which is set up to develop a set of human values defined by our own cultures, not by white culture." LASO's Tony Miranda concurred and added that contemporary education is "not simply a matter of not including what our culture is about, what our history is about. . . . It's a process of mis-education."[4]

Finally, those student leaders gathered for discussion with *Open Process* noted the importance of the model that the TWLF had established for other campuses as well as minority communities across the United States. As Roger Alvarado explained, "Third World people exist in this country in colonized ghettoes and have a colonial relationship to the established political, economic and social structures which rule this country. So it is a basic necessity that our people come together and form a united front. . . . It is only in this manner that Third World people will be able to achieve liberation."[5] Building on the words of his LASO comrade, Benny Stewart argued that "our job is to become a model and set political examples for all Third World people. . . . Third World people are natural allies." Stewart continued, "We see ourselves developing along the lines of revolutionary nationalism. . . .

So where radical whites are struggling with us . . . we see them as allies."[6] As *Open Process* journalist Peter Shapiro would reflect decades later, the strike represented "a real breakthrough" because it was "the first time you had these different nationalities cooperating. It's not just a black thing. Everybody was in on it."[7]

Rejecting the Master Plan

Even beyond the TWLF strike at San Francisco State, in the late 1960s, California became home to the most diverse and the most intense student struggles in the United States.[8] These campus-based movements spanned the range of California's public college and university campuses, from the privileged UC, and the massive California state college system, to the sprawling network of then more than eighty community colleges. Across these three levels, the 1960 California Master Plan for Higher Education had fortified the institutional racism and structural inequality against which students rebelled.[9]

Throughout the state, student protest was driven by twin forces: primary and secondary critiques of the California Master Plan. First, for the diverse cadres of Black and Brown, Asian American and Native American, and their white allies in struggle, the 1960 Master Plan represented a racist piece of legislation that channeled young people of color down California's public education hierarchy to the community colleges in an attempt to save money for the state. After all, the Master Plan had both lowered the percentage of students admitted to the UC and state colleges and reduced the use of special admissions from 10 percent to 2 percent of incoming students.[10] George Murray, a Black Panther and a leader of the BSU at San Francisco State, noted as much when he complained that "there are four and one half million black and brown people in California, and they all pay taxes for the racist departments here, but none of their taxes go to black and brown people."[11] Murray's criticism—that people of color paid the same taxes but were not afforded equal educational opportunities as white Californians— became a mainstay of the student movement's analysis. In response, student activists across California aimed to dismantle institutionalized racism by institutionalizing anti-racism in the form of Educational Opportunity Programs (EOPs) and through the establishment of programs, departments, and colleges of ethnic studies.[12]

In addition to the primary critique of the institutional racism embedded in the California Master Plan, students and faculty criticized the loss of faculty autonomy and student initiative that the Master Plan had inaugurated. This was especially true at the state college level, where the Master Plan created the state college board of trustees, a powerful institution modeled on the UC Board of Regents. Prior to the Master Plan, California's board of education had governed the state colleges. At the UC, the regents steadily encroached on campus autonomy as a dominant conservative bloc emerged within the board following the election of California governor Ronald Reagan. Conservatives on both the UC Board of Regents and state college board of trustees proved decidedly hostile to faculty attempts at workplace organizing, to the appointment of leftist faculty, and to the autonomous student control of campus institutions such as experimental colleges, activist-oriented student-run programs, and campus newspapers. Regent and trustee intrusions into such traditionally independent realms widened support for ongoing student struggles.[13]

The twin critiques of the Master Plan—focusing on its intrinsic racism and the loss of campus autonomy the plan engendered—guaranteed a diverse base of support for the student movement. While campus activism should be understood first and foremost as a response to the racism inherent in the Master Plan, striking students viewed the regents and trustees, and especially Governor Reagan, as the agents and beneficiaries of a racist social order. Rejecting such student critiques, this educational power elite played its part in a dialectic of repression and rebellion with their numerous incursions into campus affairs. Governor Reagan, the regents, and the board of trustees pressured recalcitrant campus administrators in their attempts to coordinate a unified response to student protest in the late 1960s. As such, Reagan and his allies fired or forced the resignations of numerous liberal and moderate campus presidents, while seeking to employ and empower campus administrators more amenable to their notions of law and order. In addition, Reagan and other conservatives' demands for police action in response to student protest led to thousands of arrests, the injury and hospitalization of countless students, and increased support for the embattled strikers from both previously apathetic students and diverse communities of color located across California.[14]

Rather than fostering a narrow nationalism, the racial exclusions embedded in the California Master Plan inspired a wave of multiracial activism on public campuses across the state. California's diverse population impacted its student movement in ways historians have yet to fully acknowledge.[15] In the late 1960s, interracial solidarity in the form of multiracial coalitions flourished across UC, state college, and community college campuses. Most commonly, these alliances took the form of working coalitions between Black and Chicano students struggling to establish or enlarge EOPs and programs of ethnic studies. At the same time, African American and Mexican American students typically gained support from white allies, most often in the form of campus branches of the Students for a Democratic Society (SDS). On certain campuses, this Black-Brown-white trio expanded to include Native Americans and Asian Americans. This occurred most famously with the 1968–69 TWLF strike at San Francisco State. While such coalition politics developed most fruitfully in the Bay Area, interracial solidarity flourished all around as students formed strategic alliances on California's many public campuses.

The interracial solidarity of the late 1960s student movement in California, although far from inevitable, grew out of the racialized exclusions of the Master Plan for Higher Education. Coalitions in support of campus-based EOPs sought to expand access to the top tiers of the Master Plan educational hierarchy and, succeeding in doing so, helped to mitigate the very structural racism that had inspired such alliances. With the successful implementation and expansion of EOPs and ethnic studies on virtually all of California's public campuses, a vibrant era of interracial solidarity in the California student movement would largely come to a close.

The Roots of the Educational Opportunity Program

The renewed wave of civil rights activism that came with the Greensboro, North Carolina sit-ins of February 1960 reached all the way to California. By that time, civil rights organizing in the golden state had developed most intensely in Los Angeles and the Bay Area. The Los Angeles branch of the National Association for the Advancement of Colored People (NAACP) began to organize against racism in the schools, including segregation and a lack of Black teachers, in the early 1950s.[16] As the civil rights movement picked up speed in the South between 1960 and 1964, white Californians grew increasingly aware of the racial discrimination and de facto segregation that existed within their state's borders. Within this context, Republican assemblyman Stewart Hinckley introduced a bill to the California legislature in 1963 that proposed to establish a state loan program for working-class California college students. In Hinckley's own words, his bill "aimed to discourage high school dropouts, particularly members of minority groups, who quit because they can't afford to go on to college." Yet, Hinckley's bill failed to gain traction and quickly disappeared from the historical record.[17]

Despite the fact that some of the most radical sectors of the California student movement took up the demand for EOPs in the late 1960s, the EOP had decidedly moderate roots. In December 1963, then–UC president Clark Kerr attended a meeting of the Rockefeller Foundation to examine proposals for the greater recruitment of minority students at Dartmouth and Princeton.[18] Impressed by the proposed programs, Kerr, in his own words "returned to California convinced that we should follow their example." The following month, the regents approved funds for the development of a minority scholarship program on the Berkeley campus. The program's backers framed their work as "a memorial to President John F. Kennedy's contributions to the civil rights movement and his recognition of the role of scientific and intellectual activity in our society."[19]

The first EOP in California began at UC Berkeley and soon spread to other campuses across the state. The EOP started at the UC level in the 1964–65 school year with an inaugural enrollment of approximately one hundred students. In 1966, the EOP began at the state colleges with a paltry eighty-six students. Centralized planning for EOP at the community college level began only in 1969. Despite sharing a common name, early iterations of campus-specific EOPs differed greatly from one another. At Fresno State College, as we have seen, the EOP developed out of the earlier faculty-initiated program known as Project 17. On certain campuses, members of student organizations such as the BSU and the United Mexican American Students (UMAS) took on the responsibility of running the school's EOP program. Yet, despite the labor provided by activists on such campuses, formal control ultimately remained in the hands of administrators. Depending on the specific school, EOPs provided a diverse range of services, including recruitment, preparatory summer programs, tutoring, mentoring, and work study funds. At the UC and state college level, a majority of EOP students matriculated through the use of the special exceptions rule embedded in the 1960 Master Plan's admissions standards. Not until April 1969, with the passage of Senate Bill 1072, did California provide for a statewide comprehensive EOP.[20]

The California Student Movement

One of the most important organizations dedicated to establishing and expanding EOPs across California was the BSU, the first of which formed at San Francisco State College. Originally founded as the Negro Students Association at San Francisco State in 1963 and led by Mariana Waddy, the organization changed its name to the Black Student Union in April 1966.[21] Jimmy Garrett, a twenty-year-old activist with the Student Nonviolent Coordinating Committee (SNCC) and recent transfer student, soon took on a leadership role within the newly christened BSU. Garrett and his fellow activists commenced a study of conditions at the school, focusing on the history of twentieth-century San Francisco and, in his words, "the founding of the state college system and the master plan."[22] The conditions generated by the 1960 California Master Plan for Higher Education were thus not only felt but also consciously recognized at the birth of the nation's first BSU. The following months and years saw BSUs organized on campuses including the California state colleges at Dominguez Hills, Fresno, Long Beach, Los Angeles, and San Fernando Valley; UC campuses in Davis, Los Angeles, Riverside, San Diego, and Santa Barbara; and at community colleges such as Compton City, Diablo Valley, East Los Angeles, El Camino, Fresno City, Laney, Los Angeles City, Los Angeles Southwest, Merritt, Mount St. Antonio, Pierce, Sacramento, San Bernardino Valley, and San Francisco City College.[23]

The contrast between the San Francisco State and Valley State BSUs illustrates the high degree of ideological diversity that existed between autonomous chapters. At San Francisco State, myriad ties connected the BSU to the Oakland-based Black Panther Party for Self-Defense. Graduate student George Murray served as a leader in both organizations. As the BSU member and Black Panther Terry Collins put it, "A lot of people who were in the Black Student Union were also in the Black Panther Party."[24] Given their overlapping membership, it is no surprise that the San Francisco State BSU largely shared the Oakland Panthers' embrace of socialism and revolutionary nationalism. As a political tendency, in contrast to San Francisco State, the BSU at San Fernando Valley State maintained ties with Maulana Karenga's Los Angeles–based US organization. At least one Valley State BSU member was a former member of US, and Karenga himself visited and spoke on campus.[25] As such, the BSU at Valley State remained highly influenced by the cultural nationalism of an organization the Panthers denigrated as "pork chop nationalists" and "United Slaves."[26] Despite their internal variations, as Harry Edwards noted in 1970, the emergence of BSUs represented the shift from "the integrationist-phase of the student movement" to an era of "Black liberation struggle."[27]

In the mid-1960s, Mexican American students formed a number of different campus organizations across California. As occurred with Black students, a loose division emerged between Mexican American student groups in Northern and Southern California. As Arturo Rosales notes, many "Mexican Americans became radicalized in the heady college atmosphere of the Bay Area."[28] In Southern California, at least in the early sixties, Mexican American students tended to eschew the politics of class struggle, adhering more closely to the assimilationist politics of the so-called Mexican American generation of the 1940s and 1950s. In 1964, Armando Valdez founded the nation's first Mexican American student organization, Student Initiative at San Jose State. Valdez was a member of SDS and a supporter of SNCC. By late 1967, Student Initiative reorganized as the campus branch of a larger regional network of MASC chapters. Mexican American students at UC Berkeley and the state colleges at Fresno, Hayward, Sacramento, and San Francisco likewise formed chapters of MASC. Starting in April 1967, Mexican Americans on various campuses in Southern California organized as UMAS with chapters forming at UCLA and UCSB as well as the state colleges at Long Beach, Los Angeles, and San Fernando Valley.[29] At East Los Angeles College, a predominantly Mexican American community college, students organized as the Mexican American Student Association (MASA). Mexican Americans organized as the Mexican American Youth Association (MAYA) at UC San Diego (UCSD), San Diego State, and San Diego City College, as well as Sacramento City College.[30] By the early 1970s, most of these organizations would reestablish themselves as branches of MECHA, El Movimiento Estudiantil Chicano de Aztlán.[31]

In April 1969, more than one hundred Mexican Americans from across California gathered for a three-day conference at UC Santa Barbara. Attendees included student activists, educators, and administrators who sought to increase Mexican American access to higher education. In particular, the conference planners hoped for "Chicano students and faculty from California universities and state colleges [to] come together to discuss their vision of a master plan for Chicanos in higher education comparable to the California Master Plan in Higher Education."[32] Those assembled drafted *El Plan de Santa Barbara*, which took direct aim at the shortcomings and racial exclusions of the 1960 California Master Plan. *El Plan* announced the intentions of conference participants to expand the recruitment and retention of Mexican American students at institutions of higher education. In addition, it called for the development of Chicano studies on college campuses and for organizers to work toward "redirecting university attention and resources to the needs of Mexican American students and Mexican Americans communities." Finally, conference participants recommended that existing Mexican American student organizations replace their current names to unify across California and the nation as MECHA.[33]

Throughout California, white New Leftists contributed crucial numbers and support to the struggles led by Blacks and Chicanos to establish EOPs and ethnic studies. SDS dominated the white left. Formally established in 1960, within a few years, SDS chapters were ubiquitous in California, and across much of the United States.[34] Yet by then, SDS suffered from internal conflicts with members of the Progressive Labor Party (PL) who had set about to infiltrate and take over the influential organization. In 1969, conflict with the Maoist PL would split SDS from within, first on campuses like San Francisco State and later that year at the national level.[35] The white campus left also contained a number of smaller organizations, including branches of the Independent Socialist Club (soon to become the International Socialists), the DuBois Clubs (Communist Party USA), the Young People's Socialist League (Socialist Party of America), the Young Socialist Alliance (Socialist Workers Party), and various anti-war organizations. What's more, many individual white students supported programs of affirmative action and ethnic studies much as they embraced drug use and other aspects of the burgeoning counterculture. Whether through political organizations or on their own, white students active within or on the periphery of the New Left consistently lent their support to the struggles of Black and Chicano student activists.

Chinese, Japanese, and Filipino Americans in California also contributed to ongoing student struggles that were predominantly led by Blacks and Chicanos.[36] In doing so, many came to rethink their own place in American society, giving birth to a pan-ethnic Asian American self-identification for the first time. Organizations like San Francisco State's ICSA and PACE, respectively founded in late 1967 and early 1968, organized along ethnic lines.[37] But in May 1968, UC Berkeley's Asian American Political Alliance (AAPA) was founded as the first organization to unite a diverse Asian student population as Asian Americans.[38] Over the summer, a second AAPA chapter formed at nearby San Francisco State. Such organizing efforts quickly bore fruit in the form of Asian American participation and leadership in the TWLF strike at San Francisco State and the third world strike at UC Berkeley. At Sacramento City College, Asian students participated in a campus coalition as Asian Students in Action Now (ASIAN).[39]

In Southern California, Asian American students quickly followed the lead of their Bay Area counterparts. In early 1969, five students at UCLA founded *Gidra*, an influential monthly newspaper with a focus on Asian America.[40] The establishment of *Gidra* foreshadowed a wave of Asian American activism at UCLA, including the founding of an AAPA chapter and the establishment of a "High Potential Program for young Asian Americans who are unable to meet the financial and academic requirements" established by the Master Plan.[41] In September 1969, students from UCLA, UC Davis, and UC Berkeley organized the first nationwide conference on Asian American studies, hosted on the Berkeley campus.[42] At UCSD, student activists created the Asian American Student Alliance (AASA) in 1970. The AASA formally aligned with those Black, Chicano, and white students who, since the previous year, had been organizing toward the creation of Lumumba-Zapata College at UCSD.[43] By 1970, UCSD activist Phyllis Chiu noted that "Asian-American students have organized in almost every college campus in California."[44]

As part of the wider arrival of the American Indian movement, Native Americans also participated in student struggles to diversify California campuses and institutionalize ethnic studies.[45] In the 1960s, approximately one out of every six American Indians resided in California, yet their population on California campuses remained close to nonexistent.[46] In 1968, UC Berkeley students LaNada War Jack (Shoshone Bannock) and Patty Silvas (Blackfeet) strove to overcome their isolation on campus by organizing the Native American Student Association. At San Francisco State, Native students inspired by the TWLF strike formed the Student Council of American Natives.[47] Similar organizations followed at Long Beach State College and UC Davis.[48] In November 1969, the Indians of All Tribes—a broad coalition including students from UCLA, Berkeley, and San Francisco State—seized Alcatraz Island in San Francisco Bay. Among other demands, the Indians of All Tribes called for the establishment of a Center for Native American Studies.[49] Around the same time, at UC Davis, scholars Jack Forbes (Powhatan) and David Risling Jr. (Hoopa) developed what would become the first Native American studies program to grant the doctorate.[50] Native American studies programs also emerged at UC Berkeley, UCLA, and the state colleges at Long Beach, Sacramento, San Francisco, and Sonoma.[51] Finally, in March 1971, Jack Forbes secured land for the establishment of an autonomous Native university to be controlled by Native peoples.[52]

On late 1960s California campuses, various "national" groups came together on the basis of third worldism. Alliances known as Third World Liberation Fronts formally united Black, Latina/o, Native, and Asian activists on certain campuses. Third worldism drew strength as a political current from diverse New Left struggles at home, the ongoing wave of anti-colonial rebellions abroad, and explicitly socialist movements including those in Cuba, China, and Vietnam. This political tendency blurred the lines between domestic and international politics, allowing minority activists in the United States to identify with a global majority that, for a time, seemed it might eliminate the last vestiges of colonialism, racial oppression, and an exploitative capitalist system with its bases of strength in Europe and North America. Drawing on the Marxist tradition, third worldism expanded on orthodox Marxism's singular emphasis on the proletariat as revolutionary subject to include the peasant, in the third world, and the (often racialized) lumpenproletariat, in the first world.[53] Both on and off campus, third worldists were influenced by the writings and examples of Frantz Fanon, Mao Zedong, Che Guevara, Ho Chi Minh, Amilcar Cabral, and more.[54]

Third worldism helped various racial groups understand their oppression in a comparative framework, facilitating the alliances that defined California activism in the late 1960s and early 1970s. For a time, the development of third world solidarity in California tempered a tendency toward cultural nationalism and an attendant assertion of one's in-group as unique in its experience of racial and economic oppression. As one third world activist put it, "We have made a commitment—not only to our own people, but to Third World peoples, and we are willing to stand up against the injustices and the indignities that have been shown to all people of color."[55] Much as the nations of the Global South shared the unfortunate history of a brutal and exploitative European colonialism, the various "internal colonies" within the United States—Blacks, Chicanos, Latinos, Natives, and Asians—had a common foe in racial capitalism.[56] Where racially homogenous organizing developed on both regional and California-wide bases, interracial alliances were largely campus specific, even as the TWLF at San Francisco State provided an influential model. Aside from the formal TWLFs that were organized at San Francisco State, UC Berkeley, UC Davis, Sacramento City College, and the College of San Mateo, interracial alliances developed under various other names, including the Lumumba-Zapata coalition at UCSD and the United Front at UCSB.[57]

In January 1969, members of the Young Socialist Alliance at Merritt College, a community college in Oakland, succinctly explained their support for the ongoing TWLF strike at San Francisco State by noting that "their struggle is our struggle."[58] That simple expression of solidarity best explains the network of mutual support, official alliances, and ad hoc associations that characterized the diverse California student movement of the late 1960s. As a vibrant coalition of Black, Chicano, Latino, Asian Native, and white students struck for affirmative action and ethnic studies at San Francisco State College, students at other state college campuses, at the UC, and at the state's many community colleges pledged their support. The bonds of solidarity extended horizontally across different racial and political groups as well as vertically, up and down California's three-tiered educational hierarchy. Activists at the UC strategized with their counterparts at the state colleges, organizations active on state college campuses helped establish new branches at nearby community colleges, and former community college organizers brought new experiences and insights with them when they transferred to the state colleges and UCs. Interracial solidarity and cooperation defined the student struggle in California. In the heady years of the late 1960s and early 1970s, coalition, not competition, was the rule rather than the exception.

The State Colleges

Originally teachers' colleges, the California state colleges began with the 1857 founding of what would become San Jose State. By the mid-1960s, the state colleges consisted of eighteen different campuses. Renamed the California State University in 1972, the former state colleges remain to this day the largest four-year university system in the United States. In line with the dictates of the Master Plan, the state colleges grew more selective over the course of the 1960s, reducing those admitted from upward of the top 45 percent of high school graduates to a hard 33 percent. Still, the state colleges remained more accessible than the significantly smaller UC system, and unlike the community colleges, they granted the four-year bacherlor's degree. As such, matriculation to the state colleges became the goal of broad swaths of California's minority and working-class youth for whom the elite UC often seemed decidedly out of reach.

San Francisco State represents something of an anomaly within the California state college system. The campus boasted the nation's first experimental college, the first DuBois Club, and the first BSU.[59] Founded in late 1963 as the Negro Students Association and reborn as the BSU in 1966, the organization emerged out of San Francisco State's demographic shifts. Peter Shapiro, a former student journalist at San Francisco State, notes that in the mid-1960s, "it was rapidly becoming a virtually lily white campus."[60] Prior to the Master Plan and the statewide tightening of both admissions standards and exceptions, San Francisco State had a sizable Black student population. In 1960, African Americans made up 12 percent of the student body at San Francisco State, approximately equivalent to their percentage of the population in San Francisco. Yet by 1968, years after the

Master Plan admissions standards went into effect, African Americans had dropped to 4 percent of the student body.[61] The BSU at San Francisco State struggled to halt that decline, whereas on other state college and UC campuses, activists fought to expand a Black population that had always been miniscule.[62]

The stringent entrance requirements introduced by the 1960 Master Plan made it much harder for African Americans educated in de facto segregated Bay Area schools to gain entrance to San Francisco State.[63] As former San Francisco State president John Summerskill reflected in 1971, in the 1960s, "minority students, usually from the poorest high schools, were squeezed out."[64] Proportional to their percentage in the city of San Francisco, Blacks, and people of color more generally, were drastically underrepresented on campus in the late 1960s. Although accounting for 59 percent of San Francisco's high school students, people of color made up a disproportionately small 14 percent of San Francisco State's eighteen thousand students in 1968.[65] African Americans and Asian Americans each represented roughly 13 percent of San Francisco's population but only 4 percent and 8 percent of San Francisco State students, respectively. Latinos made up 14 percent of all San Franciscans, yet accounted for a dismal 1 percent of the student body.[66] San Francisco State's dean of admissions acknowledged in 1969 that "almost half of the San Francisco people we admit come from private schools."[67] Such private institutions catered to an overwhelmingly white student population. Throughout the 1960s, working-class people of color, whose segregated and underfunded public schools often left them ill prepared for college, increasingly found themselves channeled toward local community colleges rather than UC or state college campuses.[68]

In March 1968, student organizers at San Francisco State announced the formation of the TWLF. The front functioned as "a loose coalition whose member organizations would still enjoy complete autonomy to do as they saw fit with respect to the policies established by the central committee."[69] The TWLF formally consisted of members of six race-based campus organizations: the BSU, MASC, LASO, PACE, ICSA, and AAPA.[70] Students involved in the front brought to that coalition varying histories of involvement in community and radical struggle. Some, like the BSU's Jimmy Garrett, had organized with SNCC and other Black-led civil rights organizations. LASO organizer Roger Alvarado previously developed a working relationship with the BSU while serving as the campus director for a community-based tutorial program, teaching literacy skills to local children.[71] As Peter Shapiro notes of ICSA, prior to the strike, "a couple of ex-Marines from Chinatown took over the Intercollegiate Chinese for Social Action, which had been this very stuffy academic . . . achiever type of organization. They turned it into a political thing." ICSA, alongside other nationalist student organizations on campus, was at that point "moving very rapidly to the left."[72] Such development toward revolutionary internationalist politics, rather than liberal or cultural nationalist positions, established the conditions necessary for a functioning multiracial alliance.

The TWLF engaged in a number of actions at San Francisco State prior to the decision to go on strike. On May 21, 1968, several hundred students, led by members of the TWLF and SDS, occupied the campus administration building.[73] The occupiers presented the administration with a list of four demands including the special admission of four hundred minority students in the fall of 1968; the creation of eleven teaching positions in support of minority students; the retention of Mexican American history professor Juan Martinez; and the termination of the campus Air Force Reserve Officer Training Corps (AFROTC) program.[74] In response, then-president John Summerskill agreed to rehire Martinez as the head of a planned Center for Ethnic Studies.[75] Furthermore, Summerskill promised to admit four hundred third world students through special admissions and announced that nine out of twelve new faculty hires for the coming year would be directed toward support for the incoming minority students. Regarding the matter of campus AFROTC, Summerskill announced plans for a college-wide referendum.[76] Governor Reagan and state college chancellor Glenn Dumke responded promptly by firing the campus president.[77]

The following fall semester, when Reagan and Dumke once again sought to apply pressure on campus, the TWLF responded by going on strike. On September 26, 1968, the state college board of trustees voted to request the suspension of graduate student, BSU member, and Black Panther George Murray from his position as an instructor in the English department. Chancellor Dumke had met with the newly hired San Francisco State president Robert Smith a week earlier to discuss firing Murray. Smith refused, noting that Murray had received "high marks as a very effective teacher."[78] On October 8, hundreds of students, including members of the TWLF and SDS, participated in an on-campus rally addressing a wide range of concerns, including the trustees' attack on Murray. Demonstrations organized by the TWLF and SDS in support of Murray continued throughout the month. Furthermore, having petitioned for a Black studies program for more than five years and still without faculty or funding, the BSU prepared for action.[79] On October 28, George Murray and BSU chairman Benny Stewart called for a student strike to begin on Wednesday, November 6. On November 1, President Smith reluctantly followed orders from Chancellor Dumke to suspend George Murray for the coming thirty days.[80]

On November 4, the BSU held a press conference in which they laid out a ten-point list of strike demands. To reverse the impact of the Master Plan's admissions standards at San Francisco State, they demanded open admissions for Black students in the fall of 1969. In addition to the retention of George Murray as an English instructor, the BSU called for the full and prompt development of a degree-granting Black studies department, complete with faculty positions. Wary of the steadily encroaching power of the state college board of trustees, the BSU called for Black studies to operate autonomously from the board.[81] Finally, the BSU demanded preemptive amnesty for their upcoming strike action. In support of their BSU allies, the TWLF brought not only a large group of organized student radicals but also their own five-point set of demands to supplement those of the BSU. Most importantly, the front demanded open admissions for all third world students and an entire School of Ethnic Studies.[82]

The strike began on November 6, 1968, with broad support from the TWLF, SDS, a broad swath of faculty and students, and a number of on-campus labor unions.[83] Within twenty days, the pressure Governor Reagan and the board of trustees placed on President Smith over the strike led to his resignation. He had lasted less than six months, the majority of which consisted of summer vacation.[84] For the remainder of the strike, the TWLF would have to contend with a staunch conservative in the office of president. In the wake of Smith's resignation, the board of trustees named S. I. Hayakawa acting president of San Francisco State. A part-time English instructor, Hayakawa served as the leader of a small group of right-wing San Francisco State professors known as the Faculty Renaissance. Hayakawa had previously emerged as an early critic of the Free Speech Movement (FSM). The FSM, Hayakawa wrote in late 1964, "is a travesty on the concept of free speech."[85] Frustrated with the board of trustees' sidestepping of the campus Faculty Selection Committee and standard procedure in selecting campus presidents, unionized faculty voted to request strike sanction from the San Francisco Labor Council.[86]

Strike supporters utilized the subsequent winter vacation to publicize their quest to reform the Master Plan system. Over the break, members of the front wrote and distributed a pamphlet elaborating their position and outlining the opposition they had stood down thus far. The TWLF explained to its readers that "for three years we have sought greater representation of third world peoples on the SF State campus; and for three years there have been no significant results. . . . SF State has remained a college representing only the white community, while blacks, chicanos, Phillipinos, Japanese, and Chinese are for the most part denied entrance." The TWLF stressed the hardships student strikers faced, ranging from police violence on campus to the hostility of Governor Reagan. As such, they called for greater support from third world peoples across the Bay Area, arguing that "our struggle will only be won when members of those communities come to the support of their students who have dared to stand up and confront the California political structure with demands for meaningful change."[87]

In a sign of greater faculty support to come, a number of San Francisco State professors expressed their solidarity with student strikers in a series of articles and op-eds. *Open Process* published an incisive analysis by a young philosophy professor. Anatole Anton praised what he called a "fight over mass public education" which aimed toward "creating a new future for ourselves." Rejecting what he saw as a nearsighted interpretation of the conflict, Anton claimed that "the decline of S.F. State began not with the advent of Reagan, but in 1959–60 with the institution of the Master Plan for Higher Education." The Master Plan, Anton argued, produced an unjust hierarchy that channeled working-class students downward, keeping the UC white and wealthy, while a regressive tax structure forced California's poor to pay for an educational system that further disadvantaged them.[88] Professor Arthur Bierman, a leader of San Francisco State's American Federation of Teachers (AFT) campus local, likewise published a pro-strike op-ed in the *San Francisco Bay Guardian*. Ten days later, Bierman and the rest of AFT Local 1352 went out on strike, inaugurating the first faculty strike in California history and providing a significant boost to striking students.[89]

Union solidarity and community support bolstered strikers as they continued to face arrests and police violence throughout January 1969. As many as four hundred professors joined the strike, representing one-third of the entire faculty. Indian American strike leader Hari Dillon argued that the faculty "added enormous strength to the strike."[90] At the start of the new semester, AFT members estimated that class attendance had dropped by as much as 80 percent.[91] Meanwhile, off-campus supporters planned the Community Conference to Support the San Francisco State Strike to better organize community aid for striking students and help in the fight against "institutionalized racism." Affirming "that [contrary to Ronald Reagan's opinion] higher education is a right, not a privilege," these community supporters demanded both Hayakawa's resignation and the removal of police from the campus. The conference was organized by more than forty individuals representing of a diverse range of ethnic community organizations, religious groups, and labor unions.[92]

As the strike continued, student activists were increasingly bogged down in legal troubles, and the AFT reached a tentative agreement regarding their own grievances. By February 1969, police had made a total of nearly seven hundred arrests. Following their disruption of an on-campus speech by Hayakawa, police arrested Nathan Hare, the tentative head of the Black Studies program, and three others.[93] Hayakawa suspended Hare for thirty days and warned that he had already begun interviewing potential replacements for the Black sociologist. What's more, Hayakawa announced that 187 striking faculty members had been fired, but he left often the possibility of their rehiring should they cease to support the strike.[94] At the same time, AFT Local 1352 announced a provisional strike settlement. As the *Daily Gater* noted, "One basic AFT demand . . . has been sacrificed in the compromise, [which] is the settlement of the student demands."[95] The end of the faculty strike after two months on the picket line would prove a major blow to striking students.

On March 20, 1969, student leaders from the TWLF announced the end of the strike. As early as February 26, representatives of the front had initiated secret meetings with the administration and the board of trustees.[96] The combination of police violence, looming court cases, and the settlement of the faculty strike had worn down student resolve to continue what was by then a four-and-a-half-month-long student strike. The more than seven hundred students arrested during the strike faced both disciplinary hearings on campus and cases in court.[97] No matter the grit and determination of student strikers, President Hayakawa, Governor Reagan, and the board of trustees had the full force of the state, its courts, and its police forces behind them. The strike agreement, in the words of student journalists Bill Barlow and Peter Shapiro, "was a bitter pill that the TWLF found necessary to swallow."[98]

As the revolution envisioned by some of its supporters, the strike at San Francisco State ended in failure. Yet in winning important reforms to their corner of the Master Plan system and in inspiring activism on other campuses, it proved remarkably successful. After 134 days on strike, representatives of the TWLF reached an agreement with the campus administration's six-member Select Committee.[99] The agreement acknowledged that the administration of San Francisco State had already moved to meet various strike demands and was in the process of meeting others. A number of demands, however, would remain unfulfilled. Although the strike succeeded in pressuring the administration to move toward the creation of the long-awaited Department of Black Studies, the proposed director, sociologist Nathan Hare, would play no part in its future at San Francisco State. Strike leaders Nathan Hare and George Murray, fired by President Hayakawa, never returned to the college. After announcing the settlement in a press conference on March 21, Hayakawa nonetheless refused to sign the agreement brokered by his Select Committee.[100] As *Gater* editor Dikran Karagueuzian noted in his memoirs, Hayakawa "would later say that it was only a series of recommendations."[101] Yet the EOP and ethnic studies would move forward despite Hayakawa's continuing hostility.

The TWLF strike succeeded both in increasing the enrollment of third world students at San Francisco State and in establishing ethnic studies on campus. The strike created the nation's first School of Ethnic Studies. In addition to a BA-granting Black studies department, the school included La Raza studies and Asian American studies. The college would soon add American Indian studies.[102] In this way, the strike successfully challenged the Eurocentric curriculum at San Francisco State. The TWLF also struck a blow against institutional racism by winning the expanded admission of students of color. The agreement ending the strike raised the Master Plan special admissions exceptions to 10 percent of incoming students at San Francisco State, and the campus administration promised to begin actively recruiting nonwhite students for the first time.[103] Such an agreement promised to mitigate the trend in which admissions standards set by the Master Plan had forced California's minority students into the comparatively underfunded community colleges for remedial education and vocational training. Finally, the TWLF at San Francisco State provided a model that activists across California would come to emulate.

Although San Francisco State represented a hotbed of activism in the late 1960s, student protest and interracial alliances flourished at all levels of the Master Plan system. In addition to San Francisco State, as we have seen, Black and Chicano organizers at Fresno, San Jose, and San Fernando Valley State successfully exerted mutually reinforcing pressure on their campus administrations to expand EOPs and ethnic studies. Similarly, collaborative efforts emerged around the same years at campuses as distinct as UC Berkeley, UCSB, and UCSD, on the one hand, and Merritt, San Mateo, and East Los Angeles community colleges, on the other.

The University of California

At UC Berkeley, student activists took note of developments at nearby San Francisco State to form their own TWLF and go out on strike. Although growing increasingly diverse thanks to EOP efforts, UC Berkeley remained disproportionately white in the late 1960s. The student newspaper the *Daily Californian* estimated that whites made up 90 percent of Berkeley students in the 1966–67 school year, with the rest predominantly Asian American. The campus of 26,000 then included approximately 236 Blacks, 68 Chicanos, and 36 Native Americans.[104] In September 1967, Berkeley's EOP enrolled nearly four hundred students of color, 65 percent of whom entered under the Master Plan's 2 percent admissions exception rule.[105] When UC Berkeley's third world strike began in late January 1969, the campus was home to a total of eight hundred EOP students.[106] Formed earlier that month, Berkeley's TWLF united the Afro-American Student Union, MASC, and the AAPA. Striking students consisted of Blacks, Chicanos, Latinos, Asian Americans, and Native Americans, with additional support coming from the white campus left and Berkeley's AFT Local.[107] At the start of the strike, the front presented the Berkeley administration with a list of five demands. These included funds for the establishment of a Third World College of Ethnic Studies in the fall of 1969; greater recruitment of "Third World people in positions of power"; admission, financial aid, and tutoring for third world students, and the expansion of community tutorial programs; control of third world programs by third world people; and a pledge granting amnesty to all those on strike.[108]

After almost two months, a combination of fierce repression and administrative concessions helped to bring Berkeley's third world strike to a close. The strike featured numerous arrests and police violence, including the injudicious use of billy clubs, tear gas, and even helicopters, as well as the eventual deployment of National Guardsmen equipped with bayonets.[109] In addition to the arrest of 115 students and the administrative investigation of 144 for breaking university rules, UC administrators expelled strike leaders Jim Nabors of the Afro-American Student Union and Manuel Delgado of MASC.[110] In early May, forty-two days into the strike, the UC Berkeley faculty voted 550 to 5 in favor of establishing an ethnic studies department.[111] The department included Afro-, Mexican, Native, and Asian American Studies programs that would begin offering classes in the fall of 1969.[112] For the twenty-eight-year-old Delgado, who prior to his expulsion had planned to attend law school at Berkeley in the fall, the strike represented a real success. In Delgado's view, the strike helped speed the creation of a College of Ethnic Studies at UC Berkeley "by at least a year and a half," in part because, in response to the strike, "the faculty came around" to support ethnic studies.[113] The TWLF at UC Berkeley did not win all of its aims; notably, it did not achieve full autonomy for the College of Ethnic Studies, nor did it secure amnesty for striking students. Despite such shortcomings, the coalition between Black, Chicano, and Asian American organizations at UC Berkeley demonstrates the strength of interracial alliances in the movement to diversify and democratize even the most elite of the Master Plan campuses.[114]

Blacks and Chicanos at UCSB likewise engaged in coalition building to increase their numbers on campus in spite of the Master Plan's stringent UC admissions standards. With a population of some 13,000 students, UCSB included approximately 138 Black and 136 "Mexican or Spanish American" students in 1968. These included EOP students, as the program began operation at UCSB in the spring of 1966.[115] Isolated on and alienated from the majority-white campus, Mexican American students formed a UMAS branch in early 1968. Around the same time, Black students first organized as Harambee (Swahili for "let's pull together") and later as the BSU. On October 14, 1968, BSU activists occupied the campus computer center in UCSB's North Hall. Within hours, over one thousand students had gathered outside of the building in support of the occupation and the BSU's demand for Black studies. As one UMAS leader noted of the BSU takeover, "Spiritually we were with them." In fact, the BSU invited three Chicano students to join in. As a result, at least three Chicanos participated in the nearly ten-hour-long BSU occupation. Black and Chicano activists promised mutual support moving forward, and in the coming months, BSU and UMAS organizers attended rallies in support of the EOP and ethnic studies.[116]

Frequent collaboration between Blacks and Chicanos at UCSB soon led to the developed of the United Front, which brought together the BSU, UMAS, and SDS. Together, the United Front sought to force the administration to act on a list of ten demands, including the hiring of Black and Chicano administrators and faculty, the admission of five hundred Black and five hundred Chicano students in the fall of 1969, and the expansion of the Master Plan special admissions rule to 10 percent. In February 1969, the United Front held a rally that culminated in a weeks-long occupation of the University Center building. There, student activists held classes on topics such as "Black Nationalism" and "The Chicano in the Revolution." Although the occupation eventually ended, it established an on-campus tradition that would continue as the New Free University, an institution in the mold of the experimental colleges that had first been established at San Francisco State. While UMAS soon withdrew from formal membership in the United Front, a subsequent public announcement stated that nonetheless, "Chicanos recognize and support the struggle for liberation of all oppressed people—Brown, Black, Yellow, Red and White." Subsequently, UMAS activists channeled their energy on campus toward the development of Chicano studies and the April 1969 conference that would draft *El Plan de Santa Barbara* as a "Chicano 'Master Plan'" and establish MECHA.[117] At the same time, the BSU continued its work toward the establishment of a Black studies department, which would open in the fall of 1969.[118] In addition to securing the establishment of ethnic studies, Black and Chicano activism on campus fomented what one scholar would call the EOP boom times of the 1969–70 and 1970–71 school years. Years later, May 1974 witnessed a rebirth of the United Front as Black, Chicano, Asian American, and Native American students organized for a reinvigorated campus EOP.[119]

At UCSD, a forceful rainbow coalition of Black, Chicano, white, and Asian American students emerged to fight for Lumumba-Zapata College—an effort to expand the Master Plan's special admissions rule to cover an entire college.[120] In 1960, UCSD was established some fifteen miles north of downtown, in the wealthy white enclave of La Jolla.[121] The first undergraduates arrived in 1964. The university campus developed as a series of residential colleges, and by 1969, university administrators planned the opening of the third such college for the coming school year.[122] In early March 1969, a group of sixty Black and Chicano students met with the UCSD chancellor to unveil their vision for the new college, as presented in a document read by then–graduate student Angela Davis. According to the chancellor, faculty and administrators had envisioned Third College as an "idealistic" effort geared toward "the promotion of equal educational opportunity and improvement of communication between blacks and whites." Inspired by third world Marxism and the recent struggles at San Francisco State, UC Berkeley, and elsewhere, Davis and her fellow activists put forward a highly detailed and much more combative vision for Third College.[123]

Where faculty had proposed the name of Martin Luther King College, student organizers responded with their proposal for Lumumba-Zapata College in recognition of the Black-Chicano alliance that powered the movement. The name referred to Patrice Lumumba, the first democratically elected leader of postcolonial Congo, and Emiliano Zapata, the leader—

alongside Pancho Villa—of the Mexican Revolution of the 1910s. Reading from a text coauthored by members of the Black Student Council (BSC) and MAYA, Angela Davis denounced both the "quantitative exclusion of people of color" from the university and the "quality of what is taught." As such, Davis and her BSC-MAYA comrades put forward a vision embracing the twin goals that they shared with other students of color in the Master Plan era: greater recruitment and retention of people of color to California campuses and the inauguration of ethnic studies programs. In particular, their demands called for Lumumba-Zapata College to "have an enrollment of 35% Blacks and 35% Mexican-Americans . . . selected on the basis of their potential by an admissions committee controlled by minority students." Crucially, the statement demanded that the Master Plan's "University of California admissions requirements must not be used as an instrument for excluding minority students or limiting their numbers in Lumumba-Zapata College."[124]

Like the TWLFs at San Francisco State and UC Berkeley, the Lumumba-Zapata Coalition demanded the establishment of an entire College of Ethnic Studies, rather than a single program or department. Yet, the content of Lumumba-Zapata College was to differ in key respects from the proposed colleges of ethnic studies on those Bay Area campuses. Where San Francisco State and Berkeley grouped their courses in Black, Chicano, Asian American, and Native American studies, the Lumumba-Zapata movement proposed a different format. Courses at Lumumba-Zapata College would revolve around nine key categories of study: revolutions; analysis of economic systems; science and technology; health sciences and public health; urban and rural development; communication arts; foreign languages; cultural heritage; and white studies.[125] The proposed fields represented the impact of Marxist revolutionary internationalism on the proponents of Lumumba-Zapata College. The inclusion of white studies reflected what Angela Davis described as their goal of serving the needs of not only students of color but of "white students of working-class origin" as well. As Davis noted of the effort, "White students were involved from the outset, since one very important aspect of our demands was the integration into the college of white students from working class backgrounds."[126]

With third world strikes at San Francisco State and UC Berkeley looming ominously in the background, the UCSD administration conceded to the Lumumba-Zapata demands rather than risk an outright rebellion on campus.[127] Early on, campus sentiment had swung in favor Lumumba-Zapata, with both the Associated Students Senate and the Academic Senate passing resolutions in support of the demands.[128] However, as Angela Davis would later note, "Those of us leading the movement knew that despite our victory—of which all of us were very proud—Lumumba-Zapata College would never become the revolutionary institution we had originally projected. Concessions were going to be inevitable, however the creation of the college would bring large numbers of Black, Brown and working-class white students into the university."[129] Despite the student victory, the university administration refused the proposed name of Lumumba-Zapata College.[130] Controversy over its name notwithstanding, the interracial struggle at UCSD helped change the face of the campus. Where students of color made up less than 4 percent of the student body in 1968, their number increased to 11 percent by 1970 and would reach 19 percent by 1980.[131]

The Community Colleges

In comparison with the UC and state colleges, very different circumstances existed across California's extensive network of two-year community colleges. When the Master Plan for Higher Education tightened admissions standards for the UC and state colleges, the number and percentage of high school graduates channeled into the locally funded community colleges greatly increased. Although color-blind in theory, in practice the changes often resulted in the emergence of majority-minority campuses. And as schools like Oakland's Merritt College became increasingly Black and campuses like East Los Angeles College grew more and more Brown, third world students struggled for ethnic studies and self-determination through coalition building in California's community colleges. Some community college students, like those at Sacramento City College, organized their own TWLF, explicitly modeling their efforts on the struggle at San Francisco State. The Sacramento City front brought together activists from the BSU, MAYA, ASIAN, and the predominantly white Students for Constructive Action Now.[132]

Students at the College of San Mateo organized their own TWLF in support of ethnic studies and their EOP, known there as the Campus Readiness Program. Located in one of the richest counties in California, only about one hundred minority students were enrolled on the eight-thousand-student campus in 1966. Thanks to the initiation of an EOP, that number had reached nearly one thousand by 1968. Since any high school graduate could attend, EOPs at community colleges did not offer help in admissions; instead, they recruited minority students and offered counseling, tutoring, and financial aid. In late 1968, tensions at the College of San Mateo flared when the administration failed to provide promised financial aid to EOP students, resulting in the abrupt withdrawal of almost two hundred students.[133] When college administrators responded to ongoing protests by firing the head of the Campus Readiness Program, the former SNCC activist Bob Hoover, many of the remaining third world students left as well. Hoover subsequently established the Nairobi Schools in East Palo Alto, an institution that spanned from a preschool to a community college. Although predominantly Black, Nairobi College was founded as "a 'Third World College,' reflecting the mix of Black and Mexican American students who had attended" San Mateo through the Campus Readiness Program. The Nairobi Schools represent an ambitious educational project that was one of a kind in the United States. However, the Mexican American community began to move away from the institution in the mid-1970s, and Nairobi College shuttered its doors in 1981 due to a lack of funding.[134]

At East Los Angeles College, located in a predominantly Mexican American neighborhood, Mexican American student activists supported their highly outnumbered Black counterparts. Student organizers founded a campus branch of MASA in 1967, by which point the student body of nearly twelve thousand was more than 40 percent Mexican American. In December 1967, MASA activists attended the statewide Mexican American collegiate convention. Originally planned to take place at East Los Angeles College, the convention had been relocated to the nearby University of Southern California instead. Interestingly, for a Chicano conference, the most highly attended workshop was a talk given by two BSU members on the topic of revolution. After the 1968 assassination of Martin Luther King Jr., Black and Chicano students at East Los Angeles College came together to demand ethnic studies. Chicano student activists from organizations including MASA, La Vida Nueva, and the Brown Berets aligned with and supported Black students despite African Americans making up only 6 percent of the student body. In early 1969, Chicano activists organized a student walkout in support of the BSU. Although the Chicano-Black alliance ultimately failed to establish Black studies on campus, Chicano activists won the first Mexican American studies department at any community college in the United States. In 1973, East Los Angeles College gained its first Mexican American president, only one month after San Jose City College became home to the first Mexican American college president in the state.[135]

In an inversion of the racial dynamic at play in East Los Angeles, Black community college students at Merritt College in downtown Oakland organized alongside their Chicano and white counterparts. A hotbed of activism, Merritt College helped birth the Black Panther Party for Self-Defense, as cofounders Huey Newton and Bobby Seale first met as there as students in 1962.[136] Merritt grew to such notoriety in the late 1960s that the *Wall Street Journal* described it, nestled on Oakland's Grove Street in "a sprawling black slum," as the "campus where black power won."[137] Norvel Smith, California's first Black college president, quickly pointed out in response to the *Wall Street Journal*'s less-than-laudatory coverage, that minority instructors on campus represented 20 percent of the faculty, "the highest in the state among institutions of higher learning."[138] Merritt also earned the distinction of being the first California community college to offer classes in Black studies.[139]

The transformation of Merritt College to a Black power stronghold began with the introduction of the new admissions standards mandated by the 1960 California Master Plan for Higher Education. As Master Plan admissions went into effect at the UC and state colleges, from 1964 to 1969, African Americans as a percentage of the Merritt College student body increased from 10 percent to 40 percent.[140] Student activists at Merritt in the late 1960s remained cognizant of the impact of the 1960 Master Plan's admissions standards, arguing that "under the Master Plan, social stratification has been intensified. . . . The universities handle primarily upper-income students, while third-world students are relegated to junior colleges." Such colleges, they claimed, remained plagued by "drastic classroom overcrowding" and an "average drop out rate [of] 90% in the first year."[141] As Rasheed Shabazz has documented, with demographics shifting at Merritt College, "Black students sought increased power on campus through the establishment of Black Studies, hiring Black faculty and staff, and taking over the student government."[142] Yet by 1971, in the wake of victories won by Black student activists and their allies, California education officials proposed the relocation of the community college from Grove Street in the Black North Oakland flatlands, to the white East Oakland Hills. Although the proposed move had been debated for over a decade, historian Donna Murch notes that "many speculated that campus militancy had hastened the move."[143]

In the late 1960s, a diverse coalition of Merritt College students began organizing to block the proposed relocation. In an acknowledgement of the interracial solidarity that had developed on campus, a flyer printed and distributed by Merritt SDS argued that "what has been presented to the people as a move to expand education is in fact a plan which will divide white from black students."[144] Although plans proceeded apace for the new campus, a number of student activists proposed that rather than fight the relocation, students should work toward the creation of a majority-Black university on the soon-to-be-abandoned Grove Street campus. As activists in the Soul Students Advisory Council wrote, "We feel that the black university is the next step after a black studies department."[145] With that goal in mind, the council organized a conference in the spring of 1969 toward the creation of a Black university at Merritt College. Speakers included Ruth Hagwood of the Black Panther Party, the former San Francisco State sociologist and Black studies director Nathan Hare, San Francisco State BSU chairman Benny Steward, and Berkeley councilman Ron Dellums, among others.[146] As the effort to establish community control of the college continued, Merritt BSU members raised the question "Can we buy Merritt campus?" The BSU estimated that students would need to raise approximately $3 million to purchase the campus, a large but not insurmountable sum.[147]

Despite Black leadership and the nationalist bent of the movement for community control at Merritt College, the effort remained an interracial one. Yet another flyer published and distributed by Merritt SDS called for community control by a unified front of "Blacks, Chicanos, and white working class youth" and warned students "not to let any[one] divide us."[148] Evidence suggests that organizers made real efforts toward the creation of a rainbow coalition in defense of Merritt, in part inspired by the efforts of the Black Panthers, the (Latino) Young Lords, and the (white) Young Patriots in Chicago. Arthur Turco, the cofounder of a Young Patriots splinter group, the Patriot Party, visited and spoke at Merritt College in April 1970. A flyer advertising his talk called on "poor whites [to] join forces with other oppressed liberation movements to obtain self-determination for everybody."[149] In the dying days of the Grove Street campus, activists maintained a two-day occupation of the administrative offices. The almost one hundred occupiers represented a broad coalition of campus organizations including the BSU, the Chicano Student Union, and the Revolutionary Studies Group, among others.[150] Yet when met with the force of "a platoon of 100 riot-ready police officers" and promises by President Norvel Smith to expel or suspend the "ringleaders of the takeover," the occupation came to a close.[151] Despite the best efforts of campus organizers, officials shuttered the Grove Street campus of Merritt College in 1971.

A parallel yet quite distinct movement at the community college level emerged with the efforts of Native American and Chicano activists to establish Deganawidah-Quetzalcoatl University (DQU). In March 1971, Jack

Forbes—a Native American professor of history at UC Davis—succeeded in petitioning the federal government to grant 647.9 acres of land and ten buildings with which to develop DQU on the site of a former U.S. Army facility on the outskirts of Davis.[152] Forbes's analysis of structural barriers like the Master Plan admissions standards, and the unfolding of student movements toward ethnic studies added special impetus toward the creation of DQU. As Forbes would later write in an unpublished study of admissions standards at the UC, "the University of California's admissions policies are, in fact, policies of exclusion or restriction of access. This restriction of access appears both before and since the adoption of the Master Plan." The UC, Forbes notes, "denies direct access to about 85% of high school graduates." The state colleges, he might have added, denied admission to 66 percent. As the Master Plan admissions standards worked toward what he called "the reproduction of the existing social class structure," Forbes believed that a Native-Chicano university could help counter the maintenance of inequality in California higher education.[153]

DQU opened its doors in September 1971 as a private two-year community college.[154] Seven months earlier, some four hundred Native Americans and Chicanos had participated in the election of DQU's board of directors. In its earliest years, the board included sixteen Native Americans and sixteen Chicanos.[155] During DQU's first year of operation, the student body of one hundred consisted of a mixture of "dropouts, migrants, kids from reservations and East Los Angeles, and anybody else who walks onto its campus." Recommended tuition ran at twenty dollars per unit, but with students expected to contribute as best they could afford.[156] The campus offered a mixture of the liberal arts and vocational training, all infused with "a Native American or Chicano orientation" and geared toward the betterment of reservation and barrio communities.[157] In 1972, the Western Association of Schools and Colleges accepted DQU as a candidate for accreditation. Full accreditation as a two-year college came in 1977, with DQU then authorized to award associate's degrees.[158] Despite harassment on the part of the Reagan administration in the 1980s, DQU remains on-site today, albeit unaccredited since 2005.[159]

· · · · · ·

From the TWLFs of San Francisco State and UC Berkeley, and the Lumumba-Zapata coalition at UCSD, to the cross-racial solidarity of UCSB, Merritt College, and East Los Angeles College, interracial alliances emerged at all levels of the California Master Plan system of public higher education. With the founding of institutions like Nairobi College and DQU, these coalitions went as far as establishing private community colleges that fell outside the purview of the Master Plan. By the early 1970s, however, the need for such interracial solidarity seemed increasingly less urgent. With the goals of increasing third world enrollment and establishing ethnic studies already won, incoming minority students tended to focus on their studies or on more insular in-group organizing. Largely victorious on campus, radical multiracial activism declined alongside the larger New Left in the early 1970s. As the tide turned, dramatically so by the middle part of that decade, what coalitions then remained fell apart, and individual organizations like the BSU and MECHA, and institutions like EOPs and ethnic studies programs tended to lose ground.[160]

Although student activists certainly did not win everyone over and may indeed have alienated some from their cause, their victories remain. Campus-based organizers founded new California institutions in the EOPs and ethnic studies programs that remain on campuses to this day. They also formed an important pillar of a coalition—grounded in the continuing efforts of the Vietnamese people and later American GI resistance—that ended the war in Vietnam. These were no small tasks. The institutionalization of ethnic studies has both broadened the intellectual landscape and, in counteracting a Eurocentric curriculum, made college campuses a more welcoming place for young people of color. EOPs, in turn, have helped bring thousands of Black, Chicano, Latino, Asian American, Native American, and working-class white students to college classrooms across California. In doing so, the institutionalization and expansion of campus EOPs served to rectify the California Master Plan's legacy of racial and class-based exclusions. To this day, the victories of the interracial alliances that emerged on California campuses in the late 1960s continue to breed both greater inclusion and ongoing resistance to the status quo.

Conclusion

· ·

We are in danger of producing an educated proletariat. That's dynamite!
We have to be selective on who we allow to let go through higher
education.

—Roger A. Freeman, 1970
  (adviser to Governor Reagan)

The Federal Government poured out huge amounts for higher education,
after Sputnik rose in the skies. At the same time, the states began to
raise their sights. Now a reversal is quite apparent, at a time when the
children of the poor and minority groups have just begun to hope for
college educations.

—Frederick E. Balderston, 1970
  (UC vice president)

The California student movement of the late 1960s responded to the structural conditions established, and the de facto segregation furthered, by the
1960 Master Plan for Higher Education. In doing so, student activists
changed the face of California higher education by both diversifying and
democratizing college campuses. The victories of institutionalized EOPs
and ethnic studies, however, would not go unchallenged. As the economy
declined in the mid-1970s, New Right conservatism grew stronger at the
expense of the earlier liberal consensus and the gains that students had so
recently won came under attack. This was particularly the case with the pair-
ing of twin defeats in June 1978: the passage of California's Proposition 13
and the Supreme Court's ruling in *Regents of the University of California v.*
Bakke. Both of these conservative triumphs emerged within the context of a
broad campaign against school desegregation through busing.

    Passed in June 1978, Proposition 13 guaranteed massive cuts to property
taxes for California businesses, landlords, and homeowners. Specifically, the
measure froze property assessments for taxation purposes at their 1975
levels and capped property taxes at 1 percent of those values. From then
on, properties would only be reassessed in the case of new ownership.[1]
Dramatically lowering both state and local tax revenues, Proposition 13

also "established a 'supermajority' requirement for the passage of any new taxes." This anti-tax proposition led to a significant decline in per-student expenditures for K–12 education in California. In the 1970s, California's per-pupil spending ranked in the top five states nationwide, but by 2015, it had fallen to the forty-sixth. In combination with the defeat of attempts to desegregate California schools through busing, Proposition 13 contributed to a decline in the number of minority students eligible for the UC.[2] The deleterious impact on students of color was further compounded by the Supreme Court's decision on affirmative action in the *Bakke* case.

In their June 1978 decision in *Regents of the University of California v. Bakke*, the Supreme Court ruled against the use of racial quotas in college admissions. Thirty-four-year-old Allan Bakke sued the UC after the UC Davis School of Medicine rejected his application in 1974. Although it seems likely that Bakke's advanced age was the chief factor resulting in his rejection from thirteen different medical schools, the *Bakke* case focused on the practice of race-based affirmative action, not age-based discrimination.[3] In response to the dire shortage of minority medical students and doctors in the 1970s, the medical school at UC Davis had formally set aside sixteen out of one hundred first-year slots for students of color.[4] The Supreme Court's 1978 *Bakke* ruling deemed racial quotas unconstitutional but simultaneously upheld affirmative action by allowing for the consideration of race as one of various factors. Effectively, the *Bakke* decision ended an era of rapid increase in minority access to higher education that had been inaugurated by the California student movement's promotion and expansion of EOPs in response to the de facto racial exclusions of the California Master Plan.

Even at its height, the EOP era had only begun to mitigate a long history of racial exclusion from higher education. In 1973, a California joint committee review of the Master Plan stated that "our achievements in extending equal access have not met our promises. . . . Equality of opportunity in postsecondary education is still a goal rather than a reality." The committee report quantified both the economic and racial exclusions embedded in the Master Plan structure. Economically, the average family income of a student in 1973 stood at $15,160 at the UC, $12,330 at the state colleges, and $11,420 at California's community colleges. Racially, the report noted that "Blacks, Mexican-Americans and Native Americans represent 22.9% of the state's population. However, they compromise only 17.5% of the day enrollment in the California Community Colleges, 11.9% in the California State University . . . and 10.6% in the University of California." Summarizing such results, the report's conclusion noted that "many persons believe the three-tier system with its rigid admissions quotas is inherently racist."[5] Such inherent racism became even harder to combat after 1978. Where Proposition 13 served to further increase racial disparities in early education, the *Bakke* ruling eliminated the use of racial quotas as a method of combating persistent racial inequality.

In the post-Bakke 1980s, EOPs continued at the UC and the CSU (the former state colleges) but without the racial quotas that had previously served as a straightforward method of further desegregating campuses. An applicant's potential EOP status now served as one factor within a larger matrix of admissions criteria. At the start of the decade, in 1980, EOP students at UC Berkeley were composed of working-class whites (15 percent), African Americans (28 percent), Chicanos or Latinos (31 percent), Asian Americans (20 percent), and Native Americans (3.2 percent). By the mid-1980s, the UC's admissions emphases began to change. In his study of admissions at public universities, John Aubrey Douglass notes that "in 1984, UCLA decreased its admissions of low-income students . . . to bolster the admission of minorities who came largely from middle-income families," placing "an increasingly high premium on race and ethnicity." That same year, UC Berkeley assigned targets, but not quotas, for the increased enrollment of Black, Chicano, Latino, Filipino, and Native American students. Because of such changing emphases and despite the impact of *Bakke*, the UC system "experienced an increase in minority enrollment during the 1980s."[6] For example, by 1988, Blacks, Latinos, and Native Americans made up over 30 percent of the incoming freshman class at UC Berkeley.[7]

Despite more than a decade without the use of racial quotas in university admissions, continuing efforts to eliminate racial disparities in higher education generated a massive white backlash in 1990s California.[8] The racial resentment that would ultimately end affirmative action in California took place within the context of a state that was then approaching majority-minority status. While in 1970, California's population remained 78 percent white, by 1996 the state was only 52 percent white—a white population that slanted toward the elderly and middle aged.[9] In July 1995, the UC Board of Regents voted fourteen to ten to eliminate affirmative action in university admissions. Of those eighteen regents appointed to their positions, seventeen had been chosen by Republican governors.[10]

A year and a half later, California voters passed Proposition 209, outlawing the use of affirmative action by state and local governments in hiring, contracting, and public education. Blacks, Latinos, Asian Americans, and women voted in opposition, as did Democrats on the whole. Republicans, whites, and men favored Proposition 209, along with conservative governor Pete Wilson.[11] The text of the proposition began by stating that "the state shall not discriminate against, or grant preferential treatment to, any individual or group on the basis of race, sex, color, ethnicity, or national origin in the operation of public employment, public education, or public contracting."[12] As scholar Daniel Martinez HoSang has noted, the passage of Proposition 209 represents part of a "longer history of transforming and limiting the meaning of 'civil rights' from an expansive vision of social equity toward a narrow set of concerns about individual discrimination."[13] Affirmative action, and the ethnic studies programs with which it emerged in California, would remain targets of conservatives in the decades to come.[14]

Recent trends have continued to hinder efforts toward enrolling Black students in particular. As California's Latino and Asian populations have increased over the previous decades, African Americans have come to make up an ever-smaller percentage of Californians. In addition to suffering in the wake of the *Bakke* ruling and the passage of Propositions 13 and 209, Black Californians remain disproportionately impacted by the racialized inequality that is foundational to American capitalism. As public K–12 funding decreased, as white flight contributed to a collapsing tax base, as deindustrialization limited access to remunerative employment, California's carceral archipelago grew apace. In the postwar decades, as we have seen, California prioritized building and expanding public university and college campuses. By way of contrast, the neoliberal era has seen the promotion of a far crueler kind of institution. In the years between 1984 and 2007, California became home to forty-three new prisons, contributing to a total of "thirty-three major prisons" and "fifty-seven smaller prisons and camps."[15] In the wake of the Reagan governorship, California ditched its progressive policies and began to embrace a more punitive politics. This shift reached its fruition during the Reagan presidency. No more would the state seek to provide equal opportunity for working-class people of color in any meaningful sense; instead, California's Black and Brown residents would increasingly find themselves confined to the state's growing network of prisons.[16]

Even as the end of affirmative action made it harder for many to gain admission to the UC and CSU, increasing tuition, in the guise of student fees, further hindered the aspirations of working-class youth.[17] Fees increased at the UC and CSU across the 1980s, '90s, and into the 2000s.[18] As Christopher Newfield has demonstrated in *Unmaking the Public University*, the UC's share of state general funds steadily decreased in the years from 1970 through 2007. Throughout the 1990s, in particular, Newfield notes that public higher education in California "suffered dramatic budget cuts that were never fully reversed, even during the late 1990s boom."[19] In 2011 dollars, annual fees at the UC increased from roughly $3,000 in 1990 to over $5,000 in 2000. In the same years, the increase at CSU ran from roughly $1,800 to $2,200.[20] Fees continued to rise in the early 2000s, and when California felt the impact of the Great Recession of 2008, politicians chose to increase fees once again. De facto tuition at the UC and CSU more than doubled between 2006 and 2012. UC fees more than tripled from 2002 to 2017, from $3,734 to $12,294. At the CSU, in the same years, fees increased even more drastically, from $1,572 to $5,472. However, thanks to the organizing efforts of student activists in 2009–11, fees stabilized from 2011 to 2017.[21]

The fall of 2009 witnessed the beginning of a new wave of California student struggles, this time directed against a decades-long succession of fee hikes and the steady erosion of state support for public higher education. At UC Davis, the movement found its stride with an occupation of the administration building, Mrak Hall, on November 19, 2009. That occupation resulted in the arrests of fifty-one students and one professor, henceforth known as the Mrak 52. As students across California would come to say, "Behind every fee hike, a line of riot cops."[22] Despite the looming threat of arrest or expulsion, occupations, rallies, and marches continued through the following school year. Two years later, on November 18, 2011, UC Davis police attacked and pepper sprayed students sitting on the quad in protest of a proposed 81 percent tuition increase at the UC. The fallout from the police brutality led to the dismissal of Officer John Pike, and Police Chief Annette Spicuzza, and the eventual downfall of UC Davis chancellor Linda Katehi. The UC Regents never attempted to follow through with their proposal for an 81 percent fee increase.[23]

The history of the California student movement that began in 2009—and went well beyond UC Davis to the rest of the Master Plan system—will remain a subject of inquiry for historians in the decades to come. Although most participants in that movement remained unaware of the actual content and impact of the 1960 California Master Plan for Higher Education, they were cognizant of the ways in which the promise of free higher education is now more distant than ever and of the continuing impact of racial and class exclusions on a system whose protestations of meritocracy ring ever more hollow.

Recent years have seen laudable efforts toward the promotion of ethnic studies in California and the leveling of college admissions through the elimination of standardized tests and legacy preference. At the same time, tuition and indebtedness continue to increase, and conservatives have found a new bugbear in critical race theory—however distorted or misunderstood. Affirmative action for people of color and working-class youth remains crucial for college admissions but change needs to begin much earlier. Universal pre-K, the equalization of funding across school districts, and moves to mitigate residential and educational segregation are all necessary to begin inching toward something closer to a just society. No four-year college can or should be forced to do the work of equalizing students' opportunities after eighteen years of living in a nation plagued by race and wealth-based inequality. Students and their parents should not need to go into debt to obtain an education, but the crucial work of making the United States a land of equal opportunity needs to begin long before freshman year.

· · · · · ·

The 1960 California Master Plan for Higher Education improved countless lives. At the same time, the Master Plan was riddled with de facto racial exclusions. Yet these proved generative exclusions, propelling movements for greater democratization and inclusion. That the Master Plan focused on Cold War calculations at the expense of addressing domestic racial oppression is clear enough. Within a few years, the Master Plan's shortcomings would inform the ideological contours of the Free Speech Movement at UC Berkeley. The FSM, contrary to some contemporary popular interpretations, fought not so much for an abstract right to free speech, as for the right to engage in protest in support of civil rights for African Americans and in opposition to the witch hunts of the early Cold War. The students' victory at Berkeley soon opened up a space for a vibrant movement against the American invasion of Southeast Asia. In turn, such protests contributed to a right-wing backlash, easing the election of conservative governor Ronald Reagan. Despite Reagan's attempts to stifle campus protest and rein in liberal and leftist professors, the genie was out of the lamp. During the Reagan governorship, Black student athletes brought onto campus through the Master Plan's 2 percent admissions exception rule formed a nucleus of Black struggle. In time, early efforts led by Black students and predominantly white New Left organizations would expand into broad collaboration with Chicana/o activists, newly formed Asian American student organizations, and Native Americans seeking a place in heretofore exclusionary campus settings. Through years of struggle, these interracial coalitions helped to turn California's public university campuses into something like the egalitarian spaces that the Master Plan had promised but had never truly delivered.

Acknowledgments

Writing this book has helped me to more fully appreciate the collective nature of scholarship. People whose names I will never know contributed to this book. What follows are some of the names I do know. My sincere apologies to anyone I've managed to leave out.

Lorena Oropeza has been there from the beginning to the end of this project. When I was only a second-year graduate student, Lorena suggested I make my way from Davis down to SF State to take a look at materials from the Third World Liberation Front strike. Without that suggestion, this book may never have taken shape. Lorena has been a constant source of support and critique, appropriately balanced, since we began working together. I hope I can begin to return the favor in the years to come.

At UC Davis, a wide array of people contributed to this book in myriad ways. Kathryn Olmsted and Lisa Materson deserve special thanks. Both have been big supporters of this project for years, offering insightful feedback and encouragement. In addition, their seminars helped me to think through various historiographical debates that inform this work. Clarence Walker offered strong advice and reading recommendations, as well as wonderful anecdotes from his time at SF State and UC Berkeley in the 1960s and early '70s. His support has meant a lot to me. Ed Dickinson ran the seminar where this project first began as a research paper. His early suggestions and criticisms helped guide this work from its earliest stage. Thanks as well to Omnia El Shakry and Eric Rauchway for their formative influence on my historical thinking and writing.

Pedro Regalado has been remarkably selfless with his time and advice. As the book inched toward completion, Pedro closely read chapters 1, 3, and 5. His insights made each of them notably stronger, and his enthusiasm for the project helped me push through some final reworking.

Luis Alvarez took the time—at the height of the pandemic no less—to read my full manuscript and to provide deep, thoughtful analysis of my work, making a range of suggestions for improvements. Although I was unable to address all of his concerns in the depth they merited, thinking through Luis's insights during the final months of editing allowed me to correct for a number of weaknesses and to approach certain key issues in a new light.

One of the most enjoyable parts of this process has been getting to know some of the people who participated in the history I recount. I was lucky enough to meet Peter Shapiro at a conference for the Labor and Working-Class History Association. Peter's writing on the strike at SF State has been a major influence on my thinking about the Master Plan. Upon meeting him, he was kind enough to offer to read a full draft of my manuscript, providing the sorts of correctives and suggestions that only someone deeply immersed in the struggles of 1960s California could offer. His help has been much appreciated.

I count myself quite fortunate to have connected with a number of veterans of the Free Speech Movement. Both Joel Geier and Jack Weinberg took the time to talk with me about their experiences and to read a late draft of chapter 2, offering encouragement and, where necessary, correcting my misperceptions. Sam Farber, David McCullough, and David Friedman kindly read my FSM chapter as well and contributed a range of insights.

The following people made a variety of contributions by reading chapters, discussing the project, debating the historiography, or simply offering their support. Thank you to my dear friend, interlocutor, and proofreader Lily Lucas Hodges, as well as Marco Antonio Rosales, Eran Zelnik, Robin Averbeck, Nick Perrone, Juan Carlos Medel Toro, Laura Tavolacci, Diana Johnson, Yesika Ordaz, Jordan Scavo, Chelsea Bell, Logan Clendening, Jenna Jacobson, Emily Breuninger, Stephen Silver, Steve Cox, Elad Alyagon, Rachel Reeves, Adam Brover, Mandy Cohen, Pablo Silva, Genesis Lara, Vanessa Madrigal-Lauchland, and Duane Wright. Thanks to AJ, Alyson, Magnolia, and Griffin, for all the love and support.

My earliest work toward this book began during an intense stretch of participation in the California student movement that followed on the heels of the Great Recession. I learned quite a lot from fellow campus organizers, including Sarah, Oki, Mo, Lobna, and Evan, and from my fellow reformers within AWDU—the Academic Workers for a Democratic Union—in UAW 2865. I would also be remiss not to mention a number of important influences from my undergraduate years: Catherine Stock, David Canton, Luis González, Robert Gay, Sara, Daniel, and the late Harold Juli.

Thank you to Llana Barber, Lori Flores, Victoria Langland, Matthew Garcia, Kevin Boyle, Patrick Lacroix, and Philip Mosley—all of whom offered thoughtful commentary on conference papers that helped inform this project. I would also like to thank Jason Ferreira and John Aubrey Douglass for responding to my queries with alacrity and for answering questions that likely only they could.

Numerous archivists and librarians provided indispensable support. I apologize for not keeping better track of names during the long process of researching this book. I would like to thank everyone from the archives and special collections in Shields Library at UC Davis, Catherine Powell and the folks at San Francisco State's Labor Archives and Research Center and J. Paul Leonard Library, David Olson, Kimberly Springer, and everyone else at the Columbia Center for Oral History, Lillian Castillo-Speed and the staff of the Ethnic Studies Library at the University of California, Berkeley, as well as the staffs of the Bancroft Library at the University of California, Berkeley, the California State Archives in Sacramento, the Hoover Institution, Stanford University's Greene Library, New York University's Tamiment Library and Wagner Labor Archives, and the Beinecke Rare Book & Manuscript Library at Yale University.

My experiences with the University of North Carolina Press have been, frankly, wonderful. Thank you to my editor, Brandon Proia, for being so friendly and helpful. Brandon made this process much easier than I imagine it might have been with someone less humble or attentive. Thanks as well to everyone who worked behind the scenes to get this thing on paper.

In closing, I want to convey my deep appreciation for my family, new and old. Without fail, my parents have always supported me—from the love of reading that they encouraged in me, to their enthusiasm for my pursuit of the doctorate and the publication of this book. Thank you as well to Alex, Adam, H, Cindy, Paul, Heidi, Chris, Nick, Mark, Ali, and Veronica for all of your support and love and simply for being such an important part of my life.

Wendy, what can I say? You have been such a constant source of love and encouragement for so long now. Almost single-handedly, you cared for me as I grieved the loss of one of my best friends—not once but twice. I don't know what I'd be doing if it wasn't for you, but I know I wouldn't be publishing this book. Thank you for being the incredible partner and friend that you have been. Thank you for Saya. And thank you both for bringing me so, so much joy.

Notes

Introduction

1. See, in particular, the 1969 report *The Challenge of Achievement*, 4.

2. Reagan not only sought to restrict funding to affirmative action programs, but he went so far as to propose introducing tuition, a clear violation of the California Master Plan. At the same time, some student activists advocated for open admissions, while a number of state legislators laid out a plan to reorganize the UC, state colleges, and community colleges under a single administrative board and open up the UC and state colleges to far greater numbers of Californians. On Reagan and the Master Plan, see chapter 3. On the student and legislative proposals, see Fusha Hill, "Open Admissions Stop Institutional Racism," *Daily Collegian*, April 26, 1971; and "Master Plan for Higher Education Revised," *California Aggie*, March 3, 1969.

3. Fusha Hill, "Davis Campus Community Effort in Support of a Meaningful UC Budget," *California Aggie*, March 1, 1971.

4. "BSU's 15 Demands Pertain to Davis, Too," *California Aggie*, February 11, 1969; Jerry Marr, "Faculty Forum," *California Aggie*, February 21, 1969.

5. The *Daily Collegian* republished excerpts from Hill's original article; see Hill, "Open Admissions Stop Institutional Racism."

6. In 1972, the California state colleges would be renamed the California State University.

7. Officially "fee increases." Since the 1960 Master Plan, students have only paid "fees," not "tuition." Yet, whatever the terminology, the nature of the financial transition remains the same.

8. Saving UCSB, "Save UC's Master Plan!" UCSB refers to the University of California, Santa Barbara.

9. Starr includes, alongside the Master Plan, the creation of the state's freeway system and the statewide water plan. See Kevin Starr, "California: Scorning Public Life Is Shameful," *Los Angeles Times*, September 21, 2003.

10. Charles B. Reed, "California at a Crossroads," *San Diego Union Tribune*, December 9, 2010.

11. Hemmila, "Governor Pledges to Veto."

12. Asimov, "The Golden Age."

13. Susan Gubernat, "Those Who Gained from Low Tuition Are Stiffing Today's College Students," *Sacramento Bee*, February 11, 2015.

14. Bessie, "The Trojan Horse."

15. Les Birdsall, "A Golden Age of Education," *Los Angeles Times*, May 17, 1998.

16. To be sure, vocational training serves a purpose and remedial education fills a need. However, the Master Plan reinforced the racial and class inequalities that

had long plagued all levels of education, by deepening them at the tertiary. It was then, and remains today, working-class youth, predominantly people of color, whose options for higher education are most often limited to remedial and vocational studies, while the children of the wealthy receive the best educations, paving the way for a lifetime of high earnings.

17. To be clear, I do not mean to suggest that only fifty thousand students would be diverted downward in the years from 1960 to 1975. The Master Plan's estimate of fifty thousand was for 1975 alone. That is, the plan projected that in 1975, fully fifty thousand students would need to enroll in community colleges, who previously could have begun at a four-year institution. Starting with the enactment of the Master Plan admissions standards, each year prior to 1975, lesser numbers of students—tens of thousands, if not yet fifty thousand—were denied the opportunity to begin their educations at the UC or state college levels. In this way, California sought to save money while simultaneously maintaining a form of open access to public higher education. See the Master Plan Survey Team, *A Master Plan*, 13, 89–90, 105.

18. As one scholar writing in the mid-1970s aptly noted, "California's long history of school segregation and exclusion has been virtually ignored by educators and historians, let alone politicians and the general public." See Wollenberg, *All Deliberate Speed*, 178. Segregation actually worsened as California became more diverse in the postwar decades, with high levels of residential segregation leading to highly segregated schools in the 1960s and '70s. See Douglass, *Conditions for Admission*, 65.

19. The Master Plan limited such special admissions to 2 percent of incoming students. Prior to the plan's passage, special admissions had constituted up to 10 percent of admissions. Throughout the late 1960s, student activists would fight to expand special admissions to bring more students of color and working-class youth to campus.

20. Laura Pulido and Josh Kun note that much of the scholarship on Black-Brown relations approaches the subject from a binary of "conflict" or "coalition." My own work emphasizes the victories that emerged from the coalitions developed on campuses across the Master Plan system; yet, this is not to say that conflict did not occur. But as historian Garrett Felber noted in a recent interview, coalitions are inherently difficult. Speaking of an effort at coalition building made by the Nation of Islam, Felber noted that it was "an uncomfortable coalition, and that's really what coalitions are. . . . You have to understand that coalition work is tenuous and uncomfortable. That's how you know it's a coalition." Whatever minor conflicts emerged within the context of the interracial coalitions formed by students within the Master Plan system, their victories—chiefly the establishment of ethnic studies and the formation of EOPs for affirmative action—affirm their vitality and inherent worthiness. See Kun and Pulido, *Black and Brown in Los Angeles*; and Felber, "Those Who Know Don't Say."

21. I borrow this phrase with the explicit intention of recognizing the New Left as a category far broader than the largely white, Students for a Democratic Society–dominated student movement, one that includes the Black freedom struggle, the Chicano movement, and much more. See Gosse, "A Movement of Movements."

22. HoSang and Molina, "Introduction," 1, 2.

23. Tellingly, the eleven-page bibliography helpfully provided by the editors of *Relational Formations of Race* lists only one work—out of 215—that explicitly focuses on the college campus as a site of racial formation. See Molina, HoSang, and Gutiérrez, "Further Reading"; and Ferreira, "From College Readiness to Ready for Revolution!" With the important exception of Ferreira's published and unpublished works, the vast majority of the scholarship exploring the rise of ethnic studies— though invaluable—takes as its focus a single racial group. See, for instance, Biondi, *Black Revolution on Campus*; Rogers, *Black Campus Movement*; Muñoz, *Youth, Identity, Power*; Acuña, *The Making of Chicana/o Studies*; Wei, *Asian American Movement*; and Ishizuka, *Serve the People*. Lamentably, these works' respective focuses on individual racial groups obscures the extent to which this is a shared history.

24. To be clear, that the Master Plan served as a model for other states points to the representative nature of this study. California was not the only state that would provide free, or nearly free, higher education to its residents in these years. It made, however, the largest attempt to do so and resulted in what is rightly viewed as the best such system. Likewise, the racial inequalities that plagued California's experiment in mass public higher education resembled those of other states. What's more, thanks to the efforts of those student activists covered in the book's second half, California did a better job than almost any other state enrolling diverse working-class people at its public college and university campuses. (I say almost because California's efforts toward inclusion via programs of affirmative action surely fell short of New York's experiment in open admissions.) See Breneman and Lingenfelter, "The California Master Plan." A new study of higher education—largely, although not exclusively, focused on faculty—helps put California's experience in its larger national context. See Schrecker, *The Lost Promise*.

25. See, for instance, Katznelson, *Fear Itself*; and Katznelson, *When Affirmative Action Was White*.

Chapter 1

1. *Journal of Higher Education* 29 (1958); *Journal of Higher Education* 30 (1959); *Journal of Higher Education* 32 (1961).

2. In this sense, the Master Plan is but one example of a larger trend toward greater state involvement in education in the Cold War era. See, for instance, Clowse, *Brainpower for the Cold War*; Leslie, *The Cold War and American Science*; Neusner and Neusner, *The Price of Excellence*; Schiffrin, *The Cold War and the University*; Lowen, *Creating the Cold War University*; Simpson, *Universities and Empire*; and Levin, *Cold War University*.

3. The Master Plan years would see the creation of two new UC campuses (in addition to the three new ones developed in the 1950s), four new state colleges, and upward of fifty community colleges. See Douglass, *The California Idea*, 351–54, 358.

4. An exploration of the Master Plan confirms that in the domestic sphere, the Cold War opened up certain opportunities while shutting down others. Much as

the revolutionary vision of some civil rights activists (or, for that matter, New Dealers) was tempered by McCarthyism, the radical potential of free, universal higher education was limited by Cold War priorities and consequent inattention to questions of access for people of color whose potential for upward mobility remained thwarted by racism both institutional (in the form of K–12 segregation) and interpersonal (such as the hostility young people of color often faced from white teachers and administrators).

5. Sullivan, *Assault on the Unknown*, 27, 28, 31; Killian, *Sputnik, Scientists, and Eisenhower*, 192.

6. Borstelmann, *The Cold War and the Color Line*; Dudziak, *Cold War Civil Rights*; Von Eschen, *Race against Empire*.

7. "Soviet Claiming Lead in Science: New Announcements Noted on Ballistic Missile and Rocket for Research," *New York Times*, October 5, 1957; "Who Else Can Give You a Moon?" *Sacramento Bee*, October 8, 1957; "560 Miles High: Visible with Simple Binoculars, Moscow Statement Says," *New York Times*, October 5, 1957; "Device Is 8 Times Heavier than One Planned by U.S.," *New York Times*, October 5, 1957.

8. "On Satellite's Meaning: Eisenhower's View," *New York Times*, October 13, 1957; "Ike Says Russ Satellite 'No Threat to Security," *San Francisco Chronicle*, October 10, 1957; "Ike, Top Scientists Discuss U.S. Satellite Plan Today," *San Francisco Chronicle*, October 14, 1957; John W. Finney, "3 U.S. Rocket Firings Fail in Shots for Altitude Mark: Research Team Urged to Get Missile Up 4,000 Miles to Offset Soviet Gain—President Sees Science Advisers," *New York Times*, October 16, 1957; "Could We Put Up a U.S. Sputnik?" *San Francisco Chronicle*, October 16, 1957.

9. Recent scholarship suggests that Laurence's work should not be understood as objective journalism but rather paid propaganda. While working for the *New York Times*, Laurence was simultaneously taking payments from those people and institutions he was charged with covering, including the Manhattan Project, the U.S. Army surgeon general, and the developer Robert Moses. See William J. Broad, "How a Star Times Reporter Got Paid by Government Agencies He Covered," *New York Times*, August 9, 2021.

10. William L. Laurence, "Science in Review: Soviet Success in Rocketry Draws Attention to Need for More Students in the Sciences," *New York Times*, October 13, 1957.

11. Scheuring, *Abundant Harvest*, 103; "Master Planner," *Time*, October 17, 1960; Frank Purcell, "Kerr Tells of Challenges of U.C. Task," *S.F. Examiner*, October 20, 1957, Carton 26, Folder 9, Clark Kerr Personal and Professional Papers, CU-302, Bancroft Library, University of California, Berkeley.

12. Lucy Newhall, "UC's Dr. Kerr Wins Presidency as Battler," *Los Angeles Times*, November 3, 1957.

13. Balogh, *Integrating the Sixties*, 23. The term refers to a centrist strain of liberalism in which state intervention in the economy is geared principally toward the defeat of communism rather than the eradication of myriad forms of inequality— class, racial, gender, etc.

14. The October Revolution, named according to the traditional czarist use of the Julian calendar, began on November 7, 1917.

15. "How Reds Announced 2d Sputnik," *Washington Post*, November 3, 1957; Divine, *The Sputnik Challenge*, 43; "Orbit Completed: Animal Still Is Alive, Sealed in Satellite, Moscow Thinks," *New York Times*, November 3, 1957; Miezckowski, *Eisenhower's Sputnik Moment*, 96.

16. Stewart Alsop, "The Meaning of Sputnik II," *Washington Post*, November 6, 1957.

17. James Reston, "The U.S. and Science: An Analysis of Lessons to Be Learned from Soviet Achievements in Space," *New York Times*, November 6, 1957; Killian, *Sputnik, Scientists, and Eisenhower*, xv; Eisenhower quoted in Clowse, *Brainpower for the Cold War*, 56; "Democrats Back Science Speed-Up: But Address by President Fails to Reassure Some—Johnson Cites Needs," *New York Times*, November 8, 1957; "Science and Our Society," *New York Times*, November 11, 1957.

18. "Science and Our Society," 28.

19. "Von Braun Foresees More Soviet 'Firsts,'" *Washington Post*, November 10, 1957; On Operation Paperclip, see Jacobsen, *Operation Paperclip*.

20. Homer Bigard, "Basic Research in U.S. Is Spurred by Soviet Gains: Quest for New Knowledge, Long Neglected, Will Be Aided by More Funds," *New York Times*, December 16, 1957. In 1958, the NSF would indeed secure more than three times as much, for a total of $50 million. In 1959, this skyrocketed to $136 million. See Killian, *Sputnik, Scientists, and Eisenhower*, 194.

21. Dick Turpin, "Series on Education to Begin in Times," *Los Angeles Times*, January 3, 1958.

22. Dick Turpin, "Educators Sift Russ Challenge: Public's Attitude on Schools, Teachers Discusses, Criticized," *Los Angeles Times*, January 5, 1958.

23. "How World Reacted to Sputniks," *New York Times*, November 10, 1957; Turpin, "Educators Sift Russ Challenge."

24. Turpin, "Educators Sift Russ Challenge."

25. Dick Turpin, "'Crash Programs' for Schools Hit: Leading Educators Say Results of Speed-Up Would Be Doubtful," *Los Angeles Times*, January 7, 1958.

26. Turpin, "'Crash Programs' for Schools Hit."

27. Giroux, *Theory and Resistance in Education*, 169, 217.

28. Even before Sputnik, debate over the merits of Dewey's impact proved influential in local California politics. In 1951, one Dewey disciple lost his position as school superintendent in the city of Pasadena after a three-year battle with local conservatives. A decade later, in 1962, archconservative Max Rafferty would be elected state superintendent of public instruction as an outspoken critic of Dewey's progressivism. With strong support coming from the John Birch Society, Rafferty would serve "as an advance guard for the Reagan Revolution to come." See Starr, *Golden Dreams*, 199–201.

29. Clowse, *Brainpower for the Cold War*, 14, 29.

30. Turpin, "Educators Sift Russ Challenge."

31. Dick Turpin, "Space Age Has Education Crisis: Top College Administrators Tell of School Change Need," *Los Angeles Times*, January 6, 1958.

32. Turpin, "Educators Sift Russ Challenge."

33. Turpin, "Space Age Has Education Crisis." The emphasis is my own.

34. Turpin, "Space Age Has Education Crisis."

35. Turpin, "Space Age Has Education Crisis." Here, Turpin is paraphrasing Kerr.

36. Turpin, "Space Age Has Education Crisis." DuBridge brought such views to the hearings on the development of legislation toward the National Defense Education Act (NDEA) of 1958. According to one treatment of the hearings, DuBridge clashed with Carl Elliot—a coauthor of the NDEA—over the relevant targets for federal education aid. Where DuBridge stressed the need to find and support only the best of the best, Elliot called for "increasing the numbers of poorer students in college" and "envisioned a substantial numerical increase in the total college and university student population with passage of NDEA student aid measures." Elliot, not DuBridge, would win the day. See Urban, *More than Science and Sputnik*, 60.

37. Dick Turpin, "Teaching Setup Revision Urged: Five Major Educators in Field of Education Submit Their Opinions," *Los Angeles Times*, January 8, 1958.

38. Turpin, "Teaching Setup Revision Urged." Sterling as paraphrased by Turpin.

39. Brand, "Jewish Trojans."

40. Stern, *Eugenic Nation*, 6.

41. Dick Turpin, "Educators Favor President's Plan: Proposed Program Called Good Beginning for School Needs," *Los Angeles Times*, January 9, 1958. One is reminded of Aimé Césaire's critique of colonization and Western civilization, published only three years before, in which Césaire quotes disapprovingly from French philosopher Ernest Renan: "*Let each one do what he is made for, and all will be well.*" See Césaire, *Discourse on Colonialism*, 38; emphasis in the original.

42. Dick Turpin, "Way to Improve Education Given: 5 University Heads Offer Their Ideas on Surpassing the Russians," *Los Angeles Times*, January 10, 1958.

43. Dick Turpin, "Quality Education Urged by Leaders: Top Superintendents Stress Necessity of Public Support," *Los Angeles Times*, January 12, 1958.

44. Dick Turpin, "Educators Defend Schools Programs: System Not to Blame for Russ Advances, Superintendents Say," *Los Angeles Times*, January 13, 1958.

45. Turpin, "Educators Defend Schools Programs."

46. Turpin, "Quality Education Urged by Leaders."

47. Cloud, *Education in California*, 226.

48. Roy Simpson, Subject Files—Conference on Science & Math, 1958, Department of Education Records, F3752:609, California State Archives, Secretary of State Office, Sacramento, California.

49. Roy Simpson, "Remarks by Roy. E. Simpson, Superintendent of Public Education; Conference on Science and Mathematics Education in California Public Schools, Sacramento, February 24, 1958; Subject: Purpose of the Conference," Department of Education Records, F3752:609, California State Archives, Secretary of State Office, Sacramento, California.

50. Clowse, *Brainpower for the Cold War*, 3–4.

51. Aryness Joy Wickens, "Address by Mrs. Aryness Joy Wickens; Deputy Assistant Secretary of Labor; Before a Conference on the Teaching of Mathematics and Science; California Department of Education; Sacramento, California—February 24, 1958," Department of Education Records, F3752:609, California State Archives, Secretary of State Office, Sacramento, California.

52. Leslie H. Hoffman, "Address Delivered February 24, 1958 at the Conference of Science and Mathematics Education in the Public Schools," Department of Education Records, F3752:609, California State Archives, Secretary of State Office, Sacramento, California. Although the electronics industry was California's second largest, defense reigned supreme. As noted by California historian Kevin Starr, in the postwar era it was the defense industries "driving California's economic engine." See Starr, *California*, 242. "Defense-related industries accounted for roughly half of the growth" of California's postwar (1947–57) employment boom according to Douglass, *The California Idea*, 233.

53. Hoffman, "Address Delivered February 24, 1958."

54. Given the history of higher education in the United States and the Cold War context in which this conference took place, this should not be surprising. As Christopher Newfield has wryly noted, "Historians have been unable to find a period in which colleges and universities were fully in the hands of educators who ignored business input." See Newfield, *Ivy and Industry*, 21.

55. Ellis A. Jarvis, "Sacramento Conference—February 24, 1958; Post–High Schools Mathematics, Science and Engineering Programs; Present Practices, Trends and Implications," Department of Education Records, F3752:609, California State Archives, Secretary of State Office, Sacramento, California; Nolan D. Pulliam, "Sacramento Conference—February 24, 1958; Present Status and Future Needs of the Science and Mathematics Program in California Secondary Schools," Department of Education Records, F3752:609, California State Archives, Secretary of State Office, Sacramento, California.

56. Pulliam, "Sacramento Conference."

57. C. C. Trillingham, "Address Delivered February 25, 1958, at the Conference on Science and Mathematics Education in the Public Schools," Department of Education Records, F3752:609, California State Archives, Secretary of State Office, Sacramento, California.

58. Jay D. Connor, "Address Delivered February 24 at the Conference on Science and Mathematics Education in the Public Schools," Department of Education Records, F3752:609, California State Archives, Secretary of State Office, Sacramento, California.

59. Trillingham, "Address Delivered February 25, 1958."

60. As of 1950, Mexican Americans made up 7.2 percent of California's ten million residents; African Americans—whose population had increased markedly around the war years—were 4.4 percent; Native Americans and Asian Americans—chiefly Japanese, Chinese, and Filipino—made up the then–relatively small remainder of California's nonwhite population. See Brilliant, *Color of America*, 4.

61. Stadtman, *University of California*, 383.

62. Glenn T. Seaborg, "Education in Our Age: Let's Define the Problem," Department of Education Records, F3752:609, California State Archives, Secretary of State Office, Sacramento, California. Once he himself ascended to the office of UC president, Clark Kerr named Seaborg as his replacement as the chancellor of UC Berkeley. See Lemann, *The Big Test*, 130.

63. Clowse, *Brainpower for the Cold War*, 57.

64. Killian, *Sputnik, Scientists, and Eisenhower,* 196.

65. Divine, *The Sputnik Challenge,* 164; "$887 Million Education Bill Signed by Ike," *San Francisco Chronicle,* September 3, 1958.

66. Divine, *The Sputnik Challenge,* 166.

67. Lyndon B. Johnson and the NDEA preamble quoted in Sundquist, *Politics and Policy,* 179, 180.

68. Roy E. Simpson, "Address by Roy E. Simpson, Superintendent of Public Instruction; 1959 Convention of the California Labor Federation, AFL-CIO; Balboa Park, San Diego, California; August 12, 1959," 4, Department of Education Records, F3752:640, California State Archives, Secretary of State Office, Sacramento, California.

69. Douglass, *The California Idea;* "Digital Archive: The 1960 Master Plan."

70. Hall, *Great Planning Disasters,* 153; "Memorandum concerning the Urgency of the Proposed Legislation to Establish Three New State Colleges," Department of Education Records, F3752:606, California State Archives, Secretary of State Office, Sacramento, California; Barlow and Shapiro, *End to Silence,* 22–23.

71. The report was named after report director George Strayer.

72. Douglass, *The California Idea,* 186–87. Each of the three tiers—the UC, state colleges, and the community colleges—existed before the Master Plan. However, prior to the plan, there was no real coordination between the three, and although the UC was a single institution stretched across a number of campuses, there was little that bound the autonomous locally managed state colleges or community colleges together.

73. Liaison Committee, *A Report of a Survey of the Needs of California Higher Education.*

74. Liaison Committee, *A Restudy of the Needs of California in Higher Education.*

75. Barlow and Shapiro, *End to Silence,* 24.

76. Liaison Committee, *A Restudy of the Needs of California in Higher Education,* 285.

77. Clark Kerr, "Growth of the CSU System," interview conducted by Judson Grenier, February 22, 1995, California State University Archives: Oral History Project on the Origins of the CSU System, Phase II, 11; Donald R. Gerth, "Researching Higher Education in Transition," interview conducted by Judson A. Grenier, 1987, California State University Archives: Oral History Pilot Project on the Origins of the CSU System, 9–10.

78. Douglass, *The California Idea,* 345–54; Kerr, "Growth of the CSU System," 11.

79. Gerth and Haehn, *Invisible Giant,* 8, 11–12; Coons, *Crisis in California Higher Education,* 20–21; Arthur G. Coons, "Major Steps in the Origin and Development of the Master Plan Study and Certain Consensuses of the Survey Team; 9/15/59," 1, Department of Education Records, F3752:624, California State Archives, Secretary of State Office, Sacramento, California; Douglass, *The California Idea,* 258.

80. Douglass, *The California Idea,* 259, 264; "Background: The Master Plan Survey of Higher Education in California," Department of Education Records, F3752:622, California State Archives, Secretary of State Office, Sacramento, California.

81. Douglass, *The California Idea*, 273; Coons, "Major Steps in the Origin and Development," 3; "Background: The Master Plan Survey"; Stadtman, *University of California*, 391.

82. This number included the Master Plan survey team (7 members), the Liaison Committee (10), the UC Regents (24), the state board of education (10), various state politicians (9), the Joint Advisory Committee (16), a consultant from the Assembly Education Committee (1), and technical committees focusing on enrollment projections (9), selection and retention of students (5), adult education (18), California's ability to finance higher education (4), costs of higher education (8), and institutional capacities and area needs (4). See "Organization for the Master Plan Survey of Higher Education in California," August 6, 1959, Department of Education Records, F3752:622, California State Archives, Secretary of State Office, Sacramento, California.

83. "Organization for the Master Plan Survey of Higher Education in California."

84. Stadtman, *University of California*, 392; McHenry as quoted in Douglass, *The California Idea*, 276; Coons, *Crisis in California Higher Education*, 57.

85. Coons, *Crisis in California Higher Education*, 60. Nicholas Lemann suggests that Dumke came around to supporting the Master Plan as part of a quid pro quo. Shortly after Dumke joined forces with Kerr in support of the plan, Lemann notes, he was named president of the California state college system. See Lemann, *The Big Test*, 133.

86. Dumke quoted in Gerth and Haehn, *Invisible Giant*, 22.

87. Douglass, *The California Idea*, 306, 308.

88. Rarick, *California Rising*, 148.

89. Gerth and Haehn, *Invisible Giant*, 15–16; Coons, *Crisis in California Higher Education*, 48.

90. "Brief Guide to the Master Plan"; Coordinating Council for Higher Education, "Summarized Master Plan Recommendations," January 25, 1966, Department of Education Records, F3752:181, California State Archives, Secretary of State Office, Sacramento, California.

91. This feature of the Master Plan is what's referred to as "differentiation of function." According to Glenn Dumke, a member of the Master Plan survey team, differentiation of function "was the Master Plan. Everything else was/were fringes and unimportant side issues—the admissions program, the financing program—all of that stuff were side issues." See Glenn S. Dumke, "The Evolution of the California State University System, 1961–1982," an oral history conducted in 1984 by Sarah Sharp, Regional Oral History Office, Bancroft Library, University of California, Berkeley, 1986, 10–11.

92. Free public higher education in California dated back to the Morrill Act of 1862, but mass education emerged only as a post–World War II phenomenon. The inclusion of language pertaining to tuition-free education only reaffirmed what was a long-standing commitment. This de facto tradition, however, would not meaningfully outlast Reagan's governorship in the late 1960s. Despite Reagan's introduction of increasingly prohibitive fees, access to California's public colleges and universities remained relatively affordable until the 1990s when student fees began to skyrocket.

93. Douglass, *The California Idea*, 309–10.

94. Smelser, "Growth, Structural Change, and Conflict," 56; Douglass, *The California Idea*, 322–23.

95. Because the state colleges operated autonomously before the passage of the Master Plan, some campuses had accepted upwards of the top 45 percent of California high school graduates.

96. To be clear, under the Master Plan, the UC drew from the top 12.5 percent of students (previously 15 percent) across all of California, not from each high school. The distinction is an important one. The UC and state colleges utilized a ranking system for California high schools which—given the state's de facto segregation and wealth disparities—privileged wealthy white students at the expense of the working class and people of color. Email from Douglass to the author, November 11, 2021. See Douglass, *Conditions for Admission*, 40–41.

97. Special admissions could be used for those who did not meet the Master Plan's stringent admissions requirements and included, for example, athletes, the children of alumni or donors, and promising working-class and/or minority applicants. Kerr, *The Gold and the Blue*, 1:183; and Douglass, *Conditions for Admission*, 42, 90, 99; "Progress toward Establishing Admission Requirements Specified by the Master Plan," April 28, 1962, Department of Education Records, F3752:142, California State Archives, Secretary of State Office, Sacramento, California.

98. Such was the purpose of the Master Plan's differentiation of function. Although Dumke fails to note the racial and class implications of this aspect of the Master Plan, in practice, a disproportionate number of those students consigned to the community colleges were working-class students of color previously forced to attend inferior, de facto segregated primary and secondary schools. See Dumke, "The Evolution of the California State University System, 1961–1982," 10.

99. Clark, "The 'Cooling-Out' Function," 569.

100. The cooling-out function aims to subtly convince such students to accept their fate, reframing a relative failure as something more palatable. As Clark noted, "One dilemma of a cooling-out role is that it must be kept reasonably away from public scrutiny and not clearly perceived or understood by prospective clientele. . . . If high-school seniors and their families were to define the junior college as a place which diverts college-bound students, a probable consequence would be a turning-away from the junior college and increased pressure for admission to the four-year colleges and universities that are otherwise protected to some degree. This would, of course, render superfluous the part now played by the junior college in the division of labor among colleges." See Clark, "The 'Cooling-Out' Function," 572, 575.

101. Larson, "Master Plan, Master Failure," 63.

102. Before the Master Plan, the use of standardized admissions tests had been limited to out-of-state applicants. To gauge the relative merits of in-state students, the UC maintained a graded system of high school accreditation. This system, in the words of scholars Richard Delgado and Jean Stefancic, "greatly disadvantaged Catholic and inner city schools." It was not until the 1968–69 school year that all UC applicants would be mandated to take the SAT. See Lemann, *The Big Test*, 133,

173; and Delgado and Stefancic, "California's Racial History and Constitutional Rationales for Race-Conscious Decision Making in Higher Education," 1580.

103. Clark Kerr, "The Master Plan and Its Implementation," August 6, 1962, Carton 3, Folder 29, Clark Kerr Personal and Professional Papers, CU-302, Bancroft Library, University of California, Berkeley.

104. Coons, *Crisis in California Higher Education*, 61; Stadtman, *University of California*, 392; Kerr, *The Gold and the Blue*, 1:175.

105. Roy E. Simpson, "Address by Roy E. Simpson, Superintendent of Public Instruction; 1959 Convention of the California Labor Federation, AFL-CIO; Balboa Park, San Diego, California; August 12, 1959," 3, Department of Education Records, F3752:640, California State Archives, Secretary of State Office, Sacramento, California; Roy E. Simpson, "Spring Conference; California Association of County Schools Superintendents; Asilomar; March 14, 1960," 1, 5, Department of Education Records, F3752:640, California State Archives, Secretary of State Office, Sacramento, California.

106. Roy E. Simpson, "California Elementary School Administrators Association, Conference of Elementary School Principals and Superintendents of Elementary School Districts; Sacramento, California; April 10, 1960; Subject: The Changing Face of Education," 3, 7, Department of Education Records, F3752:640, California State Archives, Secretary of State Office, Sacramento, California.

107. Clark Kerr, "The New Leisure: The New Wealth: The New Community," July 24, 1958, Carton 28, Folder 13, Clark Kerr Personal and Professional Papers, CU-302, Bancroft Library, University of California, Berkeley.

108. Clark Kerr, "Democracy, Wealth, Survival—and Education," August 30, 1958, Carton 28, Folder 14, Clark Kerr Personal and Professional Papers, CU-302, Bancroft Library, University of California, Berkeley; Clark Kerr, "Education for a Free Society: The California Experience," August 11, 1959, Carton 28, Folder 46, Clark Kerr Personal and Professional Papers, CU-302, Bancroft Library, University of California, Berkeley; Clark Kerr, "The Total Student and His Total Environment," October 3, 1958, Carton 28, Folder 18, Clark Kerr Personal and Professional Papers, CU-302, Bancroft Library, University of California, Berkeley.

109. Kerr quoted in Stuart, "Clark Kerr," 182; Clark Kerr, "1970–1980: A Decade of Reckoning?" Carton 28, Folder 28, Clark Kerr Personal and Professional Papers, CU-302, Bancroft Library, University of California, Berkeley; Clark Kerr, "1970–1980: A Decade of Reckoning?" Carton 28, Folder 34, Clark Kerr Personal and Professional Papers, CU-302, Bancroft Library, University of California, Berkeley.

Chapter 2

1. Herbert "Brad" Cleaveland's letter was originally published in the Slate Supplemental Report, vol. 1, no. 4, Berkeley, September 10, 1964; Cleaveland, "A Letter to Undergraduates."

2. Cleaveland's pamphlet was originally written and distributed in mimeographed form in September 1964; Cleaveland, "Education, Revolutions, and Citadels."

3. Herbert Cleaveland, "Free Speech Movement Oral History Project: Herbert Cleaveland," conducted by Lisa Rubens in 1998, Regional Oral History Office, Bancroft Library, University of California, Berkeley, 2013, 11, 21, 27; Heirich, *Spiral of Conflict*, 101; Goines, *Free Speech Movement*, 81.

4. Goines, *Free Speech Movement*, 79.

5. Most of the vast literature on the FSM does little to connect that rebellion against UC president Clark Kerr to Kerr's work on the California Master Plan. One exception, of course, is Hal Draper's own work, *Berkeley: The New Student Revolt*. On the FSM, see, for instance, Rorabaugh, *Berkeley at War*; Cohen, *Freedom's Orator*; Cohen and Zelnik, *The Free Speech Movement*; and Rosenfeld, *Subversives*.

6. Kerr, *The Gold and the Blue*, 1:70. The Godkin Lecture series began in 1903, in memory of Edwin L. Godkin, the Irish American journalist who founded *The Nation*. See John H. Fenton, "The Emerging U.S. University Is Called a Model: Kerr of California Delivers 3d Godkin Talk at Harvard," *New York Times*, April 26, 1963, 18; Lemann, *The Big Test*, 137; Irving S. Bengelsdorf, "Clark Kerr's Essays Define a University," *Los Angeles Times*, October 17, 1963.

7. Lemann, *The Big Test*, 137–38.

8. Kerr, *Uses of the University*, 1–2, 7.

9. Kerr, *Uses of the University*, 9.

10. Kerr, *Uses of the University*, 10, 11.

11. Kerr, *Uses of the University*, 15, 16.

12. Kerr, *Uses of the University*, 18, 37, 33.

13. Kerr, *Uses of the University*, 46, 48–49.

14. Kerr, *Uses of the University*, 86–87.

15. Kerr, *Uses of the University*, 86, 87–88,

16. Kerr, *Uses of the University*, 90, 103.

17. Kerr, *Uses of the University*, 104, 121, 124.

18. Freeman, *At Berkeley in the '60s*, 18–19, 260; Heirich, *Spiral of Conflict*, 71–73, 77, 428; Rorabaugh, *Berkeley at War*, 15.

19. Stadtman, *University of California*, 435.

20. Draper, *Berkeley*, 21. The Kerr piece was originally published in 1962 in the second volume of the student journal *The Activist*. Payne, Walls, and Berman, "Theodicy of 1984," 237.

21. Heirich, *Spiral of Conflict*, 80. Although students other than those from Berkeley participated in the HUAC protests, former Berkeley graduate student and activist Joel Geier notes that protesters included hundreds of Berkeley students, many of them previously radicalized by their participation in civil rights activism. See Geier, "Radicals and the Berkeley Free Speech Movement."

22. Wachter's parents were longtime members of the Communist Party and Wachter himself belonged to the party's youth group. See Rosenfeld, *Subversives*, 80; Freeman, *At Berkeley in the '60s*, 40.

23. Freeman, *At Berkeley in the '60s*, 40, 42; Heirich, *Spiral of Conflict*, 83; Draper, *Berkeley*, 23.

24. As FSM leader Jack Weinberg would later put it, for him, the FSM was "part of the Civil Rights Movement." "I was a civil rights activist and I wanted to mobilize

students on campus, I didn't want the university to get in the way. And I was very pissed off. At that moment in American history when everybody was forced to take a side, the University of California at Berkeley was taking the wrong side." Jack Weinberg in discussion with the author, July 28, 2021.

25. Only two years prior, in 1961, the Berkeley administration canceled a scheduled talk by Malcolm X. See Felber, "Integration or Separation?"

26. The Friends of SNCC were a northern network of support groups established to aid the Student Nonviolent Coordinating Committee (SNCC).

27. Carson, *In Struggle*, 89–91; Freeman, *At Berkeley in the '60s*, 85–86; Freeman, "From Freedom Now! to Free Speech," 73–74; Heirich, *Spiral of Conflict*, 85–86; Martin, "Holding One Another," 89; Cohen, *Freedom's Orator*, 38–39.

28. Starr, *Golden Dreams*, 202, 216.

29. Students also believed that Bank of America president Jesse Tapp, who simultaneously served as a UC Regent, lodged complaints regarding student protests at his bank. Draper, *Berkeley*, 29.

30. In 1949, the UC Board of Regents had instituted a ban on all political activity on the UC campuses. See Aptheker, *Intimate Politics*, 126.

31. Dean Katherine Towle: "I knew perfectly well that that was university property. Many people since then have claimed that they didn't know it, and I assume that they didn't, but I find it a little hard to understand that no one seemed to recognize the fact that that was university property except for myself." Heirich, *Spiral of Conflict*, 96.

32. Kerr, *The Gold and the Blue*, 2:61.

33. John Masson Smith and Richard Bridgman, "Chronology of the Free Speech Controversy on the Berkeley Campus (December 1964)," in *The FSM Papers*, ed. Hal Draper, microfilm, Shields Library, University of California, Davis, 474–76; Warshaw, *The Trouble in Berkeley*, 25; Heirich, *Spiral of Conflict*, 107; Miller and Gilmore, *Revolution at Berkeley*, xxiv; Draper, *Berkeley*, 36, 37.

34. Eighteen of the twenty-four founding members of the ISC had previously belonged to the Berkeley branch of the Young People's Socialist League (Socialist Party). Some number of them had moved to Berkeley at Draper's suggestion. Six other founders of the ISC came to the group from Campus CORE. See Geier, "Radicals and the Berkeley Free Speech Movement." Stiles Hall was a building near the campus that had become a gathering place for organizers banned from meeting on campus. See Johnson, "The Bible of the Free Speech Movement," 2.

35. His brother, Theodore, would become a well-known historian of American Communism.

36. Bureaucratic collectivism was one of a number of explanations offered by Trotsky and his followers regarding the development of the Soviet state. Where Trotsky considered the USSR a degenerated workers' state, others argued that the USSR never reached the stage of a true workers' state and thus could not have degenerated from that point. Still others maintained that the USSR was an example of state capitalism in which those in control geared the state apparatus toward greater capital accumulation. Finally, the phrase bureaucratic collectivism was first coined by Bruno Rizzi in 1939 but was popularized in the American context by Max

Shachtman. Although some early proponents of bureaucratic collectivism lurched toward the right to varying degrees—including Shachtman, Rizzi, and James Burnham—Alex Callinicos notes that "a minority led by Hal Draper resisted this evolution" by remaining firm critics of both the United States and the Soviet Union from a principled position on the left. See Callincos, *Trotskyism*, 55–60, 73–79; Johnson, "Introduction; Hal Draper," 181.

37. Quoted in Johnson, "Introduction; Hal Draper," 182.

38. In addition to Draper, the ISL leadership "at its apex" included Max Shachtman, Irving Howe, and Michael Harrington, among others. The late sociologist Stanley Aronowitz described the WP-ISL as "perhaps the most intellectually vital of all the radical formations in the 1940s and 1950s" in the United States. See Aronowitz, *Death and Rebirth of American Radicalism*, 208.

39. Johnson, "Introduction; Hal Draper," 182.

40. Geier, "Radicals and the Berkeley Free Speech Movement."

41. As Sam Farber, one of Draper's many mentees, put it, Hal "played an extremely influential role as a political mentor for many of the leaders and student activists involved" in the FSM. Farber, "The Berkeley Free Speech Movement."

42. Savio, "Introduction," 7. Despite Weinberg's famous words—an off-the-cuff remark—he himself has described the "contributions that Hal made to the FSM" as both "very significant" and "critically important." Jack Weinberg in discussion with the author, July 28, 2021.

43. Reminiscences of Mario Savio, Interview 1 (March 5, 1985), Student Movement of the 1960s Project, p. 60, Columbia Center for Oral History Archives, Rare Book & Manuscript Library, Columbia University, New York. Prior to the FSM, in addition to his work in the civil rights movement, Savio had been "an inactive YPSL [Young People's Socialist League] member." According to YPSL national secretary–turned ISC cofounder Joel Geier, Savio "agreed with our third camp politics, civil rights militancy, and emphasis on radical democracy from below, but not with our opposition to all Democratic Party candidates." See Geier, "Radicals and the Berkeley Free Speech Movement."

44. Mario Savio, "Dear Hal; December 7," Hal Draper Papers, D-373, Box 5, Folder 32, Shields Library, Special Collections, University of California, Davis; Hal Draper, "Dear Mario; 22 January 1966," Hal Draper Papers, D-373, Box 5, Folder 32, Shields Library, Special Collections, University of California, Davis. Photographic evidence suggests that Savio took up Anne Draper's offer to visit Delano, California, in support of the United Farm Workers. See Series V: Photographs, ca. 1961–1966, Box 23, Folder 2 of the Anne Draper Papers, M0228, Department of Special Collections, Stanford University Libraries, Stanford, California.

45. Kerr was the lead author of the 1960 text, which was coauthored by John Dunlop, Frederick Harbison, and Charles Myers. See Kerr et al., *Industrialism and Industrial Man*.

46. Goines later wrote, "Were any of the protesters going to sit down and read [Kerr's] books? Not a chance. Students were much accustomed to synopses of course texts and lectures, and Draper's pamphlet contained as much of Kerr's work

as we felt we needed to read. As far as we were concerned, Kerr had dug his grave with his teeth." Goines, *Free Speech Movement*, 54–55.

47. Kerr, "Postscript—1972," in *Uses of the University*.

48. Kerr, *The Gold and the Blue*, 2:53.

49. Horowitz, *Student*, 13.

50. Hal Draper, *The Mind of Clark Kerr* (Berkeley, CA: The Independent Socialist Club, 1964), 7, Shields Library, Special Collections, University of California, Davis.

51. In addition to the speeches and pamphlets they produced, student activists went as far as designing buttons announcing "I Am A Multi-Rebel" and producing a satirical play starring a thinly disguised Clark Kerr character with the nickname of Multiman. In the play, anonymous author I M Mortal Bored depicts Kerr as "Clark Urp . . . mild mannered president of the Multiversity of Cacafornia." But when he dons his suit, Urp is transformed into his "true form as MULTIMAN, COURAGEOUS MEDIATOR" and quickly defuses the free speech agitation that had developed on his campus. See "Button Designs," 1965, Free Speech Movement records, CU-309, Box 3, Folder 36, Bancroft Library, University of California, Berkeley; I M Mortal Bored, "Clark's Courageous Caper OR Another Crisis Met and Mastered???" 1964, Free Speech Movement records, CU-309, Carton 5, Folder 3, Bancroft Library, University of California, Berkeley.

52. Kerr, *Uses of the University*, 86.

53. Draper, *Berkeley*, 7–8.

54. It is interesting to note that in addition to Kerr's utilization of Aldous Huxley's phrase "a brave new world," several of the speeches Kerr gave in the years surrounding the development of the Master Plan were titled some variation on "1984." In these speeches, which varied only slightly from one another in their emphases, Kerr aimed to show that his own vision of the future was more likely than Orwell's largely discredited dystopian one; Draper, *Berkeley*, 9.

55. Draper, *Berkeley*, 9.

56. Draper, *Berkeley*, 10. Such quotes find their counterparts in a speech Kerr delivered—"1970–1980: A Decade of Reckoning"—in 1959 at Pomona and San Jose State Colleges. There, Kerr opined, "There may in fact be instances when it is better for a country to have a temporary military dictator who is honest and progressive . . . than a democracy which is run by corrupt and bungling politicians. . . . Though we cherish self-government, we should be realistic about both time and place. Degrees of 'guidance' from above may be inevitable in some situations today, and should be both expected and accepted." Although there is no reason to assume that Draper had any knowledge of these speeches, Kerr's words here go a long way toward confirming Draper's criticisms. See Clark Kerr, "Pomona College: 1970–1980 a Decade of Reckoning, February 12, 1959," Clark Kerr Personal and Professional Papers, CU-302, Carton 28, Folder 28, Bancroft Library, University of California, Berkeley; Clark Kerr, "Founders' Day, San Jose State College, May 5, 1959," Clark Kerr Personal and Professional Papers, CU-302, Carton 28, Folder 34, Bancroft Library, University of California, Berkeley.

57. Draper, *Berkeley*, 8–9, 10.

58. Draper, *Berkeley*, 11.

59. Draper, *Berkeley*, 14.

60. Savio, of course, was incorrect about the phrase knowledge factory being Kerr's own words. His attribution of "knowledge industry" to Kerr, on the other hand, was accurate; Savio quoted in Goines, *Free Speech Movement*, 151–52.

61. Savio quoted in Heirich, *Spiral of Conflict*, 133, 135.

62. In retelling this incident, Weinberg incorrectly remembered Draper's talk as being given the night before. It was actually two nights before, on September 29, not 30. Weinberg, though active on and around the Berkeley campus, was then taking time off from his graduate studies in mathematics to focus full time on civil rights organizing in the Bay Area. Weinberg had joined Draper's ISC after its founding in 1964 but left early into the FSM so as not to be seen as a mouthpiece for that organization. As he himself put it, "[I] had close relations with ISC members during the FSM and beyond. However, it soon became apparent to both the ISC leadership and me that I was not prepared to commit myself to ISC membership and they were not prepared to take responsibility for me and my actions." Weinberg would rejoin the ISC in 1966 and, after its 1969 transition into the International Socialists, remained a leading member into the late 1970s. Heirich, *Spiral of Conflict*, 123; Jack Weinberg in discussion with the author, July 28, 2021; email from Jack Weinberg to the author, September 2, 2021.

63. Unbeknownst to Weinberg or Draper, here Weinberg was channeling the language of H. Leslie Hoffman in 1958. As noted in chapter 1, the owner and CEO of Hoffman Electronics delivered a talk at Roy Simpson's Sacramento Conference on the Teaching of Mathematics and Science where he repeatedly used the term "product" when discussing students—noting, for instance, that the product suffered from a "lack of uniformity of quality" and was in need of "stricter discipline." See Hoffman, "Address Delivered February 24, 1958"; Draper *Berkeley*, 46.

64. The ranks of students surrounding the car swelled as the protest went on; estimates place the total number somewhere between three thousand and five thousand. See "A Brief History of the Free Speech Controversy," 1965, Free Speech Movement records, CU-309, Carton 1, Folder 8, Bancroft Library, University of California, Berkeley; and "Aptheker, Bettina," January 1965, CU-309, Carton 2, Folder 2, Bancroft Library, University of California, Berkeley.

65. According to Draper's own account, he spoke for approximately fifteen minutes. See Draper, *Berkeley*, 49; Heirich, *Spiral of Conflict*, 161.

66. On the pact, see Draper, *Berkeley*, 62–67.

67. Draper as quoted by Weinberg. As Weinberg noted, Hal's remark "created for me the frame in which to move forward. . . . In the next several months the Free Speech Movement leadership treated that agreement as an agreement to negotiate in good faith . . . and all of our strategies and tactics flowed from that." Jack Weinberg in discussion with the author, July 28, 2021.

68. Geier was a leader in the Berkeley ISC as well as a key organizer in the United Front and FSM. See Johnson, "The Bible of the Free Speech Movement," 3.

69. Savio, "Introduction," 7.

70. Parker was then a graduate student in the Department of Political Science. See Parker, "Mario Savio, 1942–1996."

71. The original members of the steering committee were Mario Savio, Jack Weinberg, David Friedman, Tom Miller, Brian Turner—all five of whom attended Draper's "Behind the Ban" talk—Art Goldberg, Jackie Goldberg, Bettina Aptheker, and Syd Stapleton. The three steering committee "moderates"—Turner and the Goldberg siblings—would be removed in the mid-November restructuring of the committee. All three, however, remained committed to the cause of the FSM. The steering committee, originally comprised of nine members, soon expanded. According to Hal Draper, the executive committee included more than fifty members. The executive committee consisted of two representatives from each of the "off-campus" student organizations that had originally formed the United Front, as well as representatives for independent students and religious groups. In addition to these two committees, some one hundred graduate students from twenty-five different departments met and elected representatives for what would become the graduate coordinating committee. According the Free Speech Union, the successor organization to the FSM, the steering committee, "unlike the executive committee, was chosen not to represent the spectrum of support for the FSM, but to supply the most able bargaining agents and most experienced tacticians, who would serve at the pleasure of the executive committee. By this structure, the civil rights groups were soon leading the FSM, and many of the techniques employed by these groups would be successfully employed by the FSM. . . . Through the succession of study committees set up by the administration to head off any further orderly student demonstrations, the FSM learned that it must trust to its dramatic forms of protest." Heirich, *Spiral of Conflict*, 218; Draper, *Berkeley*, 72; Cohen, *Freedom's Orator*, 122–23; Freeman, *At Berkeley in the '60s*, 169; Eric Levine, "The Berkeley Free Speech Controversy," 1965, Free Speech Movement records, CU-309, Carton 4, Folder 81, Bancroft Library, University of California, Berkeley; Free Student Union, "A Brief History of the Free Speech Controversy," 1965, Free Speech Movement records, CU-309, Carton 1, Folder 8, Bancroft Library, University of California, Berkeley. Although I did not find this information in printed sources, Friedman and Miller attended Draper's talk according to ISC cofounder Joel Geier, who was also there—this according to an email from Joel Geier to the author, April 9, 2021.

72. "Aptheker, Bettina," January 1965, Free Speech Movement records, CU-309, Carton 2, Folder 2, Bancroft Library, University of California, Berkeley.

73. The teaching assistants union, which was eventually established in December 1964, was the first effort to organize a union for graduate students in the history of the University of California. Heirich, *Spiral of Conflict*, 246, 247; Draper, *Berkeley*, 93–95; Freeman, *At Berkeley in the '60s*, 184.

74. Whereas the on-campus newspaper the *Daily Californian* put the rally at three thousand, FSM organizers maintained there were nearly five thousand protesters present. Draper, *Berkeley*, 99–100; Miller and Gilmore, *Revolution at Berkeley*, xxvii; Heirich, *Spiral of Conflict*, 251–52; Goines, *Free Speech Movement*, 337–41; Freeman, *At Berkeley in the '60s*, 201.

75. Heirich, *Spiral of Conflict*, 251.

76. Freeman, *At Berkeley in the '60s*, 202–3.

77. In the coming years, student organizers would compile several sophisticated analyses of the regents, including Marvin Garson's 1965 pamphlet *The Regents*, steering committee member Bettina Aptheker's 1966 *Big Business and the American University*, and several years later, the Radical Student Union's 1969 *The Uses of U.C. Berkeley*.

78. Bettina Aptheker put the number at "fewer than two hundred" while Draper and Heirich both argued it was closer to three hundred. Whereas Draper and Heirich refer to the "abortive sit-in" in their contemporary accounts, historian Robert Cohen calls it the "aborted sit-in." Draper, *Berkeley*, 107; Heirich, *Spiral of Conflict*, 260; Aptheker, *Intimate Politics*, 138; Cohen, *Freedom's Orator*, 167.

79. Heirich, *Spiral of Conflict*, 263.

80. Draper, *Berkeley*, 110.

81. Confusingly, in her 2006 memoirs, Bettina Aptheker lists Sandor Fuchs as one of the suspended students but does not include Mario Savio. Fuchs, a former Slate chairman and United Front organizer, does not appear to have been targeted by the administration at this time despite Aptheker's claims to the contrary. Aptheker, *Intimate Politics*, 140.

82. Goines, *Free Speech Movement*, 354.

83. The rally was the best attended protest of the FSM up to that point. Draper put the number at six thousand. Aptheker called five thousand a conservative estimate, noting that "it seemed like many more to me." However, Heirich argued that the crowd was somewhere between four thousand and five thousand. Historian Robert Cohen agrees with Draper's estimate of six thousand. Draper, *Berkeley*, 113; Aptheker, *Intimate Politics*, 142; Heirich, *Spiral of Conflict*, 270; Cohen, *Freedom's Orator*, 178.

84. Cohen, *Freedom's Orator*, 179, 183, 326.

85. Savio quoted in Cohen, *Freedom's Orator*, 327.

86. Earlier in the month, Mario Savio and Bettina Aptheker had traveled from Berkeley to Carmel, California, where they met with the pacifist Ira Sandperl who introduced them to Joan Baez. Having assured the folksinger of their commitment to nonviolence, Baez agreed to return to Berkeley in support of the FSM. See Aptheker, *Intimate Politics*, 141.

87. Savio's speech would later be published, without revision, in the December 1964 issue of *Humanity*. The speech was transcribed from an audiotape recorded during the Sproul Hall sit-in. The speech is available in full in Cohen, *Freedom's Orator*, 329–22.

88. In *The Mind of Clark Kerr*, Draper noted multiple times Kerr's references to a "brave new world." Draper, importantly, was a key theorist of bureaucratic collectivism—a theory that seems to have influenced Savio's speech. One cannot, of course, discount the likely influence of other theorists of the bureaucratic—Max Weber, C. Wright Mills, or even Franz Kafka, the last of whom Savio himself references— yet the fact that Savio had attended Draper's talk and that Draper served as a mentor to the young activist points to the centrality of Draper's influence above all others.

89. Here, Savio can be understood to critique Kerr's idea that the central figure of the modern university is the university president—Kerr's "captain of the bureaucracy." His reference to the university having "ceased evolving" also points to Kerr's teleological history of the university, with all evolution aspiring toward the multiversity.

90. With this line, Savio recalls Draper: "There are railroads and steel mills and supermarkets and sausage factories—and there are also Knowledge Factories, whose function is to service all the others and the State." Draper's factories "and the State" have become Savio's "industry or government."

91. On September 30, the day after attending Draper's talk, Savio had proclaimed that "President Kerr has referred to the University as a factory; a knowledge factory—that's his words—engaged in the knowledge industry. And just like any factory, in any industry—again his words—you have a certain product. They go in one side, as kind of rough-cut adolescents, and they come out the other side pretty smooth."

92. This can be read as a direct attack on Kerr's vision for the future. In Kerr's words, "Along with the bureaucratic conservatism of economic and political life may well go a New Bohemianism." Savio's rejection of a "consumers' paradise" is thus a rejection of Kerr's promise of "leisure of individuals." The previous quotes come directly from Draper's *The Mind of Clark Kerr* in which he quotes directly from Kerr's 1960 *Industrialism and Industrial Man*.

93. Draper, *Berkeley*, 122.

94. Aptheker, *Intimate Politics*, 145.

95. Strike organizer Joel Geier would later note that this was "the first successful student strike in the United States since the 1930s." See Geier, "Radicals and the Berkeley Free Speech Movement."

96. Draper, *Berkeley*, 125.

97. Heirich, *Spiral of Conflict*, 279.

98. Heirich, *Spiral of Conflict*, 280.

99. Draper, *Berkeley*, 128; Heirich, *Spiral of Conflict*, 282.

100. Heirich, *Spiral of Conflict*, 282.

101. In full, the Henry May resolutions read as follows: "1. That the new and liberalized rules for campus political action be declared in effect and enforced, pending their improvement. 2. That all pending campus action against students for acts occurring before the present date be dropped. 3. That a committee selected by and responsible to the Academic Senate be established, to which students may appeal decisions of the Administration regarding penalties for offenses arising from political action, and that decisions of this committee be final." The additions by Herbert McClosky were "1. Retraction of the Regents' decision that the university could prosecute students for advocating illegal off-campus action. 2. A demand that no student be prosecuted by the university for participating in any off-campus activity." Heirich, *Spiral of Conflict*, 281–83.

102. Draper, *Berkeley*, 130.

103. Draper, *Berkeley*, 133.

104. Draper, *Berkeley*, 135.

105. Draper gave a broader estimate of fifteen thousand to eighteen thousand. Aptheker, who is often on the high end of estimates, put the crowd at "more than twenty thousand." The *New York Times* put the number at a more conservative thirteen thousand. Heirich, *Spiral of Conflict*, 293; Draper, *Berkeley*, 142; Aptheker, *Intimate Politics*, 151; Wallace Turner, "Berkeley Peace Parley Upset as Police Grab Student," *New York Times*, December 8, 1964.

106. Savio later described Kerr's talk at the Greek Theatre as "half and half fabrication and platitude." See Savio, "The Berkeley Knowledge Factory," 210.

107. Turner, "Berkeley Peace Parley."

108. Kerr, *The Gold and the Blue*, 2:215. Savio was famously dragged off the stage by his tie. In response, Hal Draper soon gifted Savio a set of four clip-on ties. See "Mario Savio, Jack Weinberg & Free Speech Movement Victory."

109. Heirich wrote that reporters estimated the rally at ten thousand; Draper put the number between eight thousand and ten thousand. Heirich, *Spiral of Conflict*, 298; Draper, *Berkeley*, 145.

110. In full, the proposals read as follows: "1. That there shall be no University disciplinary measures against members or organizations of the University community for activities prior to December 8th connected with the recent controversy over political speech and activity. 2. That the time, place, and manner of conducting political activity on the campus shall be subject to reasonable regulation to prevent interference with the normal functions of the University. That the regulations now in effect for this purpose shall remain in effect provisionally pending a future report of the Committee on Academic Freedom concerning the minimal regulations necessary. 3. That the content of speech or advocacy should not be restricted by the University. Off-campus student political activities shall not be subjected to University regulation. On-campus advocacy or organization of such activities shall be subject only to such limitations as may be imposed under Section 2. 4. That future disciplinary measures in the area of political activity shall be determined by a committee appointed by and responsible to the Berkeley Division of the Academic Senate. 5. That the Division urge the adoption of the foregoing policies, and call on all members of the University community to join with the faculty in its efforts to restore the University to its normal functions." Heirich, *Spiral of Conflict*, 302.

111. Draper, *Berkeley*, 146; Heirich, *Spiral of Conflict*, 315–16.

112. Heirich, *Spiral of Conflict*, 317.

113. Heirich, *Spiral of Conflict*, 319–20.

114. Draper, *Berkeley*, 158.

115. Heirich, *Spiral of Conflict*, 322.

116. Strong remained a faculty member at UC Berkeley for two years until his retirement in 1967.

117. Aptheker, *Intimate Politics*, 152.

118. Rorabaugh, *Berkeley at War*, 91–100; Farber, "The Berkeley Free Speech Movement."

119. Rosenfeld, *Subversives*, 225.

120. Aptheker, *Intimate Politics*, 153.

121. This speech was first printed in *New Politics*, a magazine cofounded by Hal Draper. On Draper's involvement in the establishment of *New Politics*, see Johnson, "Introduction; Hal Draper," 182; Savio, "The Berkeley Knowledge Factory," 214.

122. Parker Donham, "Savio Blasts Kerr's 'Knowledge Factory,'" *Harvard Crimson*, December 12, 1964.

123. Draper notes, in a letter to Mario Savio, that his analysis was outselling two competing accounts of the FSM—*The Berkeley Student Revolt* by Lipset and Wolin and *Revolution at Berkeley* by Miller and Gilmore. All three were initially published in early 1965. See Hal Draper, "Dear Mario," October 22, 1965, Hal Draper Papers, D-373, Box 5, Folder 32, Shields Library, Special Collections, University of California, Davis. The date of publication comes from an earlier letter from Draper to Savio. See Hal Draper, "Dear Mario," September 9, 1965, Hal Draper Papers, D-373, Box 5, Folder 32, Shields Library, Special Collections, University of California, Davis.

124. Savio, "Introduction," 7.

125. Discounts ran from 40 percent off for anywhere from 25 to 199 books purchased, up to 45 percent off for purchases beyond 1,000 copies. Booth responded in kind to Draper's offer, promising to put together "a very large box of [SDS] literature" to send to Draper. Draper, enthusiastic as ever in keeping up on developments within the New Left, advised Booth that "I should like to order a complete set of all SDS literature available—I mean all pamphlets, booklets, etc. that you can find or scrounge up, INCLUDING all copies of the Bulletin and other discussion bulletins issued, INCLUDING mimeographed material as well as printed. I mean *all*: if in doubt, include it. Send a bill along with the material, and I'll send you payment immediately." See Hal Draper, "Paul Booth, SDS Chicago," September 28, 1965, Hal Draper Papers, D-373, Box 5, Folder 46, Shields Library, Special Collections, University of California, Davis; Paul Booth, "Dear Hal; 10-6-65," Hal Draper Papers, D-373, Box 5, Folder 46, Shields Library, Special Collections, University of California, Davis; Hal Draper, "Dear Paul," September 28, 1965, Hal Draper Papers, D-373, Box 5, Folder 46, Shields Library, Special Collections, University of California, Davis.

126. Paul Booth, "To SDS Worklist People," October 6, 1965, Hal Draper Papers, D-373, Box 5, Folder 46, Shields Library, Special Collections, University of California, Davis; Paul Booth, "Dear Mr. Goldfischer," October 6, 1965, Hal Draper Papers, D-373, Box 5, Folder 46, Shields Library, Special Collections, University of California, Davis.

127. "Students in Revolt: The Battle of the Berkeley Campus," *Solidarity* 18 (ca. 1965), Free Speech Movement records, CU-309, Carton 5, Folder 58, Bancroft Library, University of California, Berkeley.

128. Roussopoulos, "Canada," 39–45; Sangster, "Radical Ruptures."

129. Although Weinberg makes no direct reference to the California Master Plan for Higher Education, it seems likely that his reference to "a master plan"—the emphasis is my own—is a dig at Master Plan architect and archnemesis of the FSM Clark Kerr. Jack Weinberg, *The Wildcat Strike and the Knowledge Factory* (Toronto: Research, Information, and Publications Project, January 1965), Free Speech Movement records, CU-309, Carton 4, Folder 90, Bancroft Library, University of California, Berkeley.

130. Savio, "The University Has Become a Factory"; Savio, "The Uncertain Future of the Multiversity," 88–94.

131. Savio, "The Uncertain Future of the Multiversity," 89.

Chapter 3

1. Jeffries, *Grand Hotel Abyss*, 91, 281–82.

2. The potential outcome of such a campaign was well known in California. Less than a decade earlier, in 1961, an anti-communist gunman stormed the UC Berkeley campus targeting Professors Thomas F. Parkinson and Peter T. Drinnon. The gunman shot and wounded Parkinson, before killing twenty-nine-year-old graduate student Stephen Mann Thomas. "Suspect in UC Shootings Nabbed in Hills," *Los Angeles Times*, January 20, 1961; "Confesses He Slew Student and Shot Prof," *Los Angeles Times*, January 20, 1961; and "Fanatic in Campus Shooting Reveals 2d Intended Victim," *The Sun*, January 21, 1961.

3. McGill, *The Year of the Monkey*, 59.

4. Gennaro and Kellner, "Under Surveillance," 285, 305, 306.

5. Rosenfeld, *Subversives*, 107, 485.

6. In 1972, the Secret Army Organization—a San Diego–based militia with purported ties to the FBI—attempted the assassination of Peter Bohmer, a New Left philosophy professor at San Diego State College. On the attempt on Peter Bohmer, see Churchill and Vander Wall, *Agents of Repression*, 182. For contemporary accounts, see, for instance, David Shaw, "Vigilantes to the Right Look for a Takeover: Ranks Grow within County," *Los Angeles Times*, August 10, 1969; "Shots Fired into Bohmer's Home; Woman Hit," *Los Angeles Times*, January 7, 1972; "Secret Army, Minutemen Tied to Bombing, Sniper Arrests," *Los Angeles Times*, June 28, 1972; Steven V. Roberts, "F.B.I. Informer Is Linked to Right-Wing Violence," *New York Times*, June 24, 1973; Everett R. Holles, "A.C.L.U. Says F.B.I. Funded 'Army' to Terrorize Young War Dissidents," *New York Times*, June 27, 1975; "The FBI's 'Secret Army of Terrorists,'" *San Francisco Examiner*, January 11, 1976.

7. Harold Keen and William Tully, "'New Left' UC Professor Flees from Home after Death Threat," *Los Angeles Times*, July 11, 1968; "New Left Teacher Declares He Won't Quit Despite Death Note," *Los Angeles Times*, July 12, 1968; McGill, *Year of the Monkey*, 71.

8. Jim Bettinger, "Chancellors Deprived of Power to Approve Tenure by Slim One-Vote Margin," *El Gaucho*, April 21, 1969; Smelser, "Growth, Structural Change, and Conflict," 135.

9. Rosenfeld, *Subversives*.

10. McGill, *Year of the Monkey*, 82, 158; Dennis McCall, "Zenovich Raps Reagan for Political Interference," *Daily Collegian*, April 21, 1969.

11. It is worth noting here, given Reagan's long cooperation with J. Edgar Hoover, that the leading scholar of McCarthyism, Ellen Schrecker, has argued that McCarthyism should "probably be called 'Hooverism.' For the FBI was the bureaucratic heart of the McCarthy era." Schrecker, *Many Are the Crimes*, 203.

12. Scholarship on the New Right that has had a particular influence on my analysis—despite the relative lack of emphasis on education—includes Fones-Wolf, *Selling Free Enterprise*; Kruse, *White Flight*; Lowndes, *From the New Deal to the New Right*; and Phillips-Fein, *Invisible Hands*.

13. Skowronek, *The Politics Presidents Make*, 46.

14. Lewis, *What Makes Reagan Run?*, 173.

15. On 1978's anti-tax Proposition 13, see Schrag, *Paradise Lost*; and Self, *American Babylon*.

16. "Newspaper Descriptions of Max Rafferty," Bollinger Bruce Collection of Max Rafferty materials, BANC MSS 2000/135C, Carton 1, Folder 2, Bancroft Library, University of California, Berkeley; Gene Marine, "New Hope of the Far Right," clipping from *The Nation*, Bollinger Bruce Collection of Max Rafferty materials, BANC MSS 2000/135C, Carton 1, Folder 10, Bancroft Library, University of California, Berkeley.

17. "Rafferty Chronology," Bollinger Bruce Collection of Max Rafferty materials, BANC MSS 2000/135C, Box 1, Folder 4, Bancroft Library, University of California, Berkeley.

18. For more on the battles over Dewey's influence on public higher education in California, see chapter 1; Starr, *Golden Dreams*, 200, 201.

19. Cannon, *Reagan*, 158.

20. As the previous footnote attests, even the conservative Lou Cannon—an admirer and biographer of Ronald Reagan over several decades—describes Rafferty as an "ultraconservative." However, a recent study has proposed that an exploration of Rafferty's career "reveals . . . the inadequacy of existing labels such as 'conservative' and liberal'" and promises to "illuminate cracks in the foundation of his much-remarked conservatism." Further, the author states that "curiously . . . Rafferty proclaimed himself nonpartisan for much of his career." This fact is much less curious when one notes that the position Rafferty held for nearly a decade at the height of his career—state superintendent of public instruction—was officially a nonpartisan office. Abhorred by Democrats and moderate Republicans alike, by the time of his failed 1968 Senate run, Rafferty had alienated even conservative Republicans with his open criticism of the sitting governor. Reagan biographer Cannon notes Republican complaints that by 1968, "Rafferty was dragging down the party's legislative ticket." Cannon hints that Reagan and other top-ranking California Republicans actually voted against Rafferty in his failed 1970 run for reelection as state superintendent. Henry Salvatori, Ronald Reagan's money man, had in fact cut off all fundraising to Rafferty during his primary run against Thomas Kuchel, leaving Rafferty to "rely heavily" on out-of-state contributions. Rejected by California at the height of its Reagan revolution, Rafferty moved to Alabama where he hitched his wagon to George Wallace. Needless to say, this author remains unconvinced by the Rafferty-as-moderate thesis. See Petrzela, "Revisiting the Rightward Turn." On Reagan and Rafferty, see Cannon, *Governor Reagan*, 325–26, 346; Lewis, *What Makes Reagan Run?*, 198. To drive home the point, note the following descriptors of Rafferty in late-sixties' newspapers: "a Goldwater Republican with wide support from the radical right including the John Birch Society" (*San Jose*

Union Gazette); "[a person] whose views on practically everything are so reactionary that they make those of Gov. Ronald Reagan . . . seem progressive" (*New York Times*); "a skillful demagogue" (*Watsonville Register-Pajaronian*); "one of the most flamboyant, militant conservatives" (*Congressional Quarterly*); "darling of the far right" (*Fresno Bee*); "a rank demagogue" (*Los Angeles Times*); "a Birch-backed huckster of the right" (*National City Star News*); "at best, an ultraconservative" (*Riverside Press*); "California's rip-snorting superintendent of public instruction, whose extremism may frighten a good many Democrats and independents to the polls" (*Washington Post*); "a superconservative" (*Time* magazine); "[The] New Hope of the Far Right" (*The Nation*). See "Newspaper Descriptions of Max Rafferty," Bollinger Bruce Collection of Max Rafferty materials, BANC MSS 2000/135C, Carton 1, Folder 2, Bancroft Library, University of California, Berkeley; Gene Marine, "New Hope of the Far Right," clipping from *The Nation*, Bollinger Bruce Collection of Max Rafferty materials, BANC MSS 2000/135C, Carton 1, Folder 10, Bancroft Library, University of California, Berkeley.

21. Henry Sutherland, "School Post Held One of Most Important in State: Superintendent Simpson Tells Need for Working with Board," *Los Angeles Times*, October 16, 1962.

22. Daryl Lembke, "Ralph Richardson Gets Simpson's Endorsement," *Los Angeles Times*, October 26, 1962.

23. Jerry Gillam, "Nixon Received 65.6% of GOP Primary Votes," *Los Angeles Times*, July 12, 1962.

24. Rafferty quoted in O'Neill, *Readin, Ritin, and Rafferty!*, 5.

25. Moreau, *Schoolbook Nation*, 292.

26. Parker, "Roots of the New Right."

27. "Grins and Growls: Fascism," *Daily Bruin*, March 30, 1937, Bollinger Bruce Collection of Max Rafferty materials, BANC MSS 2000/135C, Box 1, Folder 32, Bancroft Library, University of California, Berkeley.

28. Garrigues, "Loud Bark and Curious Eyes," 56; David Shaw, "Rafferty: Agitator as a Student," *Independent Press-Telegram*, September 2, 1968, Bollinger Bruce Collection of Max Rafferty materials, BANC MSS 2000/135C, Box 1, Folder 14, Bancroft Library, University of California, Berkeley.

29. Harrison, *Parts of a Past*, 19; Gilbert A. Harrison, "Liberal Perspectives Oral History Transcript," interviewed by Joel Gardner in 1982, Oral History Program, University Library, University of California, Los Angeles.

30. Garrigues, "Loud Bark and Curious Eyes," 56; David Shaw, "Rafferty: Agitator as a Student," *Independent Press-Telegram*, September 2, 1968, Bollinger Bruce Collection of Max Rafferty materials, BANC MSS 2000/135C, Box 1, Folder 14, Bancroft Library, University of California, Berkeley.

31. La Cañada had recently left the Pasadena school district, allegedly so that the suburbs' white students would not have to attend a high school that the National Association for the Advancement of Colored People had successfully targeted for integration. See Wollenberg, *All Deliberate Speed*, 141.

32. "Educator to Discuss Patriotism," *Los Angeles Times*, September 10, 1961.

33. Schuparra, *Triumph of the Right*, 81–82, 180; David Shaw, "One Speech Shot Rafferty into Prominence," *Long Beach Independent*, September 5, 1968, Bollinger

Bruce Collection of Max Rafferty materials, BANC MSS 2000/135C, Box 1, Folder 14, Bancroft Library, University of California, Berkeley.

34. "2,000 Attend Anti-Red Town Rally in Glendale," *Los Angeles Times*, November 14, 1961.

35. Gregory Rodriguez, "Glendale's 'Racist Shadow' Shrinks as City Transforms Itself," *Los Angeles Times*, June 16, 1996.

36. Schuparra, *Triumph of the Right*, 57; "Shell Fears Socialism if Nixon or Brown Win," *Los Angeles Times*, April 13, 1962.

37. Richard Bergholz, "Rafferty Denies He's 'Far Right' Candidate," *Los Angeles Times*, May 17, 1962; "Birch Society Political Endorsement Denied," *Los Angeles Times*, September 27, 1962.

38. As many would later note during Rafferty's 1968 Senate run, the acerbic conservative had walked with a cane during the war years, yet his limp mysteriously vanished when World War II came to a close; Dick Turpin, "Simpson Warns against 'Irresponsible' Critics," *Los Angeles Times*, December 5, 1961; Ronald Moskowitz, "Simpson's Bitter Farewell," *San Francisco Examiner*, December 4, 1962.

39. The quote above is Turpin's paraphrasing of McClosky's remarks; Dick Turpin, "Extreme Rightists Hit as Threat to Education," *Los Angeles Times*, December 6, 1961.

40. "Superintendent Group Backs Richardson," *Los Angeles Times*, July 28, 1962; Dick Turpin, "Richardson Backed by State Board," *Los Angeles Times*, October 12, 1962; "Birch Society Political Endorsement Denied," *Los Angeles Times*, September 27, 1962.

41. Roy E. Simpson, "California State Department of Education, 1945–1962," conducted by Gabrielle Morris in 1978, Knight-Brown Era Oral History Project, Regional Oral History Office, Bancroft Library, University of California, Berkeley, 62.

42. Daryl Lembke, "Ralph Richardson Gets Simpson's Endorsement," *Los Angeles Times*, October 26, 1962.

43. Richard Bergholz, "Brown Leading, Kuchel Wins: Dr. Rafferty Ahead in Tight Race; Big Turnout Sets Record," *Los Angeles Times*, November 7, 1962; "Rafferty Surges Ahead in School Chief Race," *Los Angeles Times*, November 7, 1962; Richard Bergholz, "Brown's Lead Grows: Nixon Admits Defeat, Indicates Intention to Give Up Politics," *Los Angeles Times*, November 8, 1962; Henry M. Madden, "Who Is Max Rafferty?" *California Librarian* 24, no. 3 (1963): 178, Bollinger Bruce Collection of Max Rafferty materials, BANC MSS 2000/135C, Box 1, Folder 4, Bancroft Library, University of California, Berkeley.

44. The noted journalist Joseph Lewis made a similar case for Reagan's uneasy transition from anti-statist campaigner to the titular head of state government: "He had made his point with the public, but he earned the unremitting enmity of the state work force. More experienced politicians [than Reagan] knew better than to tangle with the bureaucracy . . . who are highly organized and defensive when attacked." Lewis, *What Makes Reagan Run?*, 175.

45. Daryl Lembke, "Rafferty Faces 'Sales' Job in Education Post," *Los Angeles Times*, November 9, 1962.

46. The "life adjustment movement" included the introduction of, for example, what Richard Hofstadter dismissed as "a new course in family living or home

economics." Ironically, Hofstadter placed both life adjustment courses and the far-right conservatives who opposed them in his treatment of anti-intellectualism in American life. Dewey scholar Alan Ryan has noted that life adjustment included the 1950s era "proliferation of high school classes in how to get on with other people and the obsession with personal hygiene and conventional political loyalties that marked classes in health and civics." See Hofstadter, *Anti-intellectualism in American Life*, 340; Ryan, *John Dewey*, 348–49; Hartman, *Education and the Cold War*, 133; "Dr. Rafferty Outlines 7-Point Education Place: Stress on Phonics and American History Included by Newly Elected Schools Chief," *Los Angeles Times*, November 18, 1962.

47. "Braden Debating Stay on State School Board: Attributes Rafferty's Election to Public Unhappiness over Behavior of Children," *Los Angeles Times*, November 24, 1962.

48. Wilson C. Riles, "'No Adversary Situations': Public School Education in California and Wilson C. Riles, Superintendent of Public Instruction, 1970–1982," an oral history conducted 1981–82 by Sarah Sharp, Regional Oral History Office, Bancroft Library, University of California, Berkeley, 1984, 74.

49. O'Neill, *Readin, Ritin, and Rafferty!*, 8.

50. Daryl E. Lembke, "UC Regents Face Ruling on Rebels: Whether to Submit to Campus Demonstrators Is Big Question," *Los Angeles Times*, December 10, 1964.

51. Max Rafferty, "Education and the Big Lie," Department of Education Records, F3752:855, California State Archives, Secretary of State Office, Sacramento, California.

52. Max Rafferty, "Help Wanted; Hoodlum-Preventers," *Los Angeles Times*, August 9, 1965, Department of Education Records, F3752:851, California State Archives, Secretary of State Office, Sacramento, California.

53. Max Rafferty, "Disciplining Academic Freedom," *Los Angeles Times*, October 18, 1965.

54. Max Rafferty, "Announcement of Candidacy," March 22, 1966, Department of Education Records, F3752:855, California State Archives, Secretary of State Office, Sacramento, California.

55. Between 1899 and 1959, California had only a single Democratic governor—Culbert Olson, who rode President Franklin Roosevelt's coattails to the governor's mansion for a single term in 1939. He was defeated for reelection by Republican Earl Warren. See Schuparra, *Triumph of the Right*, 3–5.

56. Schuparra, *Triumph of the Right*, 81.

57. Dallek, *The Right Moment*, 62.

58. McGirr, *Suburban Warriors*, 121, 138–39.

59. As former Reagan aide Annelise Anderson noted in an oral history, "By the time he gave the Goldwater speech in '64, it was the speech that he'd been giving on the GE tours and to Rotary and to different places." See Knott and Chidester, *At Reagan's Side*, 13; and Cannon, *Governor Reagan*, 174.

60. Whereas Cannon puts Eureka's student body population at 250, historian Garry Wills cites a 1928 article in the Eureka College newspaper, *The Pegasus*, to

place the number at 187. See Wills, *Reagan's America*, 40, 395; Cannon, *Governor Reagan*, 11, 6–7.

61. Although the UC didn't charge "tuition" in name, the increased fees that Reagan introduced had the same effect. William Trombley, "Governor and Academia Never Came to Terms," *Los Angeles Times*, September 29, 1974, in "Reagan's Quixotic Reign, 1967-1974," Ronald Reagan Subject Collection, Box 48, Hoover Institute Archives.

62. De Groot, "Ronald Reagan and Student Unrest."

63. "Excerpts of Remarks by Governor Ronald Reagan; Eisenhower College Fund Raising Dinner; Washington, D.C., October 14, 1969," 4, Ronald Reagan Subject Collection, Box 47, Hoover Institute Archives.

64. Wills, *Reagan's America*, 29, 55.

65. As Cannon notes, Archibald E. Gray, "Eureka's only teacher of economics . . . was popular because he graded leniently and did not work his students hard." See Cannon, *Governor Reagan*, 32–33; Rosenfeld, *Subversives*, 116.

66. Cannon, *Reagan*, 52; Cannon, *Ronnie and Jesse*, 31.

67. Rosenfeld, *Subversives*, 118–19; Reagan himself would go on to claim that he was exempted from military combat because of "poor eyesight." Lewis, *What Makes Reagan Run?*, 33.

68. Rosenfeld, *Subversives*, 505–12.

69. Rosenfeld, *Subversives*, 121–22.

70. Rosenfeld, *Subversives*, 127–28, 130.

71. Cannon, *Ronnie and Jesse*, 68.

72. Lewis, *What Makes Reagan Run?*, 49; Kleinknecht, *The Man Who Sold the World*, 47–48.

73. Phillips-Fein, *Invisible Hands*, 114.

74. Schuparra, *Triumph of the Right*, 41. Or as a one observer at the time put it, "In the hands of a less polished speechmaker Reagan's essential arguments might have sounded like the grousing of a dyspeptic reactionary; but Reagan came across as reasonable and well-intentioned." Joseph Lewis, *What Makes Reagan Run?*, 2.

75. Reagan's press secretary jokingly referred to these "wealthy money people" as "the conservative fat cats." See Knott and Chidester, *At Reagan's Side*, 15; Cannon, *Ronnie and Jesse*, 71. In 1958, Rubel had helped lead a failed effort to make California a right-to-work state. See Lewis, *What Makes Reagan Run?*, 8. For more on Reagan's "money people," their aims, and their impact, see Holmes, "Economic Roots of Reaganism."

76. McBirnie left Texas in 1959 with his ministerial license revoked after news broke of a scandalous affair with one of his parishioners. See Dochuk, *From Bible Belt to Sunbelt*, 259–60, 268.

77. Schuparra, *Triumph of the Right*, 111–12, 110; Dallek, *The Right Moment*, 181.

78. Dallek, *The Right Moment*, 182.

79. Dallek, *The Right Moment*, 183.

80. Schuparra, *Triumph of the Right*, 119.

81. Dallek, *The Right Moment*, 175–76.

82. Gordon Luce, "A Banker's View of State Administration and Republican Politics," an oral history conducted by Gabrielle Morris and Sarah Sharp in 1981 and 1983 in *Governor Reagan and His Cabinet: An Introduction*, Regional Oral History Office, Bancroft Library, University of California, Berkeley, 1986, 6.

83. Dallek, *The Right Moment*, 204.

84. Journalist Seth Rosenfeld has noted that in 1961, an FBI informer whom that organization had deemed "reliable" reported Reagan secretly belonged to the John Birch Society. See Rosenfeld, Subversives, 304.

85. Lewis, *What Makes Reagan Run?*, 74; Schuparra, *Triumph of the Right*, 49.

86. Dallek, *The Right Moment*, 38–39. Despite his claims to the contrary, Reagan exhibited a rather mean racist streak. In 1971, as governor of California, Reagan phoned then-president Richard Nixon to complain about the presence of African delegates at the UN. Calling them "cannibals" and "monkeys," future president Reagan quipped that "they're still uncomfortable wearing shoes." Sarah Mervosh and Niraj Chokshi, "Reagan Called Africans 'Monkeys' in Call With Nixon, Tape Reveals," *New York Times*, July 31, 2019.

87. Even as top California Republicans promoted a repudiation of Bircher extremism, Ronald Reagan spoke at a convention alongside John Birch Society member John Schmitz of Orange County. See Carl Greenberg, "State Sen. Schmitz to Address CRA Meeting: Birch Society Member to Be Keynoter at Weekend Convention in San Diego," *Los Angeles Times*, March 25, 1965; Carl Greenberg, "GOP Can't Win Governorship with 'Goldwater Campaign,' CRA Told," *Los Angeles Times*, March 26, 1965.

88. Savage, "Save Our Republic," 195.

89. The quote paraphrased comes from William F. Buckley. See Buckley, "Our Mission Statement"; Robin, *The Reactionary Mind*, 7.

90. This point draws from a similar argument made by political scientists Michael Rogin and John Shover. See Rogin and Shover, *Political Change in California*, 196–201.

91. Lewis, *What Makes Reagan Run?*, 100.

92. On the Rumford Act–Proposition 14 saga, see chapter 7 in Brilliant, *The Color of America*, 190–226. See also Dallek, *The Right Moment*, 48–61; and Schuparra, *Triumph of the Right*, 119–20.

93. Ronald Reagan, "On Becoming Governor," an oral history conducted by Sarah Sharp in 1979 in *Governor Reagan and His Cabinet: An Introduction*, Regional Oral History Office, Bancroft Library, University of California, Berkeley, 1979, 21.

94. Spencer quoted in De Groot, "Ronald Reagan and Student Unrest," 110.

95. Spencer quoted in Knott and Chidester, *At Reagan's Side*, 22.

96. Rosenfeld, *Subversives*, 333.

97. Here, once again, Reagan seemed to be employing a strategy that was previously used by Max Rafferty. As William O'Neill, University of Southern California professor of educational philosophy, wrote of Rafferty, "It is, in short, Rafferty who is most influential in forging and manipulating the will of the public, and it is, in turn, the same public opinion which Rafferty then uses to authorize his own decisions." O'Neill, *Readin, Ritin, and Rafferty!*, 10.

98. Reagan quoted in Dallek, *The Right Moment*, 180. Reagan's attempt to speak for disaffected parents is explored more deeply in Melinda Cooper, *Family Values: Between Neoliberalism and the New Social Conservatism* (New York, NY: Zone Books, 2017), 232–39.

99. Reagan himself had of course not been at the dance, nor had he spoken to persons who were. Instead, Reagan based his speech on newspaper articles that referenced the report filed by Hugh Burns, based on his committee's interviews with campus police officers who had been present at the dance. See Dallek, *The Right Moment*, 192–93, 194.

100. Rosenfeld, *Subversives*, 322, 324.

101. De Groot, "Ronald Reagan and Student Unrest," 111; Rosenfeld, *Subversives*, 328.

102. Dallek, *The Right Moment*, 194.

103. Cannon, *Ronnie and Jesse*, 86–87.

104. Dallek, *The Right Moment*, 216.

105. Dallek, *The Right Moment*, 163.

106. In the early sixties, Mike Davis describes, Yorty moved "rapidly to the right . . . [throwing] his weight behind the police and the growing white resistance to civil rights demands." See Davis, *City of* Quartz, 126. Matthew Dallek notes that Yorty fell to the right of Republican George Christopher "on the make-or-break issues that dominated the primary election." Dallek continues, "Yorty's supporters, Democrats all, were less likely to support Brown than were Christopher's" supporters. In 1960, Yorty had endorsed Nixon for president over John F. Kennedy. He formally joined the Republican Party in 1980. McGirr argues that "after [Yorty's] primary loss . . . his supporters regrouped to back Reagan." Dallek, *The Right Moment*, 217; McGirr, *Suburban Warriors*, 200.

107. Cannon, *Ronnie and Jesse*, 87.

108. This was part of a larger directive to all state agencies to cut their budgets by 10 percent. As one contemporary noted the following year, "Despite the headlines, the savings amounted to less than half of 1 per cent." What's more, at the end of his first legislative session, Reagan would sign "the largest budget in history for any state," while still opting to cut nearly $10 million from the UC and state colleges. Lewis, *What Makes Reagan Run?*, 174, 182.

109. William Trombley, "Reagan Proposes: $400 UC Tuition; Urges 10% Budget Slice and $200 Fee at State Colleges," *Los Angeles Times*, January 5, 1967. For Reagan's full remarks regarding tuition, see Reagan, "January 17, 1967 Statement" in the Ronald Reagan Presidential Library and Museum's Gubernatorial Speeches, 1967–71.

110. Ray Zeman, "Reagan: Tuition, but No Cuts," *Los Angeles Times*, January 11, 1967.

111. The words are those of Reagan's sympathetic biographer, Lou Cannon. See Cannon, *Governor Reagan*, 182.

112. "Reagan Takes the Helm," *Los Angeles Times*, January 6, 1967.

113. William Trombley, "Reagan's Cut in UC Budget 'Too Great,' Dr. Coons Declares," *Los Angeles Times*, February 9, 1967.

114. Reagan's tuition plan would have meant sending even more students to community colleges, which might well have led to significant increases in the local property taxes used to sustain them; such a tax hike, of course, would have been anathema to Reagan supporters. Lewis, *What Makes Reagan Run?*, 179; Bob Gettemy and Jack Boettner, "Tuition Proposal Rapped at UCI, Cal State," *Los Angeles Times*, January 6, 1967; "VSC Students Call Tuition Plan a Blow to Education," *Los Angeles Times*, January 6, 1967.

115. Art Berman, "Tuition Storm: Educators Blast Reagan's Plans," *Los Angeles Times*, January 6, 1967.

116. Wallace Turner, "Gov. Reagan Proposes Cutback in U. of California Appropriation: Would Impose Tuition Charge on Students from State—Kerr Weighs New Post," *New York Times*, January 7, 1967.

117. Ray Zeman, "Unruh Urges Reagan Delay Tuition Plan for Two Years," *Los Angeles Times*, January 12, 1967.

118. William Trombley, "1-Year Delay Asked on Plan for College Tuition, Budget Cuts," *Los Angeles Times*, January 17, 1967.

119. "Labor Joins Fight against Tuition at State Colleges," *Los Angeles Times*, February 9, 1967.

120. William Trombley, "UC Regents Vote $23 Million Cut," *Los Angeles Times*, February 17, 1967; William Trombley, "Bitter UC Fund Fight Looms in Legislature," *Los Angeles Times*, February 20, 1967.

121. "Crisis in Higher Education," *Los Angeles Times*, February 20, 1967.

122. Richard Bergholz, "UC's Future in Reagan's Hands," *Los Angeles Times*, February 21, 1967.

123. In the end, Reagan "forced the UC Board of Regents to trim its operating budget request by $13 million. . . . On top of that he gave the university system only 83% of its budget request." William Trombley, "Governor and Academia Never Came to Terms," *Los Angeles Times*, September 29, 1974, in "Reagan's Quixotic Reign, 1967–1974," Ronald Reagan Subject Collection, Box 48, Hoover Institute Archives.

124. "Higher Education Still in Peril," *Los Angeles Times*, March 2, 1967.

125. William Trombley, "Reagan's Tuition Action Makes Little Difference, Officials Say," *Los Angeles Times*, March 2, 1967.

126. The course instructor, lecturer Jay Ruby, confirmed to the *Los Angeles Times* that none of his students had participated in hanging an effigy of Governor Reagan that—while it happened—was "completely unrelated" to the course. See Trombley, "Reagan's Tuition Action."

127. Berrett, "The Day the Purpose of College Changed"; "The Viewpoint of the Times: The Education of Ronald Reagan," *Los Angeles Times*, March 5, 1967.

128. Lawrence E. Davies, "Kerr Ousted as President by California U. Regents," *New York Times*, January 21, 1967.

129. Wallace Turner, "Kerr Says He Will Not Quit as U. of California Head," *New York Times*, January 8, 1967.

130. Lawrence E. Davies, "Reagan Accuses University Heads," *New York Times*, January 18, 1967.

131. "The State: University: Kerr Fired by Regents," *Los Angeles Times*, January 22, 1967.

132. "Reagan Voices Surprise," *New York Times*, January 21, 1967.

133. Lawrence E. Davies "Political Move Denied by Reagan," *New York Times*, January 25, 1967.

134. Conservatives like Reagan and Hoover, of course, were not the only ones happy to see Kerr gone. The FSM leader Mario Savio remarked upon Kerr's dismissal, "Good riddance to bad rubbish." Lewis, *What Makes Reagan Run?*, 180.

135. Rosenfeld, *Subversives*, 7, 1.

136. Rosenfeld, *Subversives*, 370–71.

137. Rosenfeld, *Subversives*, 378, 489–95.

138. Cannon, *Governor Reagan*, 272.

139. Friedman's answer, and Reagan's by extension, was that they shouldn't. Yet instead of pushing for progressive taxation, Friedman pushed for a flat tax and tuition to be paid by all. See the pamphlet "A Concern for the Individual and His Right to Fulfillment; This Should Be the Preoccupation of Our Schools and Colleges," Ronald Reagan Subject Collection, Box 46, Hoover Institute Archives.

140. Only three years later, Reagan, the governor of California, would wrongly state that California schools "have always been racially integrated." This was patently untrue, as California schools *were* in fact segregated both prior to and during Reagan's tenure as governor. Reagan quoted in Wollenberg, *All Deliberate Speed*, 178.

141. Reagan's vision for tuition-funded scholarships is laid out in full in "Report to Californians: The First Eight Months of the Reagan Administration," 22–25, Ronald Reagan Subject Collection, Box 48, Hoover Institute Archives.

142. Richard Bergholz, "Governor Renews Tuition Proposals: Outlines Plans for Grants to Needy Students," *Los Angeles Times*, July 27, 1967.

143. Jerry Gilliam, "10,000 at Capitol Rally Boo Reagan," *Los Angeles Times*, February 12, 1967; "Cesar Chavez at Anti-tuition Demonstration."

144. Harry Bernstein, "Unions Begin Drive on Education Cuts," *Los Angeles Times*, February 12, 1967.

145. EOPs aimed to increase the matriculation and retention of working-class and minority students at the various levels of the Master Plan hierarchy—the UC, state colleges, and community colleges. EOPs are discussed in greater length in chapter 6.

146. For Kenneth Martyn's full report, see March 1968's *California Higher Education and the Disadvantaged: A Status Report* commissioned by the California Coordinating Council for Higher Education; William Trombley, "Tuition Plan Puzzles State Education Aides," *Los Angeles Times*, July 30, 1967.

147. Jack McCurdy, "Public School Officials Skeptical on Reagan Tuition, Loan Plan," *Los Angeles Times*, August 6, 1967.

148. Joseph Kraft, "But Will the De-Kooking Last?" *Los Angeles Times*, December 11, 1967.

149. On the tuition/fee controversy, see Cannon, *Governor Reagan*, 279–84; Cannon, *Reagan*, 153.

150. For a contemporary account of the loyalty oath controversy, which resulted in the dismissal of thirty-one UC faculty members, see Stewart, *The Year of the Oath*. For a more recent treatment, see Blauner, *Resisting McCarthyism*.

151. A liberal-moderate coalition among the UC regents dominated the board prior to Reagan, much to the chagrin of California conservatives. From 1967 through 1970, power on the board shifted to the right. See William Trombley, "New Coalition of Regents Apparent in UC Changes: Liberals Join Moderates, Back Kerr," *Los Angeles Times*, June 22, 1965; Richard Bergholz, "Rafferty Blasts Regents' Stand on Free Speech," *Los Angeles Times*, December 2, 1965; William Trombley, "Regent Challenges Group's UC Report," *Los Angeles Times*, August 9, 1966; William Trembly, "UC Split on How to Handle Reagan," *Los Angeles Times*, September 11, 1967; William Trombley, "UC's 'No Politics Test' Policy Will Be Reviewed by Regents," *Los Angeles Times*, October 17, 1969; William Trombley, "UC Regent Hits Others for Vote on Angela Davis," *Los Angeles Times*, May 18, 1970; William Trombley, "Regents Block Promotion of 2 Tied to Liberal, Radical Causes," *Los Angeles Times*, July 18, 1970; William Trombley, "Conservative Regents Assume Dominant Control over Board," *Los Angeles Times*, July 20, 1970.

152. Summerskill, *President Seven*, 54, 59.

153. John Dreyfuss, "Politicians Should Not Be UC Regents, Chancellor Declares," *Los Angeles Times*, February 1, 1969.

154. To be clear, Angela Davis was then a graduate student at UCSD, but also an instructor at UCLA. Of all these figures, only Harry Edwards and Herbert Marcuse managed to hold on to their positions. Marcuse, likely because he maintained the backing of his campus chancellor, and Edwards because of the support for his hiring generated by the strength of the third world strike at UC Berkeley. The Black Panther Party's Eldridge Cleaver, while never slated as Berkeley faculty to begin with, was denied a promised platform to deliver a series of lectures at UC Berkeley. Having consolidated power on campus through the firings of Robert Mezey and Marvin X, a revanchist administration at Fresno State College went on to fire a host of liberal faculty, generating national headlines and outrage. See Seib, *Slow Death of Fresno State*. On the regents' rejection of tenure for FSM supporter Reginald Zelnik at UC Berkeley and Angela Davis's supporter David B. Kaplan at UCLA, see "UC Regents Block Tenure for Two," *San Francisco Chronicle*, July 18, 1970, located in Hal Draper Papers, D-373, Box 17, Shields Library, Special Collections, University of California, Davis.

155. Ronald Reagan, "Transcript of Governor Ronald Reagan's Report to the People; 12-8-68; (Higher Education)," 4–5, Ronald Reagan Subject Collection, Box 47, Hoover Institute Archives.

156. "Governor Ronald Reagan—The Facts," 5, Ronald Reagan Subject Collection, Box 48, Hoover Institute Archives.

157. Litwak and Wilner, *College Days in Earthquake Country*, 51.

158. Smith, "Organizing for Social Justice," 246.

159. "A Plan to End Local Control," *Daily Gater*, November 14, 1968.

160. Barlow and Shapiro, *End to Silence*, 56, 80–81, 86, 88, 91.

161. "BSU Explanation of Today's Strike," *Daily Gater*, November 6, 1968.

162. Bob Baker, "BSU, SDS Join in Occupation of Administration Building," *Daily Sundial*, November 5, 1968.

163. Petra Fischer, "Title 5 Revision Reverts AS Power to Hayakawa," *Phoenix*, May 1, 1969; Barlow and Shapiro, *End to Silence*, 209–10.

164. "Regents to Investigate UC Campus Papers," *Triton Times*, April 4, 1969.

165. See, for instance, the folder on "Sexually Explicit Plays" on California campuses in the Ronald Reagan Subject Collection, Box 41, Hoover Institute Archives. On Reagan proxy Karl Falk and the wave faculty "purges" at Fresno State, see Seib, *Slow Death of Fresno State*.

166. De Groot, "Ronald Reagan and Student Unrest," 107, 128.

167. "CA Governor [1966]," *Our Campaigns*, accessed April 1, 2022, https://www.ourcampaigns.com/RaceDetail.html?RaceID=36416; "CA Governor [1970]," *Our Campaigns*, accessed April 1, 2022, https://www.ourcampaigns.com/RaceDetail.html?RaceID=36415.

168. William Trombley, "Governor and Academia Never Came to Terms," *Los Angeles Times*, September 29, 1974, in "Reagan's Quixotic Reign, 1967–1974," Ronald Reagan Subject Collection, Box 48, Hoover Institute Archives.

Chapter 4

1. Edwards, *Revolt of the Black Athlete*, 42.

2. Kerr, *The Gold and the Blue*, 1:183; Leon, "Racism in the University," 99; Douglass, *Conditions for Admission*, 42, 90.

3. In April 1968, under pressure from student organizers, faculty supporters, and others, the UC Board of Regents and state college board of trustees would vote to expand that number to 4 percent. William Trombley, "UC, Colleges Seek Go-Ahead for More Minority Students," *Los Angeles Times*, February 19, 1968; Douglass, *Conditions for Admission*, 99.

4. Scholars since Harry Edwards have explored the activist role taken on by many Black athletes. The phenomenon of Black student athletes as vanguard activists—as explored in this chapter—is, to my knowledge, unique to the Master Plan system. Of course, such activism was contemporaneous with, influenced, and was influenced by ongoing Black student struggles and civil rights organizing across the country. On the Black student movement, see Murch, *Living for the City*; Biondi, *Black Revolution on Campus*; and Rogers, *Black Campus Movement*.

5. First established in 1964–65, the history of California's EOPs are explored in greater detail in chapter 6. Although the student organizing covered in this chapter was largely a monoracial affair, these important struggles by Black activists helped to pave the way for similar efforts and parallel gains by Mexican American students. The Chicano student movement in California is explored in the next chapter.

6. La Nouse and Bennett, "The Impact of Desegregation"; Martin, "Jim Crow in the Gymnasium."

7. Zirin, *People's History of Sports*, 74–75; Wiggins, "With All Deliberate Speed," 329–46.

8. The National Football League had previously employed Black athletes, but African Americans were subsequently denied entrance to the league from 1934 to 1946. See Zirin, *People's History of Sports*, 98; "Significant Moments in Black Bruin History."

9. Jerry Crowe, "Some Overdue Recognition for a Basketball Trailblazer," *Los Angeles Times*, January 29, 2007.

10. Abdul-Jabbar and Knobler, *Giant Steps*, 103; Kareem Abdul-Jabbar, "Interview with Dave Zirin"; Kang, "What the World Got Wrong."

11. Smith, "It's Not Really My Country," 231, 232; Abdul-Jabbar and Knobler, *Giant Steps*, 160; Kang, "What the World Got Wrong."

12. Spivey, "The Black Athlete," 117.

13. By 1968, at the professional level "approximately one-quarter of major league baseball players, one third of professional football players, and slightly more than one-half of all professional basketball players were Afro-American." Van Deburg, *New Day in Babylon*, 83.

14. Edwards, *The Struggle That Must Be*, 106.

15. "Retired Track Coach Bud Winter Dies of Heart Attack at 76," *Los Angeles Times*, December 8, 1985; Smith, "Frozen Fists in Speed City," 395.

16. "The Olympic Jolt: 'Hell No, Don't Go!'"

17. Ken Noel, "We'll Just . . . Look Over the Scene," *Los Angeles Times*, September 22, 1968.

18. Daryl Lembke, "Cal Negro Athletes Demand Coaches Firing," *Los Angeles Times*, January 24, 1968.

19. Dwight Chapin, "Conflict at Cal: White Players Respect Coach," *Los Angeles Times*, January 30, 1968.

20. "Pete Newell Quits Athletic Director Post at Berkeley," *Los Angeles Times*, March 13, 1968.

21. "Herrerias Quits as Cal Cage Coach," *Los Angeles Times*, April 12, 1968; "Negro Situation Not Only Reason Herrerias Quit," *Los Angeles Times*, April 13, 1968.

22. "Cal Picks Padgett, Cage Coach, Adds Negro as Assistant," *Los Angeles Times*, April 25, 1968.

23. "16 Negro Athletes Boycott Spring Grid Drills at California," *Los Angeles Times*, May 16, 1968.

24. Lomax, "Revisiting *The Revolt of the Black Athlete*," 472.

25. "Erby, Former Grid Star, New Cal Aide," *Los Angeles Times*, June 6, 1968; *Life* magazine, as of March 1968, noted that "there are only seven black coaches in the over 150 major colleges" in the United States. See "The Olympic Jolt."

26. Jeff Prugh, "The Racial Problem at UCLA: Here's How It Started," *Los Angeles Times*, May 17, 1968; "The Olympic Jolt."

27. Moreno, "Of the Community, for the Community," 176–80; Marquez, "La Universidad con la Promesa del Futuro," 114–18.

28. Andy Anderson, "Coach Agrees to Apologize for His Derogatory Remark," *Daily Collegian*, December 1, 1967; Osby Davis, "Leonard McNeil . . . Brother in Exile," *Daily Collegian: Uhuru edition*, September 29, 1969; Bob Swofford, "Osby Davis: A Fighter in More Ways than One," *Daily Collegian*, March 18, 1970.

29. "Blacks Want Hare Back: Black Faculty and Black Athletes Air Grievances at Meeting Wednesday," *Phoenix*, February 27, 1969.

30. Anthony, *Time of the Furnaces*, 13. Although his history of the struggles at Valley State appears accurate when checked against other available sources, any potential reader should exercise proper caution. Earl Anthony—for some time a member of the Black Panther Party—infiltrated the Panthers as an FBI informant. See Davis and Wiener, *Set the Night on Fire*, 288.

31. The school is now known as the California State University at Northridge (CSUN), or Cal State Northridge for short.

32. "Separate State College for Valley Predicted," *Los Angeles Times*, April 21, 1957.

33. Anthony, *Time of the Furnaces*, 27; "Legislature May Get VSC Expansion Bid," *Los Angeles Times*, December 11, 1960.

34. "State College Campus Gains at Record Rate: Growing Like Topsy," *Los Angeles Times*, July 7, 1957; "San Fernando Valley College Now Official: Northridge Campus of Los Angeles State Gains Own Identity with Change of Signs," *Los Angeles Times*, July 3, 1958.

35. "Valley State Campus off to Good Start," *Los Angeles Times*, October 19, 1958.

36. "Record 5,800 Expected to Enroll at Valley State," *Los Angeles Times*, September 4, 1960.

37. John Kumbula and Leonard Greenwood, "Anatomy of a Takeover: Valley State Turmoil—Who, What, Why," *Los Angeles Times*, November 10, 1968.

38. Anthony, *Time of the Furnaces*, 28.

39. Nevin, "Uneasy Peace at Valley State."

40. Ken Fanucchi, "Reagan Hit as Stalling VSC's Minorities Plan: Governor Won't Respond to Efforts to Admit Disadvantaged Students, Faculty Chief Says," *Los Angeles Times*, June 13, 1968. The following year, Mexican American enrollment would increase to a total of forty-five. Davis and Wiener, *Set the Night on Fire*, 517.

41. Anthony, *Time of the Furnaces*, 17–19, 28–29.

42. Quoted in Anthony, *Time of the Furnaces*, 30.

43. Davis and Wiener, *Set the Night on Fire*, 506.

44. Anthony, *Time of the Furnaces*, 30–31.

45. The *Los Angeles Times* thought Cal State Los Angeles was the most diverse state college as of late 1968. There, estimates were given of 10 percent Black, 7 percent Mexican American, and 7 percent Asian. Whites, then, still made up approximately 76 percent of the Los Angeles state college campus. See Kumbula and Greenwood, "Anatomy of a Takeover."

46. Quoted in Anthony, *Time of the Furnaces*, 29.

47. Kumbula and Greenwood, "Anatomy of a Takeover."

48. The survey was conducted by Valley State's Community Involvement Project—an effort by white students on campus who aimed to enlist fellow whites in the fight against racism. See "Housing Needed for New Students," *Summer Sundial*, July 11, 1968; and Kenneth J. Fanucchi, "VSC Faculty, Students Effect Major Changes: Confrontations Produce More Shifts in Policy in Year than since Campus Was Formed," *Los Angeles Times*, June 16, 1968.

49. Karenga's group is stylized in all capital letters, despite not being an acronym. Its nationalist content, however, is clear: US, "as opposed to *them*." See Woodard, *A Nation Within a Nation*, 72; Scot Brown, *Fighting for US*, 1; Anthony, *Time of the Furnaces*, 22–24; "Letters: Black Power Erupts," *Daily Sundial*, November 9, 1967; "Karenga Coverage Biased," *Daily Sundial*, November 10, 1967.

50. Anthony, *Time of the Furnaces*, 31–32.

51. In addition to proving the driving force behind greater Black enrollment and Black studies, Chatman worked toward parallel gains for Chicano students. Rodolfo Acuña, who became head of Valley State Chicano studies in 1969, later remembered Chatman as a "decent young [man who] mentored many of the Chicana/o students who had been recruited through EOP." Chatman would later take the name Adewole Umoja and earn a PhD in political science. See Acuña, *The Making of Chicana/o Studies*, 49; BSU member quoted in Anthony, *Time of the Furnaces*, 38.

52. In the end, the number would be 220 incoming EOP students, not the 300 originally planned. The EOP drive represented the first real effort of Valley State to recruit at predominantly Black and Mexican American high schools. As such, the EOP efforts led to the matriculation of dozens of Black and Chicano students who already met the Master Plan admissions standards and thus did not need to enroll under the now-expanded 4 percent exception rule. See Ralph Sanders, "220 Enroll in Minority Plan," *Daily Sundial*, September 24, 1968.

53. For more on the collaborative effort between the BSU and UMAS to run the EOP, see Anthony, *Time of the Furnaces*.

54. Anthony, *Time of the Furnaces*, 37–39.

55. "Colleges Outline Ethnic Studies Programs and Plans," *Los Angeles Times*, April 25, 1969.

56. Fanucchi, "Reagan Hit as Stalling VSC's Minorities Plan."

57. Fanucchi, "VSC Faculty, Students Effect Major Changes"; Anthony, *Time of the Furnaces*, 39.

58. Anthony, *Time of the Furnaces*, 40.

59. Larry Pett, "Group Builds Bridge between Minority Students, Community," *Los Angeles Times*, August 25, 1968; "VSC to Admit More Minority Group Students," *Los Angeles Times*, May 19, 1968.

60. Darlene Lima, "Preparation for College Life: Ninety Minority Students Living, Studying, Working on Campus," *Summer Sundial*, July 18, 1968; Fanucchi, "Reagan Hit as Stalling VSC's Minorities Plan."

61. Quoted in Lima, "Preparation for College Life."

62. Lima, "Preparation for College Life."

63. According to a *Los Angeles Times* article, only seventy-five to eighty—or approximately 35 percent—of these 220 EOP recruits had been admitted under the Master Plan admissions exception rule. The majority, "who are qualified to enroll," met the admissions standards for entrance to the state colleges. See "VSC to Admit More Minority Group Students."

64. Quoted in Sanders, "220 Enroll in Minority Plan."

65. Anthony, *Time of the Furnaces*, 49–50.

66. "BSU, Athletic Department Confrontation Rescheduled," *Daily Sundial*, November 1, 1968.

67. Anthony, *Time of the Furnaces*, 50–51.

68. Davis and Wiener, *Set the Night on Fire*, 506.

69. "BSU, Athletic Department Confrontation Rescheduled."

70. "BSU Wants Coach Ousted: Blasts Markham," *Daily Sundial*, October 31, 1968; Anthony, *Time of the Furnaces*, 51.

71. "BSU, Athletic Department Confrontation Rescheduled"; Anthony, *Time of the Furnaces*, 52.

72. Anthony, *Time of the Furnaces*, 53–54.

73. The building occupation at San Fernando Valley State took place two days before the start of the student strike at San Francisco State. BSU and SDS members on both campuses were particularly concerned with the erosion of campus autonomy represented by the trustees' proposed Title V power-grab. Regarding San Francisco State, see chapter 6. Bill Barlow and Peter Shapiro, "State Sails Off the Edge," *Open Process*, November 6, 1968; "BSU Explanation of Today's Strike," *Daily Gater*, November 6, 1968.

74. On the topic of student versus trustee control of student funds, see chapter 6; Bob Baker, "BSU, SDS Join in Occupation of Administration Building," *Daily Sundial*, November 5, 1968.

75. Anthony, *Time of the Furnaces*, 13; Davis and Wiener, *Set the Night on Fire*, 504.

76. Baker, "BSU, SDS Join in Occupation of Administration Building"; Anthony, *Time of the Furnaces*, 55–56, 58.

77. Quoted in Anthony, *Time of the Furnaces*, 89; Davis and Wiener, *Set the Night on Fire*, 504.

78. Quoted in Anthony, *Time of the Furnaces*, 98.

79. On the advice of their lawyers, who incorrectly believed that the judge would be sympathetic, the defendants had waived their right to a jury trial. See Anthony, *Time of the Furnaces*, 90.

80. Anthony, *Time of the Furnaces*, 56, 93.

81. Anthony, *Time of the Furnaces*, 97–98.

82. Since their sentencing, Judge Mark Brandler had retired, and the Valley State 19 were released on the orders of Judge George Dell. Dell credited a report by the state Department of Corrections which had recommended that the student activists be released on probation; "25-Year Terms Modified: Judge Releases 3 Valley State Militants," *Los Angeles Times*, April 25, 1970; Anthony, *Time of the Furnaces*, 119.

83. Bob Baker, "Did CSUN Takeover Win? '69 Rebels Disagree: Two Black Leaders: One Joined Faculty, Is Accused by the Other of Settling for 'White Man's Crumbs,'" *Los Angeles Times*, June 24, 1979.

84. Anthony, *Time of the Furnaces*, 101.

85. "Colleges Outline Ethnic Studies Programs and Plans."

86. Davis and Wiener, *Set the Night on Fire*, 512.

87. Baker, "Did CSUN Takeover Win?"

88. Gerth and Haehn, *Invisible Giant*, 4.

89. Gerth and Haehn, *Invisible Giant*, 178.

90. Gerth and Haehn, *Invisible Giant*, 181; Smith, *Silent Gesture*, 75; Edwards, *Revolt of the Black Athlete*, 42.

91. Because schools kept no hard data pertaining to race and enrollment, the subjective appraisals offered by former students and faculty remain the best evidence for assessing the demographic breakdown on campus. Student athletes seemed to make up the majority of Black students on most state college and UC campuses (an important exception being San Francisco State) through the mid-to-late 1960s when schools began experimenting with EOPs; William Trombley, "UC Entrance Rules Challenged: Minorities, Poor Seek Revisions," *Los Angeles Times*, January 7, 1968.

92. Edwards, *The Struggle That Must Be*, 101, 106.

93. Edwards, *The Struggle That Must Be*, 106.

94. Abdul-Jabbar and Knobler, *Giant Steps*, 128.

95. Edwards, *The Struggle That Must Be*, 107, 108.

96. Edwards, *The Struggle That Must Be*, 108, 109.

97. Edwards, *Revolt of the Black Athlete*, 15.

98. Edwards, *The Struggle That Must Be*, 112.

99. Edwards, *The Struggle That Must Be*, 111.

100. Edwards, *Revolt of the Black Athlete*, xvi.

101. Edwards, *Revolt of the Black Athlete*, 12.

102. William Trombley, "Chicano-Black Rivalry Rises at San Jose State: Lack of Funds for Minority Students Threatens Economic Opportunity Program," *Los Angeles Times*, August 10, 1969.

103. Edwards, *The Struggle That Must Be*, 108.

104. Smith, *Silent Gesture*, 75.

105. The question of the racial breakdown of student populations in the 1960s is one that is fraught with difficulties. What remains clear is that students of color experienced California's UC and state college campuses as overwhelming white spaces and protested for the inclusion of more minority students, staff, and faculty. By the early 1970s, it would become commonplace for school administrations to track the racial demographics of their student bodies—an outcome of the very struggles we are now tracing. Unfortunately, accurate data for the years before these race-based campus uprisings remains scattered, imprecise, and hard to conclusively verify; Smith, *Silent Gesture*, 76.

106. Recipients of the Woodrow Wilson Fellowship, like Edwards, were selected by a network of nine hundred faculty members organized into fifteen regional committees. See "Search for Professors," 45.

107. Edwards, *The Struggle That Must Be*, 133, 134, 145, 150.

108. Smith, *Silent Gesture*, 82.

109. Smith, *Silent Gesture*, 110.

110. Smith, *Silent Gesture*, 117.

111. Edwards, *The Struggle That Must Be*, 158.

112. Edwards, *Revolt of the Black Athlete*, 42; Edwards, *The Struggle That Must Be*, 159.

113. Edwards, *Revolt of the Black Athlete*, 43.

114. Edwards, *The Struggle That Must Be*, 159; "Faculty Member Charges Discrimination in Housing," *Spartan Daily*, September 18, 1967.

115. Edwards, *Revolt of the Black Athlete*, 43–46; Edwards, *The Struggle That Must Be*, 159–60.

116. Edwards, *Revolt of the Black Athlete*, 45.

117. Edwards, *Revolt of the Black Athlete*, 46.

118. John Wallak, "Faculty Group Passes Discrimination Policy," *Spartan Daily*, September 20, 1967; "ASB President Admits Discrimination Charges True: Lee Promises Protesters Immediate Investigation," *Spartan Daily*, September 20, 1967.

119. Edwards, *The Struggle That Must Be*, 161.

120. Edwards, *Revolt of the Black Athlete*, 46.

121. "Dr. Clark Cancels Saturday's Game: 'Action Necessary,'" *Spartan Daily*, September 22, 1967; Edwards, *The Struggle That Must Be*, 163–64; Smith, *Silent Gesture*, 159.

122. "Cancellation of Game Draws Reagan Fire," *Sparta Daily*, September 27, 1967; "The Real Issue at San Jose," *Los Angeles Times*, September 28, 1967.

123. Edwards, *Revolt of the Black Athlete*, 47.

124. Edwards, *The Struggle That Must Be*, 165.

125. Edwards, *The Struggle That Must Be*, 174.

126. Smith, *Silent Gesture*, 159.

127. Edwards, *The Struggle That Must Be*, 175.

128. Edwards, *Revolt of the Black Athlete*, 50.

129. Smith, *Silent Gesture*, 161.

130. On campus organizing by Hoover at San Mateo Community College and Garrett at San Francisco State College are explored in chapter 6; Edwards, *Revolt of the Black Athlete*, 50.

131. Edwards, *Revolt of the Black Athlete*, 50.

132. Smith, *Silent Gesture*, 162.

133. Smith, *Silent Gesture*, 162; Edwards, *Revolt of the Black Athlete*, 49.

134. Edwards, *The Struggle That Must Be*, 180.

135. Edwards, *Revolt of the Black Athlete*, 53.

136. Smith, *The Sons of Westwood*, 114–15; Smith, *Silent Gesture*, 225.

137. The vote was, according to Edwards, three "nay" to over two hundred "yea." Edwards, *Revolt of the Black Athlete*, 54.

138. Edwards, *The Struggle That Must Be*, 217.

139. Edwards, *Revolt of the Black Athlete*, 92–94.

140. Edwards, *Revolt of the Black Athlete*, 58.

141. Bachrach, *The Nazi Olympics*, 107.

142. Large, *Nazi Games*, 55.

143. Edwards, *The Struggle That Must Be*, 186.

144. Edwards, *Revolt of the Black Athlete*, 98–100.

145. Smith, *Silent Gesture*, 237, 239; Abdul-Jabbar and Knobler, *Giant Steps*, 170–71.

146. Carlos, *The John Carlos Story*, 123–24.

147. Smith, *Silent Gesture*, 173.

148. Smith, *Silent Gesture*, 170

149. William Trombley, "UC Entrance Rules Challenged: Minorities, Poor Seek Revisions," *Los Angeles Times*, January 7, 1968; William Trombley, "UC, Colleges May Take More Poverty Students: Higher Education Council Votes to Increase Entrants from Low-Income, Minority Groups," *Los Angeles Times*, February 21, 1968; Orrick, *Shut It Down!*, 27; Barlow and Shapiro, *End to Silence*, 201.

150. Trombley, "Chicano-Black Rivalry Rises." As the title of this *Los Angeles Times* article indicates, minor tensions arose on campus in late 1969 over both the ratio of Black to Chicano students and a potential lack of funding for ever increasing numbers of EOP students.

151. Edwards, *The Struggle That Must Be*, 146.

152. "The State: Black Studies Unit to Open at San Jose State," *Los Angeles Times*, January 31, 1969.

153. "Colleges Outline Ethnic Studies Programs and Plans."

154. John Dreyfuss, "Negro Who Urged Boycott of Olympics Put on UC Faculty," *Los Angeles Times*, January 31, 1970.

155. The Third World Liberation Front strikes at San Francisco State College and UC Berkeley are explored in chapter 6.

156. Edwards, *The Struggle That Must Be*, 282.

157. Edwards, *The Struggle That Must Be*, 282–83.

Chapter 5

1. Anon., "Chicano Student/Faculty Workshop on Higher Education," March 12, 1969, Ct. 1:13, Carlos Muñoz papers, 1945–2015 (bulk 1969–1993), CS ARC 2016/1, Ethnic Studies Library, University of California, Berkeley.

2. Anon., "Chicano Workshop: Operations Report," Ct. 1:13, Carlos Muñoz papers, 1945–2015 (bulk 1969–93), CS ARC 2016/1, Ethnic Studies Library, University of California, Berkeley.

3. On Mexican American education and the history of the Chicano movement, see Gonzalez, *Chicano Education in the Era of Segregation*; Muñoz, *Youth, Identity, Power*; Acuña, *The Making of Chicana/o Studies*; García and Castro, *Blowout!*; García, *Strategies of Segregation*.

4. Ruben Salazar, "Chicanos Set Their Goals in Education," *Los Angeles Times*, May 4, 1969.

5. These numbers come from the campus newspaper, the *Daily Cal*, and are cited in Rorabaugh, *Berkeley at War*, 84.

6. Conflicting estimates put Mexican Americans at either 0.21 or 0.28 percent of the UCLA student body. Paul Houston, "Jammed Junior Colleges Seen if State Tuition Plan Passes," *Los Angeles Times*, January 11, 1967; Gómez-Quiñones, *Mexican Students por la Raza*, 20; *UCLA General Catalog*, 8.

7. The estimate comes from UCSB's dean of students who is quoted in Ann Henry, "Minorities May Find UC Admission Easier," *El Gaucho*, February 26, 1968. For the total student population, see "UCSB Headcount Enrollment: 1954–55 to 2016–17."

8. "Y eso a mi—que me importa?" *Que Tal*, September 15, 1971; Gerth and Haehn, *Invisible Giant*, 181; Smith, *Silent Gesture*, 75; Edwards, *Revolt of the Black Athlete*, 42; Ken Fanucchi, "Reagan Hit as Stalling VSC's Minorities Plan: Governor Won't Respond to Efforts to Admit Disadvantaged Students, Faculty Chief Says," *Los Angeles Times*, June 13, 1968; Estudios de la Raza, "Three Years at Fresno State," *Daily Collegian*, February 16, 1970; Raul Ruiz, "Walkout," *Chicano Student Movement*, February 1969; Godfrey, *Neighborhoods in Transition*, 97; Bob Hernandez, "Third World Studies Flap," *Daily Gater*, July 3, 1969.

9. "Minority Percentages Show Need," *El Alacran*, March 1971; "Enrollment Rises at East L.A. College," *Los Angeles Times*, October 8, 1967.

10. Gonzalez, *Chicano Education in the Era of Segregation*; Brilliant, *The Color of America*, 64–65.

11. Olson, *The Ethnic Dimension*, 69, 206–8. Olson estimates that the United States gained approximately seventy-eight thousand new citizens with the Treaty of Guadalupe Hidalgo in 1848. The large population of California Indians—approximately one hundred thousand—would not gain U.S. citizenship until decades later. Citizenship would pass, however, to California's one thousand *California* elite and to some ten thousand "mestizo artisans, soldiers, *vaqueros* (ranch hands), and small farmers."

12. Olson, *The Ethnic Dimension*, 213. The vast majority of these immigrants settled in the five southwestern states of California, Nevada, Arizona, New Mexico, and Texas.

13. Gonzalez, *Chicano Education in the Era of Segregation*, 11, 13.

14. Gonzalez, *Chicano Education in the Era of Segregation*, 13, 14; Garcia, *Strategies of Segregation*, 2.

15. McWilliams, *Factories in the Field*, 320–21.

16. Hill is quoted in Gonzalez, *Chicano Education in the Era of Segregation*, 19.

17. Brilliant, *The Color of America*, 58.

18. Unfortunately, this legal victory did little to halt the tide of anti-Mexican racism and segregation. Wollenberg, *All Deliberate Speed*, 123–24; Alvarez, "The Lemon Grove Incident."

19. Brilliant, *The Color of America*, 76, 81.

20. Gonzalez, *Chicano Education in the Era of Segregation*, 190–201; For a lesser-known case than that of the Mendez family, see Newman, "Schools for All," 81–88. For a detailed history of anti-Mexican discrimination and opposition to segregation in Oxford, California, see García, *Strategies of Segregation*.

21. Muñoz, *Youth, Identity, Power*, 62; Brilliant, *The Color of America*, 84.

22. Brilliant, *The Color of America*, 65.

23. "USA Schools," *La Hormiga*, September 12, 1968.

24. Chacón, *Radicals in the Barrio*, 57, 91.

25. Gómez, *The Revolutionary Imaginations of Greater Mexico*, 30–33.

26. On the activism of the Mexican American generation, see Oropeza, *Raza Si! Guerra No!*, 11–46; and Muñoz, *Youth, Identity, Power*, 31–58.

27. Chavez, *Mi Raza Primero!*, 42.

28. "Chicanos Jailed in Fight for Social Justice," *Brónze*, November 25, 1968. *Brónze*, the official newspaper of MASC, noted that beyond conformity with the

grape boycott, the occupiers demanded of Hitch that the "UC set up special scholarships for the children of agricultural workers," "increase [the Master Plan's] special admissions from four per cent to ten per cent," "that the increase be for 'deprived minorities' and that it reflect the ethnic make up of California," and finally, "that the university set up and finance a Mexican-American Study Center staged by Mexican-Americans selected and approved by MASC."

29. Muñoz, *Youth, Identity, Power*, 66; Pitti, *The Devil in Silicon Valley*, 187.

30. At San Jose City College, Mexican American Vietnam veterans organized alongside Guatemalans, Peruvians, and Salvadorans to form a pan-Latino organization known as Los Amigos. See Pitti, *The Devil in Silicon Valley*, 179; Muñoz, *Youth, Identity, Power*, 73; Mariscal, *Brown-Eyed Children of the Sun*, 221; "Third World Liberation Front," *Sacramento Observer*, March 27, 1969; "Professor Will Speak Thursday," *Daily Collegian*, November 13, 1967; Gómez-Quiñones and Vásquez, *Making Aztlán*, 130.

31. Although a predominantly Mexican American phenomenon, African American students at nearby schools participated in the blowouts over concerns shared with their Chicana/o counterparts. Alvarez and Widener, "A History of Black and Brown," 148; Rodriguez, *Rethinking the Chicano Movement*, 66.

32. Oropeza, *Raza Si! Guerra No!*, 73; Carlos Muñoz Jr., "Latino Leader and Scholar," conducted by Nick Garcia, 2002–2003, Regional Oral History Office, Bancroft Library, University of California, Berkeley, 2014, 179.

33. Luis Valdez, "Organizense Raza against Racism," *La Raza* 1, no. 13.

34. "Student Demands," *Chicano Student News*, March 15, 1968. This article was reprinted verbatim in various Chicano movement newspapers. See, for instance, "Student Demands," *La Hormiga*, October 7, 1968.

35. "Conspiracy for Better Education," *La Hormiga*, October 7, 1968.

36. García and Castro, *Blowout!*, 153.

37. Carlos Muñoz Jr., "Latino Leader and Scholar," 19–20, 35–36, 134; Muñoz, *Youth, Identity, Power*, 79–82; "UMAS Comes Home!" *Chicano Student News*, March 15, 1968; "UMAS," *Chicano Student Movement*, October 1968.

38. Rosales, *Chicano!*, 176–79; Gómez-Quiñones and Vásquez, *Making Aztlán*, 136. Jorge Mariscal cautions against drawing too strict a divide between a socialist north and a cultural nationalist south, pointing to the important exception of the struggle for Lumumba-Zapata College at UC San Diego. Juan Gómez-Quiñones also notes the Marxist influence on the Chicano student movement in San Diego. See Mariscal, *Brown-Eyed Children of Sun*, 217–32; Reminiscences of Juan Gómez-Quiñones, Interview 1 (June 14, 1984), Student Movement of the 1960s Project, p. 50, Columbia Center for Oral History Archives, Rare Book & Manuscript Library, Columbia University; "Time of Studies & Statistics Over! Time for Action & Revolution Now!" *La Raza*, December 25, 1967.

39. Rodriguez, *Rethinking the Chicano Movement*, 60, 62. Both Rosales and Muñoz note the predominance of Californians at this Colorado conference. See Rosales, *Chicano!*, 181; Muñoz, *Youth, Identity, Power*, 91.

40. *El Plan Espiritual de Aztlán*.

41. *El Plan Espiritual de Aztlán*.

42. Anon., "Chicano Student/Faculty Workshop on Higher Education," 1.

43. Nuñez was a "returning student." Born in 1936, Nuñez served in the army from 1959 to 1963 before enrolling at UCLA. "Obituary: René Nuñez, Ph.D. Emeritus, SDSU," *La Prensa San Diego*, August 18, 2006.

44. "Obituary: René Nuñez"; Muñoz, *Youth, Identity, Power*, 162; Acuña, *The Making of Chicana/o Studies*, 94; "Guide to the Rene Nuñez Memorial Collection"; U.S. Bureau of Education, *Search '68: Educational Talent Search Program, 1968–69* (Washington, DC: U.S. Government Printing Office, 1968), 50.

45. U.S. Bureau of Education, *Search '68*, 50.

46. Several conference participants and later scholars have noted the predominance of men within the Santa Barbara conference. Although the original planning committee was all male, the thirty-person steering committee included four women—Maria Diaz, Ludy Tapia, Ana GomezNieto, and Rosalinda Mendez. Anon., "Chicano Student/Faculty Workshop on Higher Education," 1–3; MECHA–Santa Barbara, "Estimado Carnal," July 7, 1969, Ct.1:13, Carlos Muñoz papers, 1945–2015 (bulk 1969–1993), CS ARC 2016/1, Ethnic Studies Library, University of California, Berkeley; Muñoz, "Latino Leader and Scholar," 183.

47. Moreno, "For the Community, of the Community," 201.

48. Jim Bettinger, "Mexican-American Students Attempt Unity," *El Gaucho*, January 24, 1968.

49. Moreno, "For the Community, of the Community," 205; Advertisement, "Welcome to Francisco Torres: Model Rooms and Rental Office Now Open," *El Gaucho*, March 21, 1966; UCSB purchased the privately owned Francisco Torres complex in late 2002, renaming the two buildings Santa Catalina North and South. See "UCSB Buys the Francisco Torres 19-Acre Complex."

50. Gómez-Quiñones, *Chicano Politics*, 123; Anon., "Chicano Student/Faculty Workshop on Higher Education."

51. Anon., "Chicano Student/Faculty Workshop on Higher Education."

52. Muñoz, "Latino Leader and Scholar," 183.

53. Muñoz, "Latino Leader and Scholar," 183.

54. It seems that the early conference report was written by UC Davis EOP counselor Jesus Genera, as a letter including exactly the exact language was written in his name. Anon., "Chicano Workshop," 1; Jesus Genera, "Chicano Liberation Movement," Ct.1:13, Carlos Muñoz papers, 1945–2015 (bulk 1969–1993), CS ARC 2016/1, Ethnic Studies Library, University of California, Berkeley; MECHA–Santa Barbara, "Estimado Carnal."

55. Muñoz later recalled that "we only had a handful of [Chicano] faculty and staff at that point." Muñoz, "Latino Leader and Scholar," 183. Rodolfo Acuña notes that there were only five Mexican American faculty members present at the UCSB conference. These included Gus Segade and Juan Gómez-Quiñones (San Diego State), Jesús Chavarría (UCSB), Graciela Molina Enríquez de Pick (Mesa Community College in San Diego), and Acuña himself (San Fernando Valley State). Acuña, *The Making of Chicana/o Studies*, 59; and Anon., "Chicano Student/Faculty Workshop on Higher Education," 3.

56. Muñoz, "Latino Leader and Scholar," 183.

57. Muñoz, *Youth, Identity, Power*, 95–96.

58. Muñoz, "Latino Leader and Scholar," 184.

59. Suggestions for the new organization's name ran from the likely, to the irreverent, to dirty jokes born of boredom or a lack of sleep: COSA, RAZA, POCHO, CINCO, CHUCHO, PACO, CACA, SHIT, and FUCK—the last three options the anonymous writer deemed wise to cross out. See the back of p. 3 of Anon., "Communication & Coordination Workshop," Ct.1:13, Carlos Muñoz papers, 1945–2015 (bulk 1969–1993), CS ARC 2016/1, Ethnic Studies Library, University of California, Berkeley.

60. Muñoz, "Latino Leader and Scholar," 185, 188.

61. The interim committee represented the bridge between the conference planning and steering committees and the eventual establishment of the Chicano Coordinating Council on Higher Education. See Anon., "Chicano Workshop."

62. MECHA–Santa Barbara, "Estimado Carnal"; Gómez-Quiñones and Vásquez, *Making Aztlán*, 169.

63. Anon., "Chicano Workshop"; MECHA–Santa Barbara, "Estimado Carnal."

64. Acuña, *The Making of Chicana/o Studies*, 60.

65. Muñoz, *Youth, Identity, Power*, 165. For more on Chavarría, see Moreno, "For the Community, of the Community," 173–74.

66. From a different perspective, conference participant Anna GomezNieto has since lamented the role played by the small cohort of participants who edited and published *El Plan*, noting that "I don't believe it accurately reflects the diverse thinking and visions at the conference." NietoGomez is quoted in Hidalgo, *Revelation in Aztlán*, 166.

67. Chicano Coordinating Council on Higher Education, *El Plan de Santa Barbara*, 9.

68. Chicano Coordinating Council on Higher Education, *El Plan de Santa Barbara*. On the notion of internal colonialism as it relates to the Black and Chicano struggles in the United States, see Gutiérrez, "Internal Colonialism."

69. Chicano Coordinating Council on Higher Education, *El Plan de Santa Barbara*, 9–10. The idea of a "complete man" perhaps reflects the influence of Ernesto "Che" Guevara's essay "Socialism and Man in Cuba." On the influence of Guevara on the Chicano movement, see Mariscal, *Brown-Eyed Children of Sun*, 97–139.

70. Chicano Coordinating Council on Higher Education, *El Plan de Santa Barbara*, 10.

71. Anon., "Chicano Workshop."

72. Chicano Coordinating Council on Higher Education, *El Plan de Santa Barbara*, 10.

73. Chicano Coordinating Council on Higher Education, *El Plan de Santa Barbara*, 10, 11.

74. Chicano Coordinating Council on Higher Education, *El Plan de Santa Barbara*, 77; Kerr, *The Uses of the University*.

75. Chicano Coordinating Council on Higher Education, *El Plan de Santa Barbara*, 38.

76. Chicano Coordinating Council on Higher Education, *El Plan de Santa Barbara*, 24–28.

77. Chicano Coordinating Council on Higher Education, *El Plan de Santa Barbara*, 14, 50, 60, 80.

78. Chicano Coordinating Council on Higher Education, *El Plan de Santa Barbara*, 31, 42, 44.

79. Chicano Coordinating Council on Higher Education, *El Plan de Santa Barbara*, 51–52, 58.

80. Although Chicana/o activists participated in interracial coalitions across the Master Plan system, *El Plan's* hesitancy to endorse them outright reflects the thinking of those who viewed such coalitions with skepticism. For one, Juan Gómez-Quiñones would later describe third worldism as a "threat" to the Chicano student movement, arguing that the "'Third World' tendency attempted to deny the Mexican national thrust and full development of the student movement by subordinating it to Black and Anglo movements. . . . The issue was subordination not cooperation with Asian, Indian, Anglo or Black groups." To take another example, in April 1969, the Sacramento City College branch of MAYA formally broke away from the campus Third World Liberation Front, although branch president Ernest Salinas permitted individual MAYA members who were active in the front to continue "doing their thing." Gómez-Quiñones, *Mexican Students por la Raza*, 30; "MAYA Breaks Affiliation," *Pony Express*, April 24, 1969. See chapter 6 for more on interracial coalitions at the UC, state college, and community college levels.

81. Genera, "Chicano Liberation Movement."

82. "La Raza Makes 16 Demands on Dr. Ness," *Daily Collegian*, May 21, 1968. While the city of San Jose was also more heavily Mexican American than African American, San Jose State's strong athletics and its position as an urban school in the greater Bay Area likely accounts for its ability to draw more African American students than the rural and isolated Fresno State.

83. Seib, *Slow Death of Fresno State*, 16.

84. Sylvis Selleck, "From the Sticks to the Big Shift," *Daily Collegian*, January 12, 1968.

85. Barry Hillenbrand, "The Strangulation of Fresno State: A Classic Case in the Question of Who Should Control Higher Education," *Daily Collegian*, April 16, 1971. Hillenbrand's article was reprinted from *Commonweal* magazine; "La Raza Makes 16 Demands on Dr. Ness"; Bob Swofford, "Osby Davis: A Fighter in More Ways than One," *Daily Collegian*, March 18, 1970; Estudios de la Raza, "Three Years at Fresno State."

86. Andy Anderson, "Coach Agrees to Apologize for His Derogatory Remark," *Daily Collegian*, December 1, 1967.

87. Swofford, "Osby Davis."

88. Their connection, if any, to MASA activists at East Los Angeles College is unclear.

89. Despite joining MASC, Fresno activists continued to refer to their own campus group as MASA. See "Professor Will Speak Thursday."

90. Judy Miller, "Administration Admits to De Facto Segregation," *Daily Collegian*, May 22, 1968; "EOP History, Fresno State," *CSU Fresno*. Prior to the matriculation of those seventeen students, Project 17 was known simply as the Spontaneous Project.

91. Swofford, "Osby Davis"; Estudios de la Raza, "Three Years at Fresno State."

92. Jess Rodriguez, "EOP Breaks Poverty Cycle," *Daily Collegian*, May 2, 1969; "EOP at FSC to Help Negro, Mexican-American Students," *Daily Collegian*, June 17, 1968. Later sources list the EOP numbers for the 1968–69 school year in the mid-eighties. Sources contemporary to the events, however, use the figure of seventy-six. Katherine Panas, born in 1930 to a Greek family in Guadalajara, Mexico, served as the first director of the Fresno State EOP and would later go on to earn her doctorate in clinical psychology. See "Katherine Panas," *Find a Grave*.

93. "La Raza Makes 16 Demands on Dr. Ness."

94. Miller, "Administration Admits De Facto Segregation."

95. Seib, *The Slow Death of Fresno State*, 16.

96. Phyllis Martin, "The Grape Debate: Student Senate Opposes Boycott; Chicanos Balk," *Daily Collegian*, November 14, 1968; Gerland Merrell, "Grape Boycott Issue Gives Rise of Demonstrations," *Daily Collegian*, November 15, 1968; Larry Stewart, "Fresno State Is a Great Place," *Daily Collegian*, December 12, 1967.

97. "Minority Studies Decision OKed," *Daily Collegian*, February 5, 1969.

98. "La Raza Studies Chair Announced," *Daily Collegian*, February 18, 1969; "Mexican-American Administrator Hired," *Daily Collegian*, February 26, 1969.

99. Risco, one of the East Los Angeles thirteen, is described by author and activist Frank Bardacke as a defender of the Cuban Revolution. Hunter S. Thompson, who likely knew of Risco through his Chicano activist lawyer Oscar Zeta Acosta, suggestively claimed that Risco had "participated in certain events in Havana prior to Batista's ouster." Bardacke, *Trampling Out the Vintage*, 264; Thompson, *Fear and Loathing in America*, 86.

100. Bill Martin, "Minority Group Senators Approved," *Daily Collegian*, September 26, 1968.

101. "Blacks, Chicanos Given CU Room," *Daily Collegian*, October 4, 1968.

102. "Frosh Elect DiBuduo, Haron; Bylaw Revisions Rejected," *Daily Collegian*, October 15, 1968; "Black, Chicano Students Are Given College Union Room," *Daily Collegian*, October 25, 1968.

103. "Budget Cut Will Hurt Future EOP Growth," *Daily Collegian*, April 28, 1969.

104. Frederick Ness, "Ness Makes Reply to Student Demands," *Daily Collegian*, April 8, 1969.

105. "Minority Student Rally Draws 800," *Daily Collegian*, April 14, 1969.

106. This joint takeover of the student newspaper, while unique to Fresno State, points to a larger truth about interracial coalition building in the Master Plan system. Although student activists maintained race-specific organizations, their shared experiences and goals within the structural confines of the Master Plan system led to a generative cross-pollination promoting revolutionary (inter)nationalism in the place of cultural nationalism. "Minority Demand Discussed by Publications Board," *Daily Collegian*, April 11, 1969.

107. Pat Halpern, "Minority Demand Met: Given One Collegian per Week," *Daily Collegian*, May 5, 1969.

108. John F. Ramirez, "Chicano Editorial," *Daily Collegian*, May 5, 1969.

109. *La Palabra de MASC, Regional Newsletter*, January 1969.

110. Gerald P. Merrell, "Hire Marvin or Not—Ness Says Nothing," *Daily Collegian*, October 2, 1969.

111. "Ness Refuses to OK Marvin X—Coercion by Dumke Suspected," *Daily Collegian*, October 3, 1969; "Liberal Students Vow to Support Any Action to Retain Instructor," *Daily Collegian*, October 3, 1969; "Doug Broten, Staff 'Regret Decision,'" *Daily Collegian*, October 3, 1969.

112. "Ness Quits: Blames Inexcusable Pressures for Surprise Resignation Today," *Daily Collegian*, October 7, 1969; John Dreyfuss, "Fresno State's President Ness Quits, to Head National Group," *Los Angeles Times*, September 10, 1969.

113. Seib, *Slow Death of Fresno State*, 38; Gerald P. Merrell, "Trustees Name Retired F.S.C. Prof to Interim Post," *Daily Collegian*, October 29, 1969.

114. Beverly Kennedy, "EOP Committee May Take Action on Ouster Petitions," *Daily Collegian*, February 10, 1970; Beverly Kennedy and Gloria Davis, "Questions Priorities," *Daily Collegian*, February 10, 1970.

115. Beverly Kennedy, "Munson Asks for New Assignment in EOP Turmoil," *Daily Collegian*, November 2, 1970.

116. "Hunger: Education or Revolution?" *Daily Collegian: La Voz*, March 2, 1970.

117. Burton Swope, "Chicanos Go on Hunger Strike; Issue 10 Demands," *Daily Collegian*, March 3, 1970.

118. Gloria Davis, "Fast Ends in Violence, No Response from Falk," *Daily Collegian*, March 9, 1970.

119. Sale, *SDS*, 637.

120. Vonnie Madigan, "War Protesters Present Demands to Administration," *Daily Collegian*, May 13, 1970.

121. "FSC Computer Center Firebombed: Estimated $1 Million Worth of Equipment Destroyed by Arsonists," *Daily Collegian*, May 20, 1970; "Ethnic Studies: Walker Only Recommends 4 Be Rehired," *Daily Collegian*, May 20, 1970; "FSC Gets New Computer," *Daily Collegian*, June 29, 1970.

122. "Falk Declares FSC in State of Emergency," *Daily Collegian*, May 21, 1970; "200 Students at Fresno State Vow to Close Down Campus," *Los Angeles Times*, May 22, 1970; "31 in Fresno Disorder Suspended," *Daily Collegian*, May 26, 1970; "Fresno State College Halts Funds for Paper," *Los Angeles Times*, July 5, 1970.

123. "The State: Fresno State Cancels La Raza Studies," *Los Angeles Times*, September 9, 1970.

124. Acuña, *The Making of Chicana/o Studies*, 88.

125. "Fresno State Turns Down Chicano List," *Los Angeles Times*, September 12, 1970.

126. "Protesters Attack 500 Students Registering at Fresno State," *Los Angeles Times*, September 13, 1970; Acuña, *The Making of Chicana/o Studies*, 88; "Six Students Are Suspended for Role in Demonstration," *Daily Collegian*, September 17, 1970.

127. Burton Swope, "Editorial: Reinstate Carol Bishop," *Daily Collegian*, September 17, 1970.

128. "First Arrest Made in Saturday Violence," *Daily Collegian*, September 18, 1970; Burton Swope, "Purge of Campus Leaders Underway," *Daily Collegian*,

September 21, 1970. The two remaining suspended students were both Chicano—Steve Santos and Jorge Leos.

129. Burton Swope, "Four Suspended Students Are Reinstated by Administration," *Daily Collegian*, September 25, 1970.

130. Burton Swope, "Students Charge Suspensions Are Unconstitutional, Will Sue Baxter," *Daily Collegian*, September 21, 1970.

131. "Reinstated Students Charged with Breaking Campus Rules," *Daily Collegian*, October 5, 1970; "Dean Allen Refuses to Cite Charges against Students," *Daily Collegian*, October 7, 1970.

132. Burton Swope, "Head of Philosophy Department, Two Others Face Non-retention," *Daily Collegian*, November 16, 1970; Burton Swope, "The Students' Right to Know," *Daily Collegian*, November 16, 1970; Burton Swope, "English Prof Everett Frost Is Terminated," *Daily Collegian*, December 1, 1970; John Jefferies, "Hall, Mabey Are Not Retained on Faculty," *Daily Collegian*, December 1, 1970; "Dutton, Two Others Get Their Notices," *Daily Collegian*, December 1, 1970; "Professor of Chemistry Toney Is on Firing List," *Daily Collegian*, December 1, 1970; Daniel Safreno, "Kenneth Kerr Gets Terminal Contract Notice," *Daily Collegian*, December 1, 1970; Burton Swope, "Correction," *Daily Collegian*, December 2, 1970; Seib, *The Slow Death of Fresno State*, 138–42; William Trombley, "Fresno State Professor Who Criticized Firings Gets Fired: Locked Out of Office," *Los Angeles Times*, December 5, 1970; "Zumwalt, Chittick Are Demoted; Campus Police Board-up Offices," *Daily Collegian*, December 7, 1970.

133. "La Raza Studies Program Reinstated: For Spring Semester," *Daily Collegian*, December 15, 1970.

134. "La Mesa Directiva Hits La Raza Studies Plan," *Daily Collegian*, January 5, 1970.

135. "Three Years Later . . . Nearly All Hope Destroyed," *Daily Collegian: Uhuru*, February 8, 1971.

136. "Regan Proposes Austerity Budget for State Colleges," *Daily Collegian*, February 3, 1971; James Wrightson, "Severe Curtailment in EOP Funds Is Predicted for '71–72," *Daily Collegian*, February 3, 1971; "Speculation on Proposed Cuts in EOP," *Daily Collegian: La Voz*, February 22, 1971.

137. "UHURU Endorse Boycott," *Daily Collegian: Uhuru*, March 15, 1971; Bill Schiffmann, "EOP Office Begins Fight to Restore Reagan Budget Cuts: Program Drastically Affected," *Daily Collegian*, April 2, 1971.

138. "Fresno State Elects Chicano Student Head," *Los Angeles Times*, June 5, 1972.

Chapter 6

1. "Human Rights—Not Political Privileges," *Open Process*, January 22, 1969.

2. In 1970, the combined percentage of Asian Americans (13 percent), African Americans (13 percent), and Latinos (14 percent) reached only 40 percent of the city's total population but 59 percent of the city's high schools. It is likely there were some number of other ethnic minorities—for instance, Native Americans and

Chinatown residents—left out of or underestimated in these statistics. See Godfrey, *Neighborhoods in Transition*, 97; *Strike at Frisco State!*, 37; Ishizuka, *Serve the People*; Daryl E. Lembke, "S.F. State Crisis Takes on Look of Labor Row," *Los Angeles Times*, November 25, 1968.

3. According to Jason Ferreira, as early as spring of 1966—fully three years before this interview—Roger Alvarado and other campus activists were already "grappling with the Master Plan and its implications." Email from Jason Ferreira to the author, November 10, 2021.

4. "Human Rights—Not Political Privileges."

5. Here, Alvarado was drawing on the concept of internal colonialism.

6. "Human Rights—Not Political Privileges."

7. Shapiro, I should note, did not include white students in his "everybody" despite their important involvement in the strike at San Francisco State. A sharp political thinker and observer, Shapiro was a white student New Leftist who remained skeptical of the white student left. Despite earlier activism in high school, especially in the Bay Area's civil rights movement, during his time at San Francisco State, Shapiro largely confined his activism to educational and agitational work through *Open Process*. His deep dislike for the politics and tactics of the Progressive Labor Party, which had infiltrated the Students for a Democratic Society at San Francisco State, kept him away from SDS. In the 1970s, Shapiro would continue his involvement on the left as part of the New Communist movement. In particular, Shapiro was active within I Wor Kuen and the League of Revolutionary Struggle, as a member of the Liberation School Collective, and as a rank-and-file labor movement activist after abandoning his pursuit of a PhD in labor history at UC Berkeley. In 2016, Shapiro published *Song of the Stubborn One Thousand: The Watsonville Canning Strike, 1985–87*. Reminisces of Peter Shapiro, Interview 1 (April 11, 1984), Student Movement of the 1960s Project, p. 86, Columbia Center for Oral History Archives, Rare Book & Manuscript Library, Columbia University.

8. My examination of the diverse New Left coalitions in this chapter owes much to the insights of the late Betita Martinez, especially Martinez, "Histories of the Sixties," and Martinez, "That Old White (Male) Logic." On the question of interracial coalitions, see, for instance, Pulido, *Black, Brown, Yellow, and Left*; Sonnie and Tracey, *Hillbilly Nationalists*; Behnken, *The Struggle in Black and Brown*; Kun and Pulido, *Black and Brown in Los Angeles*; Mantler, *Power to the Poor*; Williams, *From the Bullet to the Ballot*; Johnson, "Seattle in Coalition"; and Ferreira, "All Power to the People."

9. Of course, another significant sector of student revolt in the second half of 1960s stemmed from the war in Vietnam. The student anti-war movement remains intricately bound up with questions of both racist imperialism and campus complicity in the Cold War, yet does not form a central strand of my analysis of the Master Plan. As the first chapter of this book demonstrates, those who drafted the Master Plan remained firmly within the mainstream of support for the United States in the Cold War. Indeed, they saw their work on the Master Plan as a way to contribute to the struggle against the Soviets in the wake of Sputnik. On campuses

in particular, students rejected the war in Vietnam by protesting military and war industry recruitment on campus, by working to end ROTC programs, and most famously, by burning down ROTC buildings. For a succinct overview of the anti-war movement, see Hall, *Rethinking the American Anti-war Movement*.

10. Under pressure from the student struggles explored in this chapter, administrators would increase special admissions from 2 percent to 4 percent. William Trombley, "UC, Colleges Seek Go-Ahead for More Minority Students," *Los Angeles Times*, February 19, 1968; "VSC to Admit More Minority Group Students," *Los Angeles Times*, May 19, 1968.

11. As mentioned in chapter 3, even Governor Ronald Reagan appropriated Murray's critique of the racism inherent in the Master Plan system. For Reagan, who denounced Murray by name, this was a reason to introduce tuition, not to expand access for students of color; "BSU Calls for Black Strike," *Daily Gater*, October 28, 1968.

12. These goals were also adopted by students outside of the Master Plan system who, of course, were not responding directly to the Master Plan itself. In California, this included private colleges and universities such as Stanford, the University of Southern California, and Occidental, whose student activists often maintained contact with and always awareness of their state school counterparts.

13. Such tensions regarding campus autonomy are explored in chapter 3. "BSU Explanation of Today's Strike," *Daily Gater*, November 6, 1968; Bill Barlow and Peter Shapiro, "State Sails Off the Edge," *Open Process*, November 6, 1968; Summerskill, *President Seven*, 54, 58; Orrick, *Shut It Down!*, 17.

14. My reference to injuries sustained in the act of civil disobedience deliberately excludes the two police killings of protesters that occurred in the California student movement of the long 1960s. Although police violence on California campuses certainly increased over the course of the 1960s, the killings of Kevin Moran in Santa Barbara and James Rector in Berkeley took place in the context of student protest that fell outside of the Master Plan–related movements under study. On these killings, see Potter and Sullivan, *The Campus by the Sea Where the Bank Burned Down*; and Rosenfeld, *Subversives*.

15. The scholar Jason Ferreira is an important exception.

16. Theoharis, *A More Beautiful and Terrible History*, 65.

17. Gene Sherman, "L.A. Negroes Only Part of Over-all Minority Problem: Concentration of Race Here Is Fifth Largest in United States," *Los Angeles Times*, January 24, 1961; Jack Eisen, "San Francisco Schools Deeper in Racial Strife: Boards Seek 7-Month Armistice in Dispute, Gets Sit-in, Promise of More Controversy," *Los Angeles Times*, September 20, 1962; Ruben Salazar, "Civic Leaders Troubled by School Dropouts: 350,000 Mexican-Americans Who Failed to Finish Their Education Cited," *Los Angeles Times*, October 22, 1962; Jack Birkinshaw, "'Color Conscious' Policy Urged for School Districts," *Los Angeles Times*, June 16, 1963; "Segregation in Fresno's Schools Hit: Board Promises Negro Leaders It Will Take Action," *Los Angeles Times*, July 30, 1963; Jerry Gillam, "College Loan Asked for Top 15% in High School: Aims to Discourage Dropout of Bright Members of California Minority Groups," *Los Angeles Times*, February 19, 1963; "The Day in Sacramento: The Assembly," *Los Angeles Times*, February 19, 1963.

18. On the Rockefeller Foundation program, see "Foundation Gave 35 Million in '63," *New York Times*, April 27, 1964; and Gene Currivan, "Education: The Disadvantaged; New Programs Prepare Students for Advanced Schooling," *New York Times*, August 16, 1964.

19. Kerr, *The Gold and the Blue*, 1:378; "Coast School Acts to Aid Minorities," *New York Times*, January 5, 1964.

20. Leon, "Racism in the University," 88; Kitano and Miller, *An Assessment of Educational Opportunity Programs*, 1; "Help for Minority Students," *Los Angeles Times*, January 31, 1969; Estudios de la Raza, "Three Years at Fresno State," *Daily Collegian*, February 16, 1970; *The Challenge of Achievement*, 69–70; Orrick, *Shut It Down!*, 27–28.

21. Orrick, *Shut It Down!*, 77–78; Leahy, "On Strike!," 17.

22. In addition to SNCC, Garrett had previously been involved in the Congress of Racial Equality and a Communist Party USA youth group. His decision to research the history of San Francisco State and the Bay Area, he notes, was influenced by the writings of Frantz Fanon and Mao Zedong; Rogers, "Remembering the Black Campus Movement," 32.

23. This list is not definitive but draws from sources below. Angela Davis and others, in 1967, "decided to try to organize a Black Student Union" at UCSD. However, they decided on using the name of a similar organization at San Diego State College, the Black Student Council. Eventually, the organization became a BSU. See Davis, *An Autobiography*, 156–57; and Mariscal, *Brown-Eyed Children of the Sun*, 220; Students at UC Berkeley organized as the Afro-American Student Union, yet the organization was often referred to as the BSU by campus newspaper the *Daily Californian*. See Miller, "Race, Power and the Emergence of Black Studies," 85; Earl Anthony, *Time of the Furnaces*, 30–31; Rogers, *Black Campus Movement*, 109; Rogers, "Remembering the Black Campus Movement," 36; Biondi, *Black Revolution on Campus*, 68; Murch, *Living for the City*, 213, 220; Davis and Wiener, *Set the Night on Fire*, 397; Andy Anderson, "Coach Agrees to Apologize for His Derogatory Remark," *Daily Collegian*, December 1, 1967; Davis, "Leonard McNeil . . . Brother in Exile"; "SF City College Plagued by Strike of BSU, Supporters," *Daily Collegian*, December 13, 1968; "Third World Liberation Front," *Sacramento Observer*, March 27, 1969; Carol Long, "Ethnic Studies at UC," *Sun Reporter*, August 16, 1969; Collisson, "The Fight to Legitimize Blackness," 116; Lombardi, "The Position Papers of Black Student Activists," 2, 4, 5, 8, 12.

24. The Reminisces of Terry Collins, Interview 1 (April 11, 1984), Student Movement of the 1960s Project, 35, 42, 44, Columbia Center for Oral History Archives, Rare Book & Manuscript Library, Columbia University.

25. Anthony, *Time of the Furnaces*, 22–24; "Letters: Black Power Erupts," *Daily Sundial*, November 9, 1967; "Karenga Coverage Biased," *Daily Sundial*, November 10, 1967.

26. The work of the Federal Bureau of Investigation (FBI) and local police in accordance with the FBI's counterintelligence program COINTELPRO greatly exacerbated these preexisting tensions. See Bloom and Martin, *Black against Empire*, 269; Biondi, *Black Revolution on Campus*, 45; Brown, *Fighting for Us*; Ogbar, *Black Power*,

115. On Black Panther Party–US tensions at UCLA specifically, see Biondi, *Black Revolution on Campus*, 68; and Bloom and Martin, *Black Against Empire*, 216–20.

27. Or as historians have more typically delineated this shift, from the civil rights movement to Black Power. Edwards, *Black Students*, 61. For a useful contemporary look at BSUs, their diversity, and their ties to the Black Power phase of the Black freedom struggle, see Sokoya, "A Historical Analysis." As one of Sokoya's interviewees notes on p. 122, "BSUs were diverse organizations. They [BSUs] were united fronts with different tendencies and they focused primarily on campus questions."

28. Rosales, *Chicano!*, 176.

29. David A. Sanchez, "UMAS," *Daily Bruin*, January 23, 1968.

30. While a group known as MAYA formed at Sacramento City College, its ties—if any—to MAYA in San Diego remain unclear. See "Third World Liberation Front," *Sacramento Observer*, March 27, 1969. Munoz, *Youth, Identity, Power*, 66, 73; Rosenfeld, *Subversives*, 427; Mariscal, *Brown-Eyed Children of the Sun*, 221.

31. Translation: The Chicano Student Movement of Aztlán. "Aztlán" is a Nahuatl word that refers to the mythico-historical homeland of the Aztec peoples of central Mexico, believed to be located to the north of contemporary Mexico in the American Southwest.

32. The conference at UCSB is discussed extensively in chapter 5. Munoz, *Youth, Identity, Power*, 95, 101; Hidalgo, *Revelation in Aztlan*, 138.

33. The turn away from the hyphenated identity of Mexican American to Chicano signaled an embrace of nationalism. The question of cultural versus revolutionary nationalism, however, was far from settled. In MECHA, the sort of divisions that emerged between the Black Panthers and Karenga's US existed within a single organization. Tensions between Marxists and cultural nationalists, brewing since at least 1969, contributed to the deterioration of MECHA as an effective force in the aftermath of a 1973 conference at UC Riverside. In the 1970s, many Marxist Chicanos left MECHA for New Communist movement organizations such as El Comité Estudiantil del Pueblo, El Centro de Accion Social Autonomo, and the August 29th Movement. See Munoz, *Youth Identity, Power*, 96, 97, 99, 112–16.

34. Here, UC Berkeley was an important exception. A hotbed of eclectic radicalism, the Berkeley campus's left space was already occupied as SDS branches expanded elsewhere. The most comprehensive overviews of SDS remain early treatments written by members of the sixties generation. See, for instance, Sale, *SDS*; and Miller, *Democracy Is in the Streets*. For a more recent, critical analysis, see Barber, *A Hard Rain Fell*.

35. In December 1968, PL began their campaign to "defeat nationalism," embracing a narrowly defined class struggle. As the strike wore down in March 1969, PL began to push this stance more openly, denouncing the TWLF as "petit bourgeois" and "anti-working class." Barlow and Shapiro, *End to Silence*, 317–18. Beyond pushing back on the influence of the Panthers on the wider left, PL rejected the counterculture, telling its members to, like "workers," dress conservatively, keep their hair short, and refrain from drug use. Barber, *A Hard Rain Fell*, 145–48. For the perspective of PL activists, see Levin and Silbar, *You Say You Want a Revolution*.

36. These groups made up a large majority of Asian Americans in California at the time. This would, of course, change in the decades to come. There remains a

lack of parity in this study. Where organizing by Black and Chicano student activists are explored in depth, coverage of Asian Americans is minimal. There are a number of reasons why this is so, the most important being chronological. If one were to envision a timeline of organizing by students of color in California in the 1960s, the earliest efforts were made by African Americans, followed by Mexican Americans. Asian American political organizing, as such, came later. (Social organizations that focused on individual national origin groups developed on campuses before such pan-Asian political organizing.) A rough analysis suggests why this might be so. In the mid-1960s, ongoing civil rights organizing in the American South inspired Black student in California to action. Mexican Americans, while also inspired by Black organizing (North and South), found inspiration for organizing *as Chicanos* in the example of United Farm Workers, Cesar Chavez, and the Delano grape strike of 1965. Most Chicano student organizations in California emerged in 1967 in the wake of the Delano strike. Asian Americans came together *as Asian Americans* only later, inspired by the Black freedom struggle, and informed by their experiences in assorted civil rights organizations, the United Farm Workers, SDS, the Peace and Freedom Party, and the anti-war movement. The AAPA, the first pan-Asian political organization in the United States, was founded at UC Berkeley in May 1968. Subsequent chapters were founded elsewhere in the coming months. All this to say, much of the organizing done by Asian American students as such came some years after parallel organizing had begun with first, African Americans and then Mexican Americans. Perhaps one contributing factor for this comparative chronological delay was a lack of cultural cohesion. Whereas Mexican Americans ultimately had shared national origins in Mexico, African Americans united on the basis of common origins in the history of enslavement, oppression, and proud resistance to it. The Asian American student activists of the late 1960s came from families of various national backgrounds, with distinct languages and cultural traditions; yet, they would eventually come to recognize their shared pan-Asian experiences on majority-white campuses and in a stubbornly racist postwar United States. See Espiritu, *Asian American Panethnicity*, 26–27. At this point, the literature on the Asian American movement is small but growing. See Wei, *Asian American Movement*; Ishizuka, *Serve the People*; Louie and Omatsu, *Asian Americans*; Maeda, *Chains of Babylon*; Maeda, *Rethinking the Asian American Movement*; and Dong, "The Origins and Trajectory of Asian American Political Activism."

37. Umemoto, "'On Strike!': San Francisco State College Strike," 31.

38. Interestingly, the AAPA began as an "Asian Caucus" of the Peace and Freedom Party. See Wei, *Asian American Movement*, 20; Maeda, *Rethinking the Asian American Movement*, 9. The Peace and Freedom Party itself originated with a number of left formations—most importantly the Independent Socialist Club at UC Berkeley—and brought the majority-white anti-war movement into formal alliance with the Black Panther Party. My knowledge of the nearly forgotten Peace and Freedom Party comes mainly from discussions with three of its most important members: Joel Geier, Marilyn Morehead, and Jack Weinberg.

39. Such leadership included that of Mason Wong and Ed Ilamin at San Francisco State, as well as Richard Belvin and Richard Aoki at UC Berkeley. Ishizuka,

Serve the People, 82–87; Wei, *Asian American Movement*, 19; Dong, "The Origins and Trajectory of Asian American Political Activism," 50–51; "Third World Liberation Front," *Sacramento Observer*, March 27, 1969.

40. On *Gidra*, see Wei, *Asian American Movement*, 103–12.

41. "Asian American Student Alliance," *Gidra*, June 1969; "High Potential Program Starts," *Gidra*, August 1969. UCLA would also see the formation of a group known as the Asian Radical Movement. "Asian protest movement," *Daily Bruin*, October 27, 1969. To be clear, an EOP had existed on the UCLA campus since the 1966–67 school year. At the start, the High Potential Program recruited Black and Chicano students but soon expanded to include Asian- and Native Americans as well. See Collisson, "The Fight to Legitimize Blackness," 131–32. In 1971, the EOP and High Potential Program would be consolidated into a single program. UCLA's EOP program began under director Kenneth Washington, formerly a counselor at a predominantly Black high school in Compton. In the fall of 1967, Washington brought in Juvenal Gonzales, an army veteran and 1967 graduate of UC Riverside, to serve as assistant director and work with Mexican American EOP students. See "Underprivileged Get Educational Uplift," *Daily Bruin*, October 5, 1966; Irene Cardenas, "EOP Recruits, Helps Minority Students," *Daily Bruin*, October 26, 1967; "Southern Education Journal Praises UC for Recruitment of Minority Students," *University Bulletin* 16 (1967), 151. As of fall 1968, Asian Americans were disproportionately represented on UC campuses, making up approximately 5 percent of all UC students and 13 percent of all of the UC's EOP students. African Americans and Mexican Americans, by way of contrast, each comprised approximately 2 percent of UC students. Native Americans fared far worse, making up only 0.2 percent of UC students. See Kitano and Miller, *An Assessment of Educational Opportunity Programs*, 21.

42. Ishizuka, *Serve the People*, 88.

43. Kong, "Re-examining Diversity Policy," 29–52.

44. Phyllis Chiu, "Model Minority Speaks: Yellow People Are Not Bananas," *Third World*, November 4, 1970.

45. Recent investigative journalism has explored the extent to which the land grant universities originating with the Morrill Act of 1862 were, in fact, "land-grab universities" established through the theft of Native land. See Lee and Ahtone, "Land-Grab Universities." On the broader American Indian Movement, see Smith and Warrior, *Like a Hurricane*.

46. One exception, at least by 1968, was UCLA, which then enrolled as many as eighty Native American students. Across the United States, only 2,900 Native people were enrolled in higher education in 1962—that means approximately 0.5 percent of the American Indian population. See Stahl-Kovell, "Reimagining Red Power," 90, 108; Faculty Sponsoring Committee, "Proposal for a Native American Research & Development Institute and for an Interim Native American Research & Development Program on the Davis Campus of the University of California," June 1969, p. 1, David Risling Papers, Box 35, UC Davis, Special Collections.

47. De La Torre, "From Activism to Academics," 13.

48. Stahl-Kovell, "Reimagining Red Power," 96.

49. De La Torre, "From Activism to Academics," 12, 14; Dunbar-Ortiz, *An Indigenous Peoples' History*, 183–84.

50. "Native American Studies at the University of California, Davis: A Status Report, June 1970," 2, David Risling Papers, Box 35, UC Davis, Special Collections; Bernd C. Peyer, "D-Q University: A Native American Institution of Higher Learning Struggling for Existence," 3, David Risling Papers, Box 63, UC Davis, Special Collections.

51. By 1973, at least sixteen Native American Studies programs were in operation in California. Stahl-Kovell, "Reimagining Red Power," 81.

52. Despite Forbes's central role and his emphasis on Native Americans, the project initially developed as a joint venture between Chicano and Native American scholars and student activists. Robert H. Finch, "Dear Dr. Forbes," Jack D. Forbes Collection, Box 4, UC Davis, Special Collections.

53. Lumpenproletariat, as employed by Marx and later Marxists, refers to the idea of an underclass. Translated from the German, the term roughly signifies the "proletariat in rags." For Marx, the lumpenproletariat consisted of the homeless, the perpetually unemployed, thieves, pimps, and beggars, among others. The Black Panthers would later emphasize the revolutionary potential of the Black lumpen. See Marx, *The Eighteenth Brumaire*, 59. For a critical view, see Chris Booker, "Lumpenization."

54. As Jason Ferreira notes, third worldism was "animated by, and articulated itself through" the "Third Worldist concepts" of "self-determination, anti-imperialism, and Third World Unity." See Ferreira, "With the Soul of a Human Rainbow," 31. San Francisco State BSU member and Black Panther Terry Collins notes the centrality of Fanon and Mao to the organization of the TWLF. See the "Reminisces of Terry Collins," 84–85, 112, 120–21. On third world Marxism at San Francisco State, see Barlow and Shapiro, *End to Silence*, 155–56 and Ferreira, "All Power to the People." On third world Marxism more generally, see Elbaum, *Revolution in the Air*, 41–58, and Young, *Soul Power*.

55. Quoted in Kanji, "The Third World: A Response to Oppression," *Gidra*, April 1969.

56. On the concept of racial capitalism, see Robinson, *Black Marxism*.

57. To avoid the confusion inherent in using "third world" to refer to cross-race coalitions other than the TWLFs, I use the terms *interracial alliances* and *rainbow coalition*. I do so to avoid repetitive language but also to point to the influential example set by the Illinois chapter of the Black Panther Party, which founded the original Rainbow Coalition with the (Latino) Young Lords and (white) Young Patriots. Interracial alliance serves as an umbrella term encompassing both TWLFs and rainbow coalitions. The difference between the two is that TWLFs consisted only of "third world" peoples—that is, people of color—whereas rainbow coalitions included whites. To be sure, white leftists played important supporting roles in TWLF struggles, such as the one at San Francisco State. They were not, however, formal members of the fronts. Where race was the central unifier in the TWLFs, in rainbow coalitions it was class. As Bob Lee of the Chicago Panthers has noted, "Rainbow Coalition was just a code word for class struggle." Lee quoted in Sonnie and Tracey,

Hillbilly Nationalists, 80. For more on the history of the original Chicago-based Rainbow Coalition, see Williams, *From the Bullet to the Ballot* and Fernández, *The Young Lords*. "1000 Gather for Teach-in and Sit-in," *California Aggie*, May 7, 1970; "March, Rally, Senate Sit-in, Four-Hour Convocation," *Pony Express*, May 8, 1969; Lombardi, "The Position Papers of Black Student Activists," 12; and Ferreira, "From College Readiness to Ready for Revolution!"

58. Merritt College Young Socialist Alliance, "Third World Community Week, January 6–10," January 7, 1969, Merritt College Black Student Union Collection, 1964–1983, BANC MSS 2006/240 Box 1, Bancroft Library, University of California, Berkeley.

59. The DuBois Club was a Communist Party USA student group. Barlow and Shapiro, *An End to Silence*, 42; Todd Gitlin et al., "Organizations and Faculty Supporting Strike," *Strike Daily*, November 12, 1968, San Francisco State Strike Folder, Special Collections, UC Davis.

60. Reminisces of Peter Shapiro, Interview 1 (April 11, 1984), 85.

61. The UC and state colleges did not begin to collect data regarding the racial breakdown of campus populations until after the student movements under study. As such, the numbers here come from sources produced by faculty and administrators. Larson, "Master Plan, Master Failure," 76; Summerskill, *President Seven*, 79.

62. Based on the available evidence—chiefly coming from student newspapers, government reports, and later memoirs—it seems likely that San Francisco State's relatively large pre–Master Plan Black population was unique among the UC and state college campuses.

63. Barlow and Shapiro, *End to Silence*, 149

64. Summerskill, *President Seven*, 80.

65. According to Orrick, only 3 percent of San Francisco State's eighteen thousand students lived in on-campus housing; Orrick, *Shut It Down!*, 4, 76; "Strike Daily Bulletin," San Francisco State Strike Folder, Special Collections, UC Davis; Lembke, "S.F. State Crisis."

66. Godfrey, *Neighborhoods in Transition*, 97; Bob Hernandez, "Third World Studies Flap," *Daily Gater*, July 3, 1969.

67. Quoted in the pamphlet *Strike at Frisco State!*

68. Numbers regarding racial demographics at San Francisco State derive from a spring 1968 survey conducted by the school. According to strike archivist Helene Whitson, San Francisco State's was "the only such survey done by a school in the Bay Area." See Whitson, *On Strike! Shut It Down!*, 10.

69. Barlow and Shapiro, *End to Silence*, 159.

70. As noted above, these acronyms correspond to the Black Student Union, Mexican American Student Confederation, Latin American Student Organization, Philipino-Americans for Collegian Endeavor, the Intercollegiate Chinese for Social Action, and the Asian American Political Alliance. The AAPA at San Francisco State was predominantly Japanese American. See Ferreira, "All Power to the People," 78. Beyond the organizations that made up the TWLF, some white students—mainly members of SDS and PL—formally participated in the strike as members of the white student strike support committee.

71. Barlow and Shapiro, *End to Silence*, 62, 91, 155.

72. Reminisces of Peter Shapiro, Interview 1 (April 11, 1984), 74, 86.

73. Summerskill, *President Seven*, 213.

74. Orrick, *Shut It Down!*, 28; Barlow and Shapiro, *End to Silence*, 166–67.

75. Summerskill, *President Seven*, 215–16.

76. Orrick, *Shut It Down!*, 28; Smith, Axen, and Pentony, *By Any Means Necessary*, 56–57.

77. Summerskill, *President Seven*, 74.

78. Orrick, *Shut It Down!*, 31; William Drummond, "Dumke Asks S.F. State College to Explain Hiring of Panther," *Los Angeles Times*, September 20, 1968.

79. Carolyn Skaug, "Progress Slow," *Phoenix*, October 24, 1968; Richard Corville, "No Funds for Black Studies," *Daily Gater*, November 5, 1968.

80. Jacques Jourdain, "Students Attack AFROTC: Rally Shouts Down Smith, Plans Action," *Daily Gater*, October 9, 1968; Barlow and Shapiro, *An End to Silence*, 213–14.

81. The full list of BSU demands read as follows: "1. That all Black Studies courses being taught through various other departments be immediately part of the Black Studies Department and that all the instructors in this department receive full time pay. 2. That Dr. Hare, Chairman of the Black Studies Department, receive a full professorship and a comparable salary according to his qualifications. 3. That there be a Department of Black Studies which will grant a Bachelors Degree in Black Studies; that the Black Studies Department Chairman, faculty, and staff have the sole power to hire and fire without interference of the racist administration and the Chancellor. 4. That all unused slots for Black students from Fall 1968 under the Special Admissions Program be filled in Spring 1969. 5. That all Black students who wish to, be admitted in Fall 1969. 6. That twenty (20) full time teaching positions be allocated to the Department of Black Studies. 7. That Dr. Helen Bedesem be replaced in the position of Financial Aid Officer and that a Black person be hired to direct it and that Third World people have the power to determine how it will be administered. 8. That no disciplinary action will be administered in any way to any students, workers, teachers or administrators during and after the strike as a consequence of their participation in the strike. 9. That the California State College Trustees not be allowed to dissolve any Black programs on or off the San Francisco State College campus. 10. That George Murray maintain his teaching position on this campus for the 1968–69 academic year." See "Demands and Explanations," BSU Folder, San Francisco State College Strike Collection, San Francisco State University.

82. The full list of TWLF demands read as follows: "1. That a School of Ethnic Studies for the ethnic groups involved in the Third World be set up with the students in each particular ethnic organization having the authority and control of the hiring and retention of any faculty member, director or administrator, as well as the curriculum in a specific area study. 2. That 50 faculty positions be appropriated to the School of Ethnic Studies, 20 of which would be for the Black Studies program. 3. That, in the spring semester, the college fulfill its commitments to the non-white students in admitting those who apply. 4. That, in the Fall of 1969, all applications of non-white students be accepted. 5. That George Murray and any other faculty person

chosen by non-white people as their teacher be retained in their positions." See "Strike Demands," San Francisco State Strike Folder, Special Collections, UC Davis.

83. Smith, "Organizing for Social Justice," 218; "Strike Gets Wide Support," *Daily Gater*, November 6, 1968.

84. Barlow and Shapiro, *End to Silence*, 245; Sheldon J. Nyman, "Trustees Delay Decisions on SF State, to Meet Today," *Daily Gater*, November 26, 1968; "Outside Agitators: Board of Trustees Flexing Muscles Too Much on Campus," *Daily Gater*, November 19, 1968; "Trustees Run Colleges for Profit, SDS Says," *Daily Gater*, November 19, 1968.

85. S. I. Hayakawa, "The F.S.M. Demonstrations: A Statement by S. I. Hayakawa, Professor of English, San Francisco State College, December 8, 1964," Free Speech Movement Records, CU-309, Carton 3, Bancroft Library, University of California, Berkeley.

86. Karagueuzian, *Blow It Up!*, 174; Smith, "Organizing for Social Justice," 225.

87. Third World Liberation Front, "Strike Pamphlet," TWLF Folder, San Francisco State College Strike Collection, San Francisco State University.

88. Anatole Anton, "Academic Whorehouse Bankrupt, Repossessed by Finance Company," *Open Process*, December 13, 1968.

89. A. K. Bierman, "At SF State—Behind the Law and Order Facade," *San Francisco Bay Guardian*, December 24, 1968; Smith, "Organizing for Social Justice," 230; Barlow and Shapiro, *End to Silence*, 328–30.

90. Smith, "Organizing for Social Justice," 240, 244.

91. "Attendance Drops Way Off," *Daily Gater*, January 8, 1969.

92. Signatories included FSM leader Jack Weinberg, now as a representative of the Alameda County Peace and Freedom Party, and Anne Draper, a representative of the Amalgamated Clothing Workers and the wife of FSM mentor Hal Draper. "State of California, Unfair! Institutionalized Racism and Anti-unionism," San Francisco State Strike Folder, Special Collections, UC Davis.

93. Barlow and Shapiro, *End to Silence*, 301, 304.

94. John Davidson, "A Week of Losses for Strike," *Phoenix*, February 20, 1969.

95. "AFT Looks Forward to Board Approval: Teachers Strike Tentatively Settled," *Daily Gater*, February 25, 1969.

96. "TWLF Proposes a Peace Talk Plan," *Daily Gater*, February 26, 1969.

97. Barlow and Shapiro, *End to Silence*, 314.

98. Barlow and Shapiro, *End to Silence*, 320.

99. "Fact Sheet: Defend the S.F. State 700+," San Francisco State Strike Folder, Special Collections, Shields Library, UC Davis; "Joint Agreement of Representatives of the Third World Liberation Front and the Black Student Union and Members of the Select Committee," March 18, 1969, TWLF Folder, San Francisco State College Strike Collection, San Francisco State University.

100. Orrick, *Shut It Down!*, 70.

101. Karagueuzian, *Blow It Up!*, 185.

102. Whitson, *On Strike! Shut It Down!*, 53.

103. Orrick, *Shut It Down!*, 70.

104. *Daily Californian* estimates cited in Rorabaugh, *Berkeley at War*, 84. An unpublished dissertation by Harvey Dong notes a survey conducted on Berkeley's campus in 1966 that shows slightly different numbers, with 226 African Americans, 76 Chicanos, and 61 Native Americans. Either way, their combined representation on campus was exceedingly slim. Asian Americans fared better. In 1966, they seem to have made up roughly 8–9 percent of UC Berkeley's student body. See Dong, "The Origins and Trajectory of Asian American Political Activism," 52.

105. "Berkeley Gives Aid to Minority Groups," *New York Times*, November 25, 1967.

106. Rosenfeld, *Subversives*, 431.

107. Daryl E. Lembke, "Heyns Deplores Plans for Strike at UC Today," *Los Angeles Times*, January 22, 1969; Miller, "Black Studies in California," 54, 55; Rorabaugh, *Berkeley at War*, 85; Rosenfeld, *Subversives*, 428.

108. In contrast to a contemporary article in the *Los Angeles Times*, Karen Miller cites an open letter written by the Berkeley Afro-American Student Union that lists eight demands, not five. See Miller, "Black Studies in California," 54–55; Lembke, "Heyns Deplores Plans."

109. "Police Break Up Demonstration by UC Student Strikers," *Los Angeles Times*, January 31, 1969; "Berkeley Students Battle Police in Series of Clashes," *Los Angeles Times*, February 5, 1969; "30 Arrested during Berkeley Clashes," *Los Angeles Times*, February 14, 1969; "5 Injured, 25 Arrested in UC Berkeley Clash," *Los Angeles Times*, February 20, 1969; Daryl Lembke and John Dreyfuss, "Berkeley Erupts in Tear-Gas War; Reagan Alerts Guard," *Los Angeles Times*, February 21, 1969; "Police Battle Students Linked in Human Chains at Berkeley," *Los Angeles Times*, February 28, 1969; Rosenfeld, *Subversives*, 444.

110. Jerry Gillam, "Efforts to End College Strife Gaining—Reagan," *Los Angeles Times*, March 12, 1969; "The State: Two Berkeley Militant Leaders Dismissed," *Los Angeles Times*, April 6, 1969; Daryl Lembke, "Viewpoints at Odds in Aftermath of UC Strike," *Los Angeles Times*, April 24, 1969.

111. Daryl Lembke, "Faculty at UC Berkeley Votes for Ethnic Studies Department," *Los Angeles Times*, March 5, 1969; John Dreyfuss, "Ethnic Studies in State Mostly Promises, Plans," *Los Angeles Times*, April 25, 1969.

112. Miller, "Black Studies in California," 58.

113. Lembke, "Viewpoints at Odds."

114. As Harry Edwards notes, such diversification included the faculty: "It wasn't until a Third World Strike at the University of California, for example, that the issue of seriously recruiting African American, Latino professors, Native American professors, really was taken seriously by the administration. That's the auspice under which I was brought here. That's the auspice under which most of the black faculty who were here while I was here were brought here. . . . The same with Latino professors." See Harry Edwards, "Harry Edwards: An Oral History," conducted by Nadine Wilmot in 2005, Regional Oral History Office, Bancroft Library, University of California, Berkeley, 2010, 82.

115. Leon, "Racism in the University," 88.

116. Moreno, "For the Community, of the Community," 155, 157–58, 162, 170, 178, 188; Miller, "Black Studies in California," 26.

117. Moreno "For the Community, of the Community," 189–91, 195–98, 201–3.

118. Miller, "Black Studies in California," 92.

119. Leon, "Racism in the University," 93, 96.

120. Although not as prominent as the Black and Chicano activists who led the Lumumba-Zapata movement, participants included members of the AASA as well as Native American students. These included Keith Lowe (a Chinese Jamaican professor of literature), Ranadir Mitra (a Bengali graduate student), and AASA cofounders Marlene Tuyay Scott (Filipina) and Phyllis Chiu (Chinese American). See Chiu, "Model Minority Speaks"; Kong, "Re-examining Diversity Policy," 29–52.

121. Mariscal, *Brown-Eyed Children of the Sun*, 217; Moreno, "For the Community, of the Community," 236.

122. William Trombley, "Marine Base Altered to House One UC San Diego College," *Los Angeles Times*, September 3, 1967; William Trombley, "UC San Diego Enters Its Second Year of Growth," *Los Angeles Times*, October 3, 1965.

123. McGill, *Year of the Monkey*, 121, 122.

124. Both the BSC and MAYA grew out of affiliations with earlier organizations of the same name at San Diego State College. Thanks to the admissions standards introduced at the UC and state college level by the Master Plan, activists of color on both campuses were dealing with similar issues regarding minority enrollment. At UCSD, the BSC was founded in 1967 and MAYA in early 1968; "Lumumba-Zapata College: B.S.C.-M.A.Y.A. Demands"; Davis, *An Autobiography*, 157; Mariscal, *Brown-Eyed Children of the Sun*, 221; Moreno "For the Community, Of the Community," 246, 249.

125. "Lumumba-Zapata College: B.S.C.-M.A.Y.A. Demands."

126. Davis, *An Autobiography*, 196, 197.

127. For contemporary coverage of the TWLF strike at UC Berkeley, see, for instance, "Minority Students Picket at UC Berkeley," *Los Angeles Times*, January 23, 1969; "Berkeley Students Battle Police in Series of Clashes," *Los Angeles Times*, February 5, 1969; Lembke, "Faculty at UC Berkeley Votes for Ethnic Studies Department."

128. "AS Senate Resolution Gives Support to Lumumba-Zapata," *Triton Times*, April 25, 1969; "Academic Senate Hears Students on LZ College," *Triton Times*, May 2, 1969.

129. Davis, *An Autobiography*, 197.

130. Instead, the name Third College sufficed until 1993, when it was formally changed to Thurgood Marshall College in honor of the noted NAACP litigator who served as the first African American justice of the Supreme Court. See William Trombley, "'Third College'—New Goal for UC San Diego," *Los Angeles Times*, December 8, 1969; William Trombley, "'Minorities' College Called Too Radical; Regents to Decide," *Los Angeles Times*, October 11, 1970; William Trombley, "San Diego Third College Backed by UC Regents," *Los Angeles Times*, October 16, 1970.

131. UCSD, located less than thirty miles from the border, had only forty-four Chicana/o students in 1968. Black students accounted for approximately fifty UCSD students in the same year. McGill, *Year of the Monkey*, 32; Mariscal, *Brown-Eyed Children of the Sun*, 222; Moreno "For the Community, of the Community," 242.

132. "Third World Liberation Front"; "SCC Newspaper Meets with Third World," *Sacramento Observer*, April 3, 1969; "3rd Front Demands Office," *Sacramento*

Observer, April 10, 1969; "TWLF Has Convocation at SCC," *Sacramento Observer*, May 8, 1969; "TWLF Talk with SCC President," *Sacramento Observer*, May 8, 1969.

133. "Violence Forces San Mateo College to Close," *Los Angeles Times*, December 13, 1968; "The State: The College of San Mateo," *Los Angeles Times*, December 22, 1968; Earl Caldwell, "Hundreds of Police Patrol Campus of Troubled Junior College in California," *New York Times*, December 17, 1968; William Trombley, "Threat of Education Backlash: Society Will Be Loser if Blacks Are Excluded," *Los Angeles Times*, December 29, 1968.

134. Daryl Lembke, "Nairobi College Operating on a Shoestring Budget and Faith," *Los Angeles Times*, May 23, 1971; Biondi, *Black Revolution on Campus*, 220–26.

135. "Enrollment Rises at East L.A. College," *Los Angeles Times*, October 8, 1967; "ELAC President Will Meet with Student Group," *Los Angeles Times*, December 19, 1968; Stanley Siegel, "Former Pachuco Will Direct Mexican-American Study Unit," *Los Angeles Times*, February 6, 1969; "Rodriguez Assumes Top Post at East Los Angeles College," *Los Angeles Times*, August 16, 1973; Moreno, "For the Community, of the Community," 85, 92, 112, 115, 128–31, 138–39, 142.

136. Bloom and Martin, *Black against Empire*, 21.

137. David Dupree and William McAllister, "A Campus Where Black Power Won," *Wall Street Journal*, November 18, 1969.

138. Norvel Smith, "Letters: In Defense of Merritt College: A Presidential Reply," *Wall Street Journal*, December 19, 1969.

139. Dupree and McAllister, "A Campus Where Black Power Won."

140. Murch, *Living for the City*, 105.

141. Campus Mobilizer, "Strike, March; Bring All the Troops Home Now!," 2, Merritt College Black Student Union Collection, 1964–1983, BANC MSS 2006/240 Box 2, Bancroft Library, University of California, Berkeley.

142. El Shabazz, "Mau Mau Tech."

143. Murch, *Living for the City*, 116.

144. Merritt Students for a Democratic Society, "Stop the Hill Campus," ca. April 29, 1969, Merritt College Black Student Union Collection, 1964–1983, BANC MSS 2006/240 Box 1, Bancroft Library, University of California, Berkeley.

145. Soul Students Advisory Council, "Dear Brothers and Sisters," Merritt College Black Student Union Collection, 1964–1983, BANC MSS 2006/240 Box 1, Bancroft Library, University of California, Berkeley.

146. Soul Student Advisory Council, "A Black University, March 28–April 5," Merritt College Black Student Union Collection, 1964–1983, BANC MSS 2006/240 Box 1, Bancroft Library, University of California, Berkeley.

147. "Can We Buy Merritt Campus?," *Merritt BSU Newsletter* 1, no. 2, June 12, 1970, Merritt College Black Student Union Collection, 1964–1983, BANC MSS 2006/240 Box 1, Bancroft Library, University of California, Berkeley.

148. "Brothers and Sisters," November 5, 1970, Merritt College Black Student Union Collection, 1964–1983, BANC MSS 2006/240 Box 1, Bancroft Library, University of California, Berkeley.

149. "Patriot Party Chief of Staff Turco Speaking at Merritt College," April 7, 1970, Merritt College Black Student Union Collection, 1964–1983, BANC MSS 2006/240

Box 2, Bancroft Library, University of California, Berkeley. On the Young Patriots, see chapter 2 of Sonnie and Trace, *Hillbilly Nationalists, Urban Race Rebels, and Black Power*.

150. Bev Mitchell, "Merritt President Extends Closure," *Oakland Tribune*, March 16, 1971.

151. "Cops Swoop In, Oust Militants at Merritt," *Oakland Tribune*, March 17, 1971.

152. Robert H. Finch, "Dear Dr. Forbes," 1972, Jack D. Forbes Collection, Box 4, UC Davis, Special Collections.

153. Forbes, *Maintaining Inequality in a Multiethnic Society*, 98. Forbes's unpublished manuscript is available in Shields Library at the University of California, Davis.

154. Janssen, "DQU," 119.

155. In 1978, due to a funding crisis, the Chicano trustees voluntarily "elected to resign" so that DQU might be eligible for Bureau of Indian Affairs funding available for "institutions controlled by an all Indian board of directors." Bernd C. Peyer, "D-Q University: A Native American Institution of Higher Learning Struggling for Existence," 4, David Risling Papers, Box 63, UC Davis, Special Collections; "A Short History of D-QU," 1, David Risling Papers, Box 63, UC Davis, Special Collections.

156. Janssen, "DQU," 119, 123.

157. Janssen, "DQU," 123; Peyer, "D-Q University," 5.

158. Peyer, "D-Q University," 4–5.

159. Jack Forbes, "Education, Culture, and Academic Freedom: The Reagan Administration's Attack on an American Indian-Chicano College," Special Collections, UC Davis; Mike Castro, "'Indians to Consider Impeaching Reagan,' *The Sacramento Bee*," April 23, 1982, David Risling Papers, Box 63, UC Davis, Special Collections.

160. For broad discussions of the conservative turn and the decline of radical internationalist campus activism among Blacks and Chicanos, see the latter chapters of Biondi, *Black Revolution on Campus*; Rogers, *Black Campus Movement*; Mariscal, *Brown-Eyed Children of the Sun*; and Muñoz, *Youth, Identity, Power*.

Conclusion

1. Schrag, *Paradise Lost*.

2. Pusser, *Burning Down the House*, 33; Robert J. Birgeneau, "Op-Ed: To Fix California's Colleges, Reform Prop. 13 by Taxing Corporations More," *Los Angeles Times*, November 2, 2015.

3. Dreyfuss and Lawrence, *The Bakke Case*, 65.

4. According to Howard Ball, "In 1970, there were only about eight hundred minority students attending medical school in America. Almost 80 percent of that number were attending the two predominantly African-American medical schools," Howard University and Meharry Medical School. See Ball, *The Bakke Case*, 48, 49.

5. As of late 1972, African Americans were slightly overrepresented at community colleges but underrepresented at the UC and state colleges. Mexican Americans and Native Americans remained underrepresented at all three levels, whereas

whites and Asian Americans were overrepresented at all three. *Report of the Joint Committee on the Master Plan for Higher Education*, 37, 38, 41, 47.

6. Douglass, *Conditions for Admissions*, 129, 131, 134, 135.

7. Pusser, *Burning Down the House*, 29.

8. Schrag, *Paradise Lost*.

9. Pusser, *Burning Down the House*, 34.

10. Amy Wallace and Dave Lesher, "UC Regents, in Historic Vote, Wipe Out Affirmative Action Diversity," *Los Angeles Times*, July 21, 1995.

11. HoSang, *Racial Propositions*, 228; Bill Stall and Dan Morain, "Prop. 209 Wins, Bars Affirmative Action," *Los Angeles Times*, November 6, 1996.

12. "Proposition 209: Text of Proposed Law."

13. HoSang, *Racial Propositions*, 231.

14. Hartman, *War for the Soul of America*.

15. Gilmore, *Golden Gulag*, 4.

16. Between 1982 and 2000, the state's prison population quintupled. As of 2007, fully two-thirds of California's state prisoners were Black or Latino. Gilmore, *Golden Gulag*, 7.

17. Maiya Moncino has argued that the UC has charged tuition—defined as student contributions toward the cost of instruction—since 1970. See Moncino, "Tuition Is Not a Dirty Word."

18. Uebersax, "Inflation-Adjusted Tuition"; Uebersax is the force behind the organization Californians for Higher Education Reform, which calls for the "reinstatement of a California Master Plan for Higher Education." See *Californians for Higher Education Reform*.

19. Newfield, *Unmaking the Public University*, 81–82, 184.

20. Uebersax, "Inflation-Adjusted Tuition."

21. Teresa Watanabe and Rosanna Xia, "UC and Cal State Will Consider the First Tuition Hikes in Six Years," *Los Angeles Times*, November 14, 2016.

22. Bady and Konczal, "From Master Plan to No Plan."

23. For important new scholarship that provides long historical context for rising tuition costs nationwide, see Shermer, *Indentured Students*; and Shermer et al., "Up for Debate."

Bibliography

Archives

Bancroft Library, University of California, Berkeley
   Bollinger Bruce Collection of Max Rafferty materials
   Clark Kerr Personal and Professional Papers
   Free Speech Movement Oral History Project
   Free Speech Movement Records
   Governor Reagan and His Cabinet
   Knight-Brown Era Oral History Project
   Latino Leadership Series
   Merritt College Black Student Union Collection
   Reagan Gubernatorial Era Project
California State Archives
   Department of Education Records
California State University Archives, CSU Dominguez Hills
   Oral History Project on the Origins of the CSU System
Ethnic Studies Library, University of California, Berkeley
   Carlos Muñoz Papers
Hoover Institution Library & Archives
   Ronald Reagan Subject Collection
J. Paul Leonard Library, San Francisco State University
   San Francisco State College Strike Collection
   University Archives
Rare Book & Manuscript Library, Columbia University
   Student Movement of the 1960s Project
Ronald Reagan Presidential Library and Museum
   Gubernatorial Speeches, 1967–71
Special Collections, Stanford University
   Anne Draper Papers
Special Collections, University of California, Davis
   American New Left Pamphlet Collection
   David Risling Papers
   Hal Draper Papers
   Jack D. Forbes Collection
   Walter Goldwater Radical Pamphlet Collection
University Library, University of California, Los Angeles
   Oral History Program

Newspapers and Newsletters

Brónze (San Jose, CA)
California Aggie (Davis, CA)
Chicano Student Movement (Los Angeles, CA)
Chicano Student News (Los Angeles, CA)
Daily Bruin (Los Angeles, CA)
Daily Collegian (Fresno, CA)
Daily Gater (San Francisco, CA)
Daily Sundial (Northridge, CA)
El Alacran (Long Beach, CA)
El Gaucho (Santa Barbara, CA)
Gidra (Los Angeles, CA)
Harvard Crimson (Cambridge, MA)
La Hormiga (Oakland, CA)
La Palabra de MASC (Oakland, CA)
La Prensa San Diego (San Diego, CA)
La Raza (Los Angeles, CA)
Los Angeles Times (Los Angeles, CA)
New York Times (New York, NY)
Oakland Tribune (Oakland, CA)
Open Process (San Francisco, CA)
Phoenix (San Francisco, CA)
Pony Express (Sacramento, CA)
Que Tal (San Jose, CA)
Sacramento Bee (Sacramento, CA)
Sacramento Observer (Sacramento, CA)
San Diego Union Tribune (San Diego, CA)
San Francisco Bay Guardian (San Francisco, CA)
San Francisco Chronicle (San Francisco, CA)
San Francisco Examiner (San Francisco, CA)
S.F. Sunday Examiner and Chronicle (San Francisco, CA)
Spartan Daily (San Jose, CA)
Summer Sundial (Northridge, CA)
Sun Reporter (San Francisco, CA)
The Sun (Baltimore, MD)
Third World (San Diego, CA)
Triton Times (San Diego, CA)
Wall Street Journal (New York, NY)
Washington Post (Washington, DC)

Miscellaneous

Buckley, William F. "Our Mission Statement." *National Review,* November 19, 1955.
Chicano Coordinating Council on Higher Education. *El Plan de Santa Barbara: A Chicano Plan for Higher Education.* Oakland, CA: La Causa Publications, 1969.

Douglass, John Aubrey. Email to the author. November 11, 2021.

Draper, Hal, ed. *The FSM Papers* (microfilm).

Ferreira, Jason. Email to the author. November 10, 2021.

Geier, Joel. Email to the author. April 9, 2021.

Journal of Higher Education 29 (1958).

Journal of Higher Education 30 (1959).

Journal of Higher Education 32 (1961).

Kang, Jay Caspian. "What the World Got Wrong about Kareem Abdul-Jabbar." *New York Times Magazine*, September 17, 2015.

Kitano, Harry, and Dorothy Miller. *An Assessment of Educational Opportunity Programs in California Higher Education*. Sacramento, CA: Prepared for the Joint Committee on Higher Education and the California Coordinating Council for Higher Education, February 1970.

Liaison Committee. *A Report of a Survey of the Needs of California Higher Education*. Sacramento CA: Committee on the Conduct of the Study, March 1, 1948.

———. *A Restudy of the Needs of California in Higher Education*. Sacramento, CA: Joint Staff of the Liaison Committee, February 7, 1955.

Lombardi, John. "The Position Papers of Black Student Activists." Los Angeles: Graduate School of Education and the University Library, UCLA, 1970.

Lopez, Ronald W., and Darryl D. Enos. "Chicanos and Public Higher Education in California: Prepared for Joint Committee on the Master Plan for Higher Education." Sacramento: California State Legislature, 1972.

Martyn, Kenneth. *California Higher Education and the Disadvantaged: A Status Report*. Sacramento: California Coordinating Council for Higher Education, March 1968.

Nevin, David. "Uneasy Peace at Valley State." *Life*, March 14, 1969.

Orrick, William H., Jr. *Shut It Down! A College in Crisis: San Francisco State College, October, 1968–April 1969: A Staff Report to the National Commission on the Causes and Prevention of Violence*. Washington, DC: Government Printing Office, June 1969.

Report of the Joint Committee on the Master Plan for Higher Education. Sacramento: California Legislature, September 1973.

Savio, Mario. "The Uncertain Future of the Multiversity." *Harper's*, October 1, 1966.

———. "The University Has Become a Factory." *Life*, February 26, 1965.

"Search for Professors." *Time*, March 21, 1960.

Strike at Frisco State!: The Story behind It. San Francisco: Research Organizing Cooperative, 1969.

The Challenge of Achievement: A Report on Public and Private Higher Education in California. Sacramento: Joint Committee on Higher Education of the California Legislature, 1969.

The Master Plan Survey Team. *A Master Plan for Higher Education in California, 1960–1975*. Sacramento: California State Department of Education, 1960.

"The Olympic Jolt: 'Hell No, Don't Go!'" *Life*, March 15, 1968.

UCLA General Catalog: 1967–1968 issue. Los Angeles: University of California, 1967.

U.S. Bureau of Education, "Search '68: Educational Talent Search Program, 1968–69." Washington, DC: U.S. Government Printing Office, 1968.

Weinberg, Jack. Discussion with the author. July 28, 2021.

———. Email to the author. September 2, 2021.

Books, Chapters, and Journal Articles

Abdul-Jabbar, Kareem, and Peter Knobler. *Giant Steps: The Autobiography of Kareem Abdul Jabbar.* New York: Bantam, 1983.

Acuña, Rodolfo F. *The Making of Chicana/o Studies: In the Trenches of Academe.* New Brunswick, NJ: Rutgers University Press, 2011.

Alvarez, Luis, and Daniel Widener. "A History of Black and Brown: Chicana/o–African American Cultural and Political Relations." *Aztlán: A Journal of Chicano Studies* 33, no. 1 (Spring 2008): 143–54.

Alvarez, Robert R., Jr. "The Lemon Grove Incident: The Nation's First Successful Desegregation Case." *San Diego Historical Society Quarterly* 32, no. 2 (Spring 1986).

Anthony, Earl. *The Time of the Furnaces: A Case Study of Black Student Revolt.* New York: Dial Press, 1971.

Aptheker, Bettina A. *Intimate Politics: How I Grew Up Red, Fought for Free Speech, and Became a Feminist Rebel.* Emeryville, CA: Seal Press, 2006.

Aronowitz, Stanley. *The Death and Rebirth of American Radicalism.* New York: Routledge, 1996.

Bachrach, Susan D. *The Nazi Olympics: Berlin 1936.* Boston: Little, Brown, 2000.

Ball, Howard. *The Bakke Case: Race, Education, and Affirmative Action.* Lawrence: University Press of Kansas, 2000.

Balogh, Brian. *Integrating the Sixties: The Origins, Structures, and Legitimacy of Public Policy in a Turbulent Decade.* University Park: Pennsylvania State University Press, 1996.

Barber, David A. *A Hard Rain Fell: SDS and Why It Failed.* Jackson: University Press of Mississippi, 2008.

Bardacke, Frank. *Trampling Out the Vintage: Cesar Chavez and the Two Souls of the United Farm Workers.* New York, NY: Verso, 2012.

Barlow, William, and Peter Shapiro. *An End to Silence: The San Francisco State College Student Movement in the '60s.* New York: Pegasus, 1971.

———. "The Struggle for San Francisco State." In *Black Power and Student Rebellion*, edited by James McEvoy and Abraham H. Miller, 277–97. Belmont, CA: Wadsworth, 1969.

Behnken, Brian D., ed. *The Struggle in Black and Brown: African American and Mexican American Relations during the Civil Rights Era.* Omaha: University of Nebraska Press, 2012.

Berrett, Dan. "The Day the Purpose of College Changed." *Chronicle of Higher Education*, January 30, 2015.

Biondi, Martha. *The Black Revolution on Campus*. Berkeley: University of California Press, 2012.

Blauner, Bob. *Resisting McCarthyism: To Sign or Not to Sign California's Loyalty Oath*. Stanford, CA: Stanford University Press, 2009.

Bloom, Joshua, and Waldo E. Martin Jr. *Black against Empire: The History and Politics of the Black Panther Party*. Berkeley: University of California Press, 2013.

Booker, Chris. "Lumpenization: A Critical Error of the Black Panther Party." In *The Black Panther Party Reconsidered*. Baltimore, MD: Black Classic Press, 1998.

Borstelmann, Thomas. *The Cold War and the Color Line: American Race Relations in the Global Arena*. Cambridge, MA: Harvard University Press, 2001.

Breneman, David B., and Paul E. Lingenfelter. "The California Master Plan: Influential beyond State Borders?" In *Clark Kerr's World of Higher Education Reaches the 21st Century*, edited by Sheldon Rothblatt, 85–106. New York: Springer, 2012.

Brilliant, Mark. *The Color of America Has Changed: How Racial Diversity Shaped Civil Rights Reform in California, 1941–1978*. New York: Oxford University Press, 2010.

Brown, Scot. *Fighting for US: Maulana Karenga, the US Organization, and Black Cultural Nationalism*. New York: New York University Press, 2003.

Callincos, Alex. *Trotskyism*. Buckingham, UK: Open University Press, 1990.

Cannon, Lou. *Governor Reagan: His Rise to Power*. New York: Public Affairs, 2003.

———. *Reagan*. New York: Putnam, 1982.

———. *Ronnie and Jesse: A Political Odyssey*. New York: Doubleday, 1969.

Carlos, John, with Dave Zirin. *The John Carlos Story: The Sports Moment That Changed the World*. Chicago: Haymarket, 2013.

Carson, Clayborne. *In Struggle: SNCC and the Black Awakening of the 1960s*. Cambridge, MA: Harvard University Press, 2001.

Césaire, Aimé. *Discourse on Colonialism*. Translated by Joan Pinkham. New York: Monthly Review Press, 1972.

Chacón, Justin Akers. *Radicals in the Barrio: Magonistas, Socialists, Wobblies, and Communists in the Mexican American Working Class*. Chicago: Haymarket, 2018.

Chavez, Ernesto. *"Mi Raza Primero!" Nationalism, Identity, and Insurgency in the Chicano Movement in Los Angeles, 1966–1978*. Berkeley: University of California Press, 2002.

Churchill, Ward, and Jim Vander Wall. *Agents of Repression: The FBI's Secret Wars against the Black Panther Party and the American Indian Movement*. Cambridge, MA: South End Press, 2002.

Clark, Burton R. "The 'Cooling-Out' Function in Higher Education." *American Journal of Sociology* 65, no. 6 (May 1960): 569–76.

Cleaveland, Brad. "A Letter to Undergraduates." In *The Berkeley Student Revolt: Facts and Interpretations*, edited by Seymour Martin Lipset and Sheldon S. Wolin, 66–80. Garden City, NY: Anchor, 1965.

——. "Education, Revolutions, and Citadels." In *The Berkeley Student Revolt: Facts and Interpretations,* edited by Seymour Martin Lipset and Sheldon S. Wolin, 81–93. Garden City, NY: Anchor, 1965.

Cloud, Roy W. *Education in California: Leaders, Organizations, and Accomplishments of the First Hundred Years.* Stanford, CA: Stanford University Press, 1952.

Clowse, Barbara Barksdale. *Brainpower for the Cold War: The Sputnik Crisis and National Defense Education Act of 1958.* Westport, CT: Greenwood, 1981.

Cohen, Robert. *Freedom's Orator: Mario Savio and the Radical Legacy of the 1960s.* New York: Oxford University Press, 2009.

Cohen, Robert, and Reginald Zelnik, eds. *The Free Speech Movement: Reflections on Berkeley in the 1960s.* Berkeley: University of California Press, 2002.

Coons, Arthur G. *Crisis in California Higher Education: Experience under the Master Plan and Problems of Coordination.* Los Angeles: Ward Ritchie, 1968.

Cooper, Melinda. *Family Values: Between Neoliberalism and the New Social Conservatism.* New York, NY: Zone Books, 2017.

Dallek, Matthew. *The Right Moment: Ronald Reagan's First Victory and the Decisive Turning Point in American Politics.* New York: Free Press, 2000.

Davis, Angela. *An Autobiography.* New York: Random House, 1974.

Davis, Mike. *City of Quartz: Excavating the Future in Los Angeles.* New York: Verso, 2006.

Davis, Mike, and Jon Wiener. *Set the Night on Fire: LA in the Sixties.* New York: Verso, 2020.

De Groot, Gerard J. "Ronald Reagan and Student Unrest in California, 1966–1970." *Pacific Historical Review* 65, no. 1 (February 1996): 107–29.

De La Torre, Joely. "From Activism to Academics: The Evolution of American Indian Studies at San Francisco State, 1968–2001." *Indigenous Nations Studies Journal* 2, no. 1 (Spring 2001): 11–20.

Delgado, Richard, and Jean Stefancic. "California's Racial History and Constitutional Rationales for Race-Conscious Decision Making in Higher Education." *UCLA Law Review* 47 (2000): 1521–1614.

Divine, Robert A. *The Sputnik Challenge.* Oxford: Oxford University Press, 1993.

Dochuk, Darren. *From Bible Belt to Sunbelt: Plain-Folk Religion, Grassroots Politics, and the Rise of Evangelical Conservatism.* New York: Norton, 2011.

Douglass, John Aubrey. *The California Idea and American Higher Education: 1850 to the 1960 Master Plan.* Stanford, CA: Stanford University Press. 2000.

——. *The Conditions for Admission: Access, Equity, and the Social Contract of Public Universities.* Stanford, CA: Stanford University Press, 2007.

Draper, Hal. *Berkeley: The New Student Revolt.* Alameda, CA: Center for Socialist History, 1965.

——. *The Mind of Clark Kerr.* Berkeley, CA: The Independent Socialist Club, 1964.

Dreyfuss, Joel, and Charles Lawrence. *The Bakke Case: The Politics of Inequality.* New York: Harcourt Brace Jovanovich, 1970.

Dudziak, Mary. *Cold War Civil Rights: Race and the Image of American Democracy.* Princeton, NJ: Princeton University Press, 2000.

Dunbar-Ortiz, Roxanne. *An Indigenous Peoples' History of the United States.* Boston: Beacon, 2014.

Edwards, Harry. *Black Students.* New York: Free Press, 1970.

———. *The Revolt of the Black Athlete.* New York: Free Press, 1969.

———. *The Struggle That Must Be: An Autobiography.* New York: Macmillan, 1980.

El Shabazz, Rasheed. "'Mau Mau Tech': The Making of a Black University in Oakland, California, 1960–1970." *The Berkeley McNair Research Journal* (2010): 83–99.

Elbaum, Max. *Revolution in the Air: Sixties Radicals Turn to Lenin, Mao and Che.* New York: Verso, 2002.

Espiritu, Yen Le. *Asian American Panethnicity: Bridging Institutions and Identities.* Philadelphia: Temple University Press, 1993.

Felber, Garrett. "Integration or Separation? Malcolm X's College Debates, Free Speech, and the Challenge to Racial Liberalism on Campus." *Journal of Social History* 53, no. 4 (2020): 1033–59.

Fernández, Johanna. *The Young Lords: A Radical History.* Chapel Hill: The University of North Carolina Press, 2020.

Ferreira, Jason. "From College Readiness to Ready for Revolution!: Third World College Activism at a Northern California Community College, 1965–1969." *Kalfou* 1, no. 1 (Spring 2014): 117–44.

———. "'With the Soul of a Human Rainbow': Los Siete, Black Panthers, and Third Worldism in San Francisco." In *Ten Years That Shook the City: San Francisco: 1968–1978,* edited by Chris Carlsson, 30–47. San Francisco: City Lights Foundation Books, 2011.

Fones-Wolf, Elizabeth. *Selling Free Enterprise: The Business Assault of Labor and Liberalism.* Champaign: University of Illinois Press, 1994.

Forbes, Jack. *Maintaining Inequality in a Multiethnic Society: Limiting Access to the University of California, 1952–1985.* Davis, CA: Unpublished, 1996.

Freeman, Jo. *At Berkeley in the '60s: The Education of an Activist, 1961–1965.* Bloomington: Indiana University Press, 2004.

———. "From Freedom Now! to Free Speech: The FSM's Roots in the Bay Area Civil Rights Movement." In *The Free Speech Movement: Reflections on Berkeley in the 1960s,* edited by Robert Cohen and Reginald Zelnik, 73–82. Berkeley: University of California Press, 2002.

Fujino, Diane C. *Samurai among Panthers: Richard Aoki on Race, Resistance, and a Paradoxical Life.* Minneapolis: University of Minnesota Press, 2012.

García, David G. *Strategies of Segregation: Race, Residence, and the Struggle for Educational Equality.* Berkeley: University of California Press, 2018.

García, Mario T., and Sal Castro. *Blowout!: Sal Castro and the Chicano Struggle for Educational Justice.* Chapel Hill: The University of North Carolina Press, 2011.

Gennaro, Stephen, and Douglas Kellner. "Under Surveillance: Herbert Marcuse and the FBI." In *Nature, Knowledge and Negation,* edited by Harry Dahms, 283–314. Bingley, UK: Emerald Group, 2009.

Gerth, Donald R., and James O. Haehn, eds. *An Invisible Giant: The California State Colleges.* San Francisco: Jossey-Bass. 1971.

Gilmore, Ruth Wilson. *Golden Gulag: Prisons, Surplus, Crisis, and Opposition in Globalizing California.* Berkeley: University of California Press, 2007.

Giroux, Henry A. *Theory and Resistance in Education: A Pedagogy for the Opposition.* South Hadley, MA: Bergin & Garvey, 1983.

Godfrey, Brian J. *Neighborhoods in Transition: The Making of San Francisco's Ethnic and Nonconformist Communities.* Berkeley: University of California Press, 1988.

Goines, David Lance. *The Free Speech Movement: Coming of Age in the 1960s.* Berkeley: Ten Speed Press, 1993.

Gómez, Alan Eladio. *The Revolutionary Imaginations of Greater Mexico: Chicana/o Radicalism, Solidarity Politics, and Latin American Social Movements.* Austin: University of Texas Press, 2016.

Gómez-Quiñones, Juan. *Mexican Students por la Raza: The Chicano Student Movement in Southern California 1967–1977.* Santa Barbara, CA: Editorial La Causa, ca. 1978.

Gómez-Quiñones, Juan, and Irene Vásquez. *Making Aztlán: Ideology and Culture of the Chicana and Chicano Movement, 1966–1977.* Albuquerque: University of New Mexico Press, 2014.

Gonzalez, Gilbert G. *Chicano Education in the Era of Segregation.* Denton: University of North Texas Press, 1990.

Gosse, Van. "A Movement of Movements: The Definition and Periodization of the New Left." In *A Companion to Post-1945 America,* edited by Jean-Christophe Agnew and Roy Rosenzweig, 277–302. Malden, MA: Blackwell, 2002.

Gutiérrez, Ramón A. "Internal Colonialism: An American Theory of Race." *Du Bois Review* 1, no. 2 (2004): 281–95.

Hall, Peter. *Great Planning Disasters.* Berkeley: University of California Press, 1980.

Hall, Simon. *Rethinking the American Anti-war Movement.* New York: Routledge, 2011.

Harrison, Gilbert A. *Parts of a Past.* Bloomington, IN: iUniverse, 2009.

Hartman, Andrew. *A War for the Soul of America: A History of the Culture Wars.* Chicago: University of Chicago Press, 2015.

———. *Education and the Cold War: The Battle for the American School.* New York: Palgrave Macmillan, 2008.

Heirich, Max. *The Spiral of Conflict: Berkeley 1964.* New York: Columbia University Press, 1971.

Hidalgo, Jacqueline M. *Revelation in Aztlan: Scriptures, Utopias, and the Chicano Movement.* New York: Palgrave Macmillan, 2016.

Hofstadter, Richard. *Anti-intellectualism in American Life.* New York: Vintage, 1966.

Holmes, Todd. "The Economic Roots of Reaganism: Corporate Conservatives, Political Economy, and the United Farm Workers Movement, 1965–1970." *Western Historical Quarterly* 41 (Spring 2010): 55–80.

Horowitz, David. *Student.* New York: Ballantine, 1962.

HoSang, Daniel Martinez. *Racial Propositions: Ballot Initiatives and the Making of Postwar California.* Berkeley: University of California Press, 2010.

HoSang, Daniel Martinez, and Natalia Molina. "Introduction: Toward a Relational Consciousness of Race." In *Relational Formations of Race: Theory, Method, and Practice*, edited by Natalia Molina, Daniel Martinez HoSang, and Ramón A. Gutiérrez, 1–18. Oakland: University of California Press, 2019.

Ishizuka, Karen L. *Serve the People: Making Asian America in the Long Sixties.* New York: Verso, 2016.

Jacobsen, Annie. *Operation Paperclip: The Secret Intelligence Program That Brought Nazi Scientists to America.* New York: Little, Brown and Company, 2014.

Janssen, Peter A. "DQU." In *New Colleges for New Students,* edited by Laurence Hall, 119–26. San Francisco: Jossey-Bass, 1974.

Jeffries, Stuart. *Grand Hotel Abyss: The Lives of the Frankfurt School.* New York: Verso, 2016.

Johnson, Alan. "Introduction; Hal Draper: A Biographical Sketch." *Historical Materialism* 4, no. 1 (1999): 181–86.

Karagueuzian, Dikran. *Blow It Up!: The Black Student Revolt at San Francisco State College and the Emergence of Dr. Hayakawa.* Boston: Gambit, 1971.

Katznelson, Ira. *Fear Itself: The New Deal and the Origins of Our Time.* New York: Norton, 2013.

———. *When Affirmative Action Was White: An Untold History of Racial Inequality in Twentieth Century America.* New York: Norton, 2006.

Kerr, Clark. *The Gold and the Blue: A Personal Memoir of the University of California, 1949–1967. Volume One: Academic Triumphs.* Berkeley: University of California Press, 2001.

———. *The Gold and the Blue: A Personal Memoir of the University of California, 1949–1967; Volume Two: Political Turmoil.* Berkeley: University of California Press, 2003.

———. *The Uses of the University: The Godkin Lectures at Harvard University, 1963.* Cambridge, MA: Harvard University Press, 1972.

Kerr, Clark, John T. Dunlop, Frederick H. Harbison, and Charles A. Myers. *Industrialism and Industrial Man: The Problems of Labor and Management in Economic Growth.* Cambridge, MA: Harvard University Press, 1960.

Killian, James R., Jr., *Sputnik, Scientists, and Eisenhower: A Memoir of the First Special Assistant to the President for Science and Technology.* Cambridge, MA: MIT Press, 1977.

Kleinknecht, William. *The Man Who Sold the World: Ronald Reagan and the Betrayal of Main Street America.* New York: Nation Books, 2009.

Knott, Stephen F., and Jeffrey L. Chidester. *At Reagan's Side: Insiders' Recollections from Sacramento to the White House.* Lanham, MD: Rowman & Littlefield, 2009.

Kruse, Kevin. *White Flight: Atlanta and the Making of Modern Conservatism.* Princeton, NJ: Princeton University Press, 2007.

Kun, Josh, and Laura Pulido, eds. *Black and Brown in Los Angeles: Beyond Conflict and Coalition.* Berkeley: University of California Press, 2013.

La Nouse, George R., and Mark Bennett. "The Impact of Desegregation on College Choices of Elite Black Athletes." *International Journal of Higher Education* 3, no. 3 (August 2014): 142–53.

Large, David Clay. *Nazi Games: The Olympics of 1936*. New York: Norton, 2007.

Larson, Magali Sarfatti. "Master Plan, Master Failure." In *Academics on the Line*, edited by Arlene Kaplan Daniels and Rachel Kahn-Hut, 62–77. San Francisco: Jossey-Bass, 1970.

Leahy, Margaret. "On Strike! We're Gonna Shut It Down: The 1968–69 San Francisco State Strike." In *Ten Years That Shook the City: San Francisco: 1968–1978*, edited by Chris Carlsson, 15–29. San Francisco: City Lights Foundation Books, 2011.

Lemann, Nicholas. *The Big Test: The Secret History of the American Meritocracy*. New York: Farrar, Straus & Giroux, 1999.

Leon, David Jess. "Racism in the University: The Case of the Educational Opportunity Program." *Humboldt Journal of Social Relations* 8, no. 1 (Fall/Winter 1980/1981): 83–101.

Leslie, Stuart W. *The Cold War and American Science: The Military-Industrial-Academic Complex at MIT and Stanford*. New York: Columbia University Press, 1993.

Levin, John, and Earl Silbar, eds. *You Say You Want a Revolution: SDS, PL, and Adventures in Building a Worker-Student Alliance*. San Francisco: 1741 Press, 2019.

Levin, Matthew. *Cold War University: Madison and the New Left in the Sixties*. Madison: University of Wisconsin Press, 2013.

Lewis, Joseph. *What Makes Reagan Run? A Political Profile*. New York: McGraw-Hill, 1968.

Litwak, Leo, and Herbert Wilner. *College Days in Earthquake Country: Ordeal at San Francisco State, a Personal Record*. New York: Random House, 1971.

Lomax, Michael. "Revisiting *The Revolt of the Black Athlete*: Harry Edwards and the Making of the New African-American Sport Studies." *Journal of Sports History* 29, no. 3 (Fall 2002): 469–79.

Louie, Steve, and Glenn Omatsu, eds. *Asian Americans: The Movement and the Moment*. Los Angeles: UCLA Asian American Studies Center Press, 2001.

Lowen, Rebecca S. *Creating the Cold War University: The Transformation of Stanford*. Berkeley: University of California Press, 1997.

Lowndes, Joseph. *From the New Deal to the New Right: Race and the Southern Origins of Modern Conservatism*. New Haven, CT: Yale University Press, 2009.

Maeda, Daryl. *Chains of Babylon: The Rise of Asian America*. Minneapolis: University of Minnesota Press, 2009.

———. *Rethinking the Asian American Movement*. New York: Routledge, 2012.

Mantler, Gordon K. *Power to the Poor: Black-Brown Coalition and the Fight for Economic Justice, 1960–1974*. Chapel Hill: The University of North Carolina Press, 2013.

Mariscal, George. *Brown-Eyed Children of the Sun: Lessons from the Chicano Movement, 1965–1975*. Albuquerque: University of New Mexico Press, 2005.

Martin, Charles H. "Jim Crow in the Gymnasium: The Integration of College Basketball in the American South." *International Journal of the History of Sport* 10, no. 1 (April 1993): 68–86.

Martin, Waldo. "Holding One Another: Mario Savio and the Freedom Struggle in Mississippi and Berkeley." In *The Free Speech Movement: Reflections on Berkeley in the 1960s,* edited by Robert Cohen and Reginald Zelnik, 83–102. Berkeley: University of California Press, 2002.

Martinez, Elizabeth. *De Colores Means All of US: Latina Views for a Multi-colored Century.* Boston: South End Press, 1998.

——. "Histories of 'the Sixties': A Certain Absence of Color." *Social Justice* 16, no. 4 (Winter 1989): 175–85.

Marx, Karl. *The Eighteenth Brumaire of Louis Bonaparte.* Rockville, MD: Serenity, 2009.

McGill, William J. *The Year of the Monkey: Revolt on Campus, 1968–1969.* New York: McGraw-Hill, 1982.

McGirr, Lisa. *Suburban Warriors: The Origins of the New American Right.* Princeton, NJ: Princeton University Press, 2001.

McWilliams, Carey. *Factories in the Field: The Story of Migratory Farm Labor in California.* Berkeley: University of California Press, 1999.

Miezckowski, Yanek. *Eisenhower's Sputnik Moment: The Race for Space and World Prestige.* Ithaca, NY: Cornell University Press, 2013.

Miller, James. *Democracy Is in the Streets: From Port Huron to the Siege of Chicago.* Cambridge, MA: Harvard University Press, 1994.

Miller, Karen K. "Race, Power and the Emergence of Black Studies in Higher Education." *American Studies* 31, no. 2 (1990): 83–98.

Miller, Michael V., and Susan Gilmore. *Revolution at Berkeley.* New York: Dial, 1965.

Molina, Natalia, Daniel Martinez HoSang, and Ramón A. Gutiérrez. "Further Reading." In *Relational Formations of Race: Theory, Method, and Practice,* edited by Natalia Molina, Daniel Martinez HoSang, and Ramón A. Gutiérrez, 325–35. Oakland: University of California Press, 2019.

Moncino, Maiya. "'Tuition Is Not a Dirty Word': Ronald Reagan, the University of California, and the Dismantling of the Tuition-Free Principle." *Clio's Scroll* 17, no. 1 (Fall 2015): 57–98.

Moreau, Joseph. *Schoolbook Nation: Conflicts over American History Textbooks from the Civil War to the Present.* Ann Arbor: University of Michigan Press, 2003.

Muñoz, Carlos. *Youth, Identity, Power: The Chicano Movement.* New York: Verso, 2007.

Murch, Donna Jean. *Living for the City: Migration, Education, and the Rise of the Black Panther Party in Oakland, California.* Chapel Hill: The University of North Carolina Press, 2010.

Neusner, Jacob, and Noam M. M. Neusner. *The Price of Excellence: Universities in Conflict during the Cold War Era.* New York: Continuum, 1995.

Newfield, Christopher. *Ivy and Industry: Business and the Making of the American University, 1880–1980.* Durham, NC: Duke University Press, 2003.

——. *Unmaking the Public University: The Forty-Year Assault on the Middle Class.* Cambridge, MA: Harvard University Press, 2008.

Newman, Rachel Grace. "Schools for All: The Desegregation Campaign in El Monte." In *East of East: The Making of Greater El Monte*, edited by Romeo Guzmán, Carribean Fragoza, Alex Sayf Cummings, and Ryan Reft, 81–88. New Brunswick, NJ: Rutgers University Press, 2020.

Ogbar, Jeffrey O. G. *Black Power: Radical Politics and American Identity*. Baltimore: Johns Hopkins University Press, 2004.

Olson, James S. *The Ethnic Dimension in American History*. New York: St. Martin's, 1994.

O'Neill, William. *Readin, Ritin, and Rafferty!: A Study of Educational Fundamentalism*. Berkeley, CA: Glendessary, 1969.

Oropeza, Lorena. *Raza Si! Guerra No!: Chicano Protest and Patriotism during the Viet Nam War Era*. Berkeley: University of California Press, 2005.

Parker, Mike. "Mario Savio, 1942–1996." *Against the Current*, January–February 1997, 49–50.

Payne, Bruce, David Walls, and Jerry Berman. "Theodicy of 1984: The Philosophy of Clark Kerr." In *The New Student Left: An Anthology*, edited by Mitchell Cohen and Dennis Hale, 226–36. Boston: Beacon, 1966.

Petrzela, Natalia Mehlman. "Revisiting the Rightward Turn: Max Rafferty, Education, and Modern American Politics." *The Sixties* 6, no. 2 (2013): 143–71.

Phillips-Fein, Kim. *Invisible Hands: The Businessmen's Crusade against the New Deal*. New York: Norton, 2009.

Pitti, Stephen J. *The Devil in Silicon Valley: Northern California, Race, and Mexican Americans*. Princeton, NJ: Princeton University Press, 2003.

Potter, Bob, and James Sullivan. *The Campus by the Sea Where the Bank Burned Down: A Report on the Disturbances at UCSB and Isla Vista 1968–70*. Santa Barbara, CA: Faculty and Clergy Observer's Program, 1970.

Pulido, Laura. *Black, Brown, Yellow, and Left: Radical Activism in Los Angeles*. Berkeley: University of California Press, 2006.

Pusser, Brian. *Burning Down the House: Politics, Governance, and Affirmative Action at the University of California*. Albany: State University of New York Press, 2004.

Rarick, Ethan. *California Rising: The Life and Times of Pat Brown*. Berkeley: University of California Press, 2006.

Robin, Corey. *The Reactionary Mind: Conservatism from Edmund Burke to Sarah Palin*. New York: Oxford University Press, 2011.

Robinson, Cedric. *Black Marxism: The Making of the Black Radical Tradition*. Chapel Hill: The University of North Carolina Press, 2000.

Rodriguez, Marc Simon. *Rethinking the Chicano Movement*. New York: Routledge, 2015.

Rogers, Ibram H. "Remembering the Black Campus Movement: An Oral History Interview with James P. Garrett." *Journal of Pan African Studies* 2, no. 10 (June 2009): 30–41.

——. *The Black Campus Movement: Black Students and the Racial Reconstitution of Higher Education, 1965–1972*. New York: Palgrave Macmillan, 2012.

Rogin, Michael Paul, and John L. Shover. *Political Change in California: Critical Elections and Social Movements, 1890–1966.* Westport, CT: Greenwood, 1970.

Rorabaugh, W. J. *Berkeley at War: The 1960s.* New York: Oxford University Press, 1989.

Rosales, F. Arturo. *Chicano!: A History of the Mexican American Civil Rights Movement.* Houston, TX: Arte Publico, 1997.

Rosenfeld, Seth. *Subversives: The FBI's War on Student Radicals, and Reagan's Rise to Power.* New York: Farrar, Straus & Giroux, 2012.

Roussopoulos, Dimitri. "Canada: 1968 and the New Left." In *1968: Memories and Legacies of a Global Revolt,* edited by Philipp Gassert and Martin Klimke, 39–45. Washington, DC: German Historical Institute.

Ryan, Alan. *John Dewey: And the High Tide of American Liberalism.* New York: Norton, 1997.

Sale, Kirkpatrick. *SDS.* New York: Vintage, 1973.

Sangster, Joan. "Radical Ruptures: Feminism, Labor, and the Left in the Long Sixties in Canada." *American Review of Canadian Studies* 40, no. 1 (March 2010): 1–21.

Savio, Mario. Introduction to *Berkeley: The New Student Revolt,* by Hal Draper, 1–7. Alameda, CA: Center for Socialist History, 1965.

———. "The Berkeley Knowledge Factory." In *The Essential Mario Savio: Speeches and Writings That Changed America,* edited by Robert Cohen, 213–23. Berkeley: University of California Press, 2014.

Scheuring, Ann F. *Abundant Harvest: The History of the University of California, Davis.* Davis: UC Davis History Project, 2001.

Schiffrin, Andre, ed. *The Cold War and the University: Toward an Intellectual History of the Postwar Years.* New York: New Press, 1997.

Schrag, Peter. *Paradise Lost: California's Experiment, America's Future.* New York: New Press, 1998.

Schrecker, Ellen. *Many Are the Crimes: McCarthyism in America.* Princeton, NJ: Princeton University Press, 1998.

———*The Lost Promise: American Universities in the 1960s.* Chicago: University of Chicago Press, 2021.

Schuparra, Kurt. *Triumph of the Right: The Rise of the California Conservative Movement, 1945–1966.* Armonk, NY: M. E. Sharpe, 1998.

Seib, Kenneth A. *The Slow Death of Fresno State: A California Campus under Reagan and Brown.* Palo Alto, CA: Ramparts, 1979.

Self, Robert O. *American Babylon: Race and the Struggle for Postwar Oakland.* Princeton, NJ: Princeton University Press, 2005.

Shermer, Elizabeth Tandy. *Indentured Students: How Government-Guaranteed Loans Left Generations Drowning in College Debt.* Cambridge, MA: Belknap, 2021.

Shermer, Elizabeth Tandy, Claire Bond Potter, Christopher Newfield, Trevor Griffey, and Edward Balleisen. "Up for Debate: Elizabeth Tandy Shermer on the Business of Higher Ed." *Labor: Studies in Working-Class History* 18, no. 4 (December 2021): 62–119.

Simpson, Christopher, ed. *Universities and Empire: Money and Politics in the Social Sciences during the Cold War*. New York: New Press, 1999.

Skowronek, Stephen. *The Politics Presidents Make: Leadership from John Adams to Bill Clinton*. Cambridge, MA: Harvard University Press, 1993.

Smelser, Neil J. "Growth, Structural Change, and Conflict in California Public Higher Education, 1950–1970." In *Public Higher Education in California*, edited by Neil J. Smelser and Gabriel Almond, 9–141. Berkeley: University of California Press, 1974.

Smith, John Masson, and Richard Bridgman. "Chronology of the Free Speech Controversy on the Berkeley Campus (December 1964)." In *The FSM Papers*, edited by Hal Draper. Microfilm.

Smith, John Matthew. "'It's Not Really My Country': Lew Alcindor and the Revolt of the Black Athlete." *Journal of Sport History* 6, no. 2 (Summer 2009): 223–44.

———. *The Sons of Westwood: John Wooden, UCLA, and the Dynasty That Changed College Basketball*. Champaign: University of Illinois Press, 2013.

Smith, Maureen Margaret. "Frozen Fists in Speed City: The Statue as Twenty-First-Century Reparations." *Journal of Sport History* 36, no. 3 (2009): 393–414.

Smith, Paul Chaat, and Robert Allen Warrior. *Like a Hurricane: The Indian Movement from Alcatraz to Wounded Knee*. New York: New Press, 1996.

Smith, Robert, Richard Axen, and DeVere Edwin Pentony. *By Any Means Necessary: The Revolutionary Struggle at San Francisco State*. San Francisco: Jossey-Bass, 1970.

Smith, Tommie, with David Steele. *Silent Gesture: The Autobiography of Tommie Smith*. Philadelphia: Temple University Press, 2007.

Sonnie, Amy, and James Tracey. *Hillbilly Nationalists, Urban Race Rebels, and Black Power: Community Organizing in Radical Times*. New York, NY: Melville House, 2011.

Spivey, Donald. "The Black Athlete in Big-Time Intercollegiate Sports, 1941–1968." *Phylon* 44, no. 2 (1983): 116–25.

Stadtman, Verne A. *The University of California, 1868–1968*. New York: McGraw-Hill, 1970.

Starr, Kevin. *California: A History*. New York: Modern Library, 2005.

———. *Golden Dreams: California in an Age of Abundance, 1950–1963*. New York: Oxford University Press. 2009.

Stern, Alexandra. *Eugenic Nation: Faults and Frontiers of Better Breeding in Modern America*. Berkeley: University of California Press, 2005.

Stewart, George R. *The Year of the Oath*. Garden City, NY: Doubleday, 1950.

Sullivan, Walter. *Assault on the Unknown: The International Geophysical Year*. New York: McGraw-Hill, 1961.

Summerskill, John. *President Seven*. New York: World Publishing, 1971.

Sundquist, James L. *Politics and Policy: The Eisenhower, Kennedy, and Johnson Years*. Washington, DC: Brookings Institute, 1968.

Theoharis, Jeanne. *A More Beautiful and Terrible History: The Uses and Misuses of Civil Rights History*. Boston: Beacon, 2018.

Thompson, Hunter S. *Fear and Loathing in America: The Brutal Odyssey of an Outlaw Journalist.* New York: Simon & Schuster, 2000.

Umemoto, Karen. "'On Strike!' San Francisco State College Strike, 1968–1969: The Role of Asian American Students." *Amerasia Journal* 15, no. 1 (1989): 3–41.

Urban, Wayne J. *More than Science and Sputnik: The National Defense Education Act of 1958.* Tuscaloosa: University of Alabama Press, 2010.

Van Deburg, William L. *New Day in Babylon: The Black Power Movement and American Culture, 1965–1975.* Chicago: University of Chicago Press, 1992.

Von Eschen, Penny M. *Race against Empire: Black Americans and Anticolonialism, 1937–1957.* Ithaca, NY: Cornell University Press, 1997.

Warshaw, Steven. *The Trouble in Berkeley.* Berkeley, CA: Diablo Press, 1965.

Wei, William. *The Asian American Movement.* Philadelphia: Temple University Press, 1993.

Whitson, Helene. *On Strike! Shut It down!: A Revolution at San Francisco State.* San Francisco: J. Paul Leonard Library, San Francisco State University, 1999.

Wiggins, David K. "'With All Deliberate Speed': High School Sport, Race, and *Brown v. Board of Education.*" *Journal of Sport History* 38, no. 3 (Fall 2010): 329–46.

Williams, Jakobi. *From the Bullet to the Ballot: The Illinois Chapter of the Black Panther Party and Racial Coalition Politics in Chicago.* Chapel Hill: The University of North Carolina Press, 2015.

Wills, Gary. *Reagan's America: Innocents at Home.* Garden City, NY: Doubleday, 1987.

Wollenberg, Charles M. *All Deliberate Speed: Segregation and Exclusion in California Schools, 1855–1975.* Berkeley: University of California Press, 1976.

Woodard, Komozi. *A Nation within a Nation: Amiri Baraka (LeRoi Jones) and Black Power Politics.* Chapel Hill: The University of North Carolina Press, 1999.

Young, Cynthia A. *Soul Power: Culture, Radicalism, and the Making of a U.S. Third World Left.* Durham, NC: Duke University Press, 2006.

Zirin, Dave. *A People's History of Sports in the United States: 250 Years of Politics, Protest, People and Play.* New York: New Press, 2009.

Theses and Dissertations

Collisson, Craig. "The Fight to Legitimize Blackness: How Black Students Changed the University." PhD diss., University of Washington, 2008.

Dong, Harvey C. "The Origins and Trajectory of Asian American Political Activism in the San Francisco Bay Area, 1968–1978." PhD diss., University of California, Berkeley, 2002.

Ferreira, Jason. "All Power to the People: A Comparative History of Third World Radicalism in San Francisco, 1968–1974." PhD diss., University of California, Berkeley, 2003.

Garrigues, George Louis. "Loud Bark and Curious Eyes: A History of the UCLA *Daily Bruin*, 1919–1955." MA thesis, University of California, Los Angeles, 1970.

Johnson, Diana. "Seattle in Coalition: Working-Class Activism, Multiracial Unity, and Third World Activism in the Pacific Northwest, 1969–1999." PhD diss., University of California, Davis, 2017.

Kong, Angela Wai-Yin. "Re-examining Diversity Policy at University of California, San Diego: The Radical Politics of Asian Americans." PhD diss., University of California, San Diego, 2014.

Marquez, Yolanda Loza. "La Universidad con la Promesa del Futuro: A Case Study of the University of California, San Barbara Department of Chicano Studies 1965–1980." PhD diss., University of California, Santa Barbara, 2007.

Miller, Karen K. "Black Studies in California Higher Education, 1965–1980." PhD diss., University of California, Santa Barbara, 1986.

Moreno, Marisol. "'Of the Community, for the Community': The Chicana/o Student Movement in California's Public Higher Education, 1967–1973." PhD diss., University of California, Santa Barbara, 2009.

Savage, James A. "Save Our Republic: Battling John Birch in California's Conservative Cradle." PhD diss., University of Kentucky, 2014.

Smith, Sara. "Organizing for Social Justice: Rank-and-File Teachers' Activism and Social Unionism in California, 1948–1978." PhD diss., University of California, Santa Cruz, 2014.

Sokoya, Kinaya. "A Historical Analysis of the Contributions of the Black Power Movement to Higher Education: 1960–1980." PhD diss., George Washington University, 2014.

Stahl-Kovell, Daniel W. "Reimagining Red Power: Native American Community, Activism, and Academics in Postwar America." MA thesis, California State University, Long Beach, 2014.

Stuart, Mary Clark. "Clark Kerr: Biography of an Action Intellectual." PhD diss., University of Michigan, 1980.

Online Sources

Abdul-Jabbar, Kareem. "Interview with Dave Zirin." *The Nation*, January 29, 2016. https://www.thenation.com/article/kareem-abdul-jabbar-sports-taught -america-that-bigotry-is-not-a-cool-thing.

Asimov, Nanette. "The Golden Age: Higher Education Master Plan Getting Ignored." *4LAKids*. Accessed April 9, 2017. 4lakids.blogspot.com/2009/11 /bestthe-worstthe-golden-age.html (site discontinued).

Bady, Aaron, and Mike Konczal. "From Master Plan to No Plan: The Slow Death of Public Higher Education." *Dissent*, Fall 2012. https://www.dissentmagazine.org /article/from-master-plan-to-no-plan-the-slow-death-of-public-higher-education.

Bessie, Adam. "The Trojan Horse of 'Free' Community College." *Truthout*, January 21, 2015. http://www.truth-out.org/opinion/item/28637-the-trojan -horse-of-free-commun=.

Brand, Rachel. "Jewish Trojans—Oxymoron No More." *Jewish Journal*, August 21, 2003. http://www.jewishjournal.com/education/article/jewish_trojans _oxymoron_no_more_20030822/.

"Brief Guide to the Master Plan." *The History and Future of the California Master Plan for Higher Education.* Accessed July 12, 2014. http://sunsite .berkeley.edu/UCHistory/archives_exhibits/masterplan/index.html (site discontinued).

"CA Governor [1966]." *Our Campaigns.* Accessed April 1, 2022. https://www .ourcampaigns.com/RaceDetail.html?RaceID=36416.

"CA Governor [1970]." *Our Campaigns.* Accessed April 1, 2022. https://www .ourcampaigns.com/RaceDetail.html?RaceID=36415.

Californians for Higher Education Reform. http://www.caledreform.org/.

"Cesar Chavez at Anti-tuition Demonstration." *The Movement* 3, no. 3 (March 1967). https://libraries.ucsd.edu/farmworkermovement/ufwarchives /sncc/21-March%201967.pdf.

"Digital Archive: The 1960 Master Plan and Related Studies." *The History and Future of the California Master Plan.* Accessed July 8, 2014, http://sunsite .berkeley.edu/uchistory/archives_exhibits/masterplan/digitalarchive.html.

El Plan Espiritual de Aztlan, 1969. Accessed January 30, 2019. http://www.cwu .edu/~mecha/documents/plan_de_aztlan.pdf.

"EOP History, Fresno State." California State University, Fresno. Accessed August 11, 2020. http://www.fresnostate.edu/studentaffairs/eop/documents /EOP%20History.pdf.

Farber, Sam. "The Berkeley Free Speech Movement, 56 Years Later." *Jacobin,* September 3, 2020. https://www.jacobinmag.com/2020/09/berkeley-free -speech-movement-hal-draper.

Felber, Garrett. "Those Who Know Don't Say." Interview by Adam McNeil. *New Books Network,* June 12, 2020. Audio, 40:00. https://newbooksnetwork.com /garrett-felber-those-who-know-dont-say-the-nation-of-islam-the-black -freedom-movement-and-the-carceral-state-unc-press-2020.

Geier, Joel. "Radicals and the Berkeley Free Speech Movement." *Jacobin,* December 21, 2020. https://www.jacobinmag.com/2020/12/berkeley-free -speech-movement-1960s-socialist-isc-fsm.

"Guide to the Rene Nuñez Memorial Collection." *Online Archive of California.* Accessed July 8, 2020. https://oac.cdlib.org/findaid/ark:/13030/kt9r29s3qv/.

Hemmila, Donna. "Governor Pledges to Veto Any Budget Plan without Support for UC." *UCLA News Room,* April 28, 2010. http://newsroom.ucla.edu/stories /governor-promises-to-veto-any-157607.

Johnson, Alan. "'The Bible of the Free Speech Movement': Hal Draper's *The Mind of Clark Kerr* Revisited." The 19th International Congress of Historical Sciences, Oslo, August 6–13, 2000. https://www.oslo2000.uio.no/AIO/AIO16 /group%209/Johnson.pdf.

"Katherine Panas." *Find a Grave.* Accessed August 11, 2020. https://www.finda grave.com/memorial/13726701/katherine-panas.

Lee, Robert, and Tristan Ahtone. "Land-Grab Universities: Expropriated Indigenous Land Is the Foundation of the Land-Grant University System." *High Country News,* March 30, 2020. https://www.hcn.org/issues/52.4/indigenous -affairs-education-land-grab-universities.

"Lumumba-Zapata College: B.S.C.-M.A.Y.A. Demands for the Third College,
U.C.S.D." March 14, 1969. University of California, San Diego, Digital Archives.
http://libraries.ucsd.edu/speccoll/DigitalArchives/ld781_s2-l86-1969/.

"Mario Savio, Jack Weinberg & Free Speech Movement Victory." San Francisco
State University. Accessed March 6, 2019. https://diva.sfsu.edu/collections
/sfbatv/bundles/209401.

Parker, Franklin. "Roots of the New Right: School Critic Max Rafferty (1917–82)."
Self-published: West Virginia University, 1985. Accessed December 19, 2016.
http://files.eric.ed.gov/fulltext/ED257728.pdf.

"Proposition 209: Text of Proposed Law." California Secretary of State. http://
vigarchive.sos.ca.gov/1996/general/pamphlet/209text.htm.

Saving UCSB. "Save UC's Master Plan!" Care2Petitions. Accessed April 9, 2017.
http://www.thepetitionsite.com/9/save-the-university-of-californias-master
-plan/.

"Significant Moments in Black Bruin History." UCLA Alumni. February 2017.
https://alumni.ucla.edu/email/connect/2017/feb/black-history/default.htm.

"UCSB Buys the Francisco Torres 19-Acre Complex in Isla Vista." *93106: The
Faculty & Staff Newspaper*, January 6, 2003. http://www.ia.ucsb.edu/93106
_archived/2003/January6/ucsb.html.

"UCSB Headcount Enrollment: 1954–55 to 2016–17." Office of Budget and
Planning, University of California, Santa Barbara. Accessed July 8, 2020.
http://bap.ucsb.edu/institutional.research/planning.data.book/tables
/headcount.enrollment.historical.pdf.

Uebersax, John. "Inflation-Adjusted Tuition + Fees in the UC and CalState Systems
from 1965 to 2011." *Satyagraha*, December 12, 2011. https://satyagraha
.wordpress.com/2011/12/12/inflation-adjusted-tuition-fees-in-the-uc-and
-calstate-systems-from-1965-to-2011/.

Index

Bank of America, 51, 203n29
Baxter, Norman, 149
Black Athletes Committee (BAC), 102
Black Athletes of the University of
California (BAUC), 100–101
Black-Brown relations, 121, 156, 170–75,
177, 192n20, 226nn51–52, 230n150; at
Fresno State, 142, 143, 144, 146–50; at
San Fernando Valley State, 103, 106,
107, 110–11
Black Panther Party, 116, 118, 176, 177,
222n154, 225n30, 243n38, 245n53,
245n57; at San Francisco State, 154,
158, 165, 245n54
Black Student Council (BSC), 173, 241n23
Black Student Union (BSU), 94, 102–11
passim, 118, 131, 141–79 passim,
227n73, 241n23, 242n27, 245n54,
247n81
Black studies, 102, 106, 110, 121, 142,
146, 147, 165–76 passim, 226n51,
247nn81–82
Black Youth Conference (BYC), 118–19
blowouts. *See* East LA Walkouts
Brandler, Mark, 109, 227n82
Braun, Wernher von, 14
Brown, Edmund "Pat," 28, 30, 61, 75,
81, 85, 219n106
Brown v. Board of Education, 99
Brundage, Avery, 119–20
budget cuts, 85–91, 184
bureaucratic collectivism, 49, 52,
203–4n36, 208n88
Burwell, Bill, 104, 110, 111

California community colleges, 22,
25–27, 104, 111, 143, 157, 181, 220n114,
233n55; critique of, 1, 4, 32, 176,
200n98, 200n100; and the Master
Plan, 2, 4, 10, 17, 28, 30, 31, 32, 86,
192n17, 193n3, 198n72; student
demographics, 125, 174, 175, 176, 181;
student organizing at, 100, 129, 130,
147, 158, 159, 160, 162, 163, 174–78,
232n30, 235n80

California Master Plan for Higher
Education. *See* Master Plan
California state board of education, 25,
26, 27, 28, 30, 31, 74, 75, 155, 199n82
California state colleges, 4, 6, 34, 66,
69, 191n2; growth, 26, 103–4, 111, 142,
193n3; and the Master Plan, 24–33,
94, 98, 178, 192n17, 198n72, 200n95;
and Ronald Reagan, 69, 85, 86, 88,
93, 94, 95, 153, 155, 219n108; student
athletes, 100, 102, 104, 107–20, 142;
student demographics, 102, 104,
110–11, 113, 114, 125, 143, 163–64, 181;
student organizing, 97–99, 102,
103–22, 129–31, 140–50, 152–56,
157–69;
Cal State Northridge. *See* San Fernando
Valley State College
Cal State University. *See* California
State Colleges
campus autonomy, 5, 31, 68, 109, 143,
155, 227n73
Campus Committee on Political
Activity (CCPA), 55
Campus CORE, 47, 203n34
campus development, 26–27, 103, 111,
142–43
Carlos, John, 97, 100, 120
Chatman, Archie, 97, 104, 106, 107, 108,
110, 111, 226n51
Chavarría, Jesús, 133, 137, 233n55
Chavez, Cesar, 91, 129, 147, 242–43n36
Chicano Coordinating Council for
Higher Education, 124, 133, 135, 136,
234n61
Chicano Master Plan. *See* Santa Barbara
Conference
Chicano nationalism, 131, 137, 232n38,
242n33
Chicano Student Union, 177
Chicano studies, 121, 159, 169, 170, 172,
173, 175; in *El Plan de Santa Barbara*,
134, 137, 138, 140, 141; at Fresno State,
146, 148, 149, 150; at San Fernando
Valley State, 106, 107, 110, 226n51

regents, the. *See* UC Board of Regents

Regents v. Bakke, 180, 181, 182, 183, 252n4

Reserve Officers' Training Corps (ROTC), 72, 148, 165, 239–40n9

residential segregation. *See* housing discrimination

revolutionary nationalism, 153–54, 158, 165, 173, 236n106, 242n33

Revolutionary Studies Group, 177

Richardson, Ralph, 71, 74, 75

Riles, Wilson, 75, 96

Risco, Eliezer, 133, 146, 236n99

Risling, David, Jr., 161

Rousselot, John, 73, 82

Rubel, A.C., 80, 217n75

Rumford Fair Housing Act, 83

Russia. *See* Soviet Union

Sacramento, Calif., 19, 20, 26, 31, 89, 132

Sacramento City College, 158, 159, 160, 162, 174, 235n80

Sacramento Conference, 19–23

Sacramento State College, 26, 130, 144, 159, 161

Salvatori, Henry, 80, 213n20, 217n75

Sanchez, Paul, 133, 136

San Diego, Calif., 67–68, 72, 77, 85, 103, 135, 141, 172, 212n6, 232n38

San Diego City College, 130, 159

San Diego State College, 130, 137, 159, 233n55, 241n23, 250n124

San Diego Union, 67–68

San Fernando Valley State College, 100, 103–11, 125, 225n48, 233n55; student organizing, 94, 102–11, 122, 130, 158, 159, 226nn51–52, 227n73, 227n82

San Francisco, Calif., 27, 45, 81, 114, 125, 153, 161, 164

San Francisco City College, 158

San Francisco State College: professors, 69, 94, 166–67, 168, 177, 246n65; administrators, 93, 95, 164, 165, 166, 168; African American students,

152–64 passim, 166, 177, 228n91, 241n22, 247n81; Mexican American students, 130, 140, 144, 152, 153, 159; Asian American students, 160, 164–65, 167, 243n39, 246n70; Native American students, 161; student activism, 83, 102, 154, 160, 165–69, 227n73, 239n7; student demographics, 125, 163–64, 169, 246n68; Third World Liberation Front, 94, 152–54, 162, 164, 174, 245n54, 245n57, 247–48n82

San Jose City College, 100, 122, 129, 175, 232n30

San Jose State College, 27, 94, 97–98, 100, 111–29 passim, 159, 163, 235n82

San Mateo, College of, 118, 162, 169, 174–75

Santa Barbara, Calif., 81, 87, 119

Santa Barbara Conference, 6, 123–25, 132–36, 139, 140, 159, 233n46, 233nn54–55, 234n59, 234n66

Savio, Mario, 39, 46–66 passim, 204nn43–44, 207n71, 208n86, 208n88, 210n106, 210n108

Scholastic Aptitude Test (SAT). *See* standardized tests

school segregation, 4, 5, 130, 152, 164, 181, 192n18; of African Americans, 156; of Mexican Americans, 124–28, 130, 231n18

Screen Actors Guild, 79

Seaborg, Glenn T., 20, 23, 197n62

Seale, Bobby, 176

segregation. *See* school segregation; housing

Shapiro, Peter, 152, 154, 163, 164, 168, 239n7

Shell, Joe, 73, 80

Sherriffs, Alex, 47

Silvas, Patty, 161

Simon, Norton, 88

Simpson, Roy, 9, 19–36 passim, 71, 74, 75